Sir Robert Rhodes James' first book was a much acclaimed biography of Lord Randolph Churchill, first published in 1959 when the author was twenty-six. Like many of his other books – including his award-winning biographies of Lord Rosebery, Anthony Eden and Bob Boothby, and his classic history of the Gallipoli campaign – it remains in print today.

Born in 1933 and brought up in India, Rhodes James was educated at Sedbergh School and Worcester College, Oxford. He was Clerk of the House of Commons from 1955 to 1965; a Fellow of All Souls College, Oxford; Director of the Institute for the Study of International Organisations at the University of Sussex; Principal Officer in the Executive Office of the Secretary-General of the United Nations; and Conservative Member of Parliament for Cambridge between 1976 and 1992. He was also a Fellow of the Royal Society of Literature, the Royal Historical Society and Wolfson College, Cambridge; a Visiting Professor at Stanford University, California, and a Distinguished Visiting Professor at Baylor University, Texas. Knighted in 1991, he was appointed a Deputy Lieutenant for Cambridgeshire in 1993.

Sir Robert died in May 1999, leaving his wife, Angela Robertson, and their four daughters.

A SPIRIT UNDAUNTED

The Political Role of George VI

ROBERT RHODES JAMES

An *Abacus* Book

First published in Great Britain in 1998
by Little, Brown and Company
This edition published in 1999 by Abacus

Copyright © 1998 by Robert Rhodes James

A CIP catalogue record for this book
is available from the British Library.

ISBN: 0 349 11118 9

Typeset by
Palimpsest Book Production Limited,
Polmont, Stirlingshire
Printed and bound in Great Britain
by Clays Ltd, St Ives plc

Abacus
A Division of
Little, Brown and Company (UK)
Brettenham House
Lancaster Place
London WC2E 7EN

For Polly,
from all the Rhodes Jameses,
with love and gratitude.

Contents

LIST OF ILLUSTRATIONS

Alexander Hardinge (THE ROYAL ARCHIVES) and Alan ('Tommy')
  Lascelles. (ASSOCIATED PRESS/TOPHAM)
A mistake. The King and Queen with Mr and Mrs Neville Chamberlain
  on the Buckingham Palace balcony after Munich, 30 September
  1938. (HULTON GETTY)
En route to Canada and the United States, May 1939. (POPPERFOTO)
With the Roosevelts at Hyde Park, New York state, June 1939: Eleanor
  Roosevelt, the King, Mrs James D. Roosevelt (the President's
  mother), the Queen and the President. (THE ROYAL ARCHIVES)
A trust abused: the King and Chamberlain in Downing Street,
  1 September 1939. (DAILY SKETCH/THE ROYAL ARCHIVES)
'Bobbety' (Lord) Cranborne: fiery anti-Chamberlainite and friend of the
  King. (HULTON GETTY)
Sumner Welles, President Roosevelt's envoy, with Lord Halifax, March
  1940. (HULTON GETTY)
A very near miss at Buckingham Palace, 13 September 1940. Inspecting
  the damage with Churchill. (HULTON GETTY)
'The partnership': the King and Churchill in their prime. (DAILY
  HERALD/THE ROYAL ARCHIVES)
Entering Valletta Harbour, Malta, June 1943. (WAR OFFICE/THE ROYAL
  ARCHIVES)
The King with members of the War Cabinet, 1944: Lord Woolton, Sir
  John Anderson, Clement Attlee, the King, Winston Churchill,
  Anthony Eden and Ernest Bevin. (POPPERFOTO)
'A friend of Americans': the King in France, summer 1944, with US
  Generals Bradley and Eisenhower. (POPPERFOTO)
Victory in Europe, 8 May 1945. The King, Queen, Churchill and
  Princesses Elizabeth and Margaret on the precarious balcony of
  the windowless Buckingham Palace. (FOX PHOTOS/THE ROYAL
  ARCHIVES)
The King and Clement Attlee, 15 August 1945. (PLANET NEWS/THE
  ROYAL ARCHIVES)
The fatal tour: the Queen, a strained King and the Princesses in South
  Africa, 1947. (POPPERFOTO)
The last photograph. The King, with the Queen and Princess Margaret,
  waves goodbye to Princess Elizabeth and the Duke of Edinburgh
  at London Airport on 31 January 1952. (HULTON GETTY)

PREFACE

This book, like some others of my attempted contributions to an understanding of modern British history, originated quite unintentionally.

On my last day as a Member of the House of Commons in March 1992 I delivered a lecture on Prince Albert, the Prince Consort, to the Royal Institution, which was published early the following year. Perhaps it was on the basis of this that in the summer of 1993 the Royal Society of Arts invited me to deliver a lecture on the subject of the British monarchy. It was not an invitation that I welcomed, and I attempted to extricate myself from it. I eventually agreed, somewhat uneasily, and delivered the lecture on 17 November before what was, to me, a surprisingly large audience.

In the speech I emphasised what had increasingly struck me as a strangely neglected aspect of the modern British monarchy – its political role, on which I had concentrated in my biography of Prince Albert, published in 1983. Also, in the course of my researches for the lecture, it had struck me how little is known about the political significance of King George VI. Sir John Wheeler-Bennett's official biography of the King, published in 1958, had its merits, but was manifestly a work of duty rather than pleasure, as his private comments on his task made only too clear. Also, he had confided privately to Harold Nicolson, the biographer of George V, that he was depressed by the absence of any political role or initiative by the King. Admittedly, this was at a relatively early stage in his researches, but I found this opinion difficult to accept – rightly, as it proved. Sarah Bradford's admirable unofficial biography of George VI was essentially personal, and concentrated more on other aspects of the King's life than on his reign itself or its political importance.

I referred to this in the course of my lecture, almost as a side comment, but it attracted some attention then and even more later, when the lecture was published by the Royal Society in April 1994. The result was that I was encouraged to present a submission to Her Majesty the Queen and Her Majesty Queen Elizabeth the Queen Mother for permission to have access to the papers of King George VI and others in the Royal Archives and elsewhere, which was accepted.

A feature of all my books is that they have changed their character as a consequence of my researches. I gradually realised that what was envisaged as a monograph on King George VI in isolation from the experiences of his predecessors had a certain unreality, and, great though my admiration is for many royal biographers – especially Sir Philip Magnus (on Edward VII), Harold Nicolson (on George V), Wheeler-Bennett, Elizabeth Longford (on Queen Victoria), Sarah Bradford, Kenneth Rose (on George V) and Philip Ziegler (on Edward VIII and William IV) – I have sometimes found myself in disagreement with them on the political roles of these monarchs. That I have been actively involved in politics may colour my examination of the modern British monarchy, but does not, I believe, distort it.

Since I began this study I have been much encouraged and impressed by recent serious consideration given to this aspect of the monarchy by, among others, Vernon Bogdanor, Ben Pimlott and Peter Hennessy. The fact that I do not always agree with them is the result of differences of interpretation and opinion. Judgements on George VI have varied from the glowing tributes of contemporaries to the critically dismissive attitudes of some more recent commentators. Frank Hardie, the pioneer in taking the political role of the modern British monarchy seriously, wrote in 1970: 'Inevitably the evidence about George VI's [political] contribution is thinner than that for his predecessors, but the evidence already available seems to establish him firmly as, politically, the very pattern of a modern monarch.' As my account will demonstrate, there was rather more to it than that, but all the new evidence strongly confirms Hardie's understandably cautious assessment.

I have interpreted the term 'political' in the royal context quite liberally, as almost every public activity of a monarch has a political character to it. Thus, the love that Queen Victoria and Prince Albert had for Scotland had political results, as had the 1851 Great Exhibition; the ever-increasing royal involvement in charities and public institutions, largely inaugurated by Prince Albert and greatly extended during and after the reign of King George V, had a political purpose; the liking of Queen Victoria and King Edward VII for France, and the antipathy between the latter and the German Kaiser Wilhelm also had its significance. The constant visits of King George VI and Queen Elizabeth during the Second World War to bomb-damaged cities and military units had political consequences in that they dramatically raised the popularity of and respect for the institution of monarchy. Their state visits to Canada and the United States immediately before the war in 1939 had a very definite political importance. The advent of radio, and the use made of it by George V and George VI – and newsreels shown in cinemas at the height of their public popularity – gave to the Crown a voice and a character and a vast world-wide audience not available to any of their predecessors and to very few politicians in peacetime.

Thus, what began not as a biography of King George VI but as a study of his political and constitutional roles during his relatively brief, but tumultuous, reign, has developed into a considerable extension of Hardie's work on the political roles of Queen Victoria and her successors concluding with the death of King George VI in February 1952. It has proved a considerably more formidable project than I had envisaged, and I appreciate the emotions of Harold Nicolson after he had written the first sentence of his biography of King George V, that 'it is like starting in a taxi on the way to Vladivostock'.

My experience as a historian has made me sceptical of authors who provide a long list of names, distinguished or otherwise, to whom they are allegedly indebted for their researches – particularly as I have often found my own included solely on the basis of a brief conversation, correspondence, or even a single telephone call. I also have a deep suspicion of references to 'Private Information' in footnotes. I prefer the approach of R. C. K. Ensor in his Preface to his classic *England 1870–1914*:

No one could write a volume of this kind without seeking

information upon a host of particular points from individuals qualified to give it, or from the officials of various important bodies. My debts to such informants are exceedingly numerous; but believing that they will be content with the private expression of sincere gratitude, I do not propose to display their names here like a row of scalps.

But there must be a few exceptions. It was a great pleasure for me to return to the Royal Archives at Windsor Castle. I am particularly grateful to Lady de Bellaigue, Registrar of the Archives; Mr Oliver Everett, the Queen's Librarian and Assistant Keeper of the Royal Archives; and Miss Frances Dimond, whose knowledge of the royal photographic and portrait collections has been invaluable.

I have also been given access to certain private diaries and papers not in the Royal Archives relating to King George VI for my information and use, but not for quotation. I am very grateful for this. I am also grateful to Dr Piers Brendon and the Master and Fellows of Churchill College, Cambridge, for assistance with the Churchill archives.

Once again my – alas – now former secretary, Polly Andrews, to whom this work is dedicated with much affection and appreciation, has borne her part with characteristic skill and good humour; so also, as always, has my wife. I am also immensely grateful to Anthony Sheil, my literary agent and friend for so many years, and to Philippa Harrison and Andrew Gordon of Little, Brown for coping with, and necessarily curtailing, a typescript that was immensely longer than any of us had anticipated. This has been a very happy, if somewhat prolonged, undertaking, and I hope that the result will be deemed worthy of the subject, and of those who have assisted me so willingly and with such kindness.

Robert Rhodes James

The principles of the English constitution do not contemplate the absence of personal influence on the part of the sovereign: and, if they did, the principles of human nature would prevent the fulfilment of such a theory.

BENJAMIN DISRAELI, MANCHESTER, 1872

1

THE POLITICS OF SURVIVAL

olitics are about power, and usually more about its acquisition
than its useful employment. Not many who seek the gleaming
objective have clear or considered notions about how they are
to use it; what they seek so eagerly is the citadel itself. Only then can
they consider how it may be profitably used to their own advantage,
and the best methods whereby they can retain their predominance.

To state these facts is not cynicism. It is a straightforward and clear-
eyed portrayal of the lust for power, influence, fame and position that has
driven men and women of otherwise moderate qualities and abilities into
great aspirations and achievements. Some, who made misjudgements, fell
sheer; others, who calculated better, rose to great eminence, distinction
and wealth. Some were worthy of these emoluments; others were not.
But to the victors went the spoils, the riches, the titles and the glory. Their
only real achievement was that they had supported the winning side.

This was the dominant feature of the ferocious, confused and sometimes bloody contests for the English monarchy for over six hundred
years until the close of the seventeenth century, when the Protestant
Succession inflicted an exhausted, if uneasy, truce between monarch and
parliament. If the Protestant Glorious Revolution of 1689 heralded an
uncomfortable era of mixed fortunes, this was preferable to the former
ones, whose conflicts had brought to the kingdom many advantages but
also provided embittered religious strife, harsh civil wars and bloodshed, constitutional crises, much venality and corruption, foreign royal

importations at moments of desperation and crisis and a bizarre and sometimes deeply unpleasant constellation of personalities. The true histories of monarchies, to which that of England is no exception, are not for the squeamish or idealistic.

The Crown of England was a great and glittering prize, and there were many eager to secure it. The victors may have left rich benefactions and achievements, but it would be unwise for later generations to be deceived by their motivations. Normans, Plantagenets, Tudors and Stuarts had only one thing in common – seizure of power, and the authority and great wealth that accompanied it. In the course of its pursuit, the niceties were thinly observed.

In these ambitions they had many eager accomplices – and enemies. The price of failure, or of the misfortune of being on the losing side, was a heavy and sometimes lethal one. But the rewards for victory were lavish. As a result of their fealty, great palaces and mansions were built and dynasties created. The glories of English cathedrals, churches, great houses, parks and estates often had murky foundations. Adventurers and sycophants at court prospered mightily. In Bacon's words, 'by indignities men rise to dignities'. And many did.

The monarch was the provider of patronage and wealth, and the arbiter of politics and the bestower of offices, ministries and great estates. This was the situation in other monarchies too, but it was in England in the golden age of monarchy that the supreme power of the sovereign was effectively challenged and then severely reduced. This was because even at the height of the powers of the English monarchy alternative challengers had been grumbling menacingly. The events of the 1640s had long and deep antecedents – evident even in the fourteenth century – which were arrogantly ignored at a grievous price.

The modern histories of few nations can match the brutalities of the tyrannies of Henry VIII and the first Queen Elizabeth. They were despots of their time – brutal, cruel, unforgiving and totally devoid of scruple. But they were also successful and popular; and, unlike the hapless Queen Mary, they survived. But the Tudors were a deeply unpleasant, grasping and harsh confederation. Their successors, the Stuarts, lacked their ruthlessness, cold intelligence, inspired creativity and political understanding. And thus they blundered, uncomprehendingly, into disaster.

There is a strong temptation, and one to which many historians and constitutional authorities have too easily succumbed, to regard the tangled and complex history of the modern British monarchy as progressing in an easy, reasonably graceful and foreseeable manner from supreme authority and semi-despotism into a situation that the politician, essayist and historian Thomas Babington Macaulay complacently described in his *History of England* in 1855 as one in which, 'According to the pure idea of constitutional royalty, the prince reigns and does not govern; and constitutional royalty, as it now exists in England, comes nearer than in any other country to the pure idea.'

This interpretation was characteristic of an enduring view of English history that has it on a kind of confident, smooth and somewhat smug march: from Magna Carta in 1215 to the establishment of parliament; through the turmoils of the following three centuries to Sir Edward Coke's Petition of Right of 1628 and the challenge to despotic royal rule that culminated in the Civil War, the triumph of the parliamentary forces and the execution of Charles I in 1649; the ejection of James II in 1688, ending the Stuart reigns; the Protestant Succession; and the Declaration of Rights of February 1689 and the Bill of Rights of December that year that gave parliament, and not the monarch, most of the actual power – and thus, almost inexorably, moved the country towards full democracy.

The reality was infinitely more complex. Despite Magna Carta and the evolution of parliament, the era of monarch-as-despot dominated until the sixteenth and early seventeenth centuries, when Charles I came into bitter conflict with Oliver Cromwell and the parliamentary forces. The subsequent development of the English monarchy into something approaching a partnership with the other powers in the land, giving the monarch a strong if undetermined political role but not overwhelming power, was to prove its salvation. But it was a fitful, gradual and often highly controversial process which gave to all parties the time and experience to understand the new condition of affairs.

One interpretation of the changed situation was written by Bolingbroke[1]

---

[1] Henry Saint-John, first Viscount Bolingbroke (1678–1751), a highly controversial politician of erratic brilliance. Like Edmund Burke he was rather more esteemed after his death than during his lifetime. Famed during his political career as a superb orator and notorious turncoat, his writings had a much more durable impact upon the development of 'Tory Democracy', a theme later to be taken up, with considerable effect, by Benjamin Disraeli.

in 1738, in his essay 'The Idea of a Patriot King', which William IV later described as one of the most important formative influences of his life:

> As every new modification in a scheme of government and of national policy is of great importance, and requires more and deeper consideration than the warmth, and hurry, and rashness of party conduct admit, the duty of a prince seems to require that he should render by his influence the proceedings more orderly and more deliberate, even when he approves the end to which they are directed.

While neither Queen Anne nor the Hanoverians would have at all accepted that their political role was limited to 'influence', except in a very different sense from that envisaged by Bolingbroke, they understood the new political realities. Taxation had always been the most unpopular burden imposed by the monarch; that was now the function of parliament. But the monarch could and did manipulate, conspire and interfere, although no longer by diktat and decree. A more fundamental difference was that, since 1689, the Royal Family had to a considerable extent become dependent upon parliament for their income. Necessarily, the monarch-as-despot had to become the monarch-as-politician.

The Civil List Act of 1697 was intended to make the monarch totally financially dependent upon parliament (although in fact it did not). The monarchy had not been stripped of its mansions and estates, nor of the income that stemmed from the latter. Its capital wealth, in property, works of art, and other possessions, was astounding. But in the political arena it had to accept a changed situation. It was parliament that declared that King James II had abdicated and invited William of Orange and his wife Mary to fill the throne as joint sovereigns. Under the Act of Settlement of 1701, parliament provided for the succession to pass to Princess Sophia, Electress of Hanover, the grand-daughter of James I, but a Protestant. She predeceased Queen Anne by two months in 1714, and the throne of England and Scotland was inherited by her son, the Elector of Hanover, who became King George I. Thus, it has been stated by some authorities, parliament could determine who should, or should not be, the monarch. This remains technically true, but the reality has been quite different.

By this point, according to this version, the English had established a uniquely civilised and practical situation, which one eminent commentator has described as 'a parliamentary monarchy'.[2] History, and especially political history, is never as simple as this, however – largely because English sovereigns and politicians after 1688, perhaps wisely, were not much addicted either to the study of history or to constitutional law. But they knew something about politics, and they were individuals, not institutional figures. George I, who did not speak or read English, could hardly be expected to be well-versed in Magna Carta or the Bill of Rights, and nor was he. His successors certainly were not, although George III and later William IV were exceptions in that they actually studied constitutional history. But both lived in the real world of British politics, not in the abstract.

Also, the much-vaunted, nobly independent, popularly elected parliament of Macaulay's imagination was corrupt, venal, easily – and often quite cheaply – purchased, largely unelected and certainly totally unrepresentative of the people. A cool inspection of its Members' records did not invite respect. Nor did they receive it, understandably, from their contemporaries. A tiny and otherwise unprivileged majority of the population was entitled to the vote, and benefited greatly from their purchased application to their civic duty.

This received wisdom, therefore, later much enshrined and hallowed, held that, by the end of the seventeenth century and throughout the eighteenth, the monarch had little political power, which now rested solely with his ministers and parliament. This was not the case.

Although the doctrine of the Divine Right of Kings ended in England with the trial and execution of King Charles I in 1649, the immediate aftermath of the Cromwellian tyranny may actually have helped to restore the monarchy, if on very different terms. But the ambitions of the politicians were not satiated, and as the military and economic power of England increased, these were augmented. Thus, although the institution of monarchy as supreme political power survived, it did so on increasingly realistic terms. A strange understanding had developed which was unique among the monarchies of Europe. No English monarch has refused to approve parliamentary legislation since the imperious Queen Anne, and although this did not at all inhibit the Hanoverians

[2] Vernon Bogdanor, *The Monarchy and the Constitution*, p. 5.

from constant interference and influence, this fact in itself had its significance. The grim precedents of Charles I and James II were an ever-present reminder to their foreign successors of the consequences of severe political misjudgement in the most vibrant, ambitious, and successful nation of its time.

Throughout the eighteenth century, in a country with no written constitution and with a highly fluid and volatile domestic political situation, the political role of the monarch was wholly undefined. But no one engaged in politics denied its existence or its omnipresent potency. It was significant that so much of the opprobrium for the loss of the American colonies – the one disaster of that otherwise triumphant period – fell upon George III personally, who at the height of his powers was the dominating force in British politics. He dismissed and appointed ministries; he intrigued; he used his funds and patronage for political purposes; and he spent heavily in elections, most notoriously in 1781. He was the most politically active of modern monarchs since the Stuarts – and, if one of the most controversial, also one of the most respected.

Throughout this early period British politics were, and were to continue to be, corrupt. Constituencies were easily purchased – although the price could be steep – and so were Members of Parliament. There were exceptions to this rule, like Edmund Burke,[3] but their careers did not prosper, although their influence did. There were no serious party affiliations nor organisations. In this fluidity of ambition the royal influence was crucial, and although criticised was not seriously challenged.

But, as George III clearly understood, the rules had changed. The

---

[3] 1729–97. Born and educated in Ireland, he came to London to establish himself as an author, and entered politics almost by accident as private secretary to the Marquis of Rockingham (1730–82), whose Whig views included strong independence of mind and brought him into collision with George III. A writer and orator of prodigious energy and independence, Burke's political career was a failure, but his influence during and after his lifetime was immense. His denunciation of the slave trade and the role of Warren Hastings and the East India Company, and his defence of the American colonists in their disputes with the British government were not successful at the time, but left their mark. In 1790 he was able to save Britain from its delusions about the French Revolution (see p. 10). An uncomfortable genius.

severe lessons of the previous century had been learned. If the monarch could no longer dare to ignore parliament, he could, and did, ensure that it was a parliament congenial to his interests and concerns. George III's placemen in the Commons, 'The King's Friends', sometimes numbered two hundred Members. When the King made it plain that anyone who voted for Catholic Emancipation in 1801 was his enemy, this resulted in the resignation of the Younger William Pitt; in 1807, on the same issue, Grenville's government was dismissed. But although George IV fully shared his father's hostility to the measure, and even threatened to abdicate if it was carried, it was passed in 1829 despite his opposition. This was significant evidence not only that George IV did not have a fraction of the popular support of his father, nor the respect of most politicians, but that politicians no longer automatically rallied to the royal nod nor feared the royal displeasure.

The portrayal of the seven-year reign of King William IV as an interlude between the dissipations and extravagances of the lamentable and much-hated George IV and the later glories of Queen Victoria pays inadequate tribute to one of the most attractive, enlightened and underestimated of modern British monarchs.

Following the death of his elder brother, George IV, in 1830, William came to the throne at a time of acute social and political turmoil, of which the most dramatic manifestation was the proposed Reform Bill. The situation whereby the burgeoning new cities were not represented at all in the House of Commons, whereas many empty fields were, was indefensible, but it had its defenders, and the King was no radical. But he was, fortunately for the monarchy, a realist. He took the somewhat innovative view that it was his task to assist and support his ministers. He was also by nature a conciliator, and a believer in the virtues of compromise.

These qualities were to be of central importance in the convulsions of 1831 and 1832 that resulted in the eventual passing of the great Reform Act. The Duke of Wellington and the Tories would not countenance such a parliamentary revolution. The King turned to the Whigs and Earl Grey, confident that an equally aristocratic, reactionary, and property-based confederation would not propose dramatic reforms. He, and the Tories, had reckoned without Lord Durham and Lord John Russell. The products of their labours were disclosed to an astounded House

7

of Commons in March 1831. Sixty constituencies were to be totally abolished; another forty-seven were to lose one Member each. And this was only the beginning.

Members of Parliament confronted with the abolition of their seats, often purchased at considerable cost, tended to become profoundly discontented. But the opponents of reform were frightened by the huge public support for it, and the King had noted the signs. In circumstances of high drama Lord Althorp piloted the second reading of the Reform Bill brilliantly through the Commons, but when the Bill went into Committee its opponents were ready. The first hostile amendment was carried by eight votes on 18 April and the Cabinet met to agree to a formal minute to the King that he should dissolve parliament. The King initially refused, but the dissolution went ahead, much to the fury of the Tories.

The subsequent election was fought entirely, and with much intensity, on the subject of Reform. The popular pressures were such that the Whigs won easily, but in the Lords the opposition to Reform was unassuaged. In October the Second Reform Bill was defeated in the Lords by forty-one votes. There was national uproar: Derby Gaol was stormed, Nottingham Castle was burned, there were huge demonstrations in London and three days' vicious rioting in Bristol, causing great damage and some loss of life. King William, fearful of bloody revolution, had much to be fearful about. But in this chaos and disorder, this supposedly unintelligent man, surrounded by family and advisers of a distinctly reactionary hue, maintained a shrewd and sensible attitude.

On 3 January 1832 Grey travelled to Brighton to ask the King for, in the first instance, a modest creation of Peers, with perhaps more to come, to ensure the passage of the Bill. To Grey's considerable surprise the King was in principle amenable, on the conditions that only the eldest sons of existing Peers would be involved and that the government would protect the prerogative of the Crown.

As the King knew, Grey himself was extremely reluctant to make the request, and, like the King, favoured persuasion and pressure upon the Lords. But again Committee proved the government's undoing, and the Cabinet decided it must resign unless the King created the necessary number of pro-Reform new Peers to carry the measure. This time he refused, and the government resigned. The King had accepted the case for Reform, but considered that the Grey Bill went too far. But Wellington refused the King's invitation to become Prime Minister again, and the King had no choice but to restore Grey.

After this episode the King's authority was severely weakened. His only hope was to use the influence of the monarchy to ensure that enough Tory Peers absented themselves from the Reform Bill proceedings. His Private Secretary, Sir Herbert Taylor – who, as has been rightly written, 'set the pattern for the devoted band of royal servants who have followed him'[4] – was instructed by the King to write to selected potential absentees, making it plain that their absence was essential if the new creation was to be avoided.

Unhappily, one of these letters went to one of the most vehement opponents of Reform, Lord Londonderry, who promptly published it. But the King's initiative succeeded nevertheless. On 4 June the Bill passed easily, with only twenty-two Peers voting against it. The King made his views on the matter clear when he refused to give it the Royal Assent in person, but the Reform Act had passed, and the fervent agitation in the country – which had also played an important part in the pressures upon the Tory Lords – faded away.

It may be thought excessive to call William IV 'the first constitutional monarch', since he still considered that he had strong political rights. In October 1834 he dismissed the Whig government under Lord Melbourne and asked Wellington to form another. But the latter, after his past experiences, told him that the Prime Minister must be in the Commons, and that Sir Robert Peel was the outstanding candidate. Peel was eventually tracked down in Italy, and on his return asked for an immediate dissolution, which the King granted. Although it went unremarked at the time, Wellington's advice was to have long-term results. He was not to be the last Prime Minister who was a Peer, but his assessment of the new realities of political power was characteristically shrewd.

Although the subsequent election went well for the embryonic Conservatives, Peel still did not have a majority. The King stated emphatically that any censure on his government 'would be a direct censure passed upon His Majesty's conduct, by a party avowing its determination to force itself upon him, and into his councils, in opposition to his declared

[4] Philip Ziegler, *King William IV*, p. 165.

9

principles and sentiments, his wishes and his conscience'. The Whigs, although they did not formally criticise the Peel government, succeeded in forcing its resignation by a succession of defeats in the Commons. The King, who had also demonstrated considerable political reality over the Reform Act, realised that he had no choice but to accept the Whigs, while making his reluctance to do so very evident. But by then the entire political and constitutional situation had changed, and to the advantage of the monarch.

Towards the end of the eighteenth century the assumptions of royal political power had been questioned, challenged, and even denied. There had then been a formidable stroke of good fortune.

The French Revolution of 1789 was initially acclaimed by English radicals and democratic idealists, but their Republican enthusiasm was soon quenched by the awful reality of The Terror and the matchless denunciations of Edmund Burke in his *Reflections on the Revolution in France*, published in November 1790, at first derided – not least by Pitt – but which transformed English attitudes. There is a case to be made that the example of the French Revolution, with its chaotic brutality and plunge into mindless anarchy followed by militaristic despotism, played a considerable part in restoring the fortunes of the British monarchy.

As in 1649–60, the alternatives to monarchical rule, however much it was denigrated, did not appear attractive. But after the victorious conclusion to the interminable Napoleonic Wars in 1815, domestic concerns and politics had resumed their prominence, and the very purpose of monarchy was again publicly and often vehemently questioned. By the time William came to the throne, however, something remarkable had happened. The marriage of his niece, Princess Charlotte, the daughter of the Prince Regent, to Prince Leopold of Saxe-Coburg-Gotha in 1816 can now be seen as a catalytic event in the history of the British monarchy. Charlotte had been rescued from her parents and the imbroglio of a bitterly divided Court by her marriage to Leopold, who had brought with him a German doctor whom he had met by chance at a military hospital. But he was much more than a doctor. He may fairly be considered to be the genius of the modern British monarchy.

Christian Friedrich Stockmar was born in Coburg in 1787, the second son of a successful lawyer and distinguished bibliophile. Stockmar's childhood was spent in and near Coburg, where he studied medicine and practised before and after the war. But from a remarkably early age he had dedicated himself to two great political causes – the liberation and unification of Germany, and the establishment of strong links between Germany and England, an ambition that had even preceded the Anglo-Prussian coalition which had eventually defeated Napoleon. He had learned English, and, from afar, was a keen observer of the British political scene, and especially of the position of the monarchy. What he saw of the latter filled him with critical concern, but his opinion was that 'the English surpass all others in Europe in energy and vigour of character'. When he first came to England at Leopold's request in 1816 he was enraptured by London, indeed by almost everything English. As he recorded: 'The country, the houses, their arrangement, everything, especially in the neighbourhood of London, delighted me, and so raised my spirits, that I kept saying to myself, "Here you must be happy, here you cannot be ill."'

Stockmar was prone to moods, veering from almost excessive exuberance of spirits to depression, but he stood out in any company as a man of thoughtfulness and wisdom. He became in effect the political and constitutional adviser to Charlotte, heiress to the throne, and her husband. The two men had established three crucial points for the future reign of Queen Charlotte – a strict moral tone, domestic happiness, and impartiality from party politics. To these Stockmar added his own form of liberalism, which was a key aspect of his character; indeed, in some respects he was a radical, and he despised the selfishness and reactionary nature of the rest of the Royal Family, the British aristocracy and most politicians. But he also saw the threat to the institution of monarchy itself unless change came.

However, the influence of this remarkable trio was to find its ultimate expression through others. Political opposition to Leopold, and to Stockmar himself, had ensured that a foreigner would be prevented from becoming the personal physician to the future Queen of England. As a result, Stockmar was not in attendance when Charlotte went into labour in November 1817, and he could do nothing to prevent the subsequent birth of, in his words, 'a fine large dead boy'. In spite of this tragedy the Princess herself initially seemed quite well, but her condition quickly deteriorated and, although Stockmar was immediately summoned, she died five hours after her stillborn son. The plans for a rejuvenated monarchy had been shattered.

A further manifestation of this was that, as Stockmar sardonically noted, 'in opening up the prospect of succession to the throne to the younger sons of George III, [the death of Charlotte] inspired them with a desire to marry'. Among them was the Duke of Kent, George III's fourth son, who had for some time admired Leopold's widowed sister, Victoire. They married in Coburg on 27 May 1818; on 24 May 1819 she gave birth to a daughter, Princess Victoria. Soon afterwards, also in 1819, Leopold's brother Ernest, the Duke of Coburg, and his wife Louise celebrated another birth, that of their second son – christened Francis Charles August Albert Emmanuel, but known in the family as Albert. As it happened, fate had supplied Stockmar and Leopold with new material for their vision of the 'New Monarchy'.

Charlotte's death, which most obstetric experts considered then and later to have been wholly unnecessary, remains one of the great 'ifs' of modern British history. If she and her son had lived, there would have been no King William IV, and no Queen Victoria. Whether she would have developed into the kind of constitutional monarch that her husband and Stockmar had planned was not as certain, given her somewhat imperious temperament; but the auguries had seemed promising. Now Stockmar had to begin again, under what appeared to be considerably less propitious circumstances.

Prince Albert received an outstandingly good education at Coburg, under the thoughtful inspection of Leopold – who became King of the Belgians in 1831 – and Stockmar. His remarkable variety of interests impressed even the highly critical Stockmar, who had become a trusted influence with the young Princess Victoria. But, contrary to often repeated mythology, sometimes from otherwise reliable historians,[5] there was no inevitability about the marriage of Victoria and Albert, nor was it engineered by Leopold or Stockmar. The former did arrange for the Prince to visit England to meet his cousin when they were aged seventeen, but it was not a success. Both were very much aware that the Duchess of Kent and Leopold were hopeful, but there was no question of an engagement, and even less after the death of William IV on 20 July 1837, when the young Princess became Queen Victoria. Prince Albert wrote her a letter of congratulation; there is no record of any reply.

[5] Including C. Woodham-Smith, in her *Queen Victoria*.

The eighteen-year-old Queen was enchanted by her Whig Prime Minister, Melbourne, who was not only profoundly and cynically reactionary but also disliked Germans and the Coburgs, although making a notable exception for Stockmar. Prince Albert, meanwhile, finished his remarkable education and then embarked on an extended European tour. What he heard about his cousin alarmed him: she had fallen out with Leopold; was engaged in controversial politics on the Whig side; and her early popularity had declined abruptly. 'Victoria is said to be incredibly stubborn,' the Prince wrote. 'She delights in Court ceremonies, etiquette, and trivial formalities. These are gloomy prospects.'

Stockmar agreed. He had accompanied Albert on his travels, observing him closely, and was still not sure about him. What he *was* sure about was that Queen Victoria was acting against all the principles that he, Charlotte and Leopold had devised. He considered that the Queen had been poorly educated, was opinionated and arrogant, and had demonstrated few signs of political intelligence. It was an excessively severe judgement, but there was some truth in it.

Her inheritance had not been an unpromising one. The reign of William IV had been surprisingly successful; it had seen the passage of the Reform Act, and if he had used his powers to dismiss two administrations, he had at least been even-handed, one being Tory and the other Whig. It would have been a remarkably far-sighted person who could have foreseen that these would be the last occasions on which these summary powers would be used by a British sovereign. But, more surprisingly, he had actually been reasonably popular, which was a distinct change after George IV, on whose death *The Times* sourly remarked that 'no monarch will be less generally mourned'.

But within two years of her accession Queen Victoria appeared to have undone what good her predecessor had achieved. 'She has become as passionate as a spoilt child,' Stockmar gloomily reported to Leopold. 'If she feels offended, she throws everything overboard without exception.'

The influence of Melbourne was total; as Lord Aberdeen wrote, truthfully, 'He has a young and inexperienced infant in his hands, whose whole conduct and opinions must necessarily be in complete subservience to his views.' She herself, then much wiser, wrote many years later of Melbourne that 'he was an excellent man, but too much a party man, and made me a party Queen'. What made the relationship dangerous was that it was well known that the Queen, derided as 'Mrs Melbourne', fully supported a reactionary government that was determined not to give way further to democratic movements, and especially the Chartists, whose famous Six Points included such horrors as manhood suffrage, the secret ballot, abolition of the property qualification for Members of Parliament, the creation of equal electoral districts and the payment of MPs. Of all their points the only one not later attained, blessedly, was that of annual General Elections.

It was not only the Queen's ardent commitment to a government that even Melbourne recognised was deeply hated that so troubled Stockmar, now temporarily out of royal favour because of his connections with Leopold, but that she clearly had no idea of what being a constitutional monarch meant. In a notably careful letter to her he wrote, 'All trades must be learned, and nowadays the trade of a constitutional sovereign, to do it well, is a very difficult one.' The caution was not heeded.

The times were tumultuous. In addition to the agitation of the Chartists, the Anti-Corn Law League raised the banner of Free Trade. The Court too was in ferment, and the reputation of the Queen plummeted further. Her hatred for the Tories, and for their leader, Peel, became scandalous when, in the summer of 1839, Melbourne resigned, and she had to send for that 'nasty wretch' Peel to form a government. Their audience together was a disaster, and far worse was to follow. She insisted that she retain all her Ladies of the Household and Bedchamber – who were, of course, all Whigs. 'I will show them [the Tories] that I am Queen of England,' she wrote to Melbourne. Peel had to give up his attempt to form a government, the Whigs returned, and the Tories were outraged.

It so happened that this was the last occasion when a British sovereign was able to prevent the formation of a government that was personally and politically uncongenial to the monarch, but the 'Bedchamber Crisis' appalled Stockmar: 'How could they let the Queen make such mistakes, to the injury of the monarchy?' he lamented. The problem was that 'they' were not disinterested advisers. But the Queen was shaken by the ferocity of the abuse hurled at her, began to doubt Melbourne, and started to consider marriage. And then, on her second meeting with her cousin Albert, she fell passionately in love with him.

It would not be correct to describe Prince Albert, whose marriage to the Queen in February 1840 was one of the best things that ever happened to the British monarchy, as a protégé of Stockmar, or even of Leopold. The Queen was taken aback by the hostility to her choice of husband, although it did not greatly surprise Stockmar. There was uproar over his rank and precedence, and his proposed annuity was drastically cut, from which Albert drew the correct conclusion that 'the people of England are not pleased with the marriage', but which the Queen blamed entirely upon 'these infernal scoundrels', the Tories. The problems were that he was an unknown German Prince without means, a nephew of Leopold, and perceived as another foreign adventurer. In spite of his extraordinary later contributions to his adoptive country, these ignorant prejudices against him were strongly held for most of his relatively brief lifetime.

The real trouble, after their marriage, was that Queen Victoria saw no role for her husband beyond being that of her husband, whereas Prince Albert had more lofty ambitions. What his Private Secretary, George Anson – appointed by the Queen and Melbourne, without consultation with Albert, to his anger – soon realised, was that, as he told Melbourne, 'If you required a cypher in the difficult position of Consort of the Queen you ought not to have selected the Prince.' Anson was among the first to appreciate the exceptional qualities, and resolution, of this modest but determined young man.

Prince Albert's brilliance and contributions in so many areas has often obscured his really important role, which was that of a natural cerebral politician. But politics are not an intellectual business. He came to the task young and inexperienced, and was to find, after some harsh lessons, that there was rather more to British politics than his reading and Stockmar's constant advice and criticisms – although it would have been better if he had heeded the latter more.

His first concern was to ease the Queen out of her fatal commitment to the Whigs. As Stockmar wisely advised him in May 1841, when the Melbourne government was in its death-throes:

If things come to a change of ministry, then the great axiom, irrefragably one and the same for all ministries, is this, *viz*: the Crown supports frankly, honourably, and with all its might, the ministry of the time, whatever it be, so long as it commands a majority, and governs with integrity for the welfare and advancement of the country. A King, who as a constitutional King cannot or will not carry this maxim into practice, deliberately descends from the lofty position on which the constitution has placed him to the lower one of a mere party chief. Be you, therefore, the constitutional genius of the Queen; do not content yourself with merely whispering this maxim in her ear when circumstances serve, but strive also to carry it out into practice at the right time and by the worthiest means.

The Prince's political influence was for a time non-existent, that of Melbourne remaining dominant until the General Election of 1841, which resulted in the Queen's favoured government being defeated, to her astonishment and dismay; understandably, since it was unprecedented for the ministry enjoying the royal support to be defeated. The impact of the 1832 Reform Act was being felt for the first time. Peel had realised that it had totally changed the political game; Prince Albert and Stockmar had also; the Queen, who considered that the result was 'a majority returned against her', had not.

The very different attitudes of the Queen initially strained the marriage almost to breaking-point, to Stockmar's horror. Fortunately both turned to him in their distress, and from Coburg he counselled on matters large and small – 'A Queen does not drink a bottle of wine at a meal,' he once wrote rather primly – and the storms passed, to be succeeded by an almost sublime, if occasionally tempestuous, relationship.

The Queen was a passionate woman, who had fallen passionately in love with her future husband, and remained so. She was also increasingly amazed, as were so many others, by the astonishing range of his talents and interests, which ranged from music to architecture, science to garden design, academic scholarship to the condition of the poor, jewellery to international affairs, and literature to industry. He was, as Peel marvelled, 'the most extraordinary young man you will have ever met'. But Peel's awed and justified admiration for a man of such capacities, and the adoration of the Queen, were not universally shared, as Prince Albert realised, and the deepest suspicions and hostility were aroused over his political role. Albert's political sympathies and antipathies were personal rather than partisan. He considered Melbourne a bad influence on the Queen and the country; he developed a genuine personal admiration for Peel, and persuaded the Queen to revise her hostile attitude towards him. This took some time, but, once convinced, she entirely changed her opinion. But this became politically perilous when Peel, his party elected in 1841 as a Protectionist one, became converted to the repeal of the Corn Laws at the end of 1845. The Prince, a fervent advocate of Free Trade as well as a friend and ally of Peel, made his support for him and his dramatic volte-face only too obvious and public. The enraged and betrayed Tories, inspired by the young Benjamin Disraeli and his leader, mentor, and benefactor Lord George Bentinck, could not stomach Peel's perfidy. When Prince Albert made a public display of his position by personally attending the House of Commons for Peel's speech introducing the measure, Bentinck rebuked him for his partisanship in a few withering sentences.

Peel fell, and the Whigs returned. But Prince Albert, to whom political personality meant so much, perhaps too much, had made another, and deeply formidable, enemy in Lord Palmerston. The Prince disliked him personally, regarding him – quite justifiably – as a man of inferior morals; politically, he considered Palmerston's flamboyant foreign policy – and his gratuitous espousal of liberal, even revolutionary, policies in Europe – to be irresponsible, ill-considered and fraught with constitutional peril. The revolutionary surge that swept through Europe in 1848 did not reach Britain, but Palmerston's enthusiasm for it was, understandably, a cause for serious alarm to the Queen and Prince.

But the real problem concerned Palmerston's cavalier approach not only to foreign policy but to the monarchy itself. The greatest single mistake Prince Albert made was deliberately to engineer Palmerston's dismissal as Foreign Secretary in 1851. Palmerston was contemptuous, even refusing to return his seals of office in person, and then embarked upon an exceptionally skilful and malevolent press and parliamentary campaign of vilification of 'malign foreign influences'. 'Pam' was in many respects the first modern populist British politician, far ahead of his time in the techniques of personal publicity and press manipulation, and a cynical but inspired master of the House of Commons. He was a dangerous adversary. The young Prince Albert was unwise to take him on. He may have had the arguments, but he was alone; Palmerston deployed the brutal political battalions. Palmerston won. Although it had been a mistake to challenge him and to stand, however rightly, against the tides of public and political opinion – especially over the causes of the Crimean War in 1854 – that Palmerston not only followed but actively encouraged, by the mid-1850s the Prince's worth was at last beginning to be recognised, not least by Palmerston himself. In victory Palmerston had recognised an interesting and impressive contestant.

For his part Albert had now realised that royal political *influence* would have to replace political *power*, which had passed from the monarch to the politicians for ever. But if his last stand had been unsuccessful, the compromise was not insignificant. His experience was to leave, although not immediately, a lasting impression upon the British monarchy and its role.

But when he did this last service he was mortally ill. The cause of his death was typhoid fever, but what so struck his wife and his physicians was his listless and fatalistic lack of resistance. He was exhausted and depressed, and a patient who has lost the will to live usually does not survive. Prince Albert died in Windsor Castle on 14 December 1861, at the age of forty-two. His death was in itself a disaster, as well as a family tragedy, for the monarchy. He had restored its political and popular position after a period of intense controversy by his emerging understanding of what the new realities were. He had appreciated the extents, as well as the limitations, of the monarch-as-politician. He had secured, for the first time, the trust and confidence of politicians – not for the institution of monarchy, but for himself. Disraeli, at that point in his career far from being a Court favourite, considered on the Prince's death that 'he had undoubtedly a fixed determination to increase the personal power of the Crown; had he lived to add to his great industry and talent the weight which age and long experience would have given in dealing with statesmen of his own standing, he might have made himself almost as powerful as the Prime Minister of the day'.[6]

But he had gone.

In 1867 Walter Bagehot, an economist, journalist and essayist of exceptional quality, but hardly a constitutional expert, published *The English Constitution*, which has misled many later commentators as a portrait of the monarchy as it then was, whereas it was in fact a portrait of the monarchy as Bagehot wished it to be. He shrewdly emphasised the importance of a royal *family* and the requirement of a moral example. 'We have come to regard the Crown as the head of our *morality*. We have come to believe that it is natural to have a virtuous sovereign, and that domestic virtues are as likely to be found on thrones as they are eminent

6 Quoted in Bogdanor, op. cit., p. 26.

when there.' These were standards which, Bagehot observed somewhat impertinently but also perceptively, the Prince of Wales was unlikely to set before and when he became King – Albert Edward, later King Edward VII, was at the time not only alienated from his mother but pursuing a life of pleasure-seeking which brought him close to the brink of several major scandals. But Bagehot's most famous passage contained his observation that 'the sovereign has, under a constitutional monarchy such as ours, three rights – the right to be consulted, the right to encourage, the right to warn. And a King of great sense and sagacity would want no others.' Although there are dangers in ascribing excessive wisdom and shrewdness to Bagehot – he did, after all, describe George III as 'a meddling maniac', a judgement not shared by either informed contemporaries or subsequent historians – he did face the very real hazards of the hereditary principle of succession, while accepting it as the price for an unelected monarch and Head of State.

In doing so he understood the gravest weakness of the case for the hereditary monarch, the element of sheer luck – for good or ill. In recognising this he was not only exceptionally perceptive but courageous in the context of his time:

> A constitutional sovereign must in the common course of govern-ment be a man of common ability. I am afraid, looking to the early acquired feebleness of hereditary dynasties, that we must expect him to be a man of inferior ability. Theory and experience both teach that the education of a prince can be but a poor education, and that a Royal Family will generally have less ability than other families . . . Probably in most cases the greatest wisdom of a constitutional King would show itself in well-considered inaction.

This comment was, and remained, uncomfortably close to the mark. The modern British Royal Family has indeed included men and women of 'inferior ability'. So have all families, however eminent, as a glance at the record of the Churchill family demonstrates, to take but one spectacular example.

But 'ability' is a contested term. For all the limitations of her back-ground and education, Queen Victoria was unquestionably a woman of exceptional ability and talent – and, above all, of character. Her husband's qualities amounted to near genius. But in terms of character, the matter becomes more complex, and in this respect considerably more impressive, although not universally so.

The Queen's character contained many contradictions. She had her passions and prejudices and areas of ignorance, but also formidable common sense. Once she emerged from her long widowhood depression, the second period of unpopularity in her reign – as Bagehot observed, correctly, 'to be invisible is to be forgotten' – she was again an indefatigable reader and writer, and, as her ministers knew only too well, a constant if invisible presence in their deliberations and calculations. Disraeli wooed her with cynical brilliance, and won her affections and esteem. Her attitude towards the Liberal leader William Gladstone – whom Albert had greatly admired – gradually changed after 1868, when he became Prime Minister and led one of the great modern reforming governments. Not discouraged by Disraeli, the Queen became a reactionary nuisance when Liberal governments were in office, and not above keeping in close touch with Conservative Oppositions; as Lord Salisbury later discovered, she was also a burden on Conservative Prime Ministers, although an infinitely more helpful one. It has been argued that Gladstone, by loyally not revealing the Queen's blatant partisanship, saved the monarchy.[7] But the other political reality was that the fledgling Republican movement – which had started in the late 1860s, when the Queen's intolerably prolonged bereavement was causing much criticism – had been a very short-lived affair, ironically enough destroyed by the Prince of Wales's near-fatal illness in 1871. Also, Disraeli had skilfully brought the Queen back into the limelight, as the soaring triumphs of the Industrial Revolution and the return of the imperial dream made the monarchy more popular than ever.

Her relationship with Gladstone began to deteriorate only after 1870. The Queen, the Prince Consort and he had, after all, been Peelites, and she well remembered her husband's high regard for this man of moral principle and erudition. Then he offended her in August 1871 by suggesting, reasonably but tactlessly, that she should postpone her departure to Balmoral for a few days as parliament was still sitting. He

[7] Frank Hardie's sweeping assessment, that 'if Gladstone had told what he knew, almost certainly the reign, and the monarchy itself, would have ended'(*The Political Influence of the British Monarchy, 1868–1952*, p. 77), has been rather too easily accepted by historians over-impressed by the fervour of the British electorate for their elected leaders.

did not realise that she was genuinely unwell, and handled the matter clumsily.

But Gladstone's reaction may be regarded as even more extraordinary, writing to her Private Secretary, Sir Henry Ponsonby, on 16 August that: 'Upon the whole, I think it has been the most sickening piece of experience which I have had during nearly forty years of public life. *Worse* things may easily be imagined; but smaller and meaner causes for the decay of Thrones cannot be conceived. It is like the worm which bores the bark of a noble tree and so breaks the channel of its life.' The Queen's increasing conviction that Gladstone was mentally deranged looks less implausible when one contemplates such frenetic outbursts.[8]

Gladstone certainly dated the personal schism from this incident, noting that when he went to Balmoral soon afterwards he felt himself 'on a new and different footing with her . . . The repellent power which she so well knows how to use has been put in action towards me on this occasion for the first time since the formation of the government.' Gladstone began to concern himself about what he called 'the royalty question', noting that promising younger Liberals like Sir Charles Dilke and Joseph Chamberlain were publicly flirting with Republicanism. His proposal in 1872 that the Prince of Wales should serve as the Queen's representative in Dublin was rejected by her with contumely, and without much thought.

The Prince, too, was not at all attracted by the thought of spending several months each winter in Ireland, which he considered to be a form of dismal exile. More bizarrely, Gladstone suggested that he should also establish a 'pure Court' in the summer season, and provide the leadership in society that the Queen was conspicuously failing to do – this was not only tactless but unrealistic, given the Prince's character and companions at this time.

Overall, Gladstone's Irish proposal was remarkably insensitive, since he must have known – or should have known – that the Queen denied her heir all access to state and political papers, never consulted him, and considered him wholly unworthy of his father.

[8] In contrast, she agreed to Disraeli's identical request in 1874 that she should meet the Tsar of Russia, which Disraeli characteristically called 'my unrivalled triumph'.

Also, her hostility towards Ireland was, although profoundly unfortunate, understandable. She was a deeply committed Protestant. Her last visit had been in 1861 with her husband, and all had gone well, but she was subsequently deeply angered when her personal gift of a statue of the Prince Consort, unveiled in 1871 on Leinster Lawn in Dublin, was severely damaged within two months by a Fenian attempt to blow it up. This was a wound that she did not forget or forgive.

Matters were not to improve: the visit of the Prince of Wales to Ireland in 1885 was, in terms of popular approval, a disaster; in her Jubilees of 1887 and 1897 it was conspicuous that no addresses or telegrams of congratulation came from Southern Ireland. The assassination of the newly appointed Chief Secretary Lord Frederick Cavendish in Phoenix Park in Dublin in 1882, the violent horrors of the Land League, the activities of the Irish Nationalist leader Charles Stewart Parnell, and the campaign for Home Rule did not improve her opinion of her rebellious Southern Irish subjects. But although she regarded Parnell as 'a really bad and worthless man who had to answer for many lives lost in Ireland', and was 'dead against Home Rule as calamitous for Ireland, hazardous for England and tending towards separation', she also had little time for the Ulster Protestants, writing in 1888 that 'it is grievous to think what would be so good for the peace of Ireland will probably be prevented by these well-meaning but fanatical Protestants'. Also, although she hated Home Rule and had come to regard Gladstone with a special aversion, she frankly admitted his sincerity and high motives. She was a complex personality.

It would be wholly wrong, however, to depict the Queen in the last twenty-five years of her reign solely as a bigoted and interfering reactionary Tory. When the Liberal Chancellor of the Exchequer, Robert Lowe, had proposed a tax on matches for his 1871 Budget, for example, she had written to protest: 'The Queen trusts that the Govt. will reconsider this proposal, & try & substitute some other wh. will not press upon the poor.' The Cabinet agreed with her, and the proposal was dropped. Unhappily, it was revived by a later – Conservative – government, and occasioned a strike by the desperately poor match-makers, most of whom were young women, an event which was to prove one of the most important and yet underestimated events in the emergence of modern British social conscience.

Her principal dislike was for extremists, on both sides of the political arena, and she much favoured coalitions. Salisbury's last government, a Conservative–Liberal Unionist coalition, was exactly what she favoured. She wanted a strong foreign policy based on real military strength, and never forgot the lessons of the Crimean War and the terrible unpreparedness of the army. Her dominant concern was her perception of the national interest, and her mediatory role in resolving the impasse in 1884 over the Third Reform Bill, by applying pressure on Salisbury for the Conservatives to make concessions, rather belied Gladstone's son's comment that her 'lofty isolation kept her apart from all the essential dynamics of politics', an opinion that his father would not have shared. Apparently aloof from the fray in public, in reality she was deeply involved in it, so much so that Lady Ponsonby – like her husband, a committed Liberal – was fearful that Gladstone 'will show his teeth about royalty altogether, and I wouldn't answer for its lasting long after that' – a comment that severely overestimated Gladstone's popularity and the Queen's lack of it. By the last two decades of her reign she was popularly identified with British triumphs, while her politicians – especially Gladstone – took the blame for any reverses.

Her last major political battle was over Home Rule for Ireland, a subject on which, as we have seen, she was passionate and intensely partisan. She seldom opened parliament in person, but did so in January 1886 when the Queen's Speech of the short-lived first Salisbury government contained an especially strongly-worded section denouncing Home Rule, to which Gladstone had suddenly and dramatically become converted. Like most of her English subjects, she did not really understand Ireland, but what Gladstone failed to appreciate was the Queen's very understandable outrage at the proposal, given without any warning, of the division of the United Kingdom. 'Poor Ireland,' Gladstone lamented privately in 1886, 'it holds but a small place in her heart. If it held the same place as Scotland, the history of Anglo-Irish relations would have been substantially different' – a remarkable tribute in itself to the Queen's authority.

But she had at last come to understand the limitations of her political power. She could, and did, strongly influence ministerial appointments, and was very much involved in the choice of Lord Rosebery for Foreign Secretary in 1886 and 1892, and in his becoming Prime Minister when Gladstone finally, and very reluctantly, resigned in 1894. She also made herself phenomenally well-informed, and if some of her prejudices were wrong, by no means all of them were. Her common sense only occasionally slipped, as when she deliberately sent her famous *en clair* telegram to Gladstone and his principal colleagues on the death of General Gordon at Khartoum in January 1885. On that celebrated occasion she was certainly echoing the national mood of humiliation and fury, but it was a stinging public rebuke to her ministers which the Prince Consort, after his Palmerstonian battles, would not have publicly delivered. The text ran: 'These news from Khartoum are frightful, and to think that all this might have been prevented and many precious lives saved by earlier action is too fearful.'

Gladstone's reply, which only thinly masked his intense anger, was a minor masterpiece of dignified offensiveness, ending: 'Mr Gladstone does not presume to estimate the means of judgement possessed by Your Majesty, but so far as his information goes he is not altogether able to follow the conclusion which Your Majesty has been pleased thus to announce to him.' Her Private Secretary, Sir Henry Ponsonby, failed to persuade her to apologise to Gladstone, but she had assessed the public reaction to this national humiliation more acutely than either Ponsonby or the Prime Minister.

She firmly believed that she had preserved the royal prerogatives intact, with the significant caveat that monarchs would be wise not to enforce their full rights. As has been sensibly observed, if somewhat inelegantly, 'Unable to grasp the changing constitution intellectually, she nevertheless played it by ear.'[9] If her political judgements were often intuitive, they were based upon her immense commitment and unrivalled experience. As Hardie has put it, 'To be Queen of England from [the age of] eighteen to eighty-two is, to say the least, character-forming.' Through her own fortunes and personality Queen Victoria had herself totally changed the monarchy.

In the battles between herself and Prince Albert on the one side and Palmerston and the popular press on the other in the 1840s and early 1850s, the latter had decisively won, as Albert realised. The strategy had changed from one of confrontation to co-operation, from hostility to mutual confidence and influence. This worked well with Disraeli and Salisbury, if not with Gladstone after 1876, but a certain pattern had

[9] Elizabeth Longford, *Victoria R.I.*, p. 566.

been set, and this was to be Queen Victoria's most enduring political contribution. Common sense had triumphed.

The final period of Victoria's reign was shadowed by war in South Africa, when the Boer Republics, deliberately goaded by the Colonial Secretary, Joseph Chamberlain, his High Commissioner Sir Alfred Milner and the excessively ambitious and impatient Cecil Rhodes, rose in rebellion against the British partly in response to the disastrous Rhodes-inspired attempt to seize Johannesburg in 1896. It was suspected – rightly – that Rhodes had acted with the knowledge and approval of the British government. The fiasco was made worse by a telegram of congratulation to the Boer leader, Kruger, from Victoria's grandson Kaiser Wilhelm of Germany.

When war broke out in 1899, forecasts of a swift and easy British victory were soon revised. For a time, as one military disaster followed another, to undisguised glee in France, Germany and Russia, it seemed that here was another Crimea. The Queen was resolute, the tide of the war turned, but seldom was a war won at greater cost. The apparently overwhelming power of the Royal Navy precluded any European intervention, especially German. This fact was not lost on the German Emperor and his advisers. The heaviest, and near-fatal, price the British paid for this disastrous conflict was the German decision to build a great navy.

Queen Victoria did not live to see the end of the war, which lingered on miserably until 1902. She died at Osborne on 22 January 1901. The sixty-three years of her reign had seen her country and Empire rise to unparalleled eminence, and the previously discredited monarchy now seemed invulnerable.

2

TWO UNDERESTIMATED MONARCHS

Q ueen Victoria's – and Bagehot's – apprehensions about her eldest son and successor, fully shared by many others, turned out to be misplaced. King Edward VII, Rudyard Kipling's derided 'corpulent voluptuary', mocked by many sophisticates as a self-indulgent and impatient philistine, nonetheless acquired a remarkable popularity. The new King did not pretend to be anything different from what he was, and there was a warmth to him to which people responded. But there was also a shrewdness that made him greatly underestimated.

As R. C. K. Ensor, otherwise somewhat dismissive of the King, later recognised,

Edward VII had, and seized, a great opportunity to strike the public imagination. For he was not only a King succeeding a long-widowed Queen, but a brilliant man of the world succeeding a recluse. The Queen had shunned pomp and publicity; but he loved them. Along with his frank amiability went a genial delight in display, a passion for uniforms and decorations, for sumptuous entertainments and processions, and big shows of every kind. For a constitutional monarch, whose duty consists more in symbolizing power than in wielding it, an important part of that duty is to exhibit the symbol to advantage before men's eyes. This King Edward understood much better than his mother.[1]

Edward VII was the most magnificent and munificent British monarch since George IV. He brought back style and glamour to the monarchy at a time of immense national self-confidence. He was genially self-indulgent in most temptations of the flesh. His appetite was prodigious. To her subjects Queen Victoria had been awesome, respected, but distant; in total contrast, her successor was a warm-blooded man who had been in several escapades, was a successful owner of racehorses and manifestly enjoyed life. That it was a very expensive life aroused surprisingly little jealousy or criticism during a period of increasing awareness of the poverty and deprivation that contrasted so jarringly with the wealth and power of Britain and her Empire.

Edwards VII's reign saw the consolidation of the Labour Party and the development of militant trade unionism. It was a time of social and political upheaval at home and mounting tensions abroad. But the curious fact was that, unlike in other European monarchies, this discontent was not directed towards the Royal Family. The British people have never enthusiastically embraced Puritanism or self-denial. This may be regrettable in the view of many, but may also help to explain their incorrigible enthusiasm and high spirits, instinct for survival, and enjoyment of life.

It is a remarkable combination and one which King Edward VII personified. He was enormously popular, despite his many defects of character. There was on occasion a rasping unpleasantness and grossness about him that many found repugnant. But there was also kindness, amiability, and his mother's common sense, and he had inherited rather more of his father's intelligence than was usually realised. His outstanding achievement was to be the first modern British monarch who was genuinely loved. The tribute of Admiral Sir John ('Jackie') Fisher, whom the King much admired and strongly supported in his battles to reform the navy, had a point: 'He wasn't clever, but he always did the right thing, which is better than brains.' But this, also, was an underestimation: King Edward *was* clever.

Prince Albert's educational endeavours had not been entirely in vain,

[1] R. C. K. Ensor, *England, 1870–1914*, p. 342.

but in the long period between his death and his son's accession the latter had been given few opportunities by his mother. He had had no discernible role. He became easily, and famously, bored. If he was not a faithful husband, he was not an unkind one, and he was an admirable father. The death of his elder son Albert Victor, Duke of Clarence, in January 1892, at the age of twenty-eight, may now be considered a national deliverance, but he was much loved by his parents and younger brother, George, Duke of York, who now took his place in the succession and married his brother's fiancée, Princess Mary of Teck.

If Edward VII had been given serious responsibilities during the nearly forty years he was Prince of Wales – which, if Prince Albert had lived, he surely would have been – his talents would have been given their opportunity. As it was, they were largely wasted. His actual performance as King demonstrated what could have been.

He was as seriously underrated by most politicians as he had been by his mother. They remembered his past as Prince of Wales and his closeness to scandal, and many considered him a grotesque dilettante. His first Prime Minister, the cold and unreachable Unionist Arthur Balfour, refused to permit him to see Cabinet papers before decisions were reached, and his political interventions were often resented and resisted. Even after the Balfour government had fallen in December 1905 and been replaced by the Liberals, his Private Secretary and close friend Francis Knollys wrote on 29 November 1907 that 'there is no use in ministers *liking* the King if he is treated as an absolute puppet'. The King was not prepared to be treated as a puppet. The fact that Knollys was a committed Liberal was in some respects a hazard, and at least partly explains Balfour's almost contemptuous treatment of the King, but demonstrated that the Victorian era had definitely ended.[2]

King Edward's political style was considerably more subtle than most people realised, then or later. He was far better informed about public opinion than Balfour – a notably remote man who prided himself on not reading newspapers – appreciated. Understandably, there was little common ground between the non-intellectual but warm-hearted monarch and his intellectually superior, arrogant, cold and calculating

[2] Francis Knollys, created Baron Knollys in 1902, had been the King's Private Secretary and confidant since 1870. His sister Charlotte was both Lady-in-Waiting and devoted friend of Queen Alexandra, whom Edward had married in 1863.

Prime Minister. Balfour almost invariably got his political calculations wrong, but, equally invariably, emerged personally unscathed, 'like a powerful, graceful cat walking delicately and unsoiled across a rather muddy street', as Churchill felicitously put it.[3]

The King was considerably more sensitive to human problems than most of the British upper classes, and did not lack independence of thought or action. When he agreed to be a pall-bearer at the funeral of Gladstone his mother angrily demanded what precedent he had followed and what advice he had taken: he replied, magnificently, that he knew of no precedent and had taken no advice. He so loathed the atrocious policies of his kinsman King Leopold II of the Belgians in the Congo that he totally resisted all attempts by his ministers to effect a reconciliation; his outrage at the incompetence of the military medical units in the South African war also had its results. He was a deeply informed and enlightened supporter of navy and army reforms – a natural conciliator and, usually, a shrewd judge of character.

He was also an exceptionally good listener, who often pretended to know very little about the subject under discussion, a tactic that some found flattering but which confirmed others in the mistaken belief that he was ill-informed. Frederick Ponsonby[4] came to the view that, once he had become King, had seen the state papers and was part of government, he was determined to be totally discreet, a quality for which he had not been previously noted. Edward's lack of interest in domestic politics was emphasised by the fact that he loved European travel, and on average spent more than three months a year abroad. But the trip to Paris in 1903 was the single most dramatic excursion, and undertaken in almost total defiance of the unwritten limits for a constitutional sovereign.

It was the King's own idea to undertake a Mediterranean tour, with several official visits, including one, to ministerial consternation, to the Pope. He planned it in complete secrecy, without consultation

[3] Winston Churchill, *Great Contemporaries*.
[4] 1867–1935. The second son of Henry Ponsonby, he was Equerry and Assistant Private Secretary to Queen Victoria, Equerry to King Edward VII, Assistant Private Secretary to George V 1910–14, Keeper of the Privy Purse 1914–35, Lieutenant-Governor of Windsor Castle 1928–35, and created Lord Sysonby 1935. He was universally known as 'Fritz'.

with the Prime Minister, the Foreign Secretary (Lord Lansdowne) or other ministers, and he abandoned Queen Victoria's custom of inviting a Cabinet minister as one of the royal party, taking instead the rapidly rising diplomat Charles Hardinge as a more useful member. It was not until the royal yacht had left Lisbon that the King confided to Ponsonby that the tour would include Malta, Naples, Rome and Paris.

Anti-British feelings in the French capital were running high, the old animosities fuelled further by the South African war and not assisted by British political and press hostility towards France. The Ambassador did not welcome the royal visit, and nor did Lansdowne, whose relations with the King were consistently clouded. The Cabinet was not consulted, and in effect let the King do what he liked.

At first it seemed that all the official apprehensions about the King's reception were fully justified, the large Parisian crowds shouting '*Vive Marchand!*' '*Vive Fashoda!*',.'*Vivent les Boers!*' and even, Ponsonby testifies, '*Vive Jeanne d'Arc!*' But the King's speech at the Hôtel de Ville, very brief, delivered without notes in faultless French, ending with a comment about the city '*où je me trouve toujours comme si j'étais chez moi*' transformed the situation. 'The first day distinctly antagonistic, the second cold, and finally frenzied enthusiasm,' as Ponsonby wrote.

King Edward had effectively broken all the then conventions of the role of constitutional monarchy, something even his mother, at the height of her lofty authority, had never done. He had undertaken, quite deliberately and with careful planning, without even consulting his ministers, let alone seeking their approval, a highly political Grand Tour of three European capitals with outstanding success.

But if the French had been won round, the Germans were sour, and the King's visits to Germany in 1904, 1906, 1907 and 1909 were designed to reduce these tensions. But the King disliked and distrusted his nephew the Kaiser, and matters had proceeded too far for a *rapprochement* between Britain and Germany inspired at monarchical level; but at least he tried, if without enthusiasm or much optimism.

There was subsequently a deliberate attempt, notably by Balfour and Lansdowne, to play down the significance of the King's role, but it was the considered judgement of one of the Foreign Office's most intelligent members, Eyre Crowe, that the Anglo-French agreement of April 1904 would not have been attained so soon but for the French admiration and affection for the King.

The trouble was that the Entente Cordiale was not popular in England, and was heavily censured by the King's old friend, and former Foreign Secretary and Prime Minister, Lord Rosebery, who in private went even further than his public strictures, declaring that it would lead 'straight to war'. Such was the hostility towards the French that the ensuing Anglo-French military discussions were kept secret. Most members of the Cabinet did not know about them until 1912.

The King's independence of mind and action in foreign affairs were a source of constant friction between himself and the 1900–5 Unionist government. His absolute refusal to consider reconciliation with King Leopold was significant. On this he was unquestionably right, but it was another example of his refusal to be a cipher of his ministers in foreign affairs. He ardently, and successfully, pressed the claims of his son-in-law Prince Charles of Denmark to the Norwegian throne after Norway had dissolved its union with Sweden; Prince Charles was elected King of Norway in November 1905, taking the title of King Haakon VII. If it was a brilliant personal coup by the King, it was viewed without enthusiasm by the Foreign Office.

The King's lack of interest in domestic politics was a distinct liability, especially as Knollys was rightly perceived by the Unionists as a Liberal without Henry Ponsonby's ability to inspire trust among Unionist politicians. When the Balfour government was racked with deep schisms over Joseph Chamberlain's espousal of Tariff Reform in 1903, reviving all the old divisions in the Unionist Party between Protectionists and Free Traders, and five senior Cabinet ministers resigned, the King actually suggested a General Election to Balfour. It was a singularly naïve proposal, which Balfour rejected. A General Election at that stage would have been catastrophic for the riven Unionist Party, and the influence of Knollys was behind the King's suggestion.

He was a far more 'political' monarch than is usually realised. He seldom gave formal audiences to ministers, except to the Prime Minister and Foreign Secretary, and devised a circle of seven trusted friends[5] to undertake collectively the political services that his father had rendered to Queen Victoria. Perhaps the most important of them all was Mrs

[5] They were Sir Ernest Cassel, Lord Esher, Admiral Sir John Fisher, Sir Charles Hardinge, Knollys, the Marquis de Soveral, and Mrs Keppel.

Keppel, a deeply respected, shrewd and discreet woman whose strong Liberal opinions were especially useful after the Liberal triumph of 1906. She was the King's lover, but was recognised, rightly, as a person of substance in her own right.

When Balfour resigned in December 1905, calculating incorrectly that the Liberals were too divided to form an effective government, and the lowly regarded Sir Henry Campbell-Bannerman became Prime Minister, the King, on the basis of an amicable meeting with him at Marienbad, hoped for a better relationship. This was not to be. The new Prime Minister, a churlish and unwell nonentity, was even more casual than Balfour about his relations with the King, his reports of Cabinet meetings being cursory and meaningless. However, even after the Liberals had won a crushing victory in the General Election of January 1906, confirming Campbell-Bannerman as Prime Minister, it was Balfour who drew King Edward further into the domestic political vortex he so disliked.

Balfour had declared that 'the great Unionist Party should still control, whether in power or whether in Opposition, the destinies of this great Empire'. His party may have been routed in the Commons, but it still had a large majority in the Lords; with what now seems inconceivable recklessness, the electorally defeated Unionists intended to use the unelected House of Lords to destroy the legislation of the Liberal government.

The first real clash came over the new government's 1906 Education Bill. In some respects it was an ill-chosen selection by the Liberals for a contest with the Lords, since the Bill banned the teaching of any specific religious doctrine: this pleased the Nonconformists, and, no doubt, the agnostics, but aroused the ferocious opposition of the Church of England, the Roman Catholics – and the King. It had a harsh passage in the Commons, and was effectively wrecked by the Lords, to considerable acclaim.

This was only the beginning of a process of attrition that was for a time wholly successful, and which paralysed the huge Liberal majority in the Commons. The King now found himself embroiled in a domestic political situation of acute bitterness. As the fortunes of the Liberal government declined, and the Unionists became more triumphantly confident of their tactics, the ferocity of the Liberal and Labour rhetoric became more alarming. The King did not greatly regard Balfour or Campbell-Bannerman, and had his doubts about Asquith, who succeeded Campbell-Bannerman on his death in April 1908, as well as the young Liberal firebrands David Lloyd George and Winston Churchill – but these were on personal grounds. He desired a contented nation, not a divided one.

The King saw much more clearly than the Unionist leaders the perils of their strategy. When he realised that the government's Licensing Bill of 1908, which proposed a compulsory reduction in the number of public houses, was under threat by the Lords, he summoned Lansdowne to urge his Unionist Peers not to defeat the Bill, as their lack of concern for the 'evils of intemperance' would reduce the popularity of the Lords. On this he was wrong. The Bill was in fact not at all popular except in the temperance movement, which remained strong in the Liberal and Labour parties. The King's arguments were ignored, and the Bill was duly rejected by the Lords. The King's already low estimation of Lansdowne was not heightened.

But his intervention was not wholly political. He abhorred heavy drinking, which was one of the few human weaknesses he could not tolerate. He also knew that it was a major social problem, and sympathised with the essential purposes of the Bill. Admirably, he practised what he advised.

The crisis broke in April 1909, when the Chancellor of the Exchequer, the much-feared Lloyd George, introduced what became known immediately as 'The People's Budget'. Its key and most controversial element was land taxes, which brought the Lords–Commons confrontation to its climax. For the Lords to reject a Finance Bill passed by the Commons was unprecedented in modern political history, but the temper of the times was such, and heightened by unrestrained demagoguery on both sides, that the Unionists, flushed by their successes up to that point, went fatally too far.

The King saw the perils, and, after securing Asquith's approval, summoned Balfour and Lansdowne to Buckingham Palace on 12 October to urge them to persuade the Lords to pass the Budget. They too saw the dangers, but claimed that their followers were impossible to control. This was certainly true, but the personal element also played its part. Balfour and Lansdowne did not greatly respect the King, and deeply mistrusted Knollys. These suspicions were reciprocated. Thus, old resentments played their part in the subsequent drama, and the King was not without responsibility for the dilemma that he then had to face.

His initiative failed. After laboriously trawling through the Commons for over two months, the Bill was rejected by the Lords in less than a week. This provoked Lloyd George and Churchill even further, and outside Westminster the two began speaking the unmistakable language of class war, moving the debate on to a new, harder plane. Asquith, citing breach of constitutional rights by the Lords, sought and obtained a dissolution of parliament on 2 December. The issue of 'The Peers Against the People' was now taken with intense clamour to the electorate.

A decisive result from them would have eased the King's burden, but in January 1910 they returned the Liberals with a greatly reduced majority. The Irish now held the fate of the government in their hands, and their price was Home Rule. But the Lords still had their veto, and the only way around that seemed to be either the abolition of the Upper House or a massive creation of Liberal Peers to swamp the Unionist majority. The King was naturally alarmed by both options.

By April, however, a third way had appeared – the Parliament Bill, which removed the right of the Lords to reject or amend finance bills and provided for any other legislation passed by the Commons but rejected by the Lords to become law automatically after two years. To dilute the impression of overweening Commons power, the length of parliaments would be reduced from seven years to five.

In introducing the Bill Asquith stated that 'if the Lords fail to accept our policy . . . we shall feel it our duty immediately to tender such advice to the Crown as to the steps which will have to be taken if that policy is to receive statutory effect in this parliament'. The King was accordingly threatened with the possibility of a choice between a mass creation of Peers and the resignation of his government.

The King was unwell at Biarritz, and increasingly depressed, lamenting to his heir that his government's 'ways get worse and worse, and our great Empire is now being ruled by Messrs Redmond and O'Brien (in their different ways) aided and abetted by Messrs Asquith, L–George and W. Churchill! The other ministers who really know better (Crewe, Grey and Haldane) quickly agree to anything.'

This was a perfectly accurate description of the situation, which was not helped by the King's absence. But he approved Knollys' initiative for a meeting at Lambeth Palace with Balfour, Esher, and the Archbishop of Canterbury, on the afternoon of 29 April, and from which much enduring bitterness and controversy emerged.

At this meeting Balfour assumed that 'the time was not far distant when the King would be asked either to create 500 Peers for the "Veto" Bill through the present parliament, or to grant a dissolution coupled with a promise to create Peers in the event of a Liberal majority being returned after the election'. The key conclusion was that Balfour would form a government if the Liberals resigned, and would seek an immediate dissolution and election. This seemed to give the King a possible way out of the miserably difficult position into which he had been forced by two political parties, each in its own way attempting to use his authority for its own purposes.

King Edward returned to Buckingham Palace on the same evening, weary and ill, and stubbornly refusing to admit to either. He insisted on fulfilling engagements, until even he realised that he was seriously unwell. His decline was surprisingly rapid, and he died at 11.45 in the evening of 6 May 1910, at the age of sixty-nine.

Asquith was on an Admiralty yacht cruise to Spain and Portugal when he received the first ominous bulletin near Gibraltar. The ship was immediately turned to proceed home to Plymouth at maximum speed. He subsequently wrote:

I felt bewildered and indeed stunned. At a most anxious moment in the fortunes of the state, we had lost, without warning or preparation, the sovereign whose life experience, trained sagacity, equitable judgement, and unvarying consideration, counted for so much ... Now he had gone. His successor, with all his fine and engaging qualities, was without political experience. We were nearing the verge of a crisis without example in our constitutional history. What was the right thing to do?

Although the new King, George V, had adored his father – 'My best friend and the best of fathers. I never had a [cross] word with him in my life,' as he wrote in his diary immediately afterwards – he was a very different character. He had inherited none of his father's love of society, ostentation and glamour, or his addiction to foreign travel, declaring that 'England is good enough for me' and that 'there's nothing of the cosmopolitan in me. I'm afraid I'm insular.' He was a notably reticent, often apparently grumpy and private man, keen on country pursuits, a quiet life, and his stamp collection. But in private he could also be garrulous, outspoken and indiscreet. And he had formidable depths of character that became more apparent to the shrewd observer.

Both his official biographers, John Gore and Harold Nicolson, considered him undoubtedly worthy but uninspiring. The untrue canard that he was a heavy drinker, much whispered when he became King, was a total misapprehension about his florid complexion and somewhat sharp manner and language. His tastes and habits were austerely simple, and he had been perfectly happy as a Norfolk squire living at York Cottage, Sandringham, with his shy and understanding wife and growing brood of exceptionally good-looking children.[6] He had known after the death of his elder brother in 1892 that he would be King one day, but had not imagined that his father would die so unexpectedly at the age of sixty-eight.

No one could have described George V as an intellectual;[7] indeed, he would have been outraged by such a slur, but he was no fool. His tutor, and that of his elder brother, had for fourteen years been John Neale (later Canon) Dalton, whose booming voice and autocratic manner were to be faithfully replicated in his son, Hugh. Dalton was devoted to the young Princes, and the future King warmly reciprocated this affection. But Dalton was not a very accomplished man, nor a particularly demanding teacher. John Gore wrote of the King that 'in spelling and punctuation and calligraphy he was still backward, and indeed remained so for much of his life' – before hurriedly adding that many other prominent men were comparably deficient. Queen Mary later strongly criticised Canon Dalton for her husband's inadequate education, and with justification.

King George's real schooling had been in the navy, in which he rose to the rank of Captain, commanding the cruiser HMS *Melampus*

---

[6] Edward, born in 1894; Albert, born in 1895; Mary, born in 1897; Henry, born in 1900; George, born in 1902; and John, born in 1905, who died at the age of fourteen. The others were to become, respectively, the Prince of Wales, the Duke of York, the Princess Royal, the Duke of Gloucester and the Duke of Kent.

[7] Admirers of the King have rebutted the claims about his inadequate reading and intellectual interests by citing his notebook entitled 'Books I have read since May 1890', which would imply that he read a book a week. Certainly, few have claimed that he read widely or particularly deeply, but like most people, he read books on subjects that interested him, in his case royal and military – especially naval – matters, and biographies, on which he was indeed well-informed.

by the time of his marriage in 1893, and he planned for his sons the same mixture of private tutoring followed by the navy.

The new King's principal problem, infinitely more serious than nonsensical rumours of his drinking and a bigamous marriage, was that his Liberal ministers were convinced he was a Conservative. A foolish remark to Winston Churchill in 1908 that Asquith was 'not quite a gentleman' and a reference to 'that damned fellow Lloyd George' had been reported back to the victims, who were understandably displeased. As Lloyd George later wrote, 'he had the reputation of being very Tory in his views. In those days he was frank to the point of indiscretion in his talk, and his sayings were repeated in wide circles. There is no use concealing the fact that they gave offence to Liberals and his succession to the throne for that reason was viewed with misgivings.'[8]

These suspicions were particularly unfortunate in the context of the constitutional crisis between the government and the Unionist-dominated House of Lords. He also inherited a nation in shock, and politicians prepared to honour what the *Observer* editor A. J. Garvin described as 'the truce of God'. But only for a time.

The two-party constitutional conference to attempt to resolve the crisis began at a meeting in Asquith's office in the Commons on 17 June, and continued through October until there was a total breakdown on 10 November. Another General Election was imminent. All attempts to resolve the impasse, and thereby to avoid involving the new King, had foundered. Asquith had not sought guarantees from King Edward for the mass appointment of Liberal Peers, but now the situation called for such a request. It was not at all unreasonable given the Unionist intransigence, but it was the confused manner in which it was done that made matters even worse. It was a crisis which tested the new King greatly, and whose implications were so serious that his discussions with ministers were recorded in considerable detail by his joint Private Secretary, Arthur Bigge,[9] and retained in a special archive for his possible subsequent use and for that of his successors.

---

[8] Bogdanor, op. cit., p. 67.

[9] Bigge had succeeded Ponsonby as Private Secretary to Queen Victoria in 1895, but Edward VII appointed Knollys: Bigge joined the household of the Duke of York. It was at his suggestion that Knollys remained as joint Private Secretary on King George's accession.

Account of meeting between the King and Mr Asquith at Sandringham on November 11th 1910:

. . . The Government wished the PM to see the King and to state their unanimity in favour of Dissolution: & before Xmas: the sooner the better & so avoid the inevitable increased bitterness of party feeling by delay & to save expense. *He did not come to ask for anything from the King: no promises, no guarantees during this Parliament.* The King expressed himself glad to hear this, but asked whether the PM should not wait to dissolve until the Veto resolutions had been up to & rejected by the H of L: otherwise would not the Country object to a Dissolution without a definite & Constitutional reason. At first Mr Asquith thought it would waste time to do this but subsequently admitted it might be better to send Resolutions to H of L at once & he undertook to talk this point over with Lord Crewe. Looking ahead, the PM said it was impossible to continue working in a vicious circle. The H of L would have to give way. It cannot be dissolved or reduced (he does not admit legality of withholding writs of summons) it can only be increased: so there is no alternative but to create new Peers sufficient to give a Government majority & this is within the Sovereign's Prerogative.[10]

There would seem to be no doubt about the purport of this crucial discussion as recorded by Bigge, and Harold Nicolson's interpretation that 'unaccustomed as he [the King] was to ambiguous phraseology he was totally unable to interpret Mr Asquith's enigmas' remains somewhat baffling. So does the King's thankful note that 'he asked me for *no guarantees*', or Bigge's that Asquith 'did not come to ask for anything from the King: *no promises, no guarantees during this Parliament.*' This had certainly been Asquith's line at the beginning of the meeting, but not at the end of it.

The King's relief was short-lived. On 14 November the King's other Private Secretary, Knollys, after a meeting at 10 Downing Street, reported that Asquith was indeed seeking immediate guarantees for the next parliament. On the King's instructions Bigge telegraphed Asquith's Private Secretary, Vaughan Nash, to state that 'His Majesty regrets that

[10] RA GV o 2570/12. This Stamfordham–Wigram political diary covers the period 10 October 1910 to 16 May 1931. It is the principal source of this account.

it would be impossible for him to give contingent guarantees and he reminds Mr Asquith of his promise not to seek for any during the present parliament'.

This protest arrived when, on the morning of the 15th, the Cabinet was giving approval to a minute to the King stating that his ministers could not advise a dissolution of parliament 'unless they may understand that, in the event of the policy of the government being approved by an adequate majority in the new House of Commons, His Majesty will be ready to exercise his constitutional powers (which may involve the prerogative of creating Peers) if needed to secure that effect should be given to the decision of the country'. This highly unwelcome development was accompanied by the suggestion that the King's commitment should not be made public unless and until the occasion arose.

Two days later there occurred one of the most brutal meetings between sovereign and Prime Minister in modern political history, as Bigge recorded:

November 16th: The King saw the Prime Minister and Lord Crewe at Buckingham Palace.

They asked HM to give the Cabinet an understanding that, in the event of the Liberal Party being returned with a majority at the next Election & the H of L again rejecting the Veto Resolutions & HM being asked to exercise His prerogative & to create Peers sufficient to give Govt. a majority in that House, HM would do so. They also informed HM that if he did not see his way to agreeing to this arrangement, the Govt. would place their resignation in his hands. Their great wish was to prevent the King's name being brought into the controversy, & after several discussions with the Cabinet they had come to the conclusion that by making this proposition they were offering the only means of avoiding so undesirable a contingency. This understanding was to be considered as an absolute secret by the Cabinet & would never be made public: should any member of the Cabinet violate this secrecy, he would be regarded as 'a man who had cheated at cards'.

The King pointed out that he much disliked giving any understanding until after the Election was over. The PM said that his hand would then be forced & already he might have had to ask for public assurances without a dissolution & the Cabinet was unanimous that something must be done. They expressed confidence that the Liberal Party would be returned by a large Majority.

The King told the PM and Ld Crewe that he would be quite ready to agree to the understanding as between himself & them: they replied: 'But what answer can we give to the Cabinet who are waiting to know the results of this interview?' They feared that there was a serious state of unrest among the working classes, & if the King did anything to bring about the resignation of the Govt. it might do great harm to the Crown. HM said his only wish was to do what was right & constitutional & best for the country under the present circumstances. The King then reluctantly felt that it would be impossible not to act upon their advice & therefore gave them the understanding which was to be communicated to the Cabinet upon the conditions already stated.[11]

When the King turned to his closest advisers, Bigge and Knollys, he received totally different advice. Although he was unused to the wiles of politicians he was learning fast and his resentment was strong. He recognised that if he agreed to the government's demands to use his prerogative to create several hundred Peers, chosen by the Liberal Party, to ensure the drastic limitations of the powers of the Lords, and the fact became known, the monarch would become personally involved in the raging political crisis and he would be reviled not only by Unionists but by personal friends and constitutionalists; if he refused his government's ultimatum his ministers might well have carried out their threat to resign immediately, and his situation would have been even more perilous. It appeared that he would have been without a government at all, and on the unpopular side of the 'Peers Against the People' controversy.

The latter point, on which Asquith and Crewe had played so strongly, was a very valid one. The former was not. Knollys deceived the King by concealing the fact that, as he well knew, in the latter eventuality Balfour would have been prepared to form a government and advise an immediate dissolution and General Election. Bigge, as outraged as the King by the arrogance and harshness of his ministers, and as ignorant as his master of what Knollys knew, recommended defiance. Knollys advised

[11] RA GV o 2570/13. Record of meeting of 16 November 1910.

acceptance. He was the senior man, and the King was then somewhat in awe of his experience as his father's trusted guide. Thus, the King, with reluctance and deep unhappiness, decided to follow Knollys' more emollient line.

Apart from merely postponing the inevitable *dénouement*, the situation had also exemplified the problems created by having two private secretaries of different political views. Knollys was a strong Liberal, and considered that although the King could indeed advise and warn his ministers, the wisest constitutional course was to accept their decisions, however unpalatable. Whether Knollys would have taken the same approach to a Unionist government was doubtful, as his record as King Edward's Private Secretary demonstrated. This partiality, well known in political circles, was seen at its worst when he concealed from the King the fact that Balfour would have stepped in had the government resigned. When the King discovered in 1913 how cruelly he had been deceived by Knollys he was understandably indignant. However, it is fair to claim that, even if he had known the true situation, his decision would not have been different. It would indeed have been a dangerous action to deny Asquith a dissolution and then grant one to Balfour, and this was something the King never contemplated.

The real importance of this part of the crisis was that the King felt he had been cheated. He had not only been severely pressurised by 'the politicals', particularly Asquith and Crewe, but deceived by his father's Private Secretary. As Harold Nicolson languidly expressed it: 'King George remained convinced thereafter that in this, the first political crisis of his reign, he had not been accorded either the confidence or the consideration to which he was entitled.' The reality was that he was incensed by the duplicity of the politicians, and this was to leave an enduring prejudice against them – one which was not to be alleviated by later experiences. Knollys' usefulness to King George had lain in his strong Liberal connections; the reverse of the coin was that the Unionist leaders, and with even better cause than they realised, had no confidence whatsoever in him. Although Bigge – created Baron Stamfordham in 1911 – was a Conservative and believed strongly that the royal prerogatives must be faithfully preserved, he was considerably more discreet, and had his own version of the Bagehot doctrine. The King, he wrote in a memorandum that was greatly to impress King

George VI when, many years later, Alan Lascelles drew his attention to it, had 'the right to be told; to encourage; and to warn'.

When Knollys was retired after his duplicity had been exposed, leaving Stamfordham in charge, the change was greeted with dismay by the Liberal Cabinet; but these hostilities eventually faded under the pressures of war and the clear evidence of Stamfordham's political impartiality in his advice to the King. If his relations with Lloyd George were not good, it was largely the result of that later Prime Minister's casualness towards the King, and his anger at the attempts of the King to interfere in senior military appointments. George V became heavily dependent upon Stamfordham, of whom he said that 'he taught me how to be a King'. Indeed, Stamfordham did much to alleviate the sense of betrayal the episode with Knollys and 'the politicals' had caused. The King – although far from having an unrealistic opinion of the vagaries of human nature – was, after all, a straightforward and honest man, and expected the same qualities from his ministers. He had found himself in a crisis of frightening proportions with an adviser he could not trust. Stamfordham was instrumental in restoring that trust, although the King would henceforth view all politicians with a marked wariness. He had, in fact, through harsh experience, become a politician himself.

Like his father, he was by nature a conciliator, and the most important political theme of his approach to the role of monarch was to encourage settlements, sincerely believing that sensible solutions to complex matters could be arrived at if sensible men met in private to resolve their difficulties. From this perhaps ingenuous approach to political questions he never deviated – even when the true severity of his first test as monarch became clear as the thorny matter of the creation of Peers reached its climax.

The General Election of December 1910 generated little public enthusiasm; indeed, there was a sharp fall in the number of voters compared with January – over a million. But the result was an almost exact repeat of the previous one.

There were now clear indications that Balfour was resigned to the situation, and that Lords reform would be accepted without the need for the mass creation. Unfortunately, Lansdowne did not agree; even more unfortunately, the King insisted on seeing him, in spite of Asquith's oral and written objections. In a stern memorandum to the King the Prime Minister wrote that 'it is not the function of a constitutional sovereign to act as arbiter or mediator between rival parties and policies; still less to take advice from the leaders of both sides with a view to forming a conclusion of his own'.[12] This imperious and highly dubious judgement the King proceeded to ignore, then and later. Asquith in fact went even further than this in this document, stating that 'the part to be played by the Crown in such a situation as now exists has happily been settled by the accumulated traditions and the unbroken practice of more than seventy years. It is to act upon the advice of the ministers who for the time being possess the confidence of the House of Commons, whether that advice does or does not conform to the private judgment of the sovereign.'[13]

This was certainly not a doctrine accepted by either Queen Victoria or King Edward, both of whom had seen their role as far less dependent upon the advice of their ministers and, as has been related, had been willing to act as 'arbiter and mediator' at times of political crisis. Asquith's declaration would have reduced the monarch to being a political cipher of no account, confined solely to ceremonial duties. The King did not see his role in that light.

The trouble was that Lansdowne did not consider the Unionist position hopeless, and was playing for time. He still could not really believe that the Liberals would commit themselves fully, and even thought that the Unionists might force yet another General Election.

There was also the hope that, by promoting Lords reform, the Unionists might stave off the threat of massive creations, and there was a flurry of activity into this diversion. Some of the proposals were sensible, and long overdue, but the political and tactical purpose of the exercise was only too manifest, and the process came to an abrupt conclusion when Morley informed the Lords that the restrictions of the Parliament Bill, slowly proceeding through the Commons, would apply to a reformed Lords.

The King's anguish at this situation was augmented by the preparations for his Coronation, and his temper not improved by one of the hottest summers on record, although mercifully the day of the ceremony – 22 June 1911 – was cool. After this brief interval the Unionist Lords continued with their new tactic of mutilating the Parliament Bill with amendments that changed it totally. The Cabinet then turned to the

---

[12] RA GV o 2570/11.
[13] Ibid.

King. The situation that he had most dreaded had happened. The time had come, the Cabinet minute to the King stated emphatically, for the 'contingency' measures. The Commons would reject the Lords' amendments, and there was no question of a dissolution and another General Election. 'Hence, in the contingency contemplated, it will be the duty of ministers to advise the Crown to exercise its prerogative so as to get rid of the deadlock and secure the passing of the Bill. In such circumstances ministers cannot entertain any doubt that the sovereign would feel it to be his constitutional duty to accept their advice.'

This somewhat peremptory missive, very characteristic of Asquith's treatment of the King, was not received well. The King wrote that he was unwilling to agree to the creation until the Lords had been given the opportunity to assess the Commons' rejection of their amendments; he was also unhappy about the decision to reject those amendments *en bloc*, an action which he considered would merely make the most intransigent Unionist Peers more determined to resist. The King was attempting to postpone the evil hour, but his response was sensible on both counts, as Asquith and the Cabinet recognised. On 20 July, at the instigation of the King and Knollys, Asquith wrote formally to Balfour and Lansdowne to state that if the Bill was not passed in its original form the government would advise the King to use his prerogative 'and His Majesty has been pleased to accept and act on that advice'.

The more sensible Unionists now realised that Asquith had not been bluffing. Curzon was among the most conspicuous – and the most reviled – who hurriedly changed sides. The passions aroused now reached another level of near-hysteria, but the bitterness was not only between the Unionists and the government. The Opposition was now in disarray and division. There were Unionists, notably Austen Chamberlain, who still believed that the threatened creation was 'bluff, and fraudulent bluff'; and they were quite prepared to involve the King on the grounds that ministers' advice had been 'a gross violation of constitutional liberty'. Worse, Balfour spoke condescendingly of the King's lack of experience in public affairs, 'which some of his great predecessors had'; Lord Hugh Cecil went much further, and in effect denounced the King's role as partisan, irresponsible and unconstitutional.

The King was following events very closely, and was also told of reports of hostile observations made about him in the Carlton Club and other Unionist circles. He conveyed his concerns and resentments to Morley, and it was arranged that Crewe should intervene to state that the King had 'entertained the suggestion [of the creation of new Peers] as a possible one with natural, and if I may be permitted to use the phrase, in my opinion with legitimate reluctance'.

Even this did not satisfy the King, but Asquith was prepared to go no further. In this he was right, and the King wrong. It was now public knowledge that the King viewed the possibility of the mass creation with repugnance, and this fact needlessly involved him deeper in the crisis. But it did prompt the government to agree that the creation would not take place until the Lords had again decided on the Bill. This was yet another postponement, but the time for procrastination was running out. Nonetheless, Asquith's response to the King's misery had done much to restore the latter's goodwill towards his Prime Minister.

The vital debate in the Lords began on 9 August. Despite the sweltering heat of London – the temperature reaching 100 degrees – the King stayed in the capital. It was as well that he did so, because there were clear indications in the first day's debate that Crewe's statement had given the die-hards new hope that the King would baulk at the creation. Stamfordham saw the perils, and, after discussing the matter with the King, sent to Morley an urgent letter to authorise him to state that in the event of the Bill being defeated he would indeed agree 'to a creation sufficient to guard against any possible combination of the Opposition by which the measure could again be defeated'. A form of words to convey this crucial message was prepared by Morley and approved by the King and Stamfordham. Morley later claimed in his memoirs that the initiative came from him and not from the King, but the records demonstrate that although the words used in the debate were his, the initiative had come from the Palace.

In response to an intervention by Rosebery, who was well-informed about the King's feelings, Morley eventually read out the statement on the lines suggested by Stamfordham. After a deep and long silence Lord Selborne asked Morley to read it out again, which he did, adding, 'That, I think, is pretty conclusive.'

And so it was. With Stamfordham anxiously waiting close to the chamber, and in an atmosphere of intense drama, the Bill was carried by seventeen votes. The King wrote that 'I am spared any further humiliation by a creation of Peers' in his diary that night, and, on the next day, wrote that it would have been 'a humiliation which I should have never survived'. This repetition of the word is in itself instructive of his emotions during the first constitutional and political trial of his reign. It had been a torrid introduction, but further trials were ahead of him.

The next, and most grievous of the problems he confronted in the first three years after his accession, was Ireland.

The Home Rule Bill, introduced in the venomous aftermath of the Parliament Act crisis, plunged British politics into further depths of bitterness. Lord Randolph Churchill's 1886 declaration that 'Ulster will fight and Ulster will be right' now had far more than a rhetorical ring. There were preparations for armed resistance in Ulster, and for a provisional Ulster government. The spectre of civil war loomed appallingly, and no one was more appalled than the King.

By August 1913 the Home Rule Bill had been passed twice by the Commons and rejected twice by the Lords. Under the Parliament Act it had to pass the Commons only once again to become law, which would be in the summer of 1914. The Unionists, knowing of the King's reluctant role in the 1911 crisis, now resolved to employ similar tactics.

Arthur Balfour's much criticised leadership of the Unionist Party had ended with his thankful resignation in November 1911, to be succeeded, somewhat surprisingly, by the dour and enigmatic Andrew Bonar Law. In fact, Law was only the leader in the Commons; theoretically, in the event of a Unionist election victory, the King could have called upon either Lansdowne or Curzon to form a government. Although this eventuality did not arise, Law's conduct towards the King would have made it a tempting choice. As has been rightly observed, Law was not a natural Conservative, because he had no respect for, nor understanding of, traditions. He also had little esteem for established institutions, including the monarchy. We can now see why he was to become a natural ally of the equally irreverent but far more unscrupulous Lloyd George.

On the issue of Home Rule and Ulster, Law spoke and acted with passion but without scruple. After a dinner given by the King on 4 May 1912, Law told him, with characteristic bluntness, 'The situation is a grave one not only for the House but also for the throne. Our desire has been to keep the Crown out of our struggles, but the government have brought it in. Your only chance is that they should resign within two years. If they don't you must either accept the Home Rule Bill or dismiss your ministers and choose others who will support you in vetoing it – and in either case half your subjects will think you have acted against them.'[14]

This advice to the King to veto an Act of Parliament was a shock to him – and was intended to be. Law spelt it out in greater detail in a memorandum to the King in September 1912, and in a letter to Professor Dicey, in which he wrote, 'I do not think that it is a question really of using the [royal] veto; but in my view the one constitutional right which the sovereign undoubtedly still possesses is that if ministers give him advice of which he does not approve, he should then see whether he can get other ministers who would give him different advice.'

The King and Stamfordham were understandably alarmed, realising that Law was in earnest. This was confirmed by another memorandum written by him and Lansdowne in July 1913, which argued that a dissolution of parliament was the only alternative to civil war, and that if Asquith did not agree the King had the constitutional right to dismiss him and send for someone who did.

This fraught possibility prompted the King to write his own memorandum to Asquith, which he discussed with the Prime Minister on 11 August. Stamfordham recorded this, and later, discussions, as the King sought a way forward out of a constitutional and political morass that threatened civil war and the position of the monarchy. It was by far the most grave crisis that had – or has – confronted a British monarch in modern times, and the King was again in danger of being used by each side. He, and Stamfordham, saw this very clearly, but the King had his own feelings, as the dialogues demonstrate.

Stamfordham's account of the 11 August discussion is as follows:

In reply to the King's expressed regret that the Prime Minister had not even mentioned the subject, Mr Asquith said that this was because he did not consider it was etiquette for him to ask for an audience. But for some time he had been considering the advisability of having a discussion on Irish affairs & therefore was very glad of this opportunity for doing so. He had served three Sovereigns, two of them as Prime Minister & hoped that he had

[14] Robert Blake, *The Unknown Prime Minister*, p. 133.

always showed frankness and readiness to give all information and it was his wish to take the King entirely into his confidence & speak quite openly on all questions.

As to the King's position, the Prime Minister did not agree with His Majesty's view that it was *serious*. For it is absolutely unassailable so long as he does nothing unconstitutional. People may write, Unionists may talk. But since the Reign of Queen Anne the Veto has not been exercised. The Sovereign's assent to Bills is given as a matter of form. He acts merely upon the advice of his Ministers. If he thinks that his Ministers' action is wrong & likely to be harmful to the Country or to the Throne it is the Sovereign's *duty* to warn them: *and in writing*: & and the responsibility is upon *them*. He admitted that the situation is to a certain extent serious. But does His Majesty hear the other side? What will happen if the Irish do not get Home Rule? The South & West will rise. Ireland will become ungovernable. The Nationalists might even seize the money due to the Treasury on account of Land Purchase: & then who will coerce Ireland? The Prime Minister thought the *Spectator*'s article 'The King & the Constitution' (Saturday Aug 9th) was admirable. As to Ulster's 'contracting out' for a period of years he would be ready to consider any practical scheme. A General Election would do no good: for even if the Government got a majority, Sir E[dward] Carson has declared that Ulster will not have Home Rule. He does not believe in a Referendum. But he would be prepared to encourage a settlement by consent though not inclined to favour an actual Conference . . .[15]

On 4 September the King saw the Foreign Secretary, Sir Edward Grey, on the same matter; Grey, unlike Asquith, 'Fully admitted the seriousness of His Majesty's position if, in asking for his Assent to the HR Bill there were evident prospects that bloodshed in Ulster would ensue.' Stamfordham records, however, that Grey also felt that 'many things may happen before the Bill reaches its final stages' – even the collapse of the government; the Foreign Secretary was adamant, though, that some form of devolution was necessary.

The King's consultations continued. Lewis Harcourt argued against

[15] RA GV o 2570/25.

him taking any action at all and dismissed the possibility of civil war; Sir John Simon agreed, and advised firm adherence to ministerial responsibility – Stamfordham noted that Simon thought 'the Opposition are increasing the gravest dangers to the Crown by advocating that the King should intervene. Were a dissolution to be thus forced upon the government he trembles to think what the working classes would say and do against the King.'

Further meetings with Esher and Morley did little to clarify the situation. When the King saw Asquith on 15 December, he raised two possible courses to avoid or postpone violence: Ulster to be given the opportunity of deciding by referendum whether they wished to be part of the new Ireland, or a General Election. Asquith was optimistic, or perhaps disingenuous, and maintained that he did not believe it would come to bloodshed. 'But surely you realise that Ulster will fight if the Bill is passed as it is?' the King said. The Prime Minister replied that he 'trusted such an eventuality would never arise'.

The two met again on 5 February 1914. Stamfordham records that it was during this discussion that the King clarified his personal position:

The King replied that tho' constitutionally he might not be responsible, still he could not allow bloodshed among his loyal subjects in any part of his Dominions without exerting every means in his power to avert it. Tho' at the present stage of the proceedings he could not rightly intervene, his time *would* come when the Bill was presented for Assent & then he should feel it his duty to do what in his own judgment was best for his people generally.

The P. Minister expressed no little surprise at this declaration, and said, if he might speak frankly, that he earnestly trusted His Majesty did not contemplate refusing Assent: such a thing had not be[en] done since the Reign of Queen Anne and would inevitably prove disastrous to the Monarchy.

His Majesty could, however, if he chose, dismiss his Ministers; but in that case it would be most unfair to do so once this Session had begun; otherwise the whole work of the past 2 years would, through the action of the Parliament Act, be sacrificed. It ought to be done *at once*, before Parliament meets on the 10th inst. Tho' he would respectfully deprecate such a course & should offer his strong advice against it, not for his own sake so much as for that of the Crown. He hoped that he had not so far forfeited the King's confidence as to justify such a step. His Majesty said that the P. Minister had *not* forfeited his Confidence and that he had no intention of dismissing his Ministers, tho' his future action must be guided by circumstances. The King said he was ready to do anything in his power to bring about a settlement by consent: he would see the P. Minister at any time and if the latter would only give him a hint, he would send for Mr Bonar Law or even Sir E. Carson and endeavour to induce them to come to an agreement and he would not mind were he rebuffed in his efforts. With regard to the Army, the P. Minister said that the King was no more at its head than he was at the head of every Public Department, and any orders given to the troops was [*sic*] on the responsibility of Ministers. He maintained that the Sovereign without exercising his prerogative had great powers and could *warn* & *advise* Ministers altho' they might be unable to accept the views thus expressed . . .[16]

This was bordering upon insolence – the King being told that he was his ministers' puppet, and the reference to his responsibilities for the army being specially offensive. He knew that there was a real possibility of officers refusing to obey orders to exercise force to impose Home Rule in the nine Ulster counties. The answer, which had not been seriously canvassed before, was to exclude Ulster, a solution suggested to the King by one of the most fervent and extreme Unionists, F. E. Smith, in September 1913.

In this harsh and unrelenting battle the King and Stamfordham struggled to find a conciliatory role. The latter had written on the King's behalf to Law on 20 January 1914 that 'His Majesty still clings to the belief in British common sense and that by "give and take" by *all* parties concerned an amicable solution may yet be found'.[17] Law's reply was long but the key passage was unmistakably, and bluntly, clear: 'In our belief there are now only two courses open to the government: they must either submit their Bill to the judgement of the people, or prepare to face the consequences of civil war.'[18] The King's only course, he bleakly

[16] RA GV o 2570/37.
[17] RA GV o 2553(3)/69.
[18] RA GV o 2553(3)/77.

concluded, was to write to Asquith formally advising the dissolution of parliament.

But the King became persuaded by Asquith that a General Election would become one in which 'the King against the People' would be the Liberals' campaign cry. In the terrible political atmosphere that now prevailed, this was a very real threat.

As the King and politicians toiled over the grievous Irish question through the summer of 1914, with an increasing air of helplessness, another, and wholly unexpected, crisis was looming. In Churchill's vivid description, 'The parishes of Fermanagh and Tyrone faded back into the mists and squalls of Ireland, and a strange light began immediately, but by perceptible gradations, to fall and grow upon the map of Europe.'

3

THE TRAVAILS OF GEORGE V

The advent of the First World War in August 1914 now has, in retrospect, an awful inevitability. If the assassination of the Archduke Franz Ferdinand, the heir to the Austrian Imperial throne, and his wife by a Bosnian Serb in Sarajevo on 28 June had not occurred, it seems very probable that there would have been another *casus belli*. The French had thirsted for revenge against Germany and the restoration of Alsace and Lorraine for over forty years; the Germans had elaborate and well-rehearsed plans for a rapid destruction of the French army and an even more overwhelming land victory than that of 1870, and challenged British sea supremacy; the British were closely linked with France and Russia, unless they attempted to extricate themselves by an act of moral perfidy; in fact all the likely protagonists were immensely confident, and there was a war mood that surged enthrallingly throughout Europe.

But at the time, the arrival of the crisis and its rapidity in leading to war took the King, his government and his people totally by surprise. King George was still obsessed with Ireland and the failure of the latest attempt at a compromise solution, and did not mention the lowering European situation in his diary until 25 July. Three days later Austria declared war on Serbia; Russia mobilised; Germany followed.

The King hoped fervently that Britain would not be involved, and the Cabinet and the Liberal Party were deeply divided. On the 29th he noted that 'Austria has declared war on Serbia. Where will it end?

52

... the navy is all ready for war, but please God it will not come. These are very anxious days for me to live in.' He willingly agreed to approve a telegraphed appeal by Asquith to the Tsar, urging restraint, in the early hours of 1 August, but it was too late for any conceivable effect. The remorseless processes had begun. By that evening Russia and Germany were at war. Almost immediately France and Germany were as well.

The King wrote on 1 August:

Saw Sir Edward Grey. Germany declared War on Russia at 7.30 this evening & German Ambassadors left Petersburg. Whether we shall be dragged into it God only knows, but we will not send Expeditionary Force of the Army [to France] now. France is begging us to come to their assistance. At this moment public opinion here is dead against our joining in the War but I think it will be impossible to keep out of it as we cannot allow France to be smashed.

But he could also see a remarkable shift in opinion, evidenced by huge and enthusiastic crowds outside Buckingham Palace calling for war. The non-intervention group in the Cabinet dwindled to ineffectiveness, leaving Morley and John Burns isolated. On 3 August Grey invoked the treaty of 1830 guaranteeing Belgian neutrality, which the Germans had contemptuously defied. British anti-German sentiment was now immensely powerful, and on the evening of the 3rd the crowds outside the Palace were even larger and more excited, the King and Queen having to make three appearances on the Palace balcony to respond to them.

The King did not share their enthusiasm. For one thing, his second son, Prince Albert, was serving as a midshipman on HMS *Collingwood*, and was on the middle watch on the night of 4–5 August when the British declaration of war against Germany – approved by the King that morning – became effective, a fact the Prince did not forget when Britain's involvement in what was to become the Second World War began in September 1939.

The crowds outside the Palace continued to grow, and, as the King noted, 'the cheering was terrific'. But so was it in Berlin, Paris, St Petersburg and Vienna. While Europe joyously marched into oblivion,

King George wrote sombrely that 'it is a terrible catastrophe but it is not our fault . . . Please God it may soon be over and that He will protect dear Bertie's life.'

The one positive political factor that brought consolation to the King was that the Irish Nationalists had agreed to the deferment of the implementation of Home Rule until the end of the war. Like the majority, they assumed that this would be a relatively brief postponement of their ambition. The Unionists were incensed that the Bill was enacted without the exclusion of Ulster; it received the Royal Assent on 18 September, and the apparent ending of the threat of civil war was an immense relief to the King. And, although the Liberals remained in office, and there was no question of a Coalition Government, the Unionists pledged full support in the war effort. It seemed that the ferocious domestic political battles of the previous eight years were to be held in abeyance for the duration of the conflict, but the wounds were too deep, and the bitternesses too intense, for this uneasy truce to last for very long. But in August 1914, with the nation and Empire united in a common cause and with euphoric visions of a swift and decisive victory, these were strong compensations.

When things began to go badly, at sea as well as on land, the British were gripped by a hysterical anti-German phobia. One of the first conspicuous victims was the First Sea Lord, Admiral Prince Louis of Battenberg, who had been a British citizen since the age of fourteen and had served all his adult life with distinction in the Royal Navy. Haldane, his achievements as Secretary of State for War wholly forgotten, was to be another undeserved sacrifice to these passions in May 1915. The King did not share them, and his civilised objections to these man-hunts by a strident press and publicity-seeking politicians resulted in the slurs against his own German background that eventually compelled him to change the name of the Royal Family in 1917 – it was an inescapable fact that the British monarchy had very strong German antecedents, and given the ugly temper of the time the dynasty of Saxe-Coburg-Gotha seemed grotesquely inappropriate.

This was very much a political decision, made imperative by the length as well as the nature of the war. Its duration in 1917 seemed as interminable as the ghastly casualty lists from the Western Front and Mesopotamia. But when the now venerable Lansdowne proposed that same year an end to the nightmare by a negotiated peace, he was effectively howled down by a fiercely patriotic press and suddenly found himself a hate-figure.

The nominal royal German link had to be severed. It was Stamfordham who made the inspired suggestion. And thus the House of Windsor was created.

Unlike many wealthy families, the King decreed a regime of firm austerity in his own household. Strict economies were ordered, and meals at Buckingham Palace became notoriously frugal even before Lloyd George persuaded him on 29 March 1915 to set an example to the nation by total abstention from alcohol for the duration of the war. Lloyd George, who had a strong aversion to immoderate drinking, one of the few surviving remnants of his Welsh Nonconformist background, had become obsessed by the alleged effects of alcohol on munitions production, and, to the dismay of the Court and visitors to the Palace and Windsor, the King readily agreed. He had expected a government statement about general prohibition, but none was forthcoming. The King and his household were, as Harold Nicolson later put it with leaden facetiousness, left 'high and dry' for the rest of the war.

Also, the widely reported 'King's Pledge' not only had no discernible effect on others but was even a subject of widespread ridicule. Although the King was a very moderate drinker, this was a melancholy sacrifice for him and his staff and guests. His Prime Minister and most other politicians took no notice of his gesture. Only Kitchener among ministers followed the King's example; Lloyd George certainly did not.

There have been claims that both the King and the Queen occasionally broke the pledge, and there was an important ruling that cider, however potent, was a non-alcoholic drink. But Buckingham Palace, Sandringham and Windsor Castle were not places to which invitations were greatly welcomed by those who took good food and wine seriously. When the King realised that Lloyd George had made him look ridiculous rather than a national exemplar, his distaste for politicians in general, and this one in particular, was significantly augmented. Thus this episode, perhaps small in itself, had its political consequences. In the marvellous phrase of the Queen to Asquith, 'we have been carted'.[1]

---

[1] Kenneth Rose, *King George V*, p. 179.

*　　*　　*

The King took his wartime duties very seriously. The Prince of Wales was an officer in the Grenadiers serving on the Western Front, although, to his chagrin, not permitted to serve in the front line and kept carefully away from serious military action. The risks to the heir to the throne would indeed have been considerable, the life expectation of young officers in France and Flanders being tragically and terribly low, but this denial of opportunity for military experience and leadership, albeit at a relatively minor level, was the first serious occasion for the Prince's resentments against his position and his father. If his friends and contemporaries were often meeting their deaths, others were not only surviving but making their reputations and earning their self-knowledge through hard experience.

The Western Front was not all futile slaughter. It was the making of young men like the Prince's friend Oliver Lyttelton, and a future one, Duff Cooper; and they were by no means unique. Four future Prime Ministers – Churchill, Attlee, Eden and Macmillan – served with distinction in the army, as did six future Field Marshals – Montgomery, Slim, Alan Brooke, Alexander, Gort and Ironside. The First World War was a terrible destroyer of much youthful promise, but if the experience the survivors gained was at a heavy cost, it was at least gained, and from this the Prince of Wales was deprived. In fact he deliberately courted danger in his visits to the front lines, and on one such occasion emerged from the trenches to find his car riddled with bullets and his driver dead. Episodes such as this only increased official alarm about his safety. His frustration was compounded by the fact that his younger brother was given no such protection in the navy, and was to participate in the Battle of Jutland. This decision may have saved the life of the young and ebullient Prince; in other respects it damaged it severely, and in the opinion of some closest to him, irreparably.

His father was indefatigable. Rose has calculated that 'in four years of war he undertook 450 visits to troops, 300 to hospitals, almost as many to munitions factories . . . With his own hands he conferred 50,000 awards for gallantry. It was a programme to tax even the most robust of men; and by his fiftieth year the King had begun to lose resilience.'[2]

The King's visits to his troops in France and Flanders very nearly cost

[2] Rose, op. cit., p. 179.

him his life when, on 28 October 1915, at Hesdigneul, the horse supplied to him reared up at the sound of the men's cheering, and fell backwards on top of him. The doctors made rather too light of his injuries, which in fact were severe, including a fractured pelvis and three cracked ribs as well as torn muscles and bruising. When Churchill came to surrender his seals of office on his resignation from the Cabinet some weeks (and not, as he wrote in his 1936 tribute to the King, 'some months') later, he was 'shocked at his shattered condition and evident physical weakness'. The only positive aspect of this near-tragic event was that the King's doctors advised him to relax his rule about total abstinence from alcohol.

But war had not eliminated domestic politics, and certainly not the harsh partisan and personal frictions that had so defiled public life. The King was no more immune from these than the politicians. He had particularly strong views on military and naval appointments, and there was an early conflict in this regard. Far from sharing his father's admiration for the now 74-year-old Admiral Fisher, he positively abhorred him, and was horrified when Churchill, an immensely energetic and self-confident First Lord of the Admiralty, proposed to appoint Fisher as First Sea Lord to succeed the hounded Battenberg. The King agreed to Fisher's appointment on the vehement insistence of Asquith and Churchill, and only then under written protest. But for a time it seemed as though he had been wrong and the politicians right. The Churchill–Fisher combination at the Admiralty initially produced a building programme of astonishing size and an electric energy, but Fisher's megalomania and Churchill's soaring personal ambitions resulted within months in a spectacular explosion that abruptly ended Fisher's extraordinary career and also seemed to have ended Churchill's. The ultimate cause was the unsuccessful Dardanelles naval assault in March 1915, followed by the only partially successful military landings on the Gallipoli peninsula on 25 April, but the real reason was their total incompatability of temperament and strategic priorities.

Fisher's impetuous resignation on 15 May 1915 brought to a head the increasing Unionist and press criticism of the conduct of the war by the Liberal government. Bonar Law and his Unionist colleagues fully shared the King's opinion of Churchill that 'he is the real danger' and 'impossible', and his removal from the Admiralty was a *sine qua non* for their participation in a Coalition Government. Although Churchill was, and always remained, bitter about Asquith's agreement to the Opposition demands, he did not blame the King. Fisher, in contrast, lost few opportunities of denigrating him ferociously.

The significance of this episode was that it was an early example of the King's involvement in military appointments, which became increasingly resented by his ministers. Furthermore, as Asquith himself later admitted, over Fisher the King had been proved right. It certainly encouraged him to further interventions which went some way beyond the right to warn. It was a dangerous course for a constitutional monarch, and one which could have had grave consequences, but the King sincerely considered that in this field he had rights that he did not claim in the party political one.

Another senior officer of whom the King disapproved was Sir John French, the British Commander-in-Chief in France. The King's view was confirmed by French's conduct of operations in the first crisis of the war in August and September 1914. This view was widely shared, then and later; French was always swift with providing excuses for his failures; it was not until September 1915, after suffering appalling casualties with little to show for them, that he ran out of excuses and was dismissed.

As in the case of Fisher, the King's judgement had been vindicated. It also demonstrated how unfit Asquith was as a war leader, and it was only on the insistence of the King that he acted to remove French and replace him with the King's favourite and friend Douglas Haig. The first decision was unquestionably right, and scandalously long overdue by a Prime Minister ill-equipped in every respect for decisive leadership in any but a domestic political crisis; the second recommendation of the King had results that rumble angrily to this day.

The essential argument, still conducted with much passion, is whether Haig was a realist who was badly served by his political masters, and who did, after all, eventually triumph; or whether he was a cold, remote soldier who was grossly over-promoted, was devoid of tactical or strategic intelligence, and was heedless of the awful toll of casualties that destroyed the lives of hundreds of thousands of his remarkably uncomplaining soldiers. The truth, as so often, lies somewhere in the middle.

It was understandable that the King felt happier with military men than with politicians, and Haig was not only a close friend of the Royal Family – having married a Maid of Honour to Queen Alexandra in the Buckingham Palace chapel – but his record in the Boer War and in India had been outstanding. He had also conducted himself well in France under French's erratic leadership. The King was not the only man who regarded him highly.

So far, so good, but it did not end there.

The conduct of the war was marked by persistent and acrimonious differences between the political leadership and the military commanders, characterised by a mutual suspicion and contempt that has been very fully recorded by most of the participants. As the war continued to go disastrously badly, these recriminations became more venomous. The King was firmly on the side of the military, and especially Haig. Like him, he was convinced that the outcome of the war would be settled on the Western Front, and not by costly diversions in Gallipoli, Mesopotamia or Salonika. But the grim 1916 Battle of the Somme demonstrated once again the bloody limitations of infantry attacks against determined and well-entrenched defenders. Stamfordham lost his only son, John, and Asquith his son Raymond in the slaughter. The Germans at Verdun, employing the same bludgeoning tactics, fared even worse. But in Britain the mood for a change in the political leadership, rather than in the military commanders, became dominant.

If the King had never really cared for Asquith – although he respected him – he had little time for Lloyd George, rapidly emerging as his successor, and his relations with Bonar Law remained cool.

After Asquith tactically and fatally resigned in December 1916, the King sent for Law, as the leader of the major Opposition party, to ask him to form an administration. It was an unhappy meeting, indeed a singularly ill-tempered one, in which the two argued about Asquith's qualities and Lloyd George's defects (and vice versa), the King's insistence that the conduct of the war should be left to the military, and Law's request for the dissolution of parliament if he formed a government, which the King refused as a condition for Law's acceptance. Law did, however, say that he would try to form a government. Asquith having peremptorily refused Law's suggestion that he should become one of its members, there then was recourse to one of the King's favourite tactics, a Buckingham Palace conference, chaired by himself; like the others, it was wholly inconclusive except that Asquith reiterated his refusal to serve in a subordinate position under Law or anyone else. Thus Lloyd George, to the King's dismay, became Prime Minister. At first the King genuinely tried to work amicably with Lloyd George, who for his part opened his premiership with an ostensible desire to please the King by consulting him about appointments. But this loveless honeymoon was of short duration. Lloyd George, very sensibly, ended the hallowed tradition whereby the Prime Minister reported to the sovereign in his own hand the proceedings of the Cabinet – the only records that there were. His establishment of a Cabinet Secretariat under Maurice Hankey, with a proper agenda, detailed minutes, and decisions to be implemented by ministers, was considered revolutionary – as indeed it was, but the King preferred the former, more personal touch. What made matters worse was that the King often did not receive the Cabinet minutes and his letters went unanswered. (In this he was not being picked out for especially offensive treatment; Lloyd George was notorious for not even opening, let alone replying to, letters from his constituents.) But the King assumed his Prime Minister was being deliberately offensive. He had seized power; he was not going to relinquish a particle of it to a hereditary monarch. He had, after all, in one of his most virulent assaults on the hereditary principle during the conflict with the Lords, declared of primogeniture that 'you would not choose a *spaniel* on those principles'. And he had meant it.

As in the case of Prince Albert's feud with Palmerston, personalities and politics were inextricably intermingled. The two men had disliked and distrusted each other for many years; Lloyd George's conduct of his office, and the King's reactions to it, created a crisis that was equally serious. Lloyd George recognized no one superior to him in his rise, and certainly none at his zenith. He accepted no rules so far as they affected him and his ambitions; the fact that his genius was seriously flawed did not occur to him. He was, intellectually and personally, profoundly amoral. He was cynical, egocentric, devious, untruthful and dishonourable. But the sheer power of his personality was overwhelming. His admirers revered him; his enemies feared him. His oratory was incomparable, his lack of scruple well-attested. His subsequent admiration for Hitler is understandable: they came from the same mould. For a while this ferocious little demon captivated and enthralled the British people, perhaps rightly, as they were in dire need of leadership after the flaccid Asquith. But King George was not deceived, and unlike the previous contest over sixty years before, the monarch was eventually to have the last laugh.

*   *   *

Lloyd George had convinced himself of the futility of the British commanders – indeed of the entire British senior military caste, on which he
poured contemptuous scorn then and later – making claims for his greater
energy and knowledge that have conspicuously failed to stand the test
of hard and close inspection. His innate class-consciousness and arriviste
arrogance, combined with his total inexperience of military matters, led
him not only into collision with the King and the army but to some
of the greatest military disasters in British history. His attitude to the
King was fully in line with that towards the officer class – indeed, he
considered them part of the same problem.

The King's military judgements were certainly not invariably right,
but at least he had had some professional experience, which Lloyd
George had not. He was also physically a brave man, which Lloyd George
definitely was not. But, unencumbered by either courage or military
knowledge, Lloyd George blithely and with confident omniscience
donned the mantle of military genius. Arguments may still rage about
Haig, but the fact was that the British commanders included men of
considerable ability, too often under-utilised.

It was characteristic of Lloyd George that he overrode the recommendation of the Australian government that the British General Walker,
who had made his name as commander of the 1st Australian Division
at Gallipoli, should be appointed to command the Australian forces
in France. Lloyd George preferred the Australian, Monash, who had
certainly not distinguished himself on the peninsula, but had personally
entranced the Prime Minister. Lloyd George was similarly, and even
more fatally, bewitched by the confident personality of the flamboyant
French General Nivelle, who claimed that he had found the answer to
the impasse on the Western Front: advancing precisely and methodically
under a terrifying creeping barrage of overwhelming artillery power,
the German positions would be methodically annihilated, and the great
breakthrough into open country and mobile warfare would be achieved.

This inspiration required that Haig and his armies would come under
Nivelle's command. The King was not told of this development until
it was decided and agreed at a War Cabinet meeting to which neither
the Secretary of State for War, Lord Derby, nor the Chief of the
Imperial General Staff, General Sir William Robertson, had been invited.
Haig, contemplating resignation, turned to the King, who, appalled

and angered, urged him to stay and summoned Lloyd George for an explanation of why and how, without his knowledge or consent, his army had been placed under foreign command.

Perhaps unwisely, although the depth of his emotion was understandable, the King told Lloyd George that if the fact were known in the country it would be condemned, which gave his Prime Minister the opening to say that in that event he would call a General Election on the matter. Seething with impotent rage, the King backed down.

It gave him little satisfaction that the great Nivelle offensive in the spring of 1917 was one of the most spectacular disasters in military history. The Germans had created a new fortress-line some miles behind their former one, and the French advanced under their great barrage across empty and abandoned territory, although well booby-trapped and dangerous, to be irretrievably and bloodily halted. The only Allied success was the capture of Vimy Ridge by the Canadians and British, a hard-won triumph that could have been exploited, but was not. Sections of the French Army had had enough. Nivelle fell, and mutiny erupted – it was ruthlessly suppressed, but for the time being the French were a spent force.

Lloyd George's great initiative lay in ruins. The King's opposition to placing the British forces under French command had been fully justified, and his distrust of his Prime Minister had been formidably increased. Lloyd George, for his part, nursed his prejudices against Haig and Robertson, but after the Nivelle débâcle was hardly in a position to remove either of them, let alone both. He had been the chief protagonist of the Salonika campaign, moreover, which was hardly a campaign at all, and which tied down large numbers of soldiers in a virtually non-operational area, a classic 'side-show' operation of no value whatsoever. As later events were to further demonstrate, Lloyd George's capacities as a military strategist had their limitations.

But so did Haig's. His defenders have vigorously argued that he had no choice, given the parlous condition of the French, but to launch another major attack at the end of July 1917. His critics have pointed out that the cardinal, and terrible, error was to continue it regardless of chilling losses. The name Passchendaele rings a toll as terribly resonant as that of the Somme in British memories. It is for this campaign that Haig will not be easily forgiven.

The Passchendaele offensive brought the crisis between Lloyd George and Haig and Robertson to a head. Determined to fetter Haig and diminish Robertson's dominant influence in the war strategy, Lloyd George turned to another favourite, General Sir Henry Wilson, an arch-schemer and flatterer. The King shared the almost universal opinion in the army about Wilson, that he was slippery and over-ambitious. The King's judgement of character was not at all infallible, but it was often right; he may have over-valued Haig and Robertson, but his assessment of Wilson was totally correct.

The King's relations with his Prime Minister declined further when Lloyd George failed to tell him of his removal of Robertson as Chief of the Imperial General Staff. The King sent Stamfordham to remonstrate strongly on Robertson's behalf, but Lloyd George was adamant, and regarded this as monstrous royal interference, telling Stamfordham that if he persisted, 'the government could not carry on, and the King would have to find other ministers. The government must govern, whereas this was practically military dictation.' This was strong language indeed, but it was justified. Haig did not come to his champion's assistance, and by the time of Lloyd George's threat to resign on 16 February 1918 the King had reluctantly accepted the situation, while confiding to his diary his hopes that the government would fall. In fact it had been Robertson who had fallen.

It should be remembered that by this stage of the war, with the Germans poised for a massive assault in the west, no longer having to supply forces against the defeated Russians, everyone was becoming exhausted and ill-tempered. The King and the Prime Minister neither liked nor trusted each other; the latter, admittedly under immense strain, was showing strong dictatorial tendencies, and the personal relationship between him and Stamfordham was not at all good. And the one occasion on which the King prevailed over his ministers was, and remains, highly controversial.

This episode must be seen, again, in the desperate context of the times. Although the British people never broke under the strains of war, public confidence in its conduct had been seriously eroded. All that 1917 had brought the Allies had been terrible casualties on land and near-starvation at the hands of the German submarines. The French Army had suffered even greater traumatic losses than the British. Russia had collapsed into surrender and anarchy. And the Germans, so long on the defensive in the west, were now massively reinforced. At home, militant organised labour was a real and menacing force; Republicanism was now being loudly bruited in Britain as well as in Russia and Germany.

The war was a mighty destroyer of monarchies, most dramatically those of Germany, Austria–Hungary and Russia, but it was the last that most affected the British monarchy.

The unpopularity in British liberal and socialist circles of the Tsar and his regime had been only marginally lessened by the fact that Russia had been a wartime ally, and his deposition in February 1917 after almost unrelieved military disasters had not been greatly mourned in Britain. The King and Stamfordham had noted the national mood, and it had activated their acute sense of self-preservation. The story has been related before, but needs to be told again. In some respects it might appear to be to the discredit of King George V, but in others it demonstrates his political shrewdness.

The first suggestion that the Russian Imperial Family should come to England was made by Pavel Milyukov, the Foreign Minister of the provisional government, on 19 March 1917. The British Ambassador, Sir George Buchanan, at once reported it to the Foreign Office in London, and even before there had been time to consider it a second telegram arrived from Petrograd, the enquiry about asylum for the Tsar now taking the form of a formal request. The Foreign Office sent a guarded reply: the British government would be glad to see the Tsar leave Russia, but wondered whether some other destination, mentioning particularly Denmark or Switzerland, would not be a more suitable place. This provoked an even more urgent request from Petrograd that Milyukov was 'most anxious to get the Emperor out of Russia as soon as possible, the extremists having excited opinion against His Majesty . . . I earnestly trust that in spite of the obvious objections, I may be able to offer His Majesty asylum in England and at the same time assure the Russian government that he will remain there during the war.' This was discussed between Lloyd George and Stamfordham on 22 March in Downing Street, where they were joined by Bonar Law and Lord Hardinge, who had ceased to be Viceroy of India and had rejoined the Foreign Office.

Stamfordham's report reads: 'It was generally agreed that the proposal that we should receive the Emperor in this country, having come from the Russian government which we are endeavouring with all our powers to support, could not be refused.' Stamfordham then raised the practical problems of financing and accommodating the Tsar and his family, and when Lloyd George suggested that the King should place a house at their disposal, Stamfordham replied that only Balmoral was available, 'which would certainly not be a suitable residence at this time of year'. The meeting concluded that Buchanan should ask the Russian government to provide sufficient funds to allow the Tsar and his family to live in England in suitable dignity.

There was then hesitation in Petrograd, and in those days the King began to have second thoughts. This is reflected in a letter from Stamfordham to the Foreign Secretary, Balfour, on 30 March, eight days after the meeting at Downing Street:

The King has been thinking much about the Government's proposal that Emperor Nicholas and his family should come to England. As you are doubtless aware the King has a strong personal friendship with the Emperor and therefore would be glad to do anything to help him in this crisis. But His Majesty cannot help doubting not only on account of the dangers of the voyage but on general grounds of expediency whether it is advisable that the Imperial Family should take up their residency in this country. The King would be glad if you would consult the Prime Minister as His Majesty understands that no definite decision has been come to on the subject by the Russian Government.

Balfour replied that ministers did not think that it would be possible to withdraw the invitation that had been sent. Initially this seemed to settle the matter, but the King then returned to the attack, Stamfordham writing to Balfour on 7 April that 'he must beg you to represent to the Prime Minister that from all we hear, and read in the press, the residence of the Emperor and Empress in this country would be strongly resented by the public and would undoubtedly compromise the position of the King and Queen'. Buchanan agreed: 'If there is any danger of an anti-monarchist movement, it would be far better that the ex-Emperor should not come to England.'

This was *realpolitik* at a formidable level. The King, apprehensive about his own position, had overridden the advice of his ministers. But no one anticipated how dismal the fate of his relatives would be.

At the time there was no threat to the Tsar and his family from the Kerensky government; the King had asked for, and received, assurances about their safety.

After they were all brutally murdered this decision seemed heartless, and a severe scar on the King's reputation, but he was not alone in fearing the domestic political repercussions of greeting a man who was widely regarded in Britain as an evil despot. Communism had suddenly become the new enemy, at home as well as abroad; the subsequent British intervention in the Russian Civil War on the anti-Bolshevik side was vehemently denounced by the rapidly rising Labour Party and powerful trade unions, and eventually had to be abandoned.

In human terms, the decision of the King may be condemned; on political grounds at the time, it was very understandable and shrewd. The downfall of the Russian monarchy might have been regrettable, but his argument was that it should not imperil that of Britain, and his instincts were sound. It was an exercise in survival, which he and Stamfordham appreciated clearly, and remains one of the most instructive episodes in the history of the modern British monarchy.

In 1918 the seemingly interminable war reached its climax. The Germans' frighteningly successful last assault in March was eventually checked, and then decisively repulsed. Everywhere – even in Salonika – the Allies advanced, and their enemies disintegrated. By November the nightmare was over – or so it seemed.

But the difficulties with Lloyd George continued. With victory assured, the Prime Minister sought an immediate General Election. The King, remembering the unhappy long-term effects of the 'Khaki Election' of 1900, when the Unionists had cynically and successfully exploited what had appeared to be triumph in the South African war, demurred. But Lloyd George was insistent, and his Coalition won an overwhelming victory in perhaps one of the most despicable elections in British political history. His disdain for the King, and Stamfordham, remained so obvious and deliberately insulting that the King's patience was so remarkable as to be almost saintly. But the reality was that he knew that Lloyd George – 'the man who won the war' – was, for the time being, the greatest national hero since Palmerston. Thus, when the Prime Minister had not bothered to inform the King of the results of the peace conference that resulted in the Treaty of Versailles in June 1919, and had seen no reason to have done so, he was met by the King on his return at Victoria Station and they were driven together in an open carriage through cheering crowds to Buckingham Palace. It did not occur to Lloyd George, or to other commentators and historians then or later, that the King was deliberately sharing this occasion of national rejoicing with a man for whom he had little regard. But the King, once again, was playing a shrewd political role, his relief at victory tempered by the constant strain of his relations with 'the politicals'. As he wrote in his diary on 6 May 1918: 'I don't think any sovereign of these realms has had a more difficult or more troublous eight years than I have had.'

The troubles, however, were to continue – demonstrated most graphically in the immediate post-war period by the re-emergence of the Irish problem.

The Easter Rising in Dublin in April 1916 had taken the government totally by surprise, but had been quickly suppressed. It was not popular in Ireland, and in many respects was a fiasco until the British first executed the perceived ringleaders and then hanged Sir Roger Casement for treason, thereby creating new martyrs and renewed bitterness. In the 1918 General Election Sinn Féin, led by Eamon de Valera, won 73 of the 105 Irish constituencies, refused to take their seats at Westminster and declared Ireland to be an independent republic. This unilateral insurrection was accompanied by a campaign of murder and intimidation, conducted with much callousness and brutality. The British responded in kind, sending the notorious 'Black and Tans' to restore order by equally ferocious methods.

To a nation exhausted and sickened by war, this increasingly savage conflict was an additional and much resented wound. No one felt it more strongly than the King, and his opinions, as usual forcefully expressed, increased further the tensions between himself and the often insolent Lloyd George, who described him on one occasion (privately) as 'an old coward'. The King, although not particularly old and certainly no coward, was indeed frightened, and with very good cause. His pre-1914 nightmare of an Irish civil war was being made reality. As he had often stressed, he was neutral on the rights and wrongs of Irish Home Rule, unlike his grandmother, but he could not tolerate civil war in his kingdom, particularly as an independence movement was developing ominously in India.

As so often, the King's views mirrored public opinion very accurately, and the government's own supporters in the Commons and the press became increasingly uneasy and critical. By the early summer of 1921 the Irish situation had run out of control, a fact dramatically demonstrated by a successful assault by the Irish Republican Army on the Customs House in Dublin on 25 May, when they seized and destroyed not only the building but a substantial collection of the records of the Irish administration, to the bitter regret of later historians. At the time, the continuing and pervasive human slaughter and suffering throughout the country was understandably deemed infinitely more important. The King viewed the situation with mounting despair; his warnings and suggestions were ignored by his ministers, especially by Lloyd George. He was dominated by forebodings of approaching disaster, and angry at his own impotence to avert it. But on this occasion he at least had a role to play.

The British government hovered between a policy of greater repression and further attempts at negotiation. The Sinn Féin leadership was in a similar dilemma. For all their occasional spectacular successes, the conflict on the whole was not going well for the IRA, and the carnage was as unpopular in Ireland as it was in the rest of Britain, and considerably more frightening. The prospect of all-out war with the British Army, now becoming a very real possibility, was not an attractive one.

The channels of communication between the Sinn Féin leaders and the government had been maintained by the assistant under-secretary in Dublin, Alfred Cope. One of the key figures was Art O'Brien, the Irish Republican representative in Britain, and another was Tom Casement, the brother of the hanged Sir Roger. It was O'Brien who persuaded Casement to see the South African Prime Minister Jan Christian Smuts, in London for the Imperial Conference, to ask him to propose to the King that his forthcoming opening of the newly created and deeply controversial Ulster Parliament in Belfast would be an ideal opportunity for an appeal for reconciliation. Stamfordham, who knew the King's mind better than anyone, ensured that he knew of the number and quality of people urging this course. It was exactly the opportunity for intervention that the King craved.

Smuts, the former Boer Commando leader, was trusted in London. He lunched with the King on 13 June, and made the suggestion, to which the King responded with alacrity. They agreed that Smuts should write directly and immediately to Lloyd George. The key passage of Smuts' letter of 14 June, which faithfully reflected the King's views, stated: 'I believe that in the present universal mistrust and estrangement the King could be made use of to give a most important lead, which would help you out of a situation which is well nigh desperate. The Irish might accept it as coming from the King, and in that way the opening might be given you for a final settlement.'[3] Thomas Jones, whose personal knowledge of Irish politics was considerable, and whose influence with Lloyd George was greater than that of any minister, discussed the suggestion with Hankey on the 15th. There was no disagreement about the idea, although a draft that Smuts had prepared was not to these crucial officials' liking, but the question arose as to whether the King should be formally advised by 'the Imperial PM' – i.e., Lloyd George – or by the Ulster Prime Minister, Sir James Craig.

An urgent meeting of the Cabinet's Irish Situation Committee was called on the next day, chaired by Austen Chamberlain, to which, most unusually, Stamfordham was invited to attend. It was agreed that, constitutionally, the King should be advised by his government and that Craig should announce the legislation proposed for the new parliament. No one was happy with Smuts' draft and Balfour was asked to prepare a new one. The final version was the work of an exceptional civil servant, Edward Grigg, drawing upon the drafts of Smuts and Balfour, and a definite improvement on both. Although Lloyd George had not attended this key meeting, he gave his approval when the King formally sought his advice, making very clear what he wanted and expected it to be on the 17th. By then, Lloyd George had little choice. And perhaps, in that mercurial mind, he had come to the same conclusion as the King.

Many others were involved in this process, who knew of the King's anguish and sense of helplessness as his kingdom tore itself apart so bloodily, and his desire to make his own contribution to ending it. In this sense it can be reasonably described as a royal political initiative – and one that he was to follow up actively with his ministers.

The final version of the speech was a masterpiece, as the King recognised when Stamfordham put it before him.

For once, Rose has underestimated the King's role, stating that the

[3] The full text is contained in Keith Middlemas, *The Diaries of Thomas Jones*, Volume III, p. 75.

speech 'had been prepared in Downing Street and approved by the Cabinet. His only departure from custom lay in persuading the government to cast his speech in the form of a personal appeal for reconciliation in Ireland.'[4] But this 'departure from custom' – which, of course, had given the speech its entire character and purpose – had happened before, and was to happen later on many occasions when there was a genuine royal initiative and when the King's senior officials were deeply involved in the preparation of important royal speeches – and, later, broadcasts.

Nor was Smuts alone to be 'credited with implanting that visionary plan in the King's mind'.[5] It was there already, as Stamfordham knew. The decisive element was the knowledge that it was going to be welcomed by the Sinn Féin leadership – or, at least, by important elements within it.

The other political factor of deep importance, which Smuts had stressed heavily in his original letter to Lloyd George, was that it was a speech and a heartfelt appeal that only the King, with his authority and personal respect, could make, and no politician could have made with any hope of success. The wisdom of Stockmar in emphasising the vital importance of the monarch being uncontaminated with political parties, factions and disputes has seldom been better justified. And, if the actual words were, technically, 'written in Downing Street', they superbly and accurately reflected the King's deeply felt views, which he had expressed privately for so long.

There was also the fact that going to Belfast, and driving openly through the streets, was an act of great physical courage by the King. His heartfelt appeal for negotiations on 23 June formed a crucial part of the process that resulted in the Anglo-Irish Settlement which retained Ulster's separation from an independent southern Ireland. What seemed at the time to be a triumph rapidly degenerated into an Irish civil war more terrible than the Anglo-Irish one, but the King's role as a respected conciliator had been a major element in the truce that achieved what then appeared to be the only achievement of the Lloyd George Coalition.

These differences coincided with the question of honours that further soured the King's relations with his ministers, especially Lloyd George.

One very significant reason that there had not been a public uproar

4 Rose, op. cit., p. 238.
5 Ibid.

at Lloyd George's abuse of the honours system before 1922 was that one of his principal methods of securing favourable press support had been to shower honours upon newspaper proprietors – for a price. The cost of viscountcies ranged from £80,000 to £120,000; that of baronies from £30,000 to £50,000; baronetcies went for £25,000 and knighthoods for £15,000. Thus, seven members of the Harmsworth family received high honours; and peerages were conferred upon Beaverbrook, Burnham of the *Daily Telegraph*, Dalzeill of *Reynold's News*, and Riddell of the *News of the World*.

Lloyd George, with cynical brilliance, therefore simultaneously squared the press through the use of honours and acquired vast sums whose ultimate destination remain obscure. That a considerable proportion went to him personally is uncontestable, although he covered his tracks well. He bought the *Daily Chronicle* in 1918 and sold it in 1926 at a profit of £2 million; he tried to buy *The Times* in 1922 and to become its editor; he sold his memoirs to the *Daily Telegraph* for £90,000; he charged £1 per word for thousand-word articles. These were astronomical sums, and made Lloyd George immensely rich personally as well as lavishly financing his political ambitions.

King George protested vehemently against Rothermere's viscountcy and the peerages to Beaverbrook, Dalziell and Riddell. He was unaware of their purchase prices and the blatant racket that Lloyd George was running, although his knowledge of the man made him suspicious. What he loathed was conferring high honours upon very rich men whose profession he despised. The 1922 list was to him, and many others, the ultimate insult.

Lloyd George's defenders could reasonably claim that honours had been unscrupulously used as political incentives and rewards for generations, first by monarchs and then by politicians. Venality had too often been more common than merit, but Lloyd George, in his arrogance and avarice, went too far, and he and his agents were caught out.

Between Asquith taking office in 1908 and his downfall nearly nine years later, ninety political peerages had been created. The same number was secured by Lloyd George in a premiership lasting only six years. Many of them were contrary to the King's expressed views and wishes, but the list to mark the King's birthday in June 1922 was the last straw. It contained the names of five new peers: Sir Robert Borwick, Sir William Vestey, Sir Joseph Robinson, Sir Samuel Waring and Sir Archibald

Gore-Williamson. With the exception of Borwick, these completely unmerited honours created uproar in the press – which turned out not to have been wholly squared – and in parliament. All were bad, but the award to Sir Joseph Robinson, an appalling South African magnate of evil reputation but great wealth, was the worst of all. Faced with the storm, even Lloyd George realised he had over-reached himself and Robinson was forcibly persuaded to write to the King regretfully declining the honour.[6]

The enraged King wrote to Lloyd George to express his 'profound concern at the very disagreeable situation which has arisen on the question of honours', and added that 'I do appeal most strongly for the establishment of some efficient and trustworthy procedure in order to protect the Crown and the government from the possibility of similar painful if not humiliating incidents, the occurrence of which must inevitably constitute an evil, dangerous to the social and political well-being of the state'. Lloyd George, thus heavily pressed, agreed to the appointment of a Royal Commission which was to lead to the establishment of the Honours Scrutiny Committee, consisting of three Privy Counsellors, none of them members of the government.

This was not to prove a perfect safeguard against abuse of the honours system, but it did give subsequent Prime Ministers and their advisers some pause for thought. If rejections of recommendations have been rare, they have been significant. This episode was to prove a major factor in the ending of Lloyd George's premiership and his political career. The Great Moralist had been found out.

The honours scandal was only part of the mounting Conservative discontent with Lloyd George that developed rapidly in the summer of 1922. They were the majority party in the Coalition, yet were treated with neglect and disdain not only by the Prime Minister but by their own leaders, notably Balfour, Birkenhead and Austen Chamberlain. Bonar Law had left the government in March 1921 through ill-health, but even his former admiration for Lloyd George had markedly diminished. When an astonished nation found itself on the verge of war with Turkey

---

[6] Robinson, aged eighty-seven, was extremely deaf. When the unwelcome news was conveyed to him he wearily took out his chequebook and asked, 'How much more?' (Rose, op. cit., p. 251.)

in August 1922, Law emerged from his retirement to warn that Britain could not be 'the policeman of the world'. The crisis itself subsided, but for the angry Conservatives this was the final provocation. At a historic meeting at the Carlton Club on 19 October, at which the speech of the day was made by the hitherto obscure but rapidly rising President of the Board of Trade, Stanley Baldwin, they voted to withdraw from the Coalition. Lloyd George resigned that afternoon, with few, if any, of his contemporaries realising this was the end of his ministerial career.

Although Chamberlain had succeeded Law as leader of the Coalition Conservatives, his stand on behalf of Lloyd George had made his position untenable, and Law was the obvious choice for Prime Minister. But when Stamfordham telephoned him on the King's orders to ask him to come to the Palace, Law suggested that Stamfordham should come to see him at his home in Onslow Gardens instead. Considerably surprised, Stamfordham did so.

At this meeting Law 'explained that he was not the leader of the Conservative Party, that the party was for the moment broken up, and, until he knew that he could count on its undivided support, he would not accept office'. He added that even if he received it, he would only hold office for a year.

The King, having accepted the resignation of one Prime Minister, now found himself with none. Even after much telephoning Law was quietly adamant, although he did eventually agree to see the King for a discussion. A compromise was reached. Law would consult his colleagues about the formation of a new government, and would seek an immediate party meeting for election as leader: the Court Circular would merely state that Law had had an audience with the King. After a particularly hectic round of talks, Law found that he was able to form a government of sorts on the following Sunday, 22 October; the day after that, he was unanimously elected leader.

It was not at all obvious at the time that the Conservative decision to break the Coalition had been politically wise. They had not won a General Election on their own since 1900, and with many of their most prominent members openly hostile, Law's request to the King for an immediate dissolution and election seemed very hazardous indeed. But the following month the Conservatives triumphed, with Law gaining a majority of 77 over Labour and the divided Liberals.

His subsequent government, however, was notably undistinguished

– the only surprising appointment being that of Baldwin as Chancellor of the Exchequer – and almost immediately put under threat by Law's own ill-health. He had been persuaded not to make public his pledge to remain Prime Minister for only a year, but by April 1923 his voice had almost entirely gone and he was forced to rest from all official duties. The day after he attended the marriage of the Duke of York to Lady Elizabeth Bowes-Lyon, Law told the King that in his absence Curzon would preside over the Cabinet and Baldwin would lead the Commons. The King agreed to this arrangement, which inevitably and naturally gave Curzon high expectations that, if Law adhered to his plans to retire in the autumn, he would be his natural successor. But the plans went awry. In May Law was diagnosed with incurable throat cancer, and the matter of who should succeed him came to dominate his thoughts much sooner than expected.

Curzon, a towering figure of exceptional experience, intellect and ability, was the obvious choice. Baldwin, although a talented parliamentarian and the current Conservative hero through his part in Lloyd George's downfall, did not yet have the same pedigree, and Law himself certainly expected Curzon to be chosen. This was also Stamfordham's opinion.

The King, however, was already expressing his conviction that, as Stamfordham recorded, his responsibility to the country made it 'almost imperative that he should appoint a Prime Minister from the House of Commons, for were he not to do so, and the experiment failed, the country would blame the King for an act which was entirely his own, and which proved that the King was ignorant of and out of touch with public opinion'.[7]

But the King and Stamfordham then received an unsigned memorandum that, it was claimed, 'practically expressed the views of Mr Bonar Law', and which was a cogent argument in favour of Baldwin. It was written by J. C. C. Davidson, who was very close both to Law and to Baldwin. It was perhaps not as decisive as has sometimes been claimed, but it mirrored the King's own opinion, which was fortified by Balfour, who had ignored his doctors' advice to travel to London at the King's request.

The animosity between Balfour and Curzon was of long duration, but in his meeting with the King, Balfour shrewdly concentrated on

[7] Bogdanor, op. cit., p. 93.

the one point that so concerned the King – the virtual impossibility of having a Prime Minister in the Lords, where the Labour Party, now the principal Opposition, did not have a single member.

It may well be that the Davidson memorandum was a severe distortion of Law's real opinion, which was that Curzon was the inevitable choice, but its importance was that it was exactly in line with the King's political instincts and Balfour's advice. It was this combination that doomed Curzon's ambitions and expectations.

But Balfour's advice was congenial to the King not only on the constitutional aspect. The King's dislike of Curzon went back to his visit to India as Duke of York in the last days of Curzon's tempestuous Viceroyalty, on which he took the side of the Commander-in-Chief, Lord Kitchener, in the venomous dispute between the two men. But these personal feelings against Curzon had faded, and the King did appreciate what a crushing blow it would be for him to be passed over, and tried to soften it. In so doing he only made matters worse.

The situation was complicated by the fact that it was Whit weekend, and Curzon was at one of his fine residences, Montacute in Somerset, which did not have a telephone – an invention Curzon considered 'disastrous'. On the morning of Whit Monday he received a letter from Law informing him of his resignation, but it was not until the evening that he received a telegram from Stamfordham asking to see him the following day in London. Curzon telegraphed that he would be at Carlton House Terrace at 1.20 p.m.

The King had already decided to send for Baldwin, although most newspapers and political commentators expected Curzon to become Prime Minister. Certainly he did, discoursing to his wife as they travelled by train to London on appointments and domestic arrangements, and posing for photographers at Paddington Station and in front of his house. On arrival he received calls of support from an unexpected quarter, the Austen Chamberlain camp.

At 2.30 Stamfordham arrived. Few tasks entrusted to him by the King were more difficult. He explained, in Curzon's account, 'with obvious embarrassment and in halting language' that although the King fully appreciated the great strength of his claims, he had become convinced that the Prime Minister must be in the Commons and had decided to appoint Baldwin.

After Curzon had absorbed the terrible truth, he told Stamfordham of his messages from the Chamberlain supporters and claimed that only he could reunite the party. He asked Stamfordham to put these matters before the King. Stamfordham could not bring himself to say that it was too late; Baldwin was already at the Palace. It was this that made Curzon's bitterness all the greater. 'Such was the manner in which it was intimated to me that the cup of honourable ambition had been dashed from my lips and that I could never aspire to fill the highest office in the service of the Crown,' he wrote, with somewhat orotund but very understandable chagrin.

At the time, after the initial surprise, the wisdom of the King's decision was widely recognised, and Curzon himself, after his intimation that he would retire completely from public life, rallied magnificently. He agreed to serve under Baldwin as Foreign Secretary and proposed the motion to elect him leader of the party – in a speech considered by some as of notable warmth and magnanimity, by others as an example of almost sublime malice. 'In a sense,' he said, 'it may be said that the choice of Mr Stanley Baldwin as Leader of the Conservative Party has been determined by the action of the King. But we all felt, and I am sure you will agree, that it was right that the choice of the sovereign should be ratified and confirmed by the vote of the entire party.' After a notably unenthusiastic description of Baldwin's qualities, Curzon concluded that 'lastly (I breathe this almost *sotto voce*), Mr Baldwin possesses the supreme and indispensable qualification of not being a Peer'.

The virtually unanimous verdict of contemporary historians was that the King made the right decision. With a longer perspective this looks much more questionable. Baldwin's inexperience, which had so worried Law, was to be made evident very quickly, and healing the fissures in the Conservative ranks was to take time – possibly longer than under Curzon. Undoubtedly Baldwin was a more reassuring personality at a particularly difficult time of social unrest and decreasing enthusiasm for imperialism. As leader Baldwin won only two General Elections out of four, and history has given a bleak verdict upon his role in the 1930s. He was somewhat *too* reassuring when the perils began to mount after the advent of Hitler in 1933.

None of this could be remotely foreseen in 1923, but in going for inexperience over experience it is arguable that the King made the wrong decision, although perhaps for the right political reasons. Curzon lived only for another twenty-two months, and although he might have made mistakes, it is doubtful that he would have made one as momentous as Baldwin did in October–November 1923.

This resulted from a rash undertaking by Law in the 1922 election campaign that there would be no major change in fiscal policy without another General Election. By October Baldwin had become convinced that the British home market must be protected. This conversion in itself did not mean a General Election, but there were other factors involved: raising the banner of protection would bring the Chamberlain Conservatives back into the fold and deny the possibility of Lloyd George taking the issue as his own. The decision to go to the country was not Baldwin's alone; it was only when the gamble failed that all the blame fell on him. But the censure was not as unfair as his admirers have often claimed.

The King thought that it was a thoroughly bad decision, told Baldwin so, and urged him to reconsider it. The new parliament was barely a year old; the government had a clear majority in the Commons; and, until Baldwin had publicly raised it, most people had forgotten about Law's promise. Law himself had died on 20 October; five days later, at the annual Conservative Conference in Plymouth, Baldwin revived his pledge of a year before. But Baldwin told the King that things had gone too far for second thoughts, and the King, with many misgivings, agreed to grant Baldwin the dissolution of parliament that he requested. The King's political judgement – not on partisan but on practical constitutional grounds – proved much better than that of his Prime Minister and his most senior colleagues – notably Neville Chamberlain, son of Joseph and half-brother of Austen, a committed protectionist and bitter foe of Lloyd George.

The subsequent General Election in December was not conclusive, returning 257 Conservatives, 191 Labour, and 158 Liberals. But it was manifestly a Conservative defeat. The King, having told Baldwin that he thought the election precipitate and unnecessary, could have been in an awkward position if Baldwin had chosen to resign immediately. There was a scheme afoot, involving Birkenhead and Austen Chamberlain, to induce Balfour and Stamfordham to persuade the King not to send for either the Labour leader Ramsay MacDonald or Asquith but another Conservative to form a government. But Balfour would not play, and told Baldwin to face the new House of Commons, and advised a pact with Asquith to keep Labour out. This course neither Baldwin nor

Asquith would countenance, in spite of great pressure put upon them by their respective supporters, to whom the advent of a Labour government assumed the proportions of a national calamity.

Baldwin did not accept this apocalyptic prognosis. He considered that the Labour Party was now the principal Opposition party and had few fears about MacDonald. The King shared his views and also knew from Stamfordham about the right-wing Conservative attempt to dump Baldwin and use him to appoint someone – probably Austen Chamberlain – congenial to them. He accordingly asked Baldwin not to resign; he did mention the possibility of 'a working arrangement' with Asquith, but Baldwin had already rejected the idea of an anti-Socialist alliance, and had had enough of coalitions. On reflection, the King realised that his Prime Minister was entirely right, and, as he told Baldwin's closest confidant John Davidson, 'it was essential that their [the Labour Party's] rights under the constitution should in no way be impaired'.

The delay in Baldwin's resignation was initially interpreted by some Labour politicians – notably George Lansbury – as the result of the King's hostility to Socialism and Communism, which he had admittedly taken little trouble to conceal. But the more violent Labour censures on the King's conduct were diminished by the fact that the Conservatives remained significantly the largest party in the House of Commons, and there was, initially, no guarantee that the Liberals would ally with them to bring the government down.

But although the King was apprehensive about the first Labour government – 'It would be a miracle were he not', Ramsay MacDonald wrote after kissing hands in January as Prime Minister, after the government had been duly defeated in the Commons and Baldwin had resigned – he was determined to give his untried new ministers all the help he could. Within days the latter were singing his praises, and no one more than MacDonald, who kept him better informed about government matters than any of his predecessors had done. A somewhat unexpected mutual regard and even friendship grew up between the two men, and a very strong one between the King and the railway trade unionist and colonial secretary J. H. 'Jimmy' Thomas, whose salty and irreverent wit was much to the King's taste.

The first Labour government was short-lived, but was not at all undistinguished. Nor was it notably radical, let alone Socialist. It fell in September 1924 when the Liberals withdrew their support, and in the following General Election the Conservatives were easily returned with 419 Members to Labour's 151; the real losers were the Liberals, with Asquith's long career finally ended.

The defeated Labour ministers considered that the King's conduct towards them had been impeccable, and were grateful. The King continued to take a kindly personal interest in MacDonald and, when he was told of his financial problems, proposed that former Prime Ministers should receive pensions. He was not successful, but it was characteristic of his kindness, and of his political acumen. The anti-monarchical element in the Labour Party, never very significant, faded away totally. It was one of King George's most remarkable personal achievements.

The return of the Conservatives did not afford the King particular pleasure. He had come to like MacDonald more than any of his predecessors and was, in company with many others, amazed that Baldwin made Churchill Chancellor of the Exchequer on his return to the Conservative fold. But the King's antipathy to Churchill had faded. So had that towards Curzon; the King was pleased that Baldwin gave the Foreign Office to Austen Chamberlain instead, but Curzon's post as Lord President of the Council unfortunately brought him into close contact with the King and he made an unseemly and irritating fuss about minor Court appointments. But he died within four months, and this particular irritant was removed.

Rightly, the King had not thought well of the impossible Joynson-Hicks as Home Secretary, and was troubled by the continued industrial unrest that culminated in the General Strike of May 1926. He also found Baldwin's relaxed view of his duties as Prime Minister perplexing and annoying, but it was the deepening economic crisis and the bitter divisions among his subjects that were the King's deepest concerns.

As he well knew, there were elements in the Conservative Party – resisted by Baldwin – that were eager for a confrontation with the trade unions. When it came, in 1926, the King was firmly on the side of moderation and compromise. He disliked Churchill's claim in his short-lived broadsheet the *British Gazette* that the armed forces could intervene, and, through Stamfordham, made his views known to the Chief of the Imperial General Staff; he was even more critical of the government's advice to agree to an Order in Council that would have effectively frozen the finances of the unions, arguing that such action 'might cause exasperation and provoke reprisals. If money was not forthcoming to buy food, there might be looting of shops, even of banks.' His views prevailed.

The King was a compassionate man. He once growlingly told the millionaire coal-owner Lord Durham, when the latter described the striking miners as 'revolutionaries', to try living on their wages. In 1912 he had contributed 1,000 guineas to a fund to assist the families of striking miners, and in 1921 had protested to ministers about the miserably low levels of unemployment benefit. But he was not one to condone anarchy or lawlessness, and his attitudes were rather sterner on these matters than Harold Nicolson's account states.

There was no insincerity in what might appear to be a contradiction in the King's attitudes. He was a man of peace and an instinctive conciliator, but he would not tolerate indiscipline or disorder. The old naval officer in him wanted a nation and Empire that was contented and efficient; but although he desired 'a happy ship' in which there was no injustice or cause for legitimate complaint, there must be no question of mutiny. A good officer understood his men and looked after them, but there must be no misunderstanding about who was in command. To modern eyes this might seem surprising, but this was the virtually universal view. The peaceful collapse of the General Strike after a few days demonstrated how right the King's instincts were, and how widely they were shared by his subjects.

Towards the end of 1928 King George became dangerously ill with a streptococcal infection of the chest that affected his heart, and from which he very nearly died. The crisis began on 21 November; by 2 December his condition was worrying his doctors so much that the Prince of Wales was urgently summoned home from his safari in East Africa, which he abandoned with much reluctance. After the crisis had passed the King had a long period of convalescence at Craigweil, the home of Sir Arthur du Cros, near Bognor in Sussex. Here he stayed, reluctantly and irritably, from 9 February 1929 until 15 May, when he returned to Windsor, still weak.

In retrospect, it can be seen that the combination of the King's accident in 1915, the strain of the war and its difficult aftermath, a severe attack of influenza and bronchitis in 1925 and the near-fatal illness of 1928–29 had seriously, and permanently, weakened him. There have been several modern commentators who have pointed censoriously to his heavy smoking as a major contributory factor in the decline in his health, but it was septicaemia that nearly killed him in 1928 and damaged his heart, and smoking was only a peripheral factor. The King had barely recovered when another political crisis arose.

The Baldwin-led Conservative government had entered the 1929 General Election – the first in which women could vote on the same basis as men – with muted confidence and an equally muted rallying-cry of 'Safety First'. The result was that the Conservatives won 261 seats, Labour 287, and the Liberals 59. The King, Stamfordham and Baldwin all agreed that there should be no repetition of the King's December 1923 request for Baldwin not to resign until the new parliament met. As Stamfordham, now approaching eighty but still as shrewd as ever, wrote: 'We must recognise that democracy is no longer a meaningless sort of shibboleth; with the enormous increase of voters by the women's franchise it is the actual voice, for better or worse, the political voice of the state.' Baldwin therefore resigned at once and the King sent for Ramsay MacDonald on 5 June, a duty which gave him genuine pleasure and eased his continuing convalescence.

The King, although fearful of Communism and extreme Socialism, had correctly assessed that there was little danger of those forces in the deeply respectable Labour Party. He also liked MacDonald, and made a point of welcoming the first woman Privy Counsellor, Margaret Bondfield, who had been appointed Minister of Labour. His only serious disagreement with the new government occurred early, when it decided to restore full diplomatic relations with the Soviet Union. His ministers prevailed, but the King, who was admittedly still very unwell, contrived to use this as an excuse for not receiving the new ambassador and thus having to shake the hand of the representative of the regime that had murdered his cousins.

Few modern British governments have been so unfortunate in the timing of their accession to office. The calamitous crash on Wall Street marked the end of the boom years in the United States and heralded the onset of the terrible Depression. The 'economic blizzard' crossed the Atlantic, world trade slumped, and unemployment rose rapidly and inexorably, especially in Germany and Britain. By the summer of 1931 the near-frantic Labour government effectively abrogated its responsibility by appointing an independent committee to advise it on how public expenditure could be reduced; it recommended swingeing cuts. City, banking and foreign confidence in the government, never high, now evaporated; their terms for assisting it were harsh, and the Cabinet split asunder.

The King had travelled to Balmoral on 20 August, with some uneasiness, and had hardly arrived on the following morning when he received an urgent message from MacDonald that it would be necessary for him to return to London. The King immediately agreed, and was back in Buckingham Palace on the morning of the 23rd.

MacDonald came to tell him that the situation was desperate and, in his own account, 'I told him that after tonight I might be of no further use and should resign with the whole Cabinet. He asked if I would advise him to send for Henderson [for whom neither he nor the King had any respect]. I said "No", which he said relieved him. I advised him in the meantime to send for the leaders of the other two parties and have them report position from their points of view. He said he would and would advise them strongly to support me.'

The King told MacDonald that 'he believed I was the only person who could carry the country through', but it is doubtful whether this is sufficient evidence to support the contention that the King had already decided upon a National Government headed by him.

There was then a notable example of the importance of chance in history, especially political history. Baldwin, whose hold upon the leadership of his party had been tenuous since 1929, should have been the first to have been summoned to the Palace as the leader of the principal Opposition party, but he could not be found. He would not have recommended a National Government under MacDonald; most probably, given his character, he would have asked for time to consult his colleagues. What is absolutely certain is that he would have refused to serve in a government with Lloyd George, but his *bête noire* was recovering from an operation, and so the first politician the King saw after MacDonald was the temporary Liberal leader Sir Herbert Samuel, who told the King that his first preference would be for the government to put through the proposed economies, but if this was impossible the best alternative was for MacDonald to head an all-party National Government. This solution had already occurred to the King, but Samuel's arguments nonetheless made a great and favourable impression upon him.

As has been noted, most modern British monarchs have favoured coalitions, believing firmly that only such confederations truly reflect and maintain the national interest as opposed to that of individual parties. Disraeli may have been right when he declared that 'England does not love coalitions', but every monarch from Queen Victoria to King George VI has done.

When Baldwin, who had been peaceably lunching at the Travellers Club, was tracked down and eventually reached the Palace, he found that he was in effect confronted with a *fait accompli*. But his agreement to serve under MacDonald was heavily qualified. He could see the advantages to MacDonald and the Liberals of a National Government, but was doubtful about any accruing to the Conservatives. Still, he had not rejected the idea when put to him so forcefully by his King. If he had been the first to have been summoned, and Lloyd George had been the Liberal leader, the result would have been very different.

The one leading Conservative who was enthusiastic for a National Government was Baldwin's would-be successor Neville Chamberlain, a fact that did not increase Baldwin's goodwill towards it. He was prepared to take 'a helpful line' in parliament when he knew what the government proposed, but not a coalition. Indeed, he expected the government to fall, and to be invited to become Prime Minister again; when he eventually saw the King on the afternoon of the 23rd he made it plain that while he would be ready to do anything to serve the country, if MacDonald resigned he would be prepared to form a government; once the economic crisis was over he would ask for the dissolution of parliament. Although the King 'was greatly pleased with Mr Baldwin's readiness to meet the crisis which had arisen and to sink party interests for the sake of the country', Baldwin had not in fact agreed to serve under MacDonald.

The King's role now became dominant. The Cabinet was hopelessly split; eleven ministers supported the dramatic public expenditure cuts demanded by American and other bankers, and nine opposed them at an emergency Cabinet held on the evening of that momentous Sunday. MacDonald went to the Palace determined to resign, but the King again told him he was the only man to save the situation and urged him to reconsider. He also said, on very dubious evidence, that MacDonald could rely upon Conservative and Liberal support and that he would preside over a meeting of the three party leaders the following morning.

The fact was that the King held MacDonald in high esteem, and considered him a friend. It might have been thought that MacDonald's wartime pacifism, his woolly and often incomprehensible oratory and conversation, his mystical and naïve idealism and his manifold inadequacies as a political leader would have repelled the King even more than they did his colleagues and opponents. But now the King had the goal of a National Government before him, he was convinced that only MacDonald could lead it.

A further complicating factor for the King was that, sadly, he no longer had Stamfordham to guide him; his trusted ally had died the previous March, and had been replaced by his assistant Clive Wigram. The new Private Secretary was a very different character, much given to sporting metaphors, and although – as Rose has written – he served 'a long and vigorous apprenticeship' under Stamfordham, he did not have the same relationship, experience or authority. Indeed, one of the other 'ifs' of this extraordinary episode is whether the King would have conducted it as he did if Stamfordham had been at his side rather than the untried Wigram. The fact is that the King was being somewhat reckless, by Stamfordham's cautious standards, and had become the key political leader in the crisis. By the Sunday evening he had in effect refused to accept MacDonald's resignation twice, and was making all the running.

This was all the more evident on the following Monday morning (24 August), when MacDonald, Baldwin and Samuel assembled under the King's chairmanship at Buckingham Palace. The three party leaders were firmly under the impression that the Cabinet was going to resign, and MacDonald said so. But the King ruled this out, and told MacDonald that it was his duty to work out arrangements with Baldwin and Samuel for a National Emergency Government. Under this pressure it was so decided, with the qualification that it should not be termed a coalition but a 'co-operation of individuals', to resolve the immediate crisis and to be followed by a General Election in which all the political parties would revert to pre-crisis partisan politics.

The King was delighted, and lavishly praised all three. The Labour Cabinet, expecting to be told that their collective resignation had been accepted, was thunderstruck to be told by MacDonald that he was to remain Prime Minister, but of a National rather than a Labour government. He then asked them to follow his advice and his leadership; only three agreed. The second Labour government immediately collapsed in chaos and much rancour; the National Government arose from its rubble.

Controversy still continues about the King's personal role in this drama. That he was the leading advocate of a National Government is clear. Samuel certainly agreed with him, but initially neither MacDonald nor Baldwin had been enthusiastic. The new government was very much his creation, and he was solely responsible for persuading MacDonald not to resign.

It should be noted that MacDonald had not specifically advised the King to send for Baldwin to form a government, which would have been the logical sequel to the disintegration and resignation of his government, but had advised him to see Baldwin and Samuel. Constitutionally, in following that advice from his Prime Minister, the King had acted quite correctly. What is far more contestable is whether he acted properly in the personal pressure he exerted on both MacDonald and Baldwin to agree to something about which they were highly doubtful. And there is some merit in the point often made by the King's critics that he should have consulted more widely among Labour Cabinet ministers. The answer to this charge is that the King was convinced that immediate action was imperative to restore national and international confidence, and that the desperate situation required the most urgent action. This position is understandable, and can certainly be defended, but it is very probable that Stamfordham would have cast his advisory net rather wider than the King and Wigram did, and which might well have produced a different result.

Although Harold Laski exaggerated when he wrote that MacDonald 'was as much the personal choice of George V as Lord Bute was the personal choice of George III', there was enough truth in the accusation to cause the King's admirers and constitutional historians some justified uneasiness. If the shattered Labour Party, now doomed to temporary extinction in the forthcoming General Election, had fully realised the King's role in its demise, the consequences could have been grave for his reputation as a politically disinterested monarch. Furthermore, the King's involvement in the National Government did not end with its formation.

One of the principal conditions agreed by the political leaders at the Buckingham Palace conference was that 'the election which may follow the end of the government will not be fought by the government but by the parties', a pledge on which Baldwin laid considerable emphasis when securing the agreement of the parliamentary Conservative Party.

But MacDonald had been immediately and overwhelmingly repudiated by the Labour Party, only seven ministers and eight back-benchers supporting him, a fact that makes the King's initiatives even more questionable. They, and MacDonald, were expelled from the party and reviled for their treachery. Then, the National Government had to abandon the Gold Standard within weeks of its inception, and one of its principal reasons for existing vanished.

None of this diminished the King's enthusiasm for MacDonald and his government. It was not realised at the time, and indeed not for a very long time afterwards, that the King's anti-Socialist bias played a large part in his motivation. He even went so far as to tell MacDonald that 'if a Socialist government came into power and carried out their extravagant promises to the electorate, this country would be finished', and that MacDonald was the only person who could resolve the crisis. But MacDonald was by then a weak, bewildered and demoralised man, with little idea what to do next. The King, by contrast, saw the situation with unswerving clarity. His purpose had been to create, and then to maintain in power, a National Government that deliberately excluded 'the Socialists' – namely, the Labour Party.

His concept of 'a combination of all decent-minded politicians' did not include any Labour one who did not support MacDonald. King George acted throughout in what he honestly deemed to be the national interest, but it was just as well that his blatant political bias was not known until relatively recently, and even now tends to be understated.[8] The goodwill and respect shown to him by his former Labour ministers would have dissipated rapidly into harsh denunciations of his partisan role, and would have been entirely justified. If they had been aware of the King's crucial part in their destruction the Labour rage would have been even greater after the General Election in October, which was a catastrophe for their party. The National Government won 554 seats and 67 per cent of the vote; Labour won only 52 seats and 31 per cent of the vote.

It has been claimed that the King's actions throughout the two-month

[8] Bogdanor, op. cit., p. III.

crisis were not unconstitutional since he had accepted the advice of his Prime Minister. This conveniently ignores the fact that the King had given MacDonald his orders and then had accepted what was in fact his own advice. He had, at long last, found a Prime Minister he could manipulate and employ for his own purposes. As he wrote to the Duke of York, 'I mean to do everything and anything in my power to prevent the old ship running on the rocks.' It seemed that he had succeeded brilliantly; it was only later, when the old ship did indeed run on to the rocks and nearly foundered with all hands, that his usurpation of political power could be regarded considerably less favourably.

The answer to this charge has always been that the King was never anti-Labour, as he had proved in 1924 and 1929–31, and that his sole concern in August 1931 was to restore confidence in his country's ability to surmount the crisis facing it. But this conventional conclusion severely underestimates the man. The National Government was neither accidental nor unplanned. There has never been in recent British political history a more decisive intervention by a sovereign. King George did not only 'warn and encourage' during the crisis – he was the leader, the one personality who knew what was required and was single-mindedly intent upon achieving it. He had secured, virtually alone, an astounding political triumph. And he had emerged from these turbulent events not only unscathed and uncriticised but with an enhanced reputation. It was, in its way, a political masterpiece.

After so much turmoil, anguish, disappointment and frustration King George V had reached his apogee. He had at long last created his own government, the first with which he was wholly – if wrongly – content. He had never sought popularity, but it now came to him.

King George disliked change and was not so much indifferent to new developments as actively hostile to them. Although his two oldest sons learned to fly, the King abhorred aeroplanes and greatly disliked air shows. The wireless also fell into this category, but he could not prevent the BBC broadcasting his speeches; what did surprise him, and others, was that they attracted a very large listening public in Britain and abroad.

John Reith, the general manager of the BBC, had suggested in 1923 that the King might broadcast a Christmas or New Year message to the Empire; the suggestion was not welcomed. It was not until 1932 that he could be persuaded to do so. The author was Rudyard Kipling, and the text was magnificent; but it was the King's own voice that added enormously to the magic of the occasion. To his genuine surprise the King discovered he was a natural broadcaster – simple, clear, direct and conversational. So warm and enthusiastic was the national and international response that the King was reluctantly persuaded to make this an annual event, although none had the impact of the first one. As Kenneth Rose has expressed it so perfectly, 'All who gathered year after year for the King's Christmas message awaited the voice of a friend.'

4

TRANSITION

One of the sadnesses about George V was that, although irascible, and sometimes alarmingly so, he was fundamentally a kind and considerate man, much loved by those who served him, and was exceptionally good with other people's children, but was less successful as a father. But the exaggerated and self-pitying account given by his eldest son and heir of a deeply unhappy childhood, with a portrait of a harshly severe father and an indifferent and unsympathetic mother, has led many biographers seriously astray. The fact was that he delighted in his children, but found his eldest son, the attractive and popular Prince Edward, known as David, difficult to understand. Queen Mary later told Harold Nicolson that 'it was only with [him] that he did not get on well'. Kenneth Rose has put the matter sensitively and fairly:

> King George V was an affectionate parent, albeit an unbending Victorian. He loved his children, was proud of their good looks and achievements, praised as readily as he rebuked. He brought them up with impeccable manners and a total absence of that high-born arrogance which permeated so many other royal houses; only thus, he believed, could his own line survive in an age of unrest.[2]

As their correspondence and all other evidence reveals, King George

---

[2] Rose, op. cit., p. 110.

and Queen Mary were devoted to each other and to their children, but were publicly undemonstrative, often giving the wholly false impression that they were cold and aloof parents, whereas the problem was their shy incapacity to convey their love to their children. There was also the King's insistence upon an ordered and regular life and an inflexible timetable. Although this did not matter much when their children were young, it became a source of growing irritation to them later, and certainly explains their eagerness to escape from a routine that may have satisfied their parents but was suffocatingly boring to high-spirited young men. In the cases of David, the Prince of Wales, and George, the future Duke of Kent, the results were near-disastrous, and the regimen was to make even the considerably more docile and balanced Prince Albert chafe angrily.

Unfortunately, the King's genuine affection for his sons was demonstrated rather more in his letters than in his personal attention, and, having had virtually no education himself, he saw no need for it with them. It was only when he became King that he had recognised his educational limitations, and worked to rectify them, but he did not draw the obvious conclusion. This was his greatest disservice to his two eldest sons. He employed a tutor, Henry Hansell, whose time at Oxford had been more notable for his achievements on the cricket and football fields than in the examination rooms. When the Queen expressed concern about the two boys' evident backwardness the King still refused to send them to school, although he relented in the case of the two youngest ones.

This was a lamentable decision. David and Albert were intelligent boys but they received virtually no formal teaching, an oversight which gave others the entirely false impression – particularly in the case of Albert – that they were dim-witted, even stupid.

The latter had been born at York Cottage on 14 December 1895, his parents then being the Duke and Duchess of York. The timing of his arrival caused consternation in the family, as it was the anniversary of the death of the Prince Consort, and therefore a day of mourning and melancholy remembrances. To the relief of her children and grandchildren Queen Victoria took it as a good omen, but it was tactful to name the new baby Albert Frederick Arthur George, and he was always known to his family and close friends as 'Bertie'.

His elder brother, David, born eighteen months earlier, was from an early age a child of exceptional good looks, charm and fun; Bertie, however, was less fortunate: he had a poor digestion and for a time had to have splints on his legs to cure knock-knees, from which his father had also suffered. Left-handed, he was forced to write with his right, and by the age of eight had developed a stammer; he also had a fiery, almost uncontrollable, temper that developed into intense, if brief, rages of alarming ferocity. The only things he did well, to the relief of his father, were riding and shooting, at both of which he was to become outstanding.

Neither of these attainments were of any use for the destination chosen by his father, the navy. The first stage was the Royal Naval College at Osborne, where David and Bertie went at the age of thirteen, the latter finishing bottom out of sixty-eight entrants. It was an unpleasant introduction to a wider world for a shy, unconfident, stammering and rather puny boy. The Royal Naval College at Dartmouth, the next stage, was not much happier, nor was the navy itself when he became a midshipman on the battleship *Collingwood*.

He would later say that he was 'miserable in the navy', but one factor was his consistent poor health. He had severe gastric troubles at Dartmouth, then appendicitis, and a series of internal disorders which were finally, and belatedly, diagnosed as an ulcer. He also suffered from sea-sickness, an additional misery that he tried to tolerate with fortitude. But he did serve at the Battle of Jutland and was mentioned in dispatches – the first achievement of his life, and of which he was understandably proud. But then ill-health took him away from the navy for good.

Throughout these misfortunes the King had been supportive and kind, although puzzled by his son's aversion to naval life, which he had found so rewarding and enjoyable. Meanwhile, David had joined the Grenadiers, and, to his embarrassment, as he was not permitted to serve in action, had been awarded the newly created Military Cross. Prince of Wales since his father's accession in 1910, he was already the subject of head-turning adulation by the press and an adoring public. The contrast between the dashing charmer and the tongue-tied and inarticulate younger brother had now become a topic of comment in a much wider circle. Even Bertie's period in the Royal Air Force, when he became the first member of the Royal Family to acquire a pilot's licence, did not make up for what had been a depressing and frustrating period of his life.

The only persons who fully appreciated this were his parents, especially the King, whose letters to his son were sympathetic and encouraging.

When he created him Duke of York in 1920 he wrote to his son that 'I know that you have behaved very well, in a difficult situation for a young man & that you have done what I asked you to do . . . I hope you will always look upon me as yr. best friend & always tell me everything & you will always find me ever ready to help you and give you good advice.' This letter was one of several indications that the new Duke of York was becoming the King's favourite son. The Prince of Wales was undertaking exhausting Empire tours with great flair and success, but the King had already detected his waywardness, his lack of royal dignity – indeed, his active dislike of it – and friends and companions of whom the King did not approve.

The King's handling of his eldest son only became worse, and the results more unfortunate. As the Duke of York later explained to Walter Monckton: 'It was difficult for David. My father was inclined to go for him. I always thought that it was a pity that he found fault with him over unimportant things, like what he wore. This only put David's back up. But it was a pity that he did things which he knew would annoy my father. The result was that they did not discuss the important things quietly.'[3]

Freda Dudley Ward, the most important of the Prince's married mistresses before Wallis Simpson, has also recorded how the King's strictness 'only chafed David and led to rows. He became more bitter and more and more despondent as time passed, and the rows became hotter. He was a grown man now and he resented his father ordering him to button his jacket or straighten his tie.'[4]

There is one reported outburst from David that has very much the ring of truth:

I want no more of this Princing! I want to be an ordinary person. I must have a life of my own . . . What does it take to be a good King? You must be a figurehead, a wooden man! Do nothing to upset the Prime Minister or the Court or the Archbishop of Canterbury! Show yourself to the people! Mind your manners! Go to church! What modern man wants that kind of life?[5]

[3] Birkenhead, *Monckton*, p. 124.
[4] Bryan and Murphy, *The Windsor Story*, p. 69.
[5] Ibid, p. 69.

The tension between them, as their very different personalities and temperaments became more evident to both, developed ominously, while the King found his second son increasingly congenial and sensible.

It was at the King's suggestion that the Duke spent a year at Cambridge University studying constitutional history at Trinity College. The King had profited from his tutoring by a Fellow of St John's College in 1894, and particularly from reading Bagehot's *The English Constitution*, which was one of the few serious works he had perused with care, concluding from it that the monarchy was 'still a great political force and offers a splendid career to an able monarch'. Queen Mary, recalling that her husband had become heir only because of his elder brother's death, used her quiet influence to ensure that her second son had at least some rudimentary preparations. According to the Duke of York's future official biographer, Wheeler-Bennett, his studies were rather more profound than his father's, and he took special note of Bagehot's emphasis on the moral role of the monarch, with particular reference to the Prince Consort. It is doubtful whether the young Duke knew much about the extravagance, hedonism and many infidelities of his grandfather, Edward VII, but his interest in this aspect of monarchy was as interesting as was his father's initiative in sending him to Cambridge to be tutored for a role that no one, including the Duke, ever expected him to occupy.

Indeed, the King's motives in doing so are unclear, although the influence of Queen Mary may have been decisive. His relations with his eldest son had not descended to the low level that they were to, but, as the Prince of Wales enjoyed living dangerously and taking risks, an insurance policy against a tragedy to the heir before he married and had children might have been the prime cause for ensuring that his second son's inadequate education should be improved in at least one respect.

But the King, and others including Stamfordham, had noticed that the Duke of York possessed a social conscience and awareness that his elder brother did not. The Prince of Wales *spoke* a great deal on these issues, especially as they affected ex-servicemen, but then, and later, there was a conspicuous gap between fine words and actions. The Prince enjoyed the limelight, of which he was receiving much more than was good for him, but hard work offstage was not, and never would be, his strength. As he himself later recorded, whenever the King spoke to him of duty, the word itself created a barrier between them.

The Duke's social conscience was not matched by his confidence in society, however. He found the atmosphere at Buckingham Palace dreary and the routine imposed by his father immutable, and his worsening stammer seemed to preclude him not only from an active role in public life but from a normal social one as well.

It was, therefore, somewhat ironic that it should have been at a society ball that, in the early summer of 1920, he became entranced by the woman who was in many ways to prove his salvation.

Lady Elizabeth Bowes-Lyon was then aged twenty. The daughter of the Earl of Strathmore, she had recently taken London by storm, and although there were a great many young men eager to marry her, she herself was not too interested in an early engagement – and certainly not into the Royal Family, an opinion endorsed by her father. Also, although she realised that the Duke had genuine charm and kindness, and was remarkably handsome, he was also shy and inarticulate, and his attempts at courtship were initially unsuccessful.

One of the most important individuals in the story of the Duke's eventual engagement was the young Conservative politician J. C. C. Davidson, who had come to know the Duke and subsequently wrote about his involvement. Davidson had been invited by Louis Greig, the Duke's Equerry, to attend a ceremony in July 1922 to lay the foundation stone of a war memorial in Dunkirk, and before re-embarking for the journey home was taken on board the destroyer *Versatile* for an audience with the Duke. Davidson later recalled:

> During this time, sitting at ease smoking our pipes, I was permitted to glimpse into the innermost recesses of his heart and mind. I had been through the war and the years after it, on intimate terms of friendship with many of the senior members of the Royal Household, both officially and privately, and had been fortunate in having many opportunities to acquire knowledge, experience and perhaps wisdom beyond my years. I have always assumed that it was because of this, and the fact that I was only six years older than the Duke, had only recently been married, and was a pretty average type of public school and University man, that the choice had fallen on me for the honour of being taken into his confidence.
>
> I had not been in the Duke's presence more than a few minutes before I realised that he was not only worried, but genuinely

unhappy. He seemed to have reached a crisis in his life, and wanted someone to whom he could unburden himself without reserve. He dwelt upon the difficulties which surrounded a King's son in contrast with men like myself, who had always had greater freedom at school and University to make their own friends, and a wider circle to choose from. We discusssed friendship, and the relative value of brains and character, and all the sort of things that young men do talk about, in the abstract, when in reality they are very much concerned in the concrete.

He told me that sometimes the discipline and formality of the Court proved irksome, and I sensed that he was working up to something important. I felt moved with a great desire to help him if I could. He was so simple and frank and forthcoming.

Then, out it came. He declared that he was desperately in love, but that he was in despair for it seemed quite certain that he had lost the only woman he would ever marry. I told him that however black the situation looked, he must not give up hope; that my wife had refused me consistently before she finally said 'yes', and that like him, if she had persisted in her refusal, I would never have married anyone else.

To this he replied that his case was different from mine. The King's son cannot propose to the girl he loves, since custom requires that he must not place himself in the position of being refused, and to that ancient custom, the King, his father, firmly adhered. Worse still, I gathered that an emissary had already been sent to ascertain whether the girl was prepared to marry him, and that it had failed. The question was, what was he to do? He could not live without her, and certainly he would never marry anyone else.

The advice which I ventured to give him was simple. I suggested that in the year of grace 1922, no high-spirited girl of character was likely to accept a proposal made at second hand; if she was as fond of him as he thought she was, he must propose to her himself.

It was the greatest moment of his life, and although from this side, the fence seemed unjumpable, if he rode at it with determination and confidence and threw his heart over it, he would land safely, and win his bride.

'If she accepts,' I said, 'go straight to your mother, and if your mother is like mine, she will square the King.'

His despair changed, if not to joy, at least to some degree of hope, and as we talked, he seemed to be persuaded that to adopt this plan would be practicable. His mood when we parted was much brighter and more buoyant than at the beginning of our talk.

After I had left him, I heard no more until I attended a public Dinner, at which the Duke of York was receiving the guests. As my turn came to shake hands, he moved forward and said, *sotto voce*, 'All is well. There will be an announcement in the *Gazette* in a few days.'

This is the simple narrative of what to me will always remain a precious memory.

Thirty years later, after she was widowed, the then Queen Elizabeth the Queen Mother wrote to Davidson to 'thank you for the advice you gave the King in 1922'.[6]

It is impossible to exaggerate the importance of the Duke's marriage to his happiness and character. It transformed him, and was the turning-point of his life; it also had the additional advantage that his parents became devoted to his young wife, and subsequently their two grand-daughters, and this brought the Duke much closer to his father than any of his brothers.

Financial difficulties are relative, but the young Yorks certainly had them. Their first home was White Lodge, in Richmond Park – where, as it happened, the Prince of Wales had been born – but it was too large, too inconvenient, and much too expensive to maintain. Their first real home, 145 Piccadilly, was bought in 1927 on a bank loan. Most of their furniture and pictures were bought by them at second-hand shops and sales; fortunately, they both had a good eye for old furniture of quality at a time when it was unfashionable and cheap. Their personal staff was modest, although, again, this is relative, and when the King and Queen first came to lunch with the newly married couple the Duke warned them that 'our cook is not very good, but she can do the plain dishes well, & I know you like that sort'.

The myth that the Duchess came from an immensely rich family and had substantial money of her own was exactly that. Neither had

[6] Davidson Papers.

expensive tastes, nor did they want to entertain lavishly. They were happy in their London home, and lived modestly and cheerfully. The fact that they were not remotely part of the London society scene, in contrast to the Prince of Wales and the Duke of Kent, was held against them by those who considered it the epitome of civilisation, but now looks very much to their credit. It was certainly regarded as such by King George V. In 1931 he offered them The Royal Lodge in Windsor Great Park, which they gratefully accepted, and where they and their young daughters lived in great contentment.[7]

By this time the Duke's official career had begun, as President of the Industrial Welfare Society. This role had given him an insight into, and understanding of, industry and working conditions better than any member of the Royal Family since the Prince Consort. His visits to factories were of genuine interest to him, and were working ones rather than royal occasions. It was from this association that the phenomenon of the Duke of York's popular and successful annual camps for boys developed.

While carrying out duties such as these, especially after his marriage, the Duke was relaxed and happy. But at more formal functions there were two problems – his nervousness, often manifested in outbursts of explosive temper that only his wife was able to quieten, and his undefeated stammer. His speech on 31 October 1925, closing the British Empire Exhibition at Wembley – an outstanding success, which had attracted seventeen million visitors – was broadcast around the world and was a terrible ordeal for the speaker, and hardly less so for the listening audience. 'Bertie got through his speech all right,' the King recorded, 'but there were some rather long pauses.' The reactions of others were, although sympathetic, considerably more critical, and caused consternation to some.

One of the suffering listeners, however, was Lionel Logue, a 45-year-old Australian speech therapist who had established his practice in London. Born in Adelaide, he trained as an engineer before he appreciated his remarkable talents for curing speech defects, principally with returned soldiers who had been severely shell-shocked. Logue was convinced that although a total cure was probably not possible

[7] Princess Elizabeth was born on 21 April 1926; Princess Margaret Rose on 21 August 1930.

for the Duke of York, the case was far from hopeless. An appointment was arranged by Eileen Macleod, a founder-member of the Society of Speech Therapists. While the Duke agreed to an appointment with Logue, he did so without much hope. Logue's oft-quoted notes on his first session with the Duke deserve to be quoted again: 'He entered my consulting-room at three o'clock in the afternoon, a slim, quiet man with tired eyes and all the outward symptoms of a man upon whom a habitual speech defect had begun to set the sign. When he left at five o'clock, you could see that there was hope once more in his heart.'

Logue's approach was both psychological and physical. He made it clear to his patient that he had a perfectly curable condition, but one whose resolution, unlike most others, depended principally upon the patient himself. Logue taught him to breathe correctly, and prescribed exercises for an hour every day. There were regular consultations for ten weeks, when the Duke was often accompanied by his wife, who took a deep interest in her husband's treatment and encouraged him constantly. As the Duke wrote to his father, 'I am sure I am going to get quite all right in time, but twenty-four years of talking in the wrong way cannot be cured in a month.' Comparing his second son with the others, the King wrote that he had 'more guts than the rest of them put together', an excessively severe, but revealing, comment – and Logue later said that the Duke was the 'pluckiest and most determined' patient he had ever had.

As matters steadily got better, with immense dedication and determination on the Duke's part, his self-confidence grew, although it was never to be total. It was now put to a formidable test.

The Australian Prime Minister, Stanley Bruce, had asked that the official opening of the new parliament building in Canberra, the new capital of the Commonwealth of Australia, be undertaken by one of the King's sons. Having heard the Duke of York speak in public, and unaware of his progress under Logue, Bruce was understandably hoping that the King would send the Prince of Wales, whose visit in 1920 had been triumphant. But the King, as Duke of York, had opened the parliament building in Melbourne in 1900, and thought it appropriate that the son with the same title should undertake the same ceremony in Canberra.

The first test of Logue's treatment, and the Duke's progress, was a dinner given by the Pilgrims' Society, chaired by Arthur Balfour, shortly before the Yorks' departure for Australia. To general surprise, the Duke spoke easily and fluently despite being acutely nervous. It was a challenge he had deliberately set himself, and, after long and careful preparation, had passed.

The Yorks sailed on 6 January 1927 on HMS *Renown*. When they reached New Zealand the Duke was faced with three speeches at Rotorua on the first morning, which he delivered almost faultlessly. Unfortunately the Duchess contracted tonsillitis at Christchurch, and the Duke, whose reliance upon her was now a major part of his developing confidence, seriously thought of cancelling his engagements in South Island, but decided against it; the fact that everything went so well in spite of her absence demonstrated just how well Logue's treatment was working.

This first overseas visit by the Yorks had one unexpected bonus. Despite her illness, the Duchess was a sensational success. The Governor of South Australia, Sir Tom Bridges, did not greatly exaggerate when he reported to the King that she 'has left us with the responsibility of having a continent in love with her'. It was the first time it had been realised that she had a unique star quality which was undefinable but which enthralled not only the large crowds both in New Zealand and Australia but even the usually irreverent and critical Australian press. Although, as the Duke confessed to his father, 'making speeches still rather frightens me', this was not evident to his audiences, and Bruce was especially impressed by his new confidence and clear delivery.

So was the King, who ordered his other sons to greet the Yorks when they landed back at Portsmouth on 27 June. He and Queen Mary then met them at Victoria Station. This public mark of approval and regard was another sign of the King's increasing respect and affection for his second son and his wife, who could do no wrong in his eyes; even her unpunctuality, considered a heinous offence in anyone else, was forgiven. The King also found, with pleasure, that conversing with the Duke was now agreeable rather than an ordeal for both.

'Delighted to have Bertie with me [at Balmoral],' King George wrote to the Queen at this time. 'He came yesterday evening, have had several talks with him & find him very sensible, very different to D[avid].' This was a significant comment. The performances of the Prince of Wales were now causing serious anxieties not only to the King but to those close to the Prince. But there is no evidence whatsoever that the Yorks realised any of this; what they did see, and with gratitude and admiration, was the way in which the Prince took charge of the wayward Duke of Kent and managed to resolve his brother's complicated amatory and drug problems. Also, when he occasionally visited them and their young daughters, he was delightful company.

This was indicative of the Prince's contradictory character. He could perform brilliantly on some occasions, but on others he could be quite outrageous, as he was in the brutal dismissal of his two most important mistresses, Freda Dudley Ward and Thelma Furness. His conduct had already precipitated the resignation of his Assistant Private Secretary, Alan Lascelles, after the Prince – on safari in East Africa – had refused to believe reports of his father's grave illness in 1928. Now the spectre of his relationship with Mrs Wallis Simpson was looming large, and doubts about his ability to succeed his father began to surface.

After a brief hiatus, Lascelles re-entered the service of the Royal Family and became Assistant Private Secretary to the King in late 1935.

An amusing and interesting man, Alan 'Tommy' Lascelles was notably unawed by monarchs. He was an outstanding speech-writer, of considerable intellectual ability, and had always been appalled by the lamentable education received by his former employer, the Prince of Wales, and his brother. 'I can't think what Hansell, their tutor, used to teach them,' he once wrote in his diary. 'I recollect the P. of Wales, years ago, coming back from a weekend at Panshanger and saying to me, "Look at this extraordinary little book Lady Desborough says I ought to read. Have you ever heard of it?" The extraordinary little book was *Jane Eyre*.' Another such episode was the occasion when the Prince asked Thomas Hardy if he had written *Tess of the D'Urbervilles*, as he was 'sure it was by someone else' – to which, as Lascelles recorded, 'T.H., like the perfect gentleman he was, replied without batting an eyelid, "Yes, sir, that was the name of one of my earlier novels."'

When, wholly characteristically, Lascelles told the Prince the reasons for his resignation in 1929, the latter heard him out and then said, in Lascelles' account, '"Well, goodnight Tommy, and thank you for the talk. I suppose the fact of the matter is that I'm quite the wrong sort of person to be Prince of Wales" – which was so pathetically true that it almost melted me.' Now, Lascelles was to witness first-hand the results of the future King's inadequacy.

Despite his illness in 1928, the King's health at this time appeared reasonably good, although he was depressed by the deteriorating political situation in Europe, the death of his sister Princess Victoria, which affected him deeply, and by the conduct of his heir. But he was barely seventy, and although he had been unenthusiastic about the Silver Jubilee celebrations in the summer of 1935, characteristically grumbling about the number of 'too many damned parsons getting in the way' in St Paul's Cathedral, he had endured them without any notable ill effects and had been surprised and moved by the public warmth. But then after Christmas there was a sudden physical decline.

Lascelles, arriving at Liverpool Street Station for the journey to Sandringham on 16 January 1936, was surprised and somewhat embarrassed to find that a first-class carriage had been reserved for his exclusive use – 'Everybody stopped to read my name on the window & stare at me like something new in the zoo, while all the guards etc. hailed me as "My Lord",' he wrote to his wife that evening. 'About half-way down, a young man appeared in the doorway of my carriage. I was about to tell him to go away when I recognised him as the D. of York. He came in & sat with me for the rest of the journey & was very amiable. I thought him much changed for the better since I last saw him eight years ago. But he put me in a bit of a hole by asking suddenly, "What made you take this job?" – not an easy question to answer to his father's son . . .'[8]

Lascelles had hardly known the Duke at all, and this is their first recorded conversation. The Duke opened it by asking, 'What's all this about the King being ill?', the first intimation Lascelles had that his new employer was unwell. But when he and the Duke reached Sandringham the news about the King was reasonably hopeful.

However, late on the 17th he wrote to his wife: 'On the whole this is one of the least attractive places I have ever seen. House & demesne equally are irredeemably grim . . . I fear it is very likely the K. may die within the first few days . . . It has been a harrowing, anxious day, broken, as every death-bed & everything connected with the R. family always seems to be, by occasional gleams of comedy. Anyhow, the P. of W. is far better prepared for a new life than he was seven years ago in Tanganyika!' But when the Prince arrived, these hopes quickly evaporated. 'We are all rather sad at the general demeanour

[8] Lascelles Papers, 4/2/1.

of Ed. VIII,' he wrote on the 18th, before the King actually died, 'esp. myself, who had hoped for some alteration after eight years; but, *plus ça change*, etc. . . .'[9]

Thus, within days of entering the King's employment, Lascelles found himself assisting at Sandringham in the preparations for his master's lying in state at Westminster and funeral at Windsor. He also now had to contemplate the unwelcome possibility of again serving his former master as King Edward VIII.

In a characteristically effulgent tribute, Winston Churchill wrote that 'in a world of ruin and chaos, King George V brought about a resplendent rebirth of the great office which fell to his lot'. The unexpected new leader of the Labour Party, the reticent and deliberately uneloquent Clement Attlee, said: 'The movements of mass hysteria which have been noted elsewhere have passed this country by. One reason has been the presence of the King, who commanded the respect and affection of his people and was beyond the spirit of faction . . . King George showed an incomparable understanding of what is required of a King in the modern world.' It would be more realistic to state that George V had managed to save the monarchy, and that it had been a very remarkable achievement.

George V's outstanding quality was his solidity. His sons may have chafed, very understandably, at his rigid adherence to his personal routine, his stubborn loyalty to old friends and ways, and the inexorable regime of the year; his critics may have complained of, even derided, his limitations of intellect and interests. But, however valid these criticisms were, the fact was that he had the quality to persevere and to do the best he could. He was brave, honourable, decent and fair, and he loved and served his country. He would have hated to have been admired as a political monarch, but that was what he had been.

He was, above all, always himself. Perhaps it was this last attribute that was to be the most endearing and admirable of his bequeathments.

So much has been written about King Edward VIII – admiring, dismissive, hostile and sympathetic – that historical objectivity is not easy. One of the shrewdest assessments is that of Christopher Hibbert:

[9] Ibid, 4/2/3.

Restless, impatient, impulsive, frustrated, emotional, affectionate, unstable and indiscreet, he earned as Prince of Wales much popularity and some respect. He had far more charm than talent, far more capacity for feeling than for thought. His sudden enthusiasms, his discordant ambitions, were likely to die as quickly as they had been born . . . It was his tragedy that he never entirely succeeded in reconciling, as his grandfather had been ultimately able to do, his love of life with his position and responsibilities.[10]

In royal circles there were, from the outset, profound worries about the new King's commitment to his role. When he told Lascelles that he would not sell his ranch in Canada because he wanted to keep it for his retirement, Lascelles asked, 'You mean for a holiday, sir?' 'No, I mean for good,' the King replied. Both he and Wigram's successor, Sir Alec Hardinge, knew of King George's private opinion – expressed on more than one occasion – that his eldest son would not fulfil his destiny, and that the prospect of his second son becoming King had given him pleasure. But although King Edward VIII did not welcome the timing of his accession, this was the task he had waited for. As Philip Ziegler has written: 'What he hoped for when he acceded was that he would be able to run the monarchy in his own way, to preserve his privacy and his freedom of action, to live his own life within the walls of formality and tradition that encompassed him. He wanted to have his cake and eat it too; to be the King and yet retain the freedom of the ordinary mortal.'[11]

If 'private life' had meant the pursuit of useful and relaxing hobbies and the continuation of his newly acquired passion for gardening, his advisers would have entirely agreed and would have assisted him, a task much easier at a time of press restraint and respect. But 'private life' for the King meant his enjoyment of café society in London, congenial guests at Fort Belvedere, total personal freedom – and Wallis Simpson.

Situated at the edge of Windsor Great Park, Fort Belvedere had been enlarged by Wyatville in the 1820s. It was a royal property which became vacant in 1929, when the Prince of Wales asked his father for the use of it. The King consented, with some puzzlement, and the Prince then

[10] Hibbert, *The Court at Windsor*, p. 275.
[11] Ziegler, *King Edward VIII*, p. 244.

devoted much time, energy and expense to the transformation of what he called his 'peaceful, almost enchanted anchorage'. Its domestic style was as different from that of Windsor, Buckingham Palace, Balmoral and Sandringham as could be imagined. It was a real, as well as a symbolic, declaration of independence from his family. The Duke and Duchess of York and their children were very infrequent guests. The Prince's Private Secretary, Godfrey Thomas, foreseeing 'disaster' within a few days of the King's accession, wrote that 'increased responsibility may work a miracle, but I don't think he will last very long. One could prop up the façade for a Prince of Wales – not so easy for a King.' This sombre prognosis was to be proved grimly prophetic.

Edward VIII inherited the throne amid great public and press acclamation but with serious doubts among ministers, several of his acquaintances, and his former private secretaries. His action in changing the Sandringham clocks back to Greenwich Mean Time ('Sandringham Time', instituted by Edward VII, was half an hour early, to ensure more daylight in which to shoot) immediately after his father's death upset his family and royal servants to what might seem an unreasonable extent, but it was, as Frances Donaldson has written, 'a presage of all that was to follow that this man, who for so many years had seemed to have an unerring flair for doing and saying the right thing, should in the first minutes of his reign have disturbed and distressed everyone about him and alienated the sympathies of servants who had been with his family for years'.[12]

Edward had been deeply upset by his near-total omission from his father's will, although there was a clear precedent for this, but there was probably another element which contributed to his behaviour. It was Lascelles' later opinion that King George's relatively early and unexpected death had completely thrown all his eldest son's plans into disarray; he was determined to marry Mrs Simpson as soon as she was free to do so, but it was one thing to marry her as Prince of Wales, quite another as King. As Lascelles knew him only too well, this hypothesis has real credibility.

Equally serious was the fact that, as Hardinge noted, 'King Edward appeared to be entirely ignorant of the powers of a constitutional sovereign and of the lines on which a King's business should be carried

---

[12] Donaldson, *King Edward VIII*, p. 178.

on.' The King had offered the post of Private Secretary to Godfrey Thomas, his Private Secretary as Prince of Wales since 1919, who had refused it, concealing his forebodings, preferring to remain Assistant. The King's appointment of Hardinge as Private Secretary was an obvious one, but surprised those who had expected the immediate removal of what Henry 'Chips' Channon had described two years earlier as 'dreary, narrow-minded fogies', specifically naming Hardinge. As has been related, Hardinge's father had been a distinguished public servant, Viceroy of India, and Permanent Under-Secretary of State in the Foreign Office, and was highly regarded and trusted by Edward VII and George V. Hardinge was a brave and good man, of the same generation as the King (born in 1894), and, like him, the holder of the Military Cross. The fact that he was not the King's first choice did not reflect upon him: the King knew Godfrey Thomas much better. The problem was that Thomas knew the King too well to embark upon such a hazardous mission.

Hardinge was not a 'narrow-minded fogey', but after a rather lively young manhood he had become a devoted and admiring disciple of Stamfordham and George V. These influences upon him had been profound. A sensitive and very private man, dedicated to the royal service, he certainly did not give, nor did he encourage, confidences. He did not have the capacity of evoking affection among those with whom he worked, or, more importantly, those for whom he worked. He was described by one who knew him well as 'a tragic figure'. He was to play a major role in the tragi-comedy of the reign of King Edward VIII.

The appointment of Lascelles as another Assistant Private Secretary was even more strange in view of Lascelles' feelings about the new King. Given those views, Lascelles' acceptance of the offer was explicable only on the grounds that he felt that the King and the monarchy needed help. From an early point this became only too obvious.

Edward VIII, for all the years of supposed preparation, had little conception of his political role. Although the new King had strong, and to many people worrying, political opinions, as Beaverbrook later commented, 'He had made friends almost everywhere except in the political world where he now most sorely needed them.' But even if the King had had experienced political advice available to him, he did not intend to use it. He was besotted by Mrs Simpson, believed in his sycophantic publicity, and, while he wanted to be 'a reforming King', had few ideas about how to achieve it apart from populist gestures. There were ominous early indications.

In his first radio broadcast as King, on 1 March, he had proposed to insert a sympathetic phrase about Indian aspirations for greater independence which ministers had had considerable difficulty in removing. The Foreign Office, also, had early concerns about the King's favourable attitudes towards the German and Italian dictators, and there were even suspicions that Mrs Simpson was not only a Nazi sympathiser but an active agent. This was not true, but she and the King had political opinions which did not make the anxieties at all groundless.

The German Ambassador, Von Hoesch, reported to Berlin on 21 January 1936 that 'you are aware from my reports that King Edward, quite generally, feels warm sympathy for Germany. I have become convinced during frequent, often lengthy, talks with him that these sympathies are deep-rooted and strong enough to withstand the contrary influences to which they are not seldom exposed.'

This *was* true. The King had already, as Prince of Wales in 1935, publicly expressed his desire for Anglo-German reconciliation – to the fury of his father and at a time when Nazi Germany was blatantly re-arming and the ugly character of the Hitler regime was becoming very apparent. He was also more sympathetic to the Italian invader of Abyssinia, Mussolini, than to the deposed Haile Selassie – even trying to have the exiled Emperor banned from entering Britain – and saw no *casus belli* when Hitler re-militarised the Rhineland in March 1936. There may have been many who agreed with him, and none of this necessarily made him a Nazi supporter, although Churchill, for one, would later comment darkly on his 'pro-Nazi leanings'.

The King's politics were, and always continued to be, dominated by his horror of the Soviet Union and Communism. The trouble was that these opinions were not based on knowledge or careful consideration but on prejudice. He was a keen advocate of British re-armament, but as a bulwark against the USSR rather than the fascist dictators, and he certainly did not share Churchill's fears that time was rapidly running out, or the vehemently anti-German views of his friend Duff Cooper. His politics were later to become wearyingly reactionary and right-wing, increasingly reflecting the bigotries of rich Republican American friends.

The Foreign Secretary, Anthony Eden, was especially irritated by the gratuitous, unhelpful and ill-informed royal interventions in foreign affairs. Baldwin's long-standing apprehensions were being fully confirmed. The King resented and ignored advice that was unwelcome to him; too often he sought none at all. As his involvement with Mrs Simpson became public knowledge everywhere except in Britain, his hostility and impatience with his ministers – especially Baldwin – increased.

He also virtually cut himself off from the Duke of York, and said unkind things about his wife, whom he and Mrs Simpson treated with noticeable disdain, in itself a major error. As he had previously been so kind and affectionate towards his sister-in-law and nieces, this was an unexpected and wounding development for which the Yorks blamed Mrs Simpson rather than the King. Indeed, the Duchess could not abide Mrs Simpson personally, a dislike which was warmly reciprocated, and although the increasing coldness between the two brothers – or rather, coldness from the King towards the Duke – might have been transformed had the Duchess invited Mrs Simpson to their home, this she emphatically would not do. One of her great qualities was her refusal to dissimulate on really important matters, and the sanctity of marriage was something she took very seriously.

As Lady Hardinge and others had already realised, the Duchess of York's delightful smile, warmth and charm, combined with a captivating enthusiasm, sense of humour and sheer enjoyment of life, concealed to casual observers her deep Christian faith and strong personality. Those who only saw the sweet façade misjudged both her keen intellect and indomitable spirit, and critically shrewd judgement of character. She also knew how a King ought to behave, and as Edward's conduct became more careless, selfish and improper, her previous affection and warmth towards him cooled. It seemed that he had learned nothing from his father's example, or his tutors and advisers, about what being a modern constitutional monarch entailed. All this the Duchess of York observed with much greater clarity than anyone else, including her husband, apart from Queen Mary. But neither of these acutely perceptive women had assessed the true extent of the King's passion for Mrs Simpson, and his determination to make her Queen 'and Empress of India, the whole bag of tricks', as he later told the appalled Duke of Kent.

There was then a relentless deterioration.

In August the King chartered a large motor-yacht, the *Nahlin*, for a cruise in the Aegean, sailing down the Dalmatian coast and thence through the Greek islands to Istanbul. His guests included Duff and Diana Cooper, and, most important of all, Mrs Simpson. By this stage, although the British press contrived to maintain a discreet silence, American and European newspapers and magazines had become fascinated with the King's relationship with Mrs Simpson, and the cruise of the *Nahlin* was followed with intense interest. British ambassadors, and British citizens with access to American and European newspapers and magazines, began to write letters of concern and complaint.

The King's personal staff on that famous cruise – Lascelles, Thomas, and John Aird – became increasingly worried by the King's too evident, and very public, adoration of Mrs Simpson; there was also concern about the informality of his clothing, his whims – which included his insistence on dining with Lord Dudley at a small waterfront café in Piraeus – and his moods, which veered from high spirits to intense gloom and sulkiness. But their principal concern was the world-wide – except in Britain – publicity. None of them could believe that, although the King was being recklessly and brazenly indiscreet, there was any question of anything more than an affair that was being rather too blatantly advertised.

Throughout this drama the Duke and Duchess of York had no role or involvement. On 9 July they had been the guests of honour at an official dinner given by the King at Buckingham Palace, an occasion at which Mrs Simpson was not only conspicuously without her husband but placed at the head of the table. It was on this occasion that Churchill, seated next to the Duchess, brooded on the precedent of King George IV and his morganatic wife, Mrs Fitzherbert, until the Duchess retorted with a sharpness 'which was quite unlike her', as Lady Hardinge, a close observer of the scene, noted, until 'even Churchill could not mistake her meaning'.

Matters reached breaking-point in September, when the King, to the pleasure of Queen Mary, assembled a large house-party at Balmoral; to her great displeasure, it again included Mrs Simpson.

The Yorks were at Birkhall, and on 23 September deputised for the King at the opening of the new Aberdeen Infirmary, the King having declined on the grounds of Court mourning, although this period had ended on 20 July. While they were undertaking this duty the King drove his car to Aberdeen to meet Mrs Simpson, and was photographed doing so. The resulting headlines in the Scottish press, juxtaposed with accounts of the Yorks conducting their royal duties, were the first indications to British readers that something was seriously amiss.

Three days later the Duke and Duchess were invited to dinner at Balmoral. When they entered the drawing-room they were greeted not by the King but by Mrs Simpson; the Earl and Countess of Rosebery, and other guests, had already been subjected to Mrs Simpson's possessiveness and strident announcements of imminent changes in the furnishings and furniture − 'this tartan's gotta go' − as though she was already the chatelaine. At the end of dinner the Duchess led the ladies from the table without reference to Mrs Simpson, and she and the Duke left as soon as they decently could. The horrified and embarrassed Roseberys wished that they could also.

On 20 October, the morning after the Yorks had returned to London, Hardinge told the Duke that Mrs Simpson was divorcing her husband the following week, with the full support and encouragement of the King, and in spite of Baldwin's urgent request to him − prompted by Hardinge − to prevent it. Hardinge warned the Duke, to the latter's amazement and horror, that 'it might end with his brother's abdication'; the Duke was 'appalled and tried not to believe what he had been told'. Indeed, he could not believe it. His attempts to get in touch with the King were totally and humiliatingly rebuffed, and throughout the ensuing crisis he was virtually ignored by his brother.

The decree *nisi* on the Simpsons' marriage was granted at Ipswich on 27 October, but received little attention in the British newspapers as a result of a direct personal appeal by the King to Beaverbrook. No such restraint afflicted the American or European press, which openly speculated on the probability of the King marrying Mrs Simpson when the decree became absolute in six months' time. It was at this point that Hardinge, on 11 November, wrote to the King to state that the government was seriously alarmed at the situation, that the silence of the British press could not endure much longer, and to advise that Mrs Simpson leave the country immediately.

Both Baldwin, the Prime Minister, and Geoffrey Dawson, the editor of *The Times*, were made aware of Hardinge's courageous and proper intervention, but it would have been more fitting, and possibly more influential, if it had come from the Prime Minister rather than from the King's Private Secretary. But Baldwin abrogated his responsibilities.

Indeed, the Prime Minister – who had succeeded MacDonald in 1935 – acted throughout the crisis with characteristic indolence. While it is questionable whether there would have been a different outcome, Baldwin's almost total inactivity for ten vital months in 1936 can hardly be considered masterly. Ageing, bewildered, indecisive, he simply wanted the whole problem to disappear – it was only when the King arrogantly flung down the challenge of abdication that Baldwin became seriously involved, and by then it was, as Lascelles lamented, much too late.

Hardinge's was certainly a brave letter, and one with remarkable results, but part of the problem was that it came from a man the King had never liked or trusted and whose opinions on Mrs Simpson were manifestly hostile. Hardinge was promptly cast into the outer darkness, and Walter Monckton, who had been the King's principal legal adviser since 1932, in effect assumed the role that the King's Private Secretary would normally have undertaken.

By now not only Hardinge but the Cabinet were seriously agitated, and for the first time there was talk of the government resigning if the King did not change his position. Belatedly, Baldwin scented danger. Neville Chamberlain, his virtually inevitable successor, began to apply real pressure. And Baldwin's enemies – Beaverbrook, Rothermere and Churchill – were ominously bestirring themselves on the side of the King. At this point Baldwin's seriously dormant political acumen reasserted itself, and he knew his course.

The crucial episode came on 16 November, when the King told Baldwin it was his intention to marry Mrs Simpson and make her Queen, and threatened to abdicate if his will was resisted. As Lascelles noted at the time, and never forgot, the word 'abdication' came from the King, not from Baldwin, who was visibly shaken by what was an arrogant statement of confident defiance. The King had always had his way, and fully intended to have it on this matter. The years of adulation and sycophancy now extracted a terrible toll. There was a flurry of emissaries to implore the King to reconsider, most notably Hoare and Duff Cooper. Then the idea of a morganatic marriage was floated, was put to Baldwin by the King on 25 November, and, briefly, seemed to be the way out of the imbroglio; but when Baldwin told the King that legislation to make such a marriage possible would not be approved by parliament – to the King's incredulity – the problem of his determination to marry Mrs Simpson was taken on to a different plane. The King agreed to Baldwin's suggestion that the matter should be put before the Cabinet and the Dominion Prime Ministers; the prospect of the government resigning and thereby precipitating a major political crisis now became a real possibility.

The spectre of a King defying his ministers and, through them, parliament and the Dominion parliaments – which, under the 1931 Statute of Westminster, had to assent to 'any alterations in the law touching the Succession of the Throne or the Royal Style and Titles' – was now made even more fearful by that of politicians and newspapers rallying to his support. Beaverbrook, Rothermere, Lloyd George, Churchill and the self-proclaimed British fascist leader Oswald Mosley gave every indication of proposing to do just that.

This crucial aspect of the abdication crisis was best expressed by Harold Laski in the *New York Times*, three days before the matter was resolved:

> This issue is independent of the personality of the King. It is independent of the personality of the Prime Minister. It does not touch the wisdom or unwisdom of the marriage the King has proposed. It is not concerned with the pressure, whether of the churches or the aristocracy, that is hostile to this marriage. It is the principle that out of this issue no precedent must be created that makes the royal authority once more a source of independent political power in the state.

Baldwin had already ensured the support of the Labour and Liberal leaders, Attlee and Sinclair, for his stand, but Churchill's reaction had seemed distinctly ambivalent. Chamberlain was not alone in believing that Churchill was poised to form an alternative government, and he was to be one of the most conspicuous victims of the King's total failure to differentiate between his personal passions and his constitutional position. The fact that there was not a grievous constitutional crisis was due more to Baldwin's tired but still formidable political skills than to the King's self-sacrifice.

The Duke of York was kept informed, not by the King but by Baldwin, although the ending of the press silence on the morning of 3 December came as a total surprise to him. This was the result of a sermon by the appropriately named Bishop Blunt of Bradford – a totally innocent participant in the crisis, of which he was wholly unaware, as was almost everyone in Britain – which commented adversely on the King's lack of church attendance. This ended the silence of the British press, long frustrated and yearning for an excuse to reveal the story: the Duke returned to London from Edinburgh, where he had been installed as Grand Master Mason of Scotland, to confront newspaper posters blazoning 'THE KING'S MARRIAGE'.

Lascelles believed, rightly, that the King was convinced he could retain the throne and marry Mrs Simpson to public acclaim and in the teeth of the hostility of his ministers, the leaders of the two major Opposition political parties, and now, the Dominion Prime Ministers. Walter Monckton, far closer to the King than his own relatives or private secretaries, assumed until a very late stage of the hurtling crisis that 'if and when the stark choice faced them between their love and his obligations as King-Emperor, they would in the end each make the sacrifice, devastating though it might be'.[13] In the event Mrs Simpson, under intense pressure, *was* prepared to make the sacrifice; the King was not. And he still contrived to totally ignore his brother, who was distraught at the possibility of succeeding him.

In spite of everything, the Duke remained devoted to his brother, although increasingly bewildered by his conduct and his refusal to see him. Only Baldwin kept him in touch with events, and his opinion that the outcome was very uncertain only added to his plight. By the end of the crisis he was one of the two principal participants who was most strenuously opposed to abdication: the other was Mrs Simpson.

But still the King kept his brother away. The Duke telephoned him on 4 December to make an appointment, and did so repeatedly until the King agreed to see him on the 7th, by which time the crisis had reached blazing proportions. Princess Olga, the wife of Prince Paul of Yugoslavia and sister of the Duchess of Kent, described the Duke of York as 'mute and broken' and 'in an awful state of worry as David won't see him or telephone'. As Prince Paul told 'Chips' Channon, 'The Duke of York is miserable, does not want the throne and is imploring his brother to stay.' He could not accept the inevitability of the situation. Nor could Mrs Simpson. But her announcement from Cannes of her desire to

---

[13] Monckton Papers, quoted in Donaldson, op. cit., p. 207.

withdraw 'from a situation that has been rendered both unhappy and untenable' was too late, and was utterly unacceptable to the King.

On the evening of Sunday 6 December, having waited all day to hear from the King, the Duke rang the Fort, to be told that the King was in a conference and would speak to him later. The King did not call back. The Duke rang him again the next day and was told there was a possibility of a meeting that evening. At ten minutes to seven the King telephoned to ask him to come and see him after dinner; the Duke replied that he would come at once. He wrote in his account: 'The awful and ghastly suspense of waiting was over. I found him [the King] pacing up & down the room, & he told me his decision that he would go. I went back to Royal Lodge for dinner & returned later. I felt once I got there I was not going to leave. As he is my eldest brother I had to be there to try & help him in his hour of need.' In fact he left this task to his brother the Duke of Kent, and returned to London to be with his wife, who was suffering from influenza.

His nightmare got worse the following day, Tuesday 8 December. Monckton briefed him on 'all the facts', having 'not [been] allowed to see me before', an infinitely revealing comment; the Duke then saw Queen Mary and spoke to the Duke of Gloucester at The Royal Lodge before he was summoned 'urgently' to the Fort to see the King and the Prime Minister.

That dinner was to scar itself into the memories of everyone present – except the King, who, in Baldwin's account, refused to discuss anything 'but merely walked up and down the room saying, "This is the most wonderful woman in the world"' in a kind of seraphic euphoria about his now-decided abdication. As Kent related to Prince Paul, 'he never broke down and wouldn't think either of the future or of what he was giving up – only of her'. He was in superb form at dinner, to the admiration of his younger brother, who said sadly to Monckton, 'And this is the man we are going to lose.' He himself was in a deeply sombre mood, which Baldwin's Parliamentary Private Secretary, Thomas Dugdale, misinterpreted as dullness, when in fact it reflected his misery and despair, as Baldwin recognised. It was, as the Duke wrote, a dinner 'that I am never likely to forget'.

The problem of what the abdicated King should be called was swiftly decided by his successor; he must be created a Royal Duke, and suggested the title of Windsor, to which his brother at once agreed.

It was the departing King's insouciance that particularly distressed his family, even more than his infatuation with the much-detested Mrs Simpson. Queen Mary was to write to him eighteen months later that 'I do not think you ever realised the shock which the attitude you took up caused your family and the whole nation. It seemed inconceivable to those who had made such sacrifices during the war that you, as their King, refused a lesser sacrifice.'

But before the abdication drama was fully played out there was to be an episode of lasting significance, and which explains much that happened later.

As so often with King Edward, it was over money. It was also unnecessary, since ministers and his brother – strongly supported by Churchill, his long political career now damaged by his vehement advocacy of King Edward's cause – were very willing to be generous to him. His trump card, which he played, was his life interest in the royal estates, bequeathed to him in King George's will. But at a crucial meeting with the Duke and their legal advisers at Belvedere on 10 December, he claimed that his income would be only £5,000 a year, and that his total fortune was only £90,000. After what the Duke of York called 'a terrible lawyer interview' it was agreed that the King would sell his life interests in the Sandringham and Balmoral estates for an agreed sum, and that his successor would grant him £25,000 a year and would take over his responsibility for pensions. The Duke recorded that the meeting 'terminated quietly and harmoniously'. This mood did not last when it was discovered that the King's total fortune was in fact in excess of £1 million, that he had made a handsome settlement on Mrs Simpson, and that there were sharp disagreements about the value of the estates. It was when the future King and Churchill realised how abominably they had been duped that their feelings towards Edward changed sharply and irrevocably.

It was perhaps the single most disillusioning moment of the entire affair for the new King to realise that his adored brother had deliberately lied to him. It was made even worse by the fact that he and ministers were prepared to understand that an abdicated King could not be expected to live in exiled penury, however relative. It was the lie, so easily and quickly discovered, that was the crime, and that left his family and advisers aghast. For this, they could not even blame Mrs Simpson directly, although they suspected she was pressing the King hard for the highest settlement possible, a subject on which she had some experience. He had not only betrayed his country and abandoned his post, but had now also betrayed his family and closest advisers.

The shock of this revelation to the new King was immense. He had consistently overrated his eldest brother, had been tolerant about his private life, and had always admired and supported him. His grief at the King's self-immolation had not been for himself but for what he thought the nation had lost. He found it very difficult to accept that those much closer to his brother than he had been during his brief reign, and who had been so critical of him, had been right. If this came as little surprise to Lascelles and Hardinge, it came as a terrible blow to his brother and successor.

The Duchess of York, about to be Queen against her wishes, wrote: 'I don't think we could ever imagine a more incredible tragedy, and the agony of it has been beyond words. And the melancholy fact remains still at the present moment, that he for whom we agonised is the one person it did not touch.'

This remains the most perfect epitaph on the entire episode. King Edward VIII, created by his successor Duke of Windsor, departed jauntily for his new life, leaving chaos and misery behind him, and his younger brother to attempt to retrieve a situation that some thought was irretrievable. During the Commons debate on the swiftly passed Abdication Bill on 11 December, a Labour MP from Glasgow, G. D. Hardie, ended his contribution with the comment: 'Since 1914 there has been a continual building up [of support] around the throne, but what has happened recently has done more for republicanism than fifty years of propaganda could do.'

Under these extraordinary and melancholy circumstances the Duke of York acceded to the throne, taking the title of King George VI.

5

SOMBRE BEGINNINGS

——— ◆ ◆ ———

The new King, addressing his Accession Council on 12 December, within hours of his brother's departure to France, referred to 'the heavy task' confronting him. It was an understatement. He was emotionally exhausted by the strains of the previous weeks and was wholly unsure of his ability to conduct his high office successfully. He had never seen a significant state paper, knew very few politicians, and had never taken much interest in politics, either national or international. Unlike his elder brother, he had not travelled very widely. His limited confidence was not increased when, with supreme tactlessness, the Archbishop of Canterbury, Cosmo Lang, in a notorious radio broadcast on 13 December, referred to the new King's 'occasional and momentary hesitation in his speech'.

In fact, Lang had tried to be even-handed, referring to the abdicated King's qualities, but caused outrage with his criticisms of Edward's having 'sought his happiness in a manner inconsistent with the Christian principles of marriage, and within a social circle whose standards and ways of life are alien to all the best instincts and traditions of his people', and culminating in the thundering denunciation, 'Let those who belong to this circle stand rebuked by the judgement of the nation.'

Lang had hardly been consulted at all during the crisis, and was to become a warm admirer of the new King and Queen – describing them as 'indeed like waking after a nightmare to find the sun shining' – but his tactless reference to the new King's stammer fuelled rumours that he was epileptic, and that his supposedly frail health could not even endure the ordeal of the Coronation service.

The King was uncomfortably aware of these whisperings, and they did nothing to improve his self-confidence or temper. But his alleged deficiencies were more evident to himself than they were to others, who were impressed by how quickly he grasped the essentials of the modern constitutional monarchy. The new Queen, who knew how much her husband had dreaded his responsibilities, was as surprised as anyone by his decisiveness and determined application to his duties.

The fundamental reason for this unexpected resolution was that the King, although always energetic and active, had never had a full-time job. His elder brother had found his role as Heir to the Throne somewhat mysterious, and entirely undefined. That of his brothers had been even more vague. Apart from the official duties ordered by their father, and others they inherited or undertook by request or on their own initiative, they had had to make their own occupations. The Duke of Kent had left the navy in 1929, and, after his recovery from his personal problems was, although happily married, living a somewhat aimless, if luxurious, existence. The Duke of Gloucester's army career was not much helped by the official foreign visits he had had to undertake on behalf of his father. The frustrations the brothers experienced were a major part of their difficulties. The reality was that they were bored and under-employed.

George VI had ensured that, unlike his brothers, he had been neither of these things as Duke of York, but the fact was that he had not had a real occupation. Now, at the age of forty, the surprised new King certainly had. But whereas the burdens of the monarchy had oppressed his brother, his successor actively welcomed them. He was to rail constantly against the mass of paperwork, official engagements and hospitality, the formality and what he called 'high-hat' occasions, and the endless tasks that befall a British monarch, but his life suddenly had a definite purpose. As Lord Halifax later observed, 'Few people were endowed with judgement more wise and penetrating than his, rooted in simple and assured standards, and frequently salted with humour uninhibited and robust.' He had a real task to fulfil, and a genuine, full-time, and lifelong job – if the monarchy survived.

That was to be his first priority.

The King was rather more aware of his disqualifications for the job than his talents. The latter were considerable. He had actually served in combat, unlike any of his modern predecessors. He had a better knowledge of the condition of his people and the workings of industry than any member of the Royal Family since Prince Albert. He had become close to his father, and had learned from him. He had never made anything approximating to a controversial political speech, unlike his elder brother. He was exceptionally handsome and very happily married. Although he had a mind of his own, he was very ready to take advice, especially in the preparation of his speeches and radio broadcasts, both of which he hated, but over which he and others took immense pains – too immense, in Lascelles' opinion, later citing the hurriedly prepared VJ Day speech in 1945 to prove his point – and with remarkable results. He had shrewd instincts about people, and his wife's instincts were often even more shrewd, and on occasion distinctly irreverent. Also, her bubbling personality was a source of constant refreshment, as was her genius for public relations.

This capacity had been equalled by Queen Alexandra, whose popularity had been as great as her husband's, and in some quarters even greater, but not by Queen Mary, whose somewhat bleak and invariably formal public appearance belied a much warmer personality than was generally appreciated. But she had spent her entire life under constraint, and had not had the same happy childhood and family life that Queen Elizabeth enjoyed. Another limitation she had felt strongly was that she was a foreigner. This had made her more devotedly British, but it was a barrier of which she was more conscious than others; the new Queen felt no such restrictions.

The partnership between the King and Queen was also to become unparalleled since that between Queen Victoria and Prince Albert. Neither Edward VII nor George V had confided much in their wives, especially on political subjects, but King George VI told his wife virtually everything of importance or interest, and often sought her opinions and advice. She was also the best judge of his varying moods, far better than any of his Prime Ministers and most of his courtiers and private secretaries. She was his principal confidante and supporter, and provider of fun and cheerfulness at dark moments. If she was in many respects a stronger character than he was, which stemmed from a much greater self-confidence than the King ever had, the key fact was that she admired and respected as well as loved him. Her personal role can hardly be exaggerated, although her political influence has often been, but not by her.

The King also had the blessing of other interests. He was a countryman who loved and understood rural England and Scotland, and their peoples, as well as industrial Britain. This made him a realist, as all true countrymen are, and more acutely aware of the vagaries and surprises that Nature can so easily inflict. Like all countrymen he could curse and rage against these undesired misfortunes, but he could understand the total and maddening unpredictability of the British climate. There are few better backgrounds for an instinctive understanding of politics. Also, like his father and unlike his elder brother, he was a grateful and considerate employer, and spent much time on the concerns of the royal servants and tenants, to their surprise and gratitude.

But the apprehensions about his health and stamina were fuelled by his decision not to go to India for the Durbar in the winter of 1937–38, which had been announced, with considerable reluctance, in King Edward's only speech at the opening of parliament. It had been decided that the Coronation would take place on the day planned for that of his brother – 12 May – and this major event in itself was a formidable looming ordeal. The decision to postpone the Durbar was a sensible one, but it at once caused a revival of speculation about his health which was only stilled when the Coronation went faultlessly, as did his live radio broadcast that evening. But it was not until the triumphant visits to Canada and the United States in the summer of 1939 that doubts about the King's physical capacity to hold the job were finally allayed.

One of the King's first decisions had been to appoint Hardinge as his Private Secretary. He had been impressed by Hardinge's courage and devotion to the monarchy, and his wife was a good friend of the Queen. But he did not really know him well, and Hardinge was so drained by the abdication crisis that he was advised to rest. He and Lady Hardinge travelled to India and were away for three months. When he took up his duties in April 1937 he found that the King had devised his own working arrangements, which were quite different from those of George V.

The King had discovered that whereas the Court and the Household were steeped in rules of protocol, precedence, ritual, tradition and even dress, there was no manual or guidance on the political role of the sovereign. There were formulae for state occasions, prepared in meticulous detail, whether the occasion was the opening of parliament, the visit of foreign dignitaries, meetings of the Privy Council, the Trooping of the Colour, the presentation of debutantes, royal garden parties and investitures, and there were officials with long experience of how these were to be organised and conducted. The ceremonial aspect of monarchy had become near-perfect in planning and execution; the shambles of the Coronation of Queen Victoria and the misfortunes that attended her funeral were never to be repeated. On all these matters the King had truly expert advice.

But on the political side, there was virtually nothing to go on except Bagehot and Stamfordham. The example of Edward VIII was simply a model of how not to do it, but was also a warning about the perils of the King expressing his own political opinions in public, or even semi-public. The King had few, if any, political confidants, and did not know his Private Secretary or any of his assistants well, with the exception of Sir Eric Mieville, an agreeable man rather more highly esteemed in White's Club than by his Palace contemporaries. In Hardinge's absence Wigram took his place temporarily, but the differences in age and temperament were considerable, and Lascelles had not yet gained the King's confidence, friendship and trust. The King thus found himself virtually alone, if not a political innocent then certainly totally inexperienced.

One curious fact about the British monarchy had been repeated. Queen Victoria never discussed her role or experiences with her eldest son; Edward VII, for all his devotion to his heir, was similarly reticent, so that George V was wholly unprepared for the crises that he inherited; and he himself seldom discussed important matters with his heir, and only occasionally and briefly with the eventual George VI. These remarkable omissions were to a considerable extent filled by Knollys, Stamfordham, Wigram and Hardinge, but the extraordinary fact is that every modern British monarch came to the throne inadequately trained and prepared by their predecessor for their political responsibilities and duties.

In some respects this might be considered an advantage, as political circumstances change so rapidly, and often so fundamentally, that the lessons learned by George V were not entirely applicable to those his second son confronted. Also, the different personalities of modern monarchs moulded their approach and their actions. Edward VIII was unusual in that he had firm ideas of his own about the job from the outset, but, as has been seen, these were general rather than particular, with an element of vague sentimentalism combined with obstinacy that made him believe that he could function without the need for advice. The new King's initial weakness was the very opposite. He had never thought seriously about the position at all, and his lack of self-confidence was evident. But this sense almost of awe and humility about his new situation made him very willing to seek and to absorb advice. Thus, the weakness became quite quickly a source of strength.

In many respects he returned to the routine and traditions of his father, to the relief of the Household. Unlike his brother he loved Balmoral and Sandringham, and Windsor Castle was a welcome relief from Buckingham Palace. But he was not going to make his father's mistakes about his family; he wanted his wife and daughters to be close to him and to see as much of them as possible. And he was demonstrative in his devotion to them, and wished for his young children to continue to have the happy informal childhoods they had enjoyed before he became King.

In the difficult early months of his reign a disproportionate amount of the King's time, and that of his advisers, was unhappily dominated by the problem of the Duke of Windsor.

The adrenalin, almost the elation, that the Duke had experienced immediately after the abdication was short-lived. He had given up the throne; most of his servants had refused to accompany him into exile; virtually his sole companion was the raffish Major Edward 'Fruity' Metcalfe; and he was debarred from seeing Mrs Simpson until her decree became absolute – and for some time there were serious doubts whether it would be. The intervention of the King's Proctor into the affair was a considerably more serious matter than it has sometimes been subsequently regarded, as the King well knew. The truth was concealed, but it was a hazardous business. Unquestionably, despite vehement denials – on occasions legally enforced – there was no doubt that Mrs Simpson had been the former King's mistress, but the evidence was quietly dealt with and silenced. Lascelles tartly and knowledgeably wrote that he believed in the innocence of the relationship between his former master and Mrs Simpson as in 'a herd of unicorns grazing in Hyde Park and a shoal of mermaids swimming in the Serpentine'. In this scepticism he was not alone. But there was no guarantee that someone would not reveal the truth and cause another explosion. In the event, those in the know kept their secrets.

The Duke had established himself at the country house of Baron Eugène de Rothschild, Schloss Enzesfeld, near Vienna. From this eyrie he bombarded the King with incessant telephone calls and was subjected in turn by those from Mrs Simpson in Cannes. The King, understandably, became seriously worried about his brother's state of mind, and eventually had to ask him to stop telephoning. The stay at the Rothschild castle was not a happy one, and the Duke, with the ever-loyal Metcalfe, moved in March to the Landhaus Appesbach, near St Wolfgang, where his sense of grievance was not diminished.

There were no precedents at all for dealing with a voluntarily abdicated monarch, and certainly not with one who was to prove so exceptionally difficult and demanding.

The Duke had started his exile with a long letter to the King professing his affection and promising his full support, while already complaining about the government 'and the Court and other officials who are against us', which was to become a very familiar refrain. At first he and Mrs Simpson concentrated their complaints against Baldwin, Hardinge and Lascelles; when the King decided that he could no longer tolerate the fusillade of telephone calls, and in effect cut the Duke off, they turned their anger upon the King and Queen. Brotherly relations deteriorated with surprising rapidity, and were never to be restored.

The King was justifiably angered to discover that his brother had not revealed to him his very considerable personal wealth, and the negotiations on this matter were long, complex and increasingly unpleasant. Agreement was not reached until 1938. But whereas the Duke had little else to do, and was obsessed with money, as was his future wife, the King was already carrying an arduous burden of duties in addition to preparing himself for his Coronation. Monckton did his best, as the eternal intermediary, but noted that each brother increasingly doubted the good intentions of the other, and the Duke made it plain that he considered he was being cheated out of his patrimony. But this wearying and lengthy dispute, which tested the King's temper mightily, was not the only cause of the estrangement.

The second issue of contention concerned the wedding of the Duke to Mrs Simpson. Both Queen Mary and the Queen were understandably adamant that they would never receive Mrs Simpson as the Duchess of Windsor. They would certainly not attend the wedding, and this ban was extended to all other members of the family after the Chancellor of the Exchequer, Neville Chamberlain, and the Home Secretary, Sir John Simon, had been consulted – although, oddly enough, Baldwin was not. Chamberlain had been particularly helpful and sympathetic in the complex financial negotiations over the Duke of Windsor's demands, and had secured the warm gratitude of the King for his achievement and patience.

It was left to the King to break the news to the Duke, which he eventually did on 11 April 1937, after many anguished drafts, writing that 'this is a matter where I can't act like a private person and I have had to get advice from ministers'. It is very doubtful whether he *had* to do anything of the sort, but it was a wise decision, as the presence of any member of the family would have had considerable political as well as religious ramifications, especially as the Church of England did not recognise Mrs Simpson's first American divorce, which had been on the grounds of incompatibility, as legal; consequently, it was the judgement of the church authorities that her marriage to Ernest Simpson was itself invalid. The press commentaries alone would have been deeply harmful to the monarchy. The Duke was enraged, writing that 'I will never understand how you could ever have allowed yourself to be influenced by the present government and the Church of England and their continued campaign against me'.

It has been suggested that, left to himself, the King might have been more sympathetic, but the fact was that his devotion to his brother had come under intense strain already, and, as a devout Christian, he fully shared the abhorrence of his mother and wife at what they regarded as a travesty of a marriage. He also saw, with great clarity, the constitutional consequences if he, as Defender of the Faith, or any member of his family, were to be present at an occasion that the Church of England did not recognise, and especially so shortly before he was to take his Coronation oath, which was something he took deeply seriously. The claim that he weakly surrendered to the pressures of two strong-willed ladies and his private secretaries is not sustainable.

The Windsor camp blamed Hardinge; in fact, having been in India on sick leave, he had not been involved at all. It was the King's decision, and was not only understandable, but right. The next step was more controversial, and concerned the future Duchess of Windsor's title.

The problem culminated when the Duke of Windsor wrote to the King on 13 April to say that, 'Although Wallis' royal title comes automatically with marriage in our case, I hope you will spare us the last and only remaining embarrassment, by having it announced that she will be styled "Her Royal Highness".' This was very much on the promptings of Mrs Simpson, who wanted what she called 'the extra chic' of being HRH, but the fact was that the Duke was right; indeed, it has been suggested, if he had not himself raised the matter the whole issue, which was to destroy irretrievably the relations between the brothers, might possibly never have arisen.

This is not true. The matter had been discussed in the Royal Family and with the King's advisers, particularly Wigram and Lascelles, in Hardinge's absence as early as January.

The King had been under the impression that the royal title required his consent, which he was certainly not going to give. But when Wigram sought the advice of Granville Ram, a member of the Office of the Parliamentary Counsel, the response was categoric that it did not, citing the precedent of Queen Elizabeth herself on her marriage. Ram did suggest that Wigram refer the matter to Sir John Simon, adding, 'I sincerely hope that the Home Secretary's ingenious mind may find some way of reaching a more satisfactory conclusion, but for the life of me, I cannot see how ever he will achieve it.'

The King was dismayed at this advice, and Wigram admitted that the case was not strong, but told Simon that 'HM hopes you will find some way to avoid this title being conferred'. Even Simon's celebrated 'ingenuity' was put to a hard test. At first he could see only one way out, which was to deprive the Duke of his royal status, which was not an option that the King could, or would, consider. Then he wrote a somewhat tortuous memorandum that argued that the title of HRH should be applied only to members of the Royal Family who were within the line of succession.

This was very poor law, and had no discernable logic, as Simon himself admitted, even asking Wigram if it would not be best to let matters proceed normally, a view shared not only by Baldwin and Chamberlain but also by the senior civil servants, Warren Fisher and Horace Wilson, who were consulted. But the problem was that the

King, strongly supported by the Queen and Queen Mary, was determined not to permit this adulterous American divorcee to be formally recognised as a member of his family. He also vehemently took the view that although he recognised that the sovereign's powers were now severely limited in many respects, he must surely have a decisive voice in matters affecting his own family. This point was unanswerable, except that his determination to exclude the future Duchess had no precedent.

The repeated claims that the new Queen was actively involved in what seemed then and later to be a deliberate humiliation of the Duke of Windsor and the future Duchess are unfounded. She was ill throughout the final stages of the abdication crisis and its immediate aftermath. She then had to cope with the dizzying practical aspects of the unexpected and unwelcome changes in the life and circumstances of her husband, daughters and herself. To move her family and relatively small staff from their London house to the bleak grandeur of Buckingham Palace, with its army of servants, retainers and equerries, and from the comfort and domesticity of The Royal Lodge to the vastness of Windsor Castle, was in itself a major logistical and emotional operation. In this turmoil she was not concerned about Mrs Simpson.

She would not have been human if she had not felt resentment against the Duke and his paramour and the former King's abandonment of his position. It is also true that she had thought little of Mrs Simpson before the débâcle, and now thought even less. But, like Queen Mary, she still had strong feelings for Edward. And, like her mother-in-law and the rest of the Royal Family, she still could not really believe what had happened.

The King took titles seriously, as he did honours and decorations, especially when they directly affected the Royal Family. Another fact was that neither he nor many others expected the Windsor marriage to last very long. The Duke was clearly passionately in love, but there were many who seriously doubted whether she was, and her record as an avaricious 'bolter' was not encouraging. If the marriage ended in divorce and the Duke married again, would the second Duchess also be an HRH? These conundrums and questions were not as absurd as they might now appear.

The Duke's biographer, Philip Ziegler, has written: 'The legal justification was minimal, but they would get away with it, seems to have been the resigned conclusion of the law officers of the Crown.'[1] It was also the view of Wigram, Hardinge and Lascelles, who clearly felt uncomfortable about the impression of pettiness that the public might receive, although none of them had any time whatsoever for Mrs Simpson, and increasingly little for the Duke.

The King's feelings against the Duke were, of course, fully shared by Hardinge, Lascelles and Wigram. They had dedicated much of their lives to the royal service and felt abominably betrayed by the former King. If Lascelles had anticipated disaster, the reality was not made any less unpleasant by this fact. Ministers tended to be more sympathetic to the Duke, but very few of them knew of the financial aspect of the dispute between the brothers which was the crux of the problem.

For someone of the King's character and background, and with the influence, if not the guidance, of his father still heavily upon him, the Duke's conduct at first amazed, then bewildered, and finally disgusted him. To have been betrayed by a friend would have been incomprehensible enough; to be thus treated by his own brother was a wound that never healed. The Duke's friends and admirers, then and later, never understood how deep was this sense of outrage. But nor did the Duke, who always portrayed himself as the injured party, and genuinely believed it.

Monckton, once again, had the difficult task of preparing the Duke for the bad news. 'The Duke was at first rather excited, but afterwards asked Walter Monckton to see the King and tell him how much he would resent it,' Hardinge noted. Unexpectedly, the only senior politician who thought that the King had a case was Churchill, who told Wigram that any government would advise the King not to create Mrs Simpson HRH.

The only possible explanation for this unhappy episode lies in the realities and personalities involved. What is interesting is that the King had started the process almost immediately after his accession to the throne, and before his relations with his brother had begun to worsen. But the Duke's behaviour, his intemperate telephone calls, letters and accusations against the King and his family had only increased his determination. As the Duke's letter to him of 13 April demonstrates, he had clearly picked up what was going on in London.

[1] Ziegler, op. cit., p. 359.

The Duke's rage when he received the King's verdict for once had real justification, and the issue rankled with him for the rest of his life. He virtually severed all relations with his family, and wrote to his mother a letter of such bitterness that she showed it to the King, who wrote to the Duke that it had never been his intention to humiliate him, and that the action was '*absolutely* necessary for the sake of the country'. He added: 'How do you think I liked taking on a rocking throne, and trying to make it steady again? It has not been a pleasant job, and it is not finished yet.'

Unsurprisingly, the Duke was not remotely placated by this explanation. He blamed his brother exclusively for this public snub to his wife, and never forgave him, particularly incensed by the reference to 'the rocking throne', which was interpreted by the King, rightly, as further evidence that his brother had totally lost touch with reality and still had no conception of the enormity of what he had done.

But the King's actions, dubious though they were in strict constitutional legality, had a political as well as a personal element. It was his opinion that Mrs Simpson had caused immense damage to the status of the monarchy already, and he had noted how press comment had turned violently against her; so, to judge from letters and the reports of ministers and Members of Parliament, had the British people. The Duke still had his devotees – alarmingly numerous, in the view of Hardinge and Lascelles – but Mrs Simpson did not. To the anger of the Duke, who was also keeping a close eye on the British press, she was being depicted, on occasion with some savagery, as the cause of his downfall and as his evil genius. Mild though this comment might appear now, in the age of unfettered tabloid newspapers – whose treatment of the abdication and its aftermath today scarcely bears thinking about – it was severe by the standards of the time, and no politician could ignore it. Even Churchill was changing his opinion; as he remarked to his wife at King George's Coronation, 'I now realise that the other one wouldn't have done.'

Churchill's unexpected help did much to restore the King's view of him after his role in the abdication. It was not that Churchill had so ardently espoused his brother's case that had created the rift, but the firm conviction in the minds of Baldwin and Chamberlain that Churchill had intervened from personal political motives. But Churchill's letter of support, and his advice, touched the King, who wrote to him in his own hand on 18 May:

> My dear Mr Churchill,
>   I am writing to thank you for your very nice letter to me. I know how devoted you have been, and still are, to my dear brother, and feel touched beyond words by your sympathy and understanding in the very difficult problems that have arisen since he left us in December. I fully realise the great responsibilities and cares that I have taken on as King, and I feel most encouraged to receive your good wishes, as one of our great statesmen, and from one who has served his country so faithfully. I can only hope and trust that the good feeling and hope that exists in the Country and Empire will prove a good example to other nations in the world.
>   Believe me,
>   Yours very sincerely,
>   George R.I.

Not many people considered Churchill 'one of our great statesmen' at that time; he himself considered that his influence 'had fallen to zero', and was not alone in thinking that his political career was finished. He had not held office since 1929, and it was almost universally thought that, like Lloyd George, he never would again. His violent and sustained opposition to concessions to Indian nationalism had overshadowed his warnings about the revival of German militarism after the Nazi coup of 1933; just when his position and reputation were reviving in 1936, and Baldwin's were in sharp decline, the abdication crisis had totally reversed their fortunes. Churchill was a disconsolate and reviled figure in 1937, with his own normal confidence badly shaken. Always subject to moods of depression, in 1937 he had much to be depressed about. He was in his sixty-third year, the brilliant early promise and eminence now in what seemed total eclipse. His following was minuscule, and unimpressive both in quality and influence. In this dark period in his fortunes the King's letter had a remarkable effect upon him. It may be seen as the beginning of the most fruitful and positive relationship the King was to have with any British politician.

Beaverbrook was experiencing a similar recantation, as his newspapers graphically demonstrated. Mrs Simpson still sold newspapers, but not in the way she or the Duke desired.

It was this political reality that loomed heavily in the King's mind, and in those of his ministers and advisers. Their concern was that the decision itself would smack of vindictiveness, but in the event there was a marked degree of public understanding that it had been the right one. There were, of course, those who felt differently. This commentator confesses to serious ambiguity in his assessment, but considers that it was the right decision in the circumstances of the time; that it was never rescinded, in spite of Churchill's attempts to do so when he was Prime Minister, is another matter.

The oft-repeated claim that the King and Queen were apprehensive of the Duke of Windsor attempting to reverse the events of December 1936 and returning to the throne is totally unsustained by the King's papers and diaries. The King well knew that it was a preposterous suggestion. What did trouble him, and with good reason, was that his brother and his brother's new wife would cause him and the monarchy grave embarrassment by their pro-Nazi views and friends – which is exactly what happened. But the obloquy fell not upon the King, but on the Duke, whose foray to Germany within months of the abdication, ostensibly to study German 'housing projects' and much fawned upon by Hitler, Goering, and the appalling Robert Ley – a man disgusting even by Nazi standards – was a notable disaster for his reputation. His projected visit to the United States, again under the auspices of the odious Charles Bedaux, had to be abandoned humiliatingly, but not before serious people on both sides of the Atlantic had lost whatever respect they had had for the Windsors.

Thus, the deliberate decision of the King to distance himself and the monarchy from these erratic and insensate performances was the first important political decision of his reign.

The King and Duke at least agreed about Hardinge, on whose personality there were very different judgements. It is somewhat startling to discover in the memoirs of Oliver Lyttelton that 'Alec Hardinge, afterwards the most correct of courtiers, was perhaps the wildest of our set [at Cambridge]'; these youthful high spirits and frivolities were wholly unsuspected by those who knew him. When Lyttelton told George VI about his Private

Secretary's undergraduate adventures the King replied that he thought the better of him for these escapades; for once, Lyttelton missed the irony of the comment.[2] Harold Macmillan described him in his 1943 diary, grossly unfairly, as 'beyond the pale. He is idle, supercilious, without a spark of imagination or vitality,' whereas the diplomat Oliver Harvey considered him to be 'strong, sensible [and] progressive-minded' – no doubt because he became strongly anti-Munich and anti-Chamberlain.

No one who worked with Hardinge ever accused him of idleness, as Macmillan did; the problem was that he was a solitary and self-contained man and, as Lascelles' diaries repeatedly emphasised, a difficult and uncommunicative colleague. Another close colleague wrote that

> Alec is a tragic figure. He is an old friend of both of us & it is truer of him than anybody else that he is his own worst enemy. The highest principles, long experience, great capacity & infinite attention to duty – such a makeup shld combine to make the ideal occupant of his position, but, alas, the gods have withheld too much. A contempt for *servility* has left hardly standing room for *civility*; & what profiteth a man in his position to be irreproachable, if he is even more unapproachable?

The incompatibility of temperament between the King and Hardinge was apparent from a very early stage of their relationship. The problem was that the King had not only confirmed Hardinge in his position as one of the first acts of his reign but had conferred on him the GCVO for services to the sovereign and the KCB for services to the state. But he had never worked with him, and when he realised that they had remarkably little in common, instead of courteously moving him to another position, he sought his political and constitutional advice from other sources. Baldwin's small dinner parties for the King to meet politicians was one method; his friendships with Halifax and Lord

---

[2] *The Memoirs of Lord Chandos*, p. 20. Lyttelton served in the Grenadiers with the Prince of Wales, of whom he later wrote that 'for me his spell has never been broken', and that 'he was the most charming and delightful human being that I had ever known'. (Ibid, pp. 46–7.)

Another fellow Grenadier in the war was Arthur Penn, future courtier and Private Secretary to Queen Elizabeth, and who, when wounded in February 1915, recorded in his game book: 'BEAT: Cour du Avoué; BAG: Self.' (Ibid, p. 42.)

Cranborne were valuable; and he tried, not always successfully, to meet, and get on with, trade union and Labour leaders, the reluctance being on their side and not on his.[3]

Hardinge appears to have been the only person in the royal service who did not realise what was going on. Perhaps it would have been kinder to let Hardinge go, but the King and Queen shrank from such an action, which would have been a humiliation for an immensely loyal public servant. This was to their credit. The King much valued loyalty, and Hardinge certainly had no faults on that score. But they grated on each other's nerves, and especially Hardinge's upon the King's, who once burst out, 'What can you do with a man who always says "*No*"?' This episode also brought to light a problem that was to become a source of considerable difficulty.

George V, so reticent to his own children, enjoyed conversations with politicians, although they often complained that they were more like monologues. Immediately after a meeting with a minister the King would dictate a record of it. King George VI at once decided to work in his own way, which was to apply himself diligently to his papers and not to be content with submissions and summaries by his private secretaries. Also, he considered that private conversations were private, and should remain so. Except on certain occasions his diaries, intermittent until September 1939, were discreet, and in any event Hardinge and Lascelles did not have access to them. The result was that the King's private secretaries found themselves cut off from knowledge of the King's talks with his principal ministers except when he chose to inform them, and there were few written records of them.[4]

So, while Hardinge had real qualities of loyalty and experience, he was

[3] The King recorded in his diary on 15 May 1940: 'I met Mr [Ernest] Bevin of the Transport Workers' Union who has become Minister of Labour & a Privy Councillor. He had always excused himself from coming to see me when I had met other trade union leaders, now I shall be able to send for him. He looks a strong man and a leader.'

[4] Harold Nicolson, then engaged on his biography of George V, recorded in his diary for 5 February 1951 that 'Tommy [Lascelles] tells me that the present King never tells him exactly what happens at his interviews with ministers . . . [he] just says to Tommy, "Oh, he was optimistic as usual," or "He was worried about the coal situation," and never goes into any detail.' (Nigel Nicolson, *Harold Nicolson, Diaries and Letters*, Vol. II, p. 204.)

excessively cautious and negative. The King and Queen quickly found that when they wanted to do something Hardinge almost invariably argued against it. They therefore tended to go ahead anyway, not always with good results, as will be seen. Lascelles, a much more relaxed figure who could see what was happening at first hand, later marvelled that Hardinge had lasted so long. The essential reason was that while the King appreciated Hardinge's loyal service to his father and brother, and his total integrity, he in effect usually ignored his advice. The myth that the Queen, Hardinge, Lascelles and Wigram ran the monarchy and dominated a weak King, much propagated by the Duke and Duchess of Windsor, is amusing to the constitutionalist because the exact reverse was the case.

The King's private office soon however received an important, if junior, addition. Michael Adeane was twenty-seven. His father had been killed serving with the Coldstream Guards in 1914; his mother, Victoria, was the elder daughter of Stamfordham. After Eton and Cambridge – where he achieved a First in History – he was commissioned into the Coldstream Guards and appointed ADC to Lord Tweedsmuir (John Buchan), the Governor-General of Canada.

It is not clear whether it was Hardinge or Lascelles who proposed that Adeane should become an Assistant Private Secretary, although it was most probably Lascelles. But both men had got to know the young Adeane through his eminent grandfather, and no royal pedigree could have been bettered. Adeane also physically resembled Stamfordham, being small in height, slim, thoughtful, and impassively discreet. But, like Lascelles and unlike Hardinge, he moved easily in literary, club and political circles, and entertained no hostility to cocktail or dinner parties. But his calm and inscrutable discretion, which was to become legendary, was as evident in the younger man as it was to become much later when he succeeded Lascelles as Private Secretary to Queen Elizabeth II.

Adeane's initial period in the King's service was destined to be relatively short, as on the outbreak of war in 1939 he returned, on his own insistence, to his regiment. The only recorded occasion when the King reprimanded him was when he was summoned to Buckingham Palace in 1945 and forgot to put on his officer's pips. The King spotted this grave omission at once, but then rummaged in a drawer to find a set, which he handed to Adeane, who was ordered to withdraw and not to return until he was properly dressed.

In a curious way Adeane was a mixture of Hardinge and Lascelles. As Kenneth Rose has vividly recorded, when Adeane became the Queen's Private Secretary, 'From a mournful little office cheered only by a painting of a fat white dog and an old-fashioned grate adorned with pleated white paper, Adeane bore a vast burden . . . By his own wish, for he disliked delegation, his staff was tiny.'[5] This is almost a portrait of Hardinge, but Adeane shared Lascelles' mischievous sense of humour, his gregariousness and enjoyment of the ridiculous. He was invariably dignified, but wholly devoid of pomposity.

In the pantheon of exceptional royal private secretaries Adeane stands at the top, challenged for the very first place only by his grandfather. Whether it was Hardinge or Lascelles who recruited him does not much matter, but it was to prove an inspired selection.

But this talented and dedicated team faced the problem, not resolved until 1943, of the King's working methods and Hardinge's bleak and unsympathetic personality. Indeed, the two problems were inseparable. As he was to prove later, the King could work closely and harmoniously with congenial spirits, and was far less interested in formalities than is usually realised.

The principal difficulty of working for the King lay in his own complex and volatile personality. In a phrase of true insight, Wheeler-Bennett was to write that 'perhaps more than any monarch of modern times, King George maintained an even balance between the aloof position of a sovereign and the "homespun dignity of man"'. But the problem for his closest advisers was that they were never sure which aspect was to be predominant at any time. He could be relaxed, amusing and tolerant. He could also be taut, hyper-critical and wounding to the point that some people were frightened of him. He had a particularly cold look when out of humour that was positively intimidating.

Except in the company of his wife and daughters and their friends – his true relaxation – to other observers he often seemed to be a lonely, ill-tempered and unhappy man. And then, in total contrast, they beheld the happy countryman, sportsman and considerate host and employer, whose wife, with his full approval, always kept a good table until the exigencies of war. As Lascelles once noted – and he was not alone in this

[5] Rose, *Kings, Queens, and Courtiers*, p. 141.

observation – the King in a good mood was the best and most amusing of company; when not, it was wise to undertake essential business as rapidly as possible.

But the important point is that the King, from the beginning of his unexpected and unwanted reign, was determined to conduct matters himself, in his own way, and on his own terms. He was acutely aware – at the outset, perhaps too acutely aware – of his constitutional responsibility to depend upon his ministers for their advice and judgements. He turned to them, and on occasion the Queen, rather than to his private secretaries. But he grasped the essentials of his political role swiftly, and, above all, his own personal responsibility for it, which could not be delegated to anyone else. If mistakes were made, they were to be his mistakes. One understands why he subsequently warmed to men of the same school of thought, notably Churchill, Roosevelt and Harry Truman.

But he had worked all this out for himself. Bagehot did not come into it. He had no intention of becoming a suppliant figurehead, although few understood better the symbolic roles of the sovereign. Hardinge was the first of many who failed to recognise this essential fact.

6

CHAMBERLAIN AND ROOSEVELT

B aldwin had retired from the premiership and public life with an earldom in May 1937, and was succeeded by Neville Chamberlain. Chamberlain had been Baldwin's obvious and natural successor since 1931, and his election as leader of the Conservative Party – proposed by Churchill – was unanimous. There was no need for the King to take soundings or receive advice. Although the King wrote Baldwin a warm letter of gratitude, their association had been brief, and Chamberlain was in effect the King's first Prime Minister. On his death-bed in November 1940, just after the King and Queen had visited him, Chamberlain told Halifax that 'he had been in a sense their Godfather – or something like it'. It was a significantly characteristic comment. His freezing public manner, which made him so detested by his opponents and critics, and which earned him Brendan Bracken's nickname of 'The Coroner', was belied by a quite different one in private, as the King realised when Chamberlain stayed at Balmoral in August 1937. Chamberlain was genuinely impressed by the King, and so was the Foreign Secretary, Anthony Eden – rather to the latter's surprise – although the King found him difficult to talk to; the reality was that Chamberlain's increasing interference in foreign policy and his mounting self-confidence that he had the measure of the German and Italian dictators grated on Eden's nerves, and led to his resignation. Their relations had not been particularly good, and the King considered that Eden hardly ever departed from his Foreign Office brief; also, he was beginning to lean towards Chamberlain's more optimistic view of the European scene.[1]

But the impression from the King and Chamberlain's correspondence that Chamberlain was condescending to the King was strongly confirmed by his conduct. On the morning of Sunday, 20 February 1938, the King read in the Beaverbrook newspapers that there was a crisis involving the Foreign Secretary, which was the first he knew of it. Later in the day he heard from the radio that Eden had resigned. The King was understandably incensed with Hardinge, who had only told him that it was very unusual to have a Cabinet meeting on a Saturday, but he was especially angry with Downing Street. His Prime Minister had not only failed to consult him, he had not even been told that his Foreign Secretary was threatening resignation, and then had to learn of this event from the press and his radio.

Hardinge was instructed to find out was going on. He had considerable difficulty in contacting any Cabinet minister until he telephoned Oliver Stanley, who told him that 'the situation is as bad as it could be'. This was intolerable: as Hardinge wrote to Hankey on the 21st, this meant that 'any opportunity for His Majesty to make a helpful contribution of any kind, in consultation with the Prime Minister, is delayed until the situation becomes irretrievable and intervention useless . . . I feel sure you will agree that some arrangement should be devised to enable the King to receive immediate intimation of any serious developments of this nature and I would welcome the opportunity of discussing this matter with you.'[2] In an additionally farcical moment Hardinge addressed his letter wrongly, and it only reached the intended recipient a day later. The invention of the telephone appeared to have passed by the Prime Minister's secretariat and that of the King. But there was no mistaking the King's legitimate fury. Chamberlain hastened to make amends, proper arrangements for informing the Palace of looming crises were promised, and it was agreed that in future the King should receive draft copies of Cabinet minutes rather than having to wait for the final version, which usually arrived several days later. 'I think, and I hope

---

[1] It should be noted that in this he was not alone, Churchill writing in the *Evening Standard* on 15 September 1937 that: 'I declare my belief that a major war is not imminent, and I still believe there is a good chance of no major war taking place in our time.'

[2] RA PS GVI C 067/02.

you will agree,' Hardinge wrote to Hankey on the King's instructions on 25 February, 'that the onus of keeping the King informed should rest on the Prime Minister and those who work under his direction, as always used to be the case in the time of Lord Stamfordham.'[3] So it appeared that something positive emerged from this lamentable but highly revealing episode. In reality, however, little changed; it was not until November 1938 that the King was sent the draft Cabinet minutes.[4]

When Eden came to the King on the 22nd to surrender his Seal of Office he was startled, and pleased, when the King told him that 'he had great sympathy for his point of view and did not think it would be long before he saw him again as one of his senior ministers'. Some historians have interpreted this as an example of the King's courtesy rather than of his real views, but although he had found Eden rather difficult to get on with personally, he admired his intellect and knew of his outstanding record in the war and in public life. The King was also still seething at his offhand treatment by Downing Street.

There was another factor, however. The King and Queen had few close friends in politics, but Lord and Lady Cranborne were exceptions. 'Bobbety' Cranborne, Eden's junior Foreign Office minister, resigned with Eden, and became a ferocious opponent of Chamberlain's foreign policy from the Conservative back-benches. His wife, a truly formidable and equally outspoken personality, left the King in no doubt about her opinions, and, in the words of one of her family, 'gave him a hard time'. They, and Eden, had raised doubts in the King's mind about Chamberlain's foreign policies, which were to mature and develop.

This episode might have caused a serious rift between the King and Chamberlain, but the latter's abject apologies and the excuse that the fault had lain at a lower level placated the King. He also found Eden's successor, Halifax, one of the few politicians apart from Cranborne whom he knew well, far more congenial; indeed, Halifax's wife was a lady-in-waiting to the Queen, and he and the King were very similar personalities, with the same interests in country life and sport; there was also the fact that Halifax, as his biographer concedes, did not 'find the study of foreign affairs a matter of absorbing interest'. His naïveté, which

[3] RA PS GVI C 067/04.
[4] RA PS GVI C 067/10.

was to persist until he was among the first to realise that the Munich agreement of September was far from the triumph it appeared, made him initially a dangerous guide for the King.

There have been few instances, if any, in modern British political history of a Prime Minister treating a monarch with greater duplicity than the way in which Chamberlain dealt with George VI. Following the events of February, there occurred in May another example of Chamberlain's deliberate habit of keeping the King ill-informed and then misleading him. This episode concerned the fate of Lord Swinton, Secretary of State for Air since 1935.

The one glittering exception to the general mediocrity of the Baldwin and Chamberlain governments apart from Eden, Swinton had served as President of the Board of Trade in the 1920s and early 1930s and then as Secretary of State for the Colonies before going to the Air Ministry. His achievements were, and have been, gravely underestimated. While Churchill was publicly and consistently lamenting the condition of the Royal Air Force, and being as unhelpful in private as he was in public, Swinton was re-creating it. It was due to his energy, drive and leadership that the eight-gun monoplane Spitfire and Hurricane fighters were ordered and rushed into production; also the Wellington and Blenheim bombers which, however inadequate, were to be the precursors of the heavy bombers of Bomber Command; the vital radar development and chain, and its incorporation into RAF Fighter Command; a substantial recruitment and training programme for flying crew; and the 'Shadow Factory' scheme whereby car and lorry factories could be converted into manufacturing aircraft engines, supplies and parts.

All these were the results of Swinton's brilliant, and, as it happened, war-saving stewardship of the Air Ministry and the outstanding team that he created. The King was to write in his diary on 4 October 1940, after the Battle of Britain had been narrowly won, that 'men like Lord Swinton will be remembered'. Alas, that was not to be the case.

But, remarkable though these achievements were, a totally new Air Force was difficult to create quickly, particularly in the teeth of Treasury reluctance to spend money and parliamentary and press criticism of the alleged slow progress. And Swinton's position was made more difficult by the fact that he was no longer in the Commons – MP for Hendon since 1918, he had in 1935 accepted the offer of a viscountcy, a decision he later bitterly regretted.

Also, Swinton was a splendidly abrasive character. As Lord Winterton, the cause of his downfall, later wrote, he had 'never in his long life in both Houses of Parliament sought or obtained popularity'. This was being rather kind. Swinton had a remarkable capacity for treating fools, and even some who were not, with withering contumely, impatience and asperity. His admirers were not as numerous as those who had felt the lash of his fierce tongue. He was rightly incensed by the ignorant criticisms of his policies – notably Churchill's – and did not handle his critics gently. But there was another problem; even if he had still been in the Commons it would have been difficult to explain publicly what was being done without jeopardising national security.

His new minister in the Commons was Winterton, whose appointment on 12 May had amazed everyone, including himself. There may have been something endearing about this genial, literate and not unintelligent man, although this is somewhat difficult to grasp, but his appointment demonstrated the firm grip that the Government Whips' Office under David Margesson and James Stuart had. His speech on the Air Estimates went disastrously, and gave Chamberlain and the Chancellor of the Exchequer, Simon, their opportunity.

Swinton went, although not voluntarily, and Winterton was promoted to the Home Office. Swinton was replaced by the more pliant, amenable, unbelligerent and ultimately useless Sir Kingsley Wood, one of whose first actions was to abandon the Shadow Factory programme under pressure from Lord Nuffield. The King, who liked abrasive and strong-willed personalities, and who had admired Swinton and his dedicated work for the RAF, was dismayed, writing to the Prime Minister on 16 May:

My dear Chamberlain,

I am so sorry to hear of your attack of gout, which prevented you from coming to see me today & I do hope that you will soon be well again.

I saw Swinton this evening & I was very sorry to have to say goodbye to him as Secretary of State for Air, he has done so well in the Air Ministry I feel, & he will be a great loss to the country at this time . . .

I am just going off to the station for our tour in Lancashire for four days.

I hope it will not be too tiring & that we will shall be able to meet next week for a talk.

Believe me,

Yours very sincerely,

George R.I.[5]

This letter demonstrates how politically and personally remote was their relationship. Chamberlain's explanation of the event that caused the King so much regret came in a notably disingenous, indeed dishonest, letter of 17 May, when he wrote, 'I have parted with Lord Swinton very regretfully. He has done wonders for the Air Force but I was fighting a losing battle in trying to retain him. The House simply would not have it . . .'[6]

This was untrue in every respect.

As the terrible year of 1938 unfolded its horrors, from the German occupation of Austria in March to the Czechoslovak crisis in September, the King's principal sources of information were Chamberlain and Halifax, especially the latter. And Hardinge took a totally different view of the Chamberlain policy of appeasement, echoing those of Churchill and Vansittart.

It is impossible to underestimate the degree of disillusionment about the Great War in Britain and France. Indeed, in the former, a small but highly significant and much-read literary industry of generally high and arresting quality denouncing the war and its conduct had grown up. For years Churchill's reputation was shadowed by the Dardanelles defeat; Lloyd George's fame as 'the man who won the war' had swiftly evaporated, and Bonar Law's intervention over Chanak and his statement that Britain could not be 'the policeman of the world' had been strongly applauded; Duff Cooper's generally supportive biography of Haig was denounced, not least by *The Times*'s military correspondent Basil Liddell Hart; the Labour Party was largely pacific, as was the League of Nations, then at its zenith in membership and influence.

Of the other principal belligerents, none of this happened in Germany, especially after the Nazi seizure of power in 1933. War was glorified, and the veterans held up to admiration and respect; the war had not been

[5] RA PS GVI C 047/06.
[6] RA PS GVI C 047/09.

lost, the army had been betrayed, and Versailles had been a humiliation that must be extirpated. It was on these legends that the Nazis fed. Erich Maria Remarque's *All Quiet on the Western Front*, one of the most powerful anti-war books ever written, was banned in Germany, as was the equally influential American film of the book. The glories, not the horrors, of war were extolled – the exact opposite of the situation in Britain and France.

German propaganda was also skilful; any politician who dared to call for rearmament, especially the reviled Churchill, was denounced as a warmonger; British fears of Soviet Communism, rife in the Conservative ranks, were exploited, as were their distinct anti-Semitic prejudices. The German assumption that the British had no stomach for another war was correct, at least up to the summer of 1938. There were many Germans, including senior officers, who were in the same mood, but their voices were ruthlessly silenced.

This was the political context in which British politicians had to operate, and the anti-war mood was even greater in France. There were those in Britain who shared Churchill's alarm over the ever-growing German Air Force, and took the vital steps towards combating this threat, and the Royal Navy was unquestionably the largest and best surface fleet afloat.

There was also the fact that Britain could no longer count upon the unquestioned support of the Commonwealth – especially Canada and Australia – in a European war. The Australians felt so deeply about Gallipoli that the British official history's fully justified criticisms of the Australians' performance during and immediately after the Anzac landings had to be substantially omitted or watered down, political factors being deemed far more important than historical accuracy. The mythology of Gallipoli – gallant Australians condemned to slaughter by incompetent British commanders – had been born, and could not be challenged. It is difficult to do so even over eighty years later.

The Canadians, also, had reflected upon their heavy losses. The epic capture of Vimy Ridge that had caused such pride, now appeared to have been another sanguinary episode in a war that seemed to have settled nothing. The Canadian Prime Minister, Mackenzie King, was an ardent pacifist, and this did him no harm with the Canadian electorate. In South Africa these emotions were augmented by the violent anti-British feelings still held by many Boers.

These emotions featured strongly at the 1937 Commonwealth Conference in London. At that point even Churchill thought that the danger of war had passed, and a government headed by Neville Chamberlain was unlikely to give a strong alarmist lead. It was to be one of Hitler's great achievements that by 1939 this mood had totally changed.

The United States did not feature in anyone's calculations. American politicians were isolationists because their constituents were. American involvement in the war was now deemed to have been a useless sacrifice of young men, and Wilson's memory treated with contempt; the League of Nations was a European trap; the British had not paid their war bills. And then the hideous Depression dominated their concerns. Utterly preoccupied with their own ills, Americans neglected military matters to the extent that by 1939 the American armed forces were rated fourteenth in the world, below those of Holland.

To state these facts is not to condone British foreign and defence policies in the mid- and late 1930s, but to give a clearer background to the events of 1938.

The only positive episode of that year, and one that looks poignant in the light of future events, was the success of the State Visit of the King and Queen to France in July, after it had to be postponed because of the sudden death of the Queen's mother. In the enthusiasm and excitement the shadows of war seemed to have been temporarily lifted, but by August they had gathered again; and by September, over Czechoslovakia, they dominated Europe.

It has been wrongly claimed that George V at the end of his reign 'embraced an extreme pro-appeasement stance which was to percolate through his family'.[7] The phrase itself was unknown before the death of the King, and was not linked to a policy until 1938, when it became inextricably and permanently associated with Chamberlain's attempts to avert war by concessions to the fascist dictators.

It is true that George V had dreaded another war as much as he had the previous one. So did his two eldest sons, but the difference between the Duke of Windsor and George VI was that the former had a strong personal affinity with Germany which the latter did not. Nor did his father. Nor had Queen Elizabeth, who had lost a brother in the war.

---

[7] Roberts, *Eminent Churchillians*, p. 5.

The King certainly wanted Chamberlain to be right. He even suggested that he should write a personal letter to Hitler as 'one ex-serviceman to another', but Halifax persuaded him not to. The crisis, which culminated in Chamberlain's meeting at Munich with Hitler, Mussolini and Daladier, the hapless French Premier, and the abandonment of the Czechs to their fate, was initially greeted with ecstatic relief, in which the King fully shared.

After Chamberlain triumphantly returned from Munich on 30 September with his infamous 'scrap of paper', the King wanted to meet him in person at Heston aerodrome but was dissuaded by Hardinge; he did send a handwritten letter to be given to the Prime Minister inviting him to Buckingham Palace immediately, so that he could express to Chamberlain personally his 'most heartfelt congratulations'.[8] A huge crowd gathered outside the Palace when this was reported on the radio and in the evening papers. The King suggested that he and Chamberlain should appear on the balcony to respond to their enthusiasm, which they did.

But afterwards, to the dismay of Halifax and Chamberlain's Parliamentary Private Secretary, Lord Dunglass – himself a future Prime Minister as Sir Alec Douglas-Home – Chamberlain, recalling Beaconsfield's phrase in 1878 after the Congress of Berlin, told an equally excited crowd in Downing Street that 'this is the second time in our history that there has come back from Germany to Downing Street peace with honour. I believe it is peace for our time.' Dunglass had specifically urged him not to use the fatal phrase, and thought that he had succeeded. As he later recalled:

On our return to London Downing Street was packed with people waiting to acclaim the Munich achievement. I was with Chamberlain as we approached the foot of the staircase in No. 10, where Cabinet colleagues and others were assembled. Out of the crowd someone said, 'Neville, go up to the window and repeat history by saying "Peace in our time".' I could not identify the voice but Chamberlain turned rather icily towards the speaker, and said, 'No, I do not do that kind of thing.' He was right, because by nature he was the most reticent and the least flamboyant of men. I then lost

[8] RA PS GVI C 047/13.

touch with him on the staircase, and the next thing I knew was that he had spoken the fateful words. Somebody in the last few yards to the window must have overtaken and over-persuaded him. He knew at once that it was a mistake, and that he could not justify the claim. It haunted him for the rest of his life.[9]

This was not to be the last occasion on which the King and Queen stood on the Palace balcony with a Prime Minister at a time of national rejoicing, but it was by far the most controversial. The King was genuinely surprised at the subsequent extent of the hostility to Munich, denounced not only by prominent Conservatives but by the Labour Party. Most disturbing of all was the fact that Halifax was already having serious doubts, reflecting strong feelings within the Foreign Office and his own scepticism about Hitler's personality. Also, whereas Chamberlain had been greatly impressed by Hitler, Dunglass had found him repellent. Hardinge was vehemently anti-Munich, but his influence on the King was nothing to that of Halifax.

The King was spared what could have proved a major embarrassment, largely due to the shrewdness of Halifax. His first reaction to any outstanding act was to think of honours or other signs of royal recognition, and he immediately considered honouring Chamberlain. He asked Hardinge to take soundings, and his Private Secretary reported that

with regard to the question of an honour for the Prime Minister, I consulted Lord Baldwin and Lord Halifax (as personal friends). The former was quite certain that the Prime Minister would refuse and if the King was to make the offer it must be made very judiciously. *Lord Halifax on the whole advised against any immediate offer in view of the strong criticism of the Munich settlement which was sure to arise in Parliament.* I subsequently ascertained from the Prime Minister's Private Secretary that Mr Chamberlain had mentioned he would never accept anything, at any rate as long as he was in office.[10]

Munich was an event that divided families, broke friendships, and led

[9] Home, *The Way the Wind Blows*, p. 65.
[10] Author's italics. RA PS GVI C 235/20.

to fierce arguments and violent emotions. In this unhappy context the King's apparent endorsement of Chamberlain's actions aroused strong criticism; it was muted in public, but it certainly existed, and the King was informed of it by Hardinge and Lascelles.

At first, believing in Chamberlain, he tended to dismiss the anti-Munich sentiment. But it is clear that he quickly came to appreciate its strength, and although the documentary evidence is not strong – the King was not at that time keeping a diary, and there are few records kept of his discussions with ministers – the doubts of Halifax and the violent opposition of the Cranbornes must have played a major part in the King's change of mind. Before Hitler annexed the rest of Czechoslovakia in March 1939 the King was convinced that war was virtually inevitable. Chamberlain did not accept this, but retreated in the face of a new mood in the country, and one in which the name of Churchill was increasingly mentioned.

The King's actions have been cited as evidence of his naïveté, but should be judged more sympathetically in the context of the time. In a message issued on 2 October he said, 'After the magnificent efforts of the Prime Minister in the cause of peace, it is my fervent hope that a new era of friendship and prosperity may be dawning among the peoples of the world.' He may have been wrong, but he soon changed his mind.

As the Czechoslovak crisis progressed, there was an increasing divergence of view between the Foreign Office and Downing Street, and between Halifax and Chamberlain. Halifax can reasonably be described as perhaps the most underestimated and unfairly maligned of modern British politicians, and this despite two outstanding biographies of him, by Lord Birkenhead and Andrew Roberts. He has been cast by Churchillian mythology – although not by Churchill himself – as one of the principal apostles of appeasement. The reality was very different.

Halifax did not accompany Chamberlain on any of his three missions to see Hitler in September 1938. Whereas Chamberlain complacently told the Cabinet after his disastrous confrontation with Hitler at Godesberg that 'he thought that he had now established an influence over Herr Hitler', Halifax was appalled at Hitler's blatant bullying of the British Prime Minister and the latter's craven acquiescence. To Chamberlain's astonishment, thunderstruck by what he described as 'a horrible blow to me', Halifax denounced the Godesberg terms in the Cabinet, and Oliver Harvey wrote in his diary that Halifax 'has lost all his delusions about

Hitler and now regards him as a criminal lunatic. He loathes Nazism.' As Roberts has written, Halifax had had 'an almost Damascene conversion from appeaser to resister'.

Halifax became a key political figure before and, even more importantly, after the Munich crisis. He was convinced that Munich had only bought time, and that time should be used for urgent rearmament. Unlike other leading Conservatives he consistently kept in close touch with Churchill, Eden, Amery, Cranborne and other Tory pariahs. He also had excellent personal contacts with the Labour and Liberal leaders. Chamberlain was slow to appreciate just how far his Foreign Secretary was distancing himself from him in advocating a more aggressive foreign policy than he himself thought either necessary or desirable. When he did he was intensely resentful, particularly of Halifax's repeated insistence that he should form a National Government with Labour and the Liberals, including the principal Conservative dissidents, and introduce not only a massive rearmament programme but military conscription. Those who still wonder why Halifax was the overwhelming favourite to succeed Chamberlain in May 1940 have underestimated or ignored his role in late 1938 and in 1939.

Halifax's conviction, fortified by Munich, that Hitler and Nazism could be defeated only by war or the threat of war buttressed by military strength, which Chamberlain vehemently resisted, had an immense effect upon the King.

Edward and Dorothy Halifax were among the relatively few personal friends involved in active politics that the King and Queen had. The four of them regularly dined together in private, the King gave Halifax a key to the Palace gardens and increasingly relied upon his advice and information. Indeed, it would be right to describe Halifax as the King's principal political adviser in 1939. He urged upon Chamberlain the Halifax line – a National Government, urgent rearmament, and a Ministry of Supply. Halifax consistently gave the King the Foreign Office view of the deteriorating situation as a wholly effective counterweight to the continuing optimism radiating from Downing Street. In the debates on Munich in the Commons, Chamberlain applauded his own achievement and spoke of further disarmament; in the Lords, Halifax described Munich as only the better of 'a hideous choice of evils'.

Halifax was convinced that war was inevitable and that Britain and

France should prepare jointly and urgently for it. He also saw, rather better than most Conservative politicians, the fundamental evil of Nazism and its savage ambitions. There was also the fact that, contrary to the expectations of the Conservative hierarchy, the realities of what had really happened at Munich were soon appreciated. Euphoria was replaced with a sense of shame and humiliation. The Conservatives lost two by-elections immediately – to Labour at Dartford and to the anti-Munich Independent Vernon Bartlett at Bridgwater – and held Oxford with a greatly reduced majority, where Quintin Hogg uncomfortably held off the anti-Munich challenge of the Master of Balliol, who was keenly supported by many Conservatives including Harold Macmillan and the young Edward Heath. By an interesting irony, Hogg, the Chamberlainite hero in November 1938, was to be one of their villains on 8 May 1940, when his vote against the government assisted in Chamberlain's downfall and the salvation of his country.

Neither Halifax nor the King was disloyal to Chamberlain between Munich and May 1940. Halifax brooded over resignation, but put that possibility aside, however attractive it seemed, considering that his influence inside the government was infinitely more important than outside it. Although lacking in personal vanity, if not totally, Halifax knew that his resignation would have brought the government down.

Whether Chamberlain appreciated this is doubtful, but he became increasingly resentful of Halifax's dramatic change of attitude. His ally had become a critic, and to Chamberlain and his coterie a critic ceased to be an ally. What he and they failed to understand was that the King, who loomed very low in their calculations, had also changed sides. Munich was the first major political turning-point of the King's reign. He had, with the best intentions, made a mistake. Few blamed him at the time for his enthusiastic personal endorsement of Munich. Before long he blamed himself. It was not an episode on which he would have wished his biographers to linger. But, largely due to his friend Halifax, he woke up to the realities sooner than his ministers did.

When he saw Chamberlain on 19 October he urged that 'the future policy must be the cultivation of friendly relations combined with intensified rearmament. One must be strong in order to negotiate.' Chamberlain assured the King that he was 'determined to get more aeroplanes, better

ARP, and some kind of National Register'. But he also said that 'the USA must be left alone. They will never take a more active line if we preach at them . . . The PM considered that it was better to leave the Soviets alone.' When the question of creating a Ministry of National Service or Supply – much favoured by Churchill – was raised by the King, Chamberlain replied that 'it was undesirable except in wartime, and would upset the manufacturers who were just settling down to production of armaments. The manufacturers had a horror of government interference.'

Halifax had unsuccessfully urged Chamberlain to make his government a truly national one by including Churchill, Eden and Cranborne. Knowing this, the King raised the matter with Chamberlain at the same meeting. The Prime Minister was dismissive of the idea of having the Opposition in government, as they 'would criticise the PM's foreign policy as being a paradox to [the] rearmament programme' – which was certainly true.[11] Chamberlain's only concession to Halifax's advice and the King's questioning was to invite the Liberal Herbert (now Lord) Samuel, a supporter of Munich, to become Lord Privy Seal; the offer was rejected.

In October 1938 the government decided to issue an appeal for volunteers for national service 'in time of need', and that the King should inaugurate it in a national broadcast that had the approval of the leaders of the Opposition parties. This was obtained, and the speech prepared. But the Governor of the Bank of England, Montagu Norman, protested that this might be interpreted that war was imminent and lead to panic on the Stock Exchange.[12] The idea was dropped. It was a significant example of the fatal dichotomy of the government's policy. It was not until April 1939 that the appointment of a Minister of Supply was announced; the holder was the lacklustre National Liberal Leslie Burgin, and not Churchill.

The King had been given the impression by Chamberlain that rearmament was to be a priority for the 'negotiation from strength' policy. In fact it proceeded without urgency. The army was to go to war with essentially Great War equipment; the RAF with the much-vaunted Spitfires and Hurricanes with two-bladed wooden propellors and no

[11] RA PS GVI C Conf/239/03.
[12] RA PS GVI C 047/21.

rear-view mirrors[13] and with disastrously bad bombers which were to condemn many brave young airmen to their deaths. The navy was without radar, had inadequate anti-aircraft weapons and an excessive faith in ASDIC to combat the submarine menace, which was in itself grossly underestimated. These and other terrible failings were soon to be brutally exposed. Only in the provision of air-raid shelters – especially the simple, cheap, but effective Anderson shelter – was real urgency and efficiency demonstrated.

It would have been impossible for the British to have rectified two decades of neglect of their armed services in twelve months, but far more could, and should, have been done to reduce the perils in which Britain found herself in 1940. What was required was the obsessive dynamism of a youthful Lloyd George or an older Churchill. Such people had no place in a Baldwin or Chamberlain government.

But appeasement, this time to Mussolini, still flourished, and in January 1939 Chamberlain returned from Rome, reporting to the King in a notably long and self-congratuatory letter that 'both Halifax and I were favourably impressed by Mussolini. Talking with him is a much pleasanter affair than with Hitler. You feel that you are dealing with a reasonable man, not a fanatic, and he struck us both as straightforward and sincere in what he said. Moreover he has a sense of humour which occasionally breaks out in an attractive smile, whereas it would take a long surgical operation to get a joke into Hitler's head.'[14] To be fair to Chamberlain, many other British politicians, including Churchill and Duff Cooper, had been impressed by Mussolini. In his reply the King noted that 'nothing concrete has come out of it [the visit] in the way of pacts, etc.', but that 'I am sure that your visit has done good in the way of personal contact with Mussolini & [Galeazzo] Ciano'.[15] When Chamberlain's strategy crashed in ruins in March 1939, closely followed by the 'Pact of Steel' between Germany and Italy, the King was sympathetic to Chamberlain's 'feelings about the recent behaviour of the German government' and appreciated his 'deep distress', but maintained that his 'labours have been anything but wasted, for they can have left no doubt

[13] This fatal deficiency was realised by the pilots themselves in France after the war had begun, and they bought rear-view car mirrors and attached them to their windscreens.
[14] RA PS GVI C 047/14.
[15] RA PS GVI C 047/19.

in the minds of ordinary people all over the world of our love of peace & of our readiness to discuss with any nation whatever grievances they may think they have'.[16] He was now convinced that war was unavoidable. His private secretaries and the Queen knew this, and agreed with him.

It has been a characteristic of modern Prime Ministers to become obsessed with the press – Attlee being a spectacular exception – but Chamberlain's methods were unique in their scope and ruthless cynicism. James Margach, a veteran parliamentary and political correspondent, called him 'the most authoritarian, intolerant and arrogant of all the premiers I have known',[17] and has described his methods to ensure that his case got favourable attention. Later revelations demonstrate that, if anything, Margach understated his exposure to Chamberlain's deliberate, and largely successful, manipulation of the newspapers and their readers, most notably *The Times*.[18]

A particularly notorious example of this occurred on 9 March 1939, when Chamberlain informed a group of lobby correspondents that the international situation had seldom looked better. He was working actively to halt the arms race; his relations with Herr Hitler were most cordial; the Spanish situation was about to be resolved, which would gratify Signor Mussolini; and he was working on the creation of better relations between France and Italy.

This was the line meekly followed by the bulk of the newspapers, to consternation in the Foreign Office and much surprise at Buckingham Palace. The King instructed Hardinge to discover the source of this rosy view of the grim European situation. Halifax, equally amazed, did the same. The true author, not the Foreign Office but Chamberlain himself, was then revealed. The Foreign Secretary had not even been told that the Prime Minister was meeting the lobby, let alone what he intended to say. Halifax wrote a letter of protest; Chamberlain apologised and promised never to do it again, yet within weeks was assuring the lobby they could promise their readers that there would be no more shocks or surprises from the dictators. Within twenty-four hours Mussolini had invaded Albania.

[16] RA PS GVI C 047/15.
[17] Margach, *The Abuse of Power*, p. 51.
[18] See Cockett, *The Twilight of Truth*.

The 9 March briefing had been followed by the German occupation of the rest of Czechoslovakia on the night of 14–15 March, and even the most docile and supportive newspaper editors – with the exception of Dawson of *The Times* – were becoming uneasy about looking ridiculous when their roseate claims were so swiftly overtaken by another example of the dictators' ruthlessness.

Margach has described the sequel:

A few of us therefore had a private lunch with Chamberlain during which the point was firmly made that editors were becoming sceptical of our sources, Prime Ministerial or not. Chamberlain pronounced himself astounded that journalists should be so short-sighted as to take such a self-centred view of their national responsibilities. Did we not realise how Herr Hitler and Signor Mussolini objected to the constant attacks upon them in the British press? He had reason to believe, he added plaintively, that Herr Hitler and Signor Mussolini appreciated his efforts to improve the atmosphere and to correct the mischievous criticisms in the British newspapers – all too often, he feared, inspired by Communist sympathisers in Britain in order to frustrate his efforts to find peace. Didn't we realise, too, that the real threat to European civilisation came from Russian communism? If only we could be patient and help him in his endeavours, he was confident that Herr Hitler and Signor Mussolini would reach agreement with him to satisfy their demands and ambitions.[19]

The King's forebodings, fully shared and articulated by Hardinge, remorselessly increased. But it is difficult for a monarch to tell a Prime Minister he does not believe him. The King, although deeply worried, did not possess the necessary self-confidence, and the private Chamberlain he saw – described by the hostile Margach as being, before he became Prime Minister, 'the most shy, kindly, generous-minded and warm-hearted of men, always friendly and understanding although by nature cold, indrawn, and lonely'[20] – was very different from the public

[19] Margach, op. cit., p. 59.
[20] Ibid.

one. The King saw his duty as a constitutional monarch to assist his Prime Minister, not to make his life more difficult, but his doubts about his judgement had increased further. And although most of the British press still slavishly followed the Chamberlain line, there were exceptions, notably the *Daily Telegraph*, the *Daily Mirror*, and the *Yorkshire Post*, which were increasingly giving publicity to the sombre warnings of Churchill and his Conservative allies. And the facts spoke for themselves.

On 18 March Hardinge submitted a memorandum to the King:

Talk with Sir A. Cadogan.

1. The optimistic announcement which was issued from official quarters during the weekend of March 11th emanated from 10 Downing Street without the knowledge of the Foreign Secretary or the Foreign Office. Lord Halifax has sent a protest to the PM who had expressed profound regret. It is presumed that Horace Wilson was responsible for it. *Later:* It was the PM himself.

AC was not at all pleased with the PM's speech in the House of Commons. It was supposed to be based on the statement which the FO had prepared before the necessity for a debate arose, but No. 10 put in the statement the PM was determined to pursue his policy which entirely spoilt the effect of the speech.

The member of the German Embassy to whose activities we have taken exception is the Commercial Counsellor, Weber, who carries on propaganda against us among the press. I hear that a number of German correspondents are likely to be expelled from London shortly – a fate which also awaits the *News Chronicle* correspondent in Berlin.[21]

It appeared at first that appeasement had been abandoned. Chamberlain had unexpectedly denounced Hitler in a speech in Birmingham on 17 March, and two weeks later announced a British guarantee to Poland. Despite his burst of chagrined belligerency, he still believed that war could be averted. The King and Queen did not. The public and press approval – with the interesting exception of the *Daily Express* – reflected the changed mood, but the guarantee made little sense unless it

[21] RA Hardinge Papers.

was in concert with the Russians. But dealing with the Communists was abhorrent to Chamberlain, and the British negotiating team proceeded dilatorily and unenthusiastically to Moscow.

On 27 March Hardinge reported to the King:

I saw Anthony Eden tonight, and found him very perturbed about the situation both at home and abroad. It is very doubtful if the countries with whom we are trying to make an alliance to resist further aggression will have sufficient confidence in the determination of our government, as at present constituted, to justify the risk which is inevitably attached to their coming out into the open on our side. He has had a message from Col. Beck saying that he wants to have a long talk with him during his visit next week, and he does not doubt that this is the aspect of the matter which he wishes to discuss.

From the 'Home' point of view he is convinced that the government will not be able to hold the country unless they give some sign of action, of which there has been none since the plunder of Czechoslovakia ten days ago. His mailbag has risen to the heights that it reached at the time of his resignation and afterwards of Munich. The ovation given to Winston Churchill at the Guildhall last Wednesday was most significant, and I myself heard the reception given to Eden by the crowd when he left the opera the same night. He also tells me that in his constituency he has received, during last week, regular ovations in the districts where he usually gets booed, and that even the docile supporters of the government in the House of Commons are becoming extremely restive. He does not believe that it would be impossible to agree on a home policy with the Opposition, as well as the foreign policy of which they now approve and he thinks that it would be quite feasible to form a government of all Parties on a policy of 'conscription of industry, wealth and manpower' but whether they would take office under Mr Chamberlain of course he does not know. He is very anxious for Winston to be brought in anyhow. He quite appreciates that it is difficult for the Government to make an immediate declaration of their new foreign policy, but he thinks that if they do not take any immediate action inside the country that there may be serious trouble.

I cannot help personally having doubts whether a Government

which includes Simons and Hoares can pursue the new foreign policy with sufficient resolution, for which the inclusion of people like Winston and Eden would be a guarantee before the whole world.[22]

Although the King's relations with Hardinge were formal rather than close, and tensions continued to exist between them, the King, fortified by Halifax's increasing forebodings, took his Secretary's opinions on the domestic and international situations much more seriously than before. But he was still doubtful about Churchill, and had found Eden a difficult man to talk to, and even more difficult to understand. He could not forget that, as Foreign Secretary, Eden had always seemed 'to speak from a brief' rather than openly and informally, and the Queen, although recognising Eden's charm and cultured intelligence, had her doubts about his strength of character – doubts which were to be enduring. The King came to change his opinion of Eden, and of Churchill, but in the case of the former there always remained an element of doubt. Nonetheless, as the grim year of 1939 opened, and while he firmly maintained the constitutional proprieties of loyalty to his Prime Minister, the King was moving rapidly in the direction of the Churchill–Eden view of the international situation.

These were given a substantial boost by an unplanned and unexpected development in the summer of 1939 that was to be the King's most important political experience to date.

The King was anxious to visit as many of his dominions as possible, particularly India, Canada, Australia, New Zealand and South Africa, and in the aftermath of the Coronation and the state visit to France he had given much thought to this, and discussed his plans with Chamberlain. The fundamental problem was the menacing situation in Europe, even after the temporary euphoria of Munich. But a visit to Canada was a real possibility, and Mackenzie King was eager that one should be made as soon as was reasonably possible. There were some dangers in this, as the King fully realised. The Duke of Windsor, as Prince of Wales, had been captivated by the beauty and spaciousness of the western prairies of Alberta, and had bought the Bedingfeld Ranch, near Pekisko, in 1922. He had also captivated the

[22] RA Hardinge Papers.

Canadians, and his popularity there was even greater than in Australia. The contrast with the ebullient Prince Charming could well cause problems, as the King and his advisers appreciated. But he decided to accept Mackenzie King's invitation, and the visit was scheduled for May 1939.

President Roosevelt was told of these plans by King during a visit to Canada in August 1938, and then devised one of his own, writing to King George from the White House on 17 September:

My dear King George,

When I was in Canada a few weeks ago, Prime Minister Mackenzie King told me, in confidence, that there is a possibility that you and Her Majesty will visit the Dominion of Canada in the Summer of 1939.

If this visit should become a reality, I hope very much that you will extend your visit to include the United States. I need not assure you that it would give my wife and me the greatest pleasure to see you, and, frankly, I think it would be an excellent thing for Anglo-American relations if you could visit the United States.

If you should be here in June or July you might like to avoid the heat of Washington, and in such a case it would give us the greatest pleasure to have you and Her Majesty come to visit us at our country home at Hyde Park, which is on the Hudson River, about eighty miles north of New York and therefore, on the direct route between New York City and Canada. Also, it occurs to me that the Canadian trip would be crowded with formalities and that you both might like three or four days of very simple country life at Hyde Park – with no formal entertainments and an opportunity to get a bit of rest and relaxation.

In case you would care to come to Washington, however, and to see the Capital, you would, of course, stay with us at the White House. This would of necessity be somewhat more formal and, in the event of the Congress being still in session, there would be great pressure for you to be received by the Congress.

You and I are fully aware of the demands of the Protocol people, but, having had much experience with them, I am inclined to think that you and Her Majesty should do very much as you personally want to do — and I will see to it over here that your decision becomes the right decision.

I have had, as you know, the great privilege of knowing your splendid Father, and I have also known two of your brothers. Therefore, I am greatly looking forward to the possibility of meeting you and the Queen.

There is, of course, no hurry about plans for next year, but I want you to know how sincerely welcome you would be if you could arrange to come to the United States.

I am asking Mr Kennedy to give you this, but I think that we can keep any talk of your visit out of diplomatic channels for the time being. Your Ambassador, Ronald Lindsay, is a very old and close personal friend of mine.

I forgot to mention that if you bring either or both of the children with you, they will also be very welcome, and I shall try to have one or two Roosevelts of approximately the same age to play with them!

With my sincere regards,
Faithfully yours,
Franklin D. Roosevelt[23]

The King consulted Lascelles, who contacted Halifax; the advice of the British Ambassador in Washington, Sir Ronald Lindsay, was also sought. He cabled the Foreign Office on 10 October: 'General tone is already in the sense that such a visit will be made and it is my view that in the absence of any unforeseen obstacles it would be highly advisable. Of course a welcome of the utmost cordiality could be counted on.'[24]

Meanwhile, the King had written to Roosevelt, in his own hand, from Balmoral on 8 October:

My dear President Roosevelt,
    Your letter which Mr Kennedy handed to me last week, came

[23] RA PS GVI PS 03400/003/01/001. Only part of this remarkable letter was published in Wheeler-Bennett, op. cit., p. 372. Roosevelt had met King George V only once, and briefly, in 1919. The claim to 'Knowing your splendid Father' was vintage Roosevelt.
[24] RA PS GVI PS 03400/003/01/005.

as a pleasant relief at a time of great anxiety, and I thank you warmly for it.

The Queen and I appreciate most sincerely your kind invitation to visit Mrs Roosevelt and you in the United States in the event of our going to Canada next summer. I can assure you that the pleasure which it would in any case give to us personally, would be greatly enhanced by the thought that it was contributing in any way to the cordiality of the relations between our two countries.

I hope that it will not be inconvenient if I delay my answer until the plans for Canada are further advanced, and I am in a position to judge how long it will be possible for me to be absent from this country. I will then communicate with you again.

Although the plans you make for the visit sound very attractive I am afraid that we shall not be taking the children with us to Canada as they are much too young for such a strenuous tour.

Before I end this letter, I must say how much I welcomed your interventions in the recent crisis. I have little doubt that they contributed largely to the preservation of peace.

With all good wishes and many thanks for your kind invitation.

Believe me, yours very sincerely,

George R.I.[25]

Already there were misunderstandings. Roosevelt had not contemplated an official state visit by the royal couple but three days as his private guests at Hyde Park. As always with Roosevelt, his motives were complex, and had a political content.

His own popularity was not high at this point, and his relations with his Republican critics in Congress and parts of the press were acerbic to the point of savagery. Isolationism was a major political factor, and many Americans had sympathised with the former King during and after the events of December 1936. But Roosevelt had noticed a shift of opinion both in Britain and the United States about his successor, and the impact of their visit to Paris had not escaped him. And there was the kudos of entertaining the King and Queen of Great Britain in his own home. He did not lack vanity, as well as guile.

[25] Roosevelt Papers.

But Lindsay was thinking of a visit to Washington 'as the principal part of the plan', to Roosevelt's intense annoyance, whose plan was for the Hyde Park visit to be the highlight – at that point the only highlight – of the trip. But now Lindsay was mentioning New York and Chicago in addition to Washington.

It was with some reluctance that the President agreed, writing to the King on 2 November:

> I know that you will not mind my telling you that in my judgement, to the American people, the essential democracy of yourself and the Queen makes the greatest appeal of all. Probably the official visit to the Capital should be made, and also a visit to New York, but if you could stay with us at Hyde Park for two or three days, the simplicity and naturalness of such a visit would produce a most excellent effect – in addition to giving my wife and me the greatest possible pleasure in getting to know you both . . .[26]

The King immediately accepted his invitation, and it was announced in his speech at the opening of parliament on 8 November, it being emphasised, with Mackenzie King's notorious prickliness and Canadian susceptibilities much in mind, that it would take place 'after the conclusion of my Canadian tour', the King adding that 'I warmly welcome this practical expression of the good feeling that prevails between our countries'.

There seemed little evidence to confirm this opinion. Chamberlain's attitude towards the United States bordered upon contempt; the only American he regarded highly was the ambassador in London, the egregious Joseph P. Kennedy, who had all the prejudices of the Irish–American Bostonian and was a slavish advocate of appeasement; Roosevelt himself had strong anti-imperial sentiments, and other Americans had even stronger ones. The era of mass travel between the two countries had not yet dawned, and the ignorance of each about the other was almost total. The United States was a negligible military and economic power, her only visible exports to Britain being tobacco, music and films – the latter giving a somewhat distorted

---

[26] RA PS GVI PS 03400/003/01/015.

picture of a nation only slowly recovering from the Depression and with its self-confidence only partially restored. Even after the New Deal programmes, there was much poverty and unemployment.

But, for reasons that are somewhat difficult to explain, the King had not inherited the anti-American bias of his father, nor did he share that of Chamberlain. His personal enthusiasm for the American adjunct to his Canadian visit was genuine, as was Roosevelt's. If neither had anticipated that it would develop into a full-blown state visit, they accepted the fact. But, for both, the Hyde Park visit was the most important. And so it proved to be.

And then Roosevelt apparently failed to send an official invitation, and there was consternation in London when nothing had been received by the beginning of February 1939. Hardinge urgently enquired of Lindsay what was happening, and received the somewhat laconic reply, 'I can't help fearing that the President, who is something of an impish schoolboy, has forgotten all about it.'[27] In fact the President's letter had been written on 18 January, and, with a dilatoriness remarkable even in those more leisurely days, arrived somewhat languidly in London on 5 February. This casualness was a foretaste of the visit itself.

Lindsay had already met the King and Queen, and had, rather to his surprise, been impressed by them, writing to his wife that 'the King is lithe, brown, and walks like a mountaineer, the very picture of health. He talks a great deal and you would never think he could be tongue-tied before a crowd except for an occasional and momentary check noticeable to anyone on the look-out for a stammer. He talks quite well and vigorously.'[28]

The original plan had been for the King and Queen to travel to Canada on HMS *Repulse*, but because of the European situation the Admiralty was concerned that such a valuable warship should be out of British waters at a time of crisis, an opinion in which the King entirely concurred.

The royal couple, accompanied by Lascelles, sailed from Southampton on 5 May on the liner *Empress of Australia*, not at all sure about their reception on the other side of the Atlantic. The King would be the first British monarch ever to visit the United States, and there were

[27] RA PS GVI PS 03400/003/001/038.
[28] Bradford, *King George VI*, p. 344.

unpleasantly critical articles already appearing in the American press in which he and the Queen were being unfavourably compared to his elder brother, who broadcast an appeal for world peace from the battlefields of Verdun, addressed to the American people, while the King and Queen were at sea on their way to Canada. This was considered by the royal party as quite deliberate and malicious, and the Duke's subsequent explanations totally lacked conviction. They also knew, through a letter from the Duke to Queen Mary, that he considered the King as being 'under the influence of that common little woman', his wife.

Queen Elizabeth has often been accused of conducting a vendetta against the Duchess of Windsor; all the evidence is that the Duchess was not only the instigator of the harsh estrangement but fuelled the Duke's increasingly intemperate language about his sister-in-law, which enraged the King even more than his brother's constant imperious demands for money and his ill-judged forays into international politics.

The crossing of the *Empress of Australia* was further marred by thick fog as the ship approached the Newfoundland coast, and the liner had to negotiate an ice-field alarmingly close to the place where the *Titanic* had foundered. As the Queen noted in a lively letter to Queen Mary, the ship's Captain 'was nearly demented because some kind cheerful people kept reminding him' of the fact. The ship hardly moved for three and a half days, enshrouded by fog and surrounded by icebergs; the King and Lascelles reflected that although it was a strange way to have three days' holiday, the rest was very welcome. They did not reach Wolfe's Cove, Quebec, until 17 May.

After this inauspicious beginning the initial reception was politely cool, but then the atmosphere dramatically improved, to the surprise not only of the hosts and the Governor-General, Lord Tweedsmuir, but of the royal couple themselves. A gathering of ex-servicemen in Ottawa, during which, at the suggestion of the Queen, they went down spontaneously to speak to the veterans, was a particular triumph. Tweedsmuir was a notorious arch-flatterer, but when he wrote in a letter after the visit that 'I have always been attached to the King, and I realise now more than ever what a wonderful mixture he is of shrewdness, kindliness and humour. As for the Queen, she has a perfect genius for the right kind of publicity,' these praises were echoed by others, and, most significantly, by the critical American press.

Indeed, the great success of the Canadian part of the tour was threatened only by the presence of Mackenzie King himself, who caused some difficulties.

A bachelor, King was a hyper-sensitive political veteran who considered – with some justification – that he had been ill-treated by Governor-General Byng in 1926, when he refused him a dissolution of parliament only to promptly grant one to the Conservative leader, Meighen. King was a Gladstonian Liberal with a horror of war and any possibility of Canada being involved in a European conflict ever again. He was also markedly inconsistent. He was a monarchist, not only loyal to the Crown but sometimes almost mawkishly sentimental about his royal friendships and connections. He was strongly opposed to Canadians receiving British honours, and refused to make any recommendations on principle, although this stand did not inhibit him from accepting the Order of Merit from George VI and numerous other foreign decorations and honours. He had agonised over the abdication, but so had many Canadians, torn between their anti-Americanism, their almost Victorian attitudes towards divorce, their distrust of Beaverbrook, and strong feelings of affection towards Edward VIII.

Tweedsmuir played King brilliantly, flattering his very considerable ego and understanding his corresponding insecurity and vanity, while lamenting to the King in a private letter on 16 March 1939 that 'the crying need for Canada is for some national leader who would really guide the thought and touch the imagination of the whole country . . . the lack of such a figure explains the incomplete integration of the country and the danger of provincial sentiment being stronger than national . . . But great personalities are the gift of Providence, they cannot be manufactured.'[29] King, for his part, was jealous of Tweedsmuir's popularity, and the Governor-General, although he played a considerable part in preparing the King's speeches on the Canadian leg of the tour, wisely kept a low profile. Mackenzie King did not, travelling on the royal train and leaping out first at every station to greet the King and Queen formally on their arrival at their latest destination, with all the attendant publicity. If he was surprised by the remarkable warmth and enthusiasm of the large crowds that greeted and cheered the royal visitors, he did not neglect to capitalise on it.

[29] Janet Adam Smith, *John Buchan*, p. 421.

This regular ritual caused the royal couple considerable private hilarity, which they valiantly suppressed in public. Well-briefed by Tweedsmuir and Lascelles – who had done a preliminary reconnaissance in February – they understood Mackenzie King well and treated him with immense respect and warmth. This was to pay handsome dividends in September 1939.

The Canadian tour was a very considerable personal and political success, for the monarchy and British interests as well as for Mackenzie King. As the King wrote to Tweedsmuir on his return to Britain, 'Our tour has done *me* untold good in every way.'

The American leg posed even greater difficulties, not least because Mackenzie King insisted on taking part in it, incensed at the possibility that his role would end at the Canadian–American border. He also ensured that the royal party travelled to Washington in Canadian Pacific Railway carriages (a perfectly acceptable change, since they were actually superior to the American ones).

The King had prepared himself very carefully for the American visit, and the Foreign Office had briefed him exceptionally well. A lengthy document of thirty-four pages had been prepared by F. R. Hoyer Millar, based on information supplied by the Washington Embassy, and which described the American political scene with remarkable detail and insight. With some courage it stated that, after Munich, there were American fears that 'we may rat again', but the King had long passed his brief Munich period, and took the point.

The professionalism of the King and Queen was demonstrated by their ability to recognise and converse with Congressmen, who were naturally flattered by their knowledge of them and their constituencies and achievements. The King and Queen, and Lascelles, had been nervous about their reception in Canada, but were considerably more apprehensive about that in the United States. But the tiring official part of the American visit in Washington and New York, conducted in broiling heat, went far better than anyone had expected, and the Roosevelts, and others, were particularly impressed by the King's careful preparation and knowledge. The reception they received in New York was tumultuously enthusiastic, although by this stage both were showing signs of exhaustion, and Lascelles, who had been knighted by the King on American soil – another novelty – had found the New York visit, particularly that to the World's Fair on Flushing Island on 12 June, almost unendurable. But the crowds both in Washington and New York had been astonishingly large, the press coverage almost uniformly positive, and if the royal couple reached Hyde Park hours late and somewhat wearily limp, they did so after a tour which had been a personal triumph.

They had also received tributes from Eleanor Roosevelt, someone not much given to hailing visiting dignitaries. Somewhat waspishly she preferred the King to the Queen, as 'I think he feels things more than she does & knows more. She is perfect as a Queen, gracious, informed, saying the right thing & kind but a little self-consciously regal.' She perhaps did not know that the Queen, learning that the President's closest aide at that time, Harry Hopkins, had a young daughter who longed to meet a real 'Fairy Queen', had seen the little girl specially in all her regal finery before dinner at the British Embassy, with political consequences that no one could have possibly envisaged, least of all the Queen. Those who have adjudged, with justification, that the Queen was not all sweetness and light, have often underestimated her innate kindness and warmth, which had so entranced her husband and which was so unfeignedly natural.

Roosevelt greeted his guests at his country home with a tray of cocktails. 'My mother,' he said, 'thinks you should have a cup of tea; she doesn't approve of cocktails.' 'Neither does mine,' the King replied, taking one.

Hyde Park is, like so many American grand houses, startlingly small by European standards. The bedroom provided for the King and Queen would be considered very small in even a modest English country house, and was suffocatingly hot and humid. This was to be one of the Queen's most vivid memories of a period the King considered perhaps the most important during the initial period of his reign.

After dinner that evening the ladies retired – although, in the case of the Queen, not to sleep in her sweltering bedroom – and the King, the President and Mackenzie King, fortified by whisky and cigarettes, discussed the menacing international situation. It was a discussion the King never forgot.

He found that the President and Mackenzie King now accepted the virtual inevitability of war, and Roosevelt had a number of ideas about what the role of the United States might be, which made a deep impression upon the King. But what struck him even more was that Roosevelt spoke to him so frankly, easily and intimately. Afterwards, the King said to Mackenzie King, 'Why don't my ministers talk to me as the President did tonight?'

The King's official biographer states that at 1.30 in the morning, after a very long and tumultuous day, the President said to the King, 'Young man, it's time for you to go to bed.' The recollection of the Queen is that it was considerably later, but the King had had a further talk with Mackenzie King before joining her.

On the following day – a Sunday – the King and the President had another long conversation, in which Mackenzie King, to his considerable anger, was not invited to participate. When the royal party left by train to return to Canada the King had much to reflect upon, and which he recorded at length to be communicated to his ministers.

Although his notes have been quoted at length by Wheeler-Bennett they deserve to be recorded again, as his role has been somewhat derided by some commentators and was far more important than has been recognised. The King wrote, on White House notepaper:

Notes re: President.

A really go-ahead man. Insists on getting things done. Full of ideas of the right kind. Right man in right place at the moment.

New Deal assistants all know their job, & personally chosen by FDR. Have done in 6 years what we have been doing in Social Services for 25 years. Results just showing. Out of 10 billion dollars lent 8 billion have been repaid. This sum rotates for new schemes. 450,000 boys a year go through CCC camps. All happy & well-fed. All volunteers work in camp. Boys come from families on relief.

FDR very frank with me. Hopes Neutrality Act will be altered. So does Hull, Garner & others.

Suggests US Navy shld patrol W. Indies on outbreak of War & so relieve our Fleet of responsibility. Same on W. Coast, Canada from Japan.

Anxious USA & us shld cooperate in Antarctic. Coal there, probably oil as well.

[FDR's ideas in case of War:]

Trinidad Patrol

Base for his fleet at Trinidad to fuel & replenish stores. From this base he can patrol the Atlantic with ships & aeroplanes on a radius of approximately 1,000 miles on a sector of latitude of Haiti to latitude of Brazil. This patrol should locate any enemy fleet which tried to get to S. Am. or the West Indies. *Bermuda Patrol* Base as above. To patrol N. Atlantic from Cape Cod to Florida, with ships & aeroplanes to prevent submarines from attacking convoys.

Brazil

Germans have an air base at Natal Cape St Roque, also a landing ground of the island of Fernando Noronha, 200 miles from the coast. Brazil is pretty sure to kick out the Germans. He would then use it himself.

Haiti, Cuba & West Indies are potential friendly bases.

The idea is that USA should relieve us of these reponsibilities, but can it be done without a declaration of war.

Debts

Better not re-open the question. Congress wants repayment in full, which is impossible, & a small bit is of no use, as they will want more later.

Credits

USA will want nickel from Canada. They will buy our surplus rubber. In return they can send steel sheets which can be cut for aeroplane wings. Rough castings with bored cylinders to be machined at home. Can be used for aeroplanes or motor-boats.

Notes on USA

FDR. Charming personality. Very frank person. Easy to get to know, & never makes one feel shy. As good a listener as a talker. Through New Deal realises Govt. must take a hand in putting country right after 1929 crash. . . .

The old order has been superseded, & the Govt. will in future have to run the country.

There was another note by the King in his own handwriting, again with no reference, and again undated. 'I had two good conversations with the President besides many opportunities for informal talks on current matters in the car driving with him. He was very frank &

friendly & seemed genuinely glad that I had been able to pay him this visit. He gave me all the information in these notes either in answer to my questions or he volunteered it.'

The King then described a meeting with the President at which Mackenzie King *was* present, in which Roosevelt described how he was persuading the farmers in the west to abandon their isolationism.

I was alone with him for the 2nd conversation. We discussed Europe in a general way. He hoped France & Italy would try & get together.

He was doing his best to get New York to loan money to Roumania. I told him how difficult it was for us to help the Balkans as there was the Mediterranean to convoy things through & they would want all they had got in a war. I explained to him Roumania's position as to frontiers having 4 to cope with. Because of the air we were only just becoming frontier-conscious ourselves. In the whole of N. America he has none. He was definitely anti-Russian. I told him so were we but if we could not have an understanding with her Germany probably would make one.

He showed me his naval patrols in greater detail, about which he is terribly keen. If he saw a U-boat he would sink her at once & wait for the consequences.

If London was bombed USA would come in. Offensive air warfare was better than defensive & he hoped we should do the same on Berlin.[30]

In the follow-up discussions between Roosevelt and Lindsay in Washington on 30 June, the former said, 'In case of war in which the United States government would be neutral, it would be his desire that the United States government should establish a patrol over the waters of the western Atlantic with a view to denying them to warlike operations of belligerents. This purpose will be publicly declared on the outbreak of war . . .' Roosevelt then said that it would be necessary to have American naval bases in Trinidad, Santa Lucia, Bermuda and Halifax.[31]

Lindsay was informed on 6 July that 'His Majesty's Government gladly

[30] RA GVI Conf. (misc.).
[31] RA PS GVI C 139/02.

accept their proposal', but by the 8th Lindsay reported that Roosevelt was retreating, citing American public opinion, and that

> the suggested patrol has receded in point of time. Instead of coming into existence on the outbreak of war, it is postponed until action by an Axis Power furnishes pretext . . . But this postponement is hardly a surprise to me. In discussion with my staff we had all been aghast at the light-hearted manner in which the President was proposing to defy all conceptions of neutrality at the very outset of a war . . . Upshot is that from military point of view His Majesty's Government cannot expect that important help at the outset of war which plan in its first form seemed to promise.
>
> But from the political point of view the project is now in a far more healthy shape. Danger that the President may get ahead of his public opinion is greatly diminished . . .[32]

This was deeply disappointing, but Lindsay had more experience than the King had of Roosevelt's habit of expansive offers and promises in genial conversation, followed by qualifications, in which the phrase 'public opinion' occurred only too often. He was prepared to ask for the bases, but not to commit the United States to the patrol unless 'as a result of some event which would have the requisite effect on public opinion here . . . [such as] belligerent action against commerce by an Italian submarine or by a German raider in waters sufficiently near to the American continent'.[33]

These excuses were to happen – and made to happen – but not for a long time. But the crucial fact was that Roosevelt was now moving, if rather too slowly and cautiously for the British, in the right direction.

Just as important as these meetings was the significant effect they and the tour in general had had upon the King. As Wheeler-Bennett later wrote, with truth, 'Henceforth [he] was determined to trust to his own judgement and to size up men for himself. With reluctance and uncertainty he had gone forth, to return in buoyant confidence.'[34]

[32] RA PS GVI C 139/05, 06.
[33] RA PS GVI C 139/05.
[34] Wheeler-Bennett, op. cit., p. 393.

Lindsay put the results of the visit soberly. 'While we cannot at present feel certain of receiving an immediate [political] dividend, we can be assured that our hidden reserves have been immensely strengthened.'[35]

Justifiably exhilarated, the King and Queen had sailed back to Britain to another ecstatic reception in London. On 23 June the King had spoken in the Guildhall with a new authority and eloquence that surprised his distinguished audience. 'It was very interesting to watch the effect of his words on such hardened experts as Winston Churchill, Baldwin & the Archbishop of Canterbury,' Lascelles reported to Mackenzie King. 'It was patent that each of them & indeed everybody else in that historic place was deeply moved.'

By this time, however, the war-clouds were gathering and darkening.

The King, following Halifax's public and private declarations that Hitler must realise that there would be no more Munichs, suggested that his cousin Prince Philip of Hesse, who had been the personal liaison officer between Hitler and Mussolini, might be an appropriate conduit for a similar message of warning. It was a perfectly sensible proposal, but was turned down by Chamberlain and Halifax. Significantly, Hardinge knew nothing about it.

The last few weeks of peace saw the first meeting between Princess Elizabeth and Prince Philip of Greece on a royal trip to Dartmouth – the King's first visit since he had left the College – and the last of the boys' camps, held in the grounds of Abergeldie Castle, and which closed with the traditional bonfire with the Balmoral pipers playing as they circled the Royal Family. A sense of ending was palpable. On 22 August what feeble hopes that the autumn might pass without an international crisis vanished when the Soviet–German non-aggression pact was announced. The King returned to London at once from Balmoral.

[35] RA PS GVI PS 03400/003/01/054.

7

FROM CHAMBERLAIN TO CHURCHILL

T he Cabinet met urgently after 22 August to decide that the Polish Guarantee must be publicly and firmly adhered to and parliament recalled. Characteristically of Chamberlain, the announcement was made before the King was told. Recognising that the Japanese would be astounded by the abandonment of the 1936 Anti-Comintern Pact, he suggested that he should send a personal message to Emperor Hirohito; Halifax advised against it, fearing the possibility of a humiliating rebuff. Then the King suggested to Chamberlain that he should send a direct appeal to Hitler on the lines he had proposed in September 1938, as 'one ex-serviceman to another', but Chamberlain replied, rather bafflingly, that it would be wiser 'to await a more suitable moment'. By this stage the King himself had little faith in an appeal to Hitler, but was under considerable pressure from national leaders, including Roosevelt, to do so. The 'more suitable moment' rapidly passed.

On 1 September the Germans invaded Poland. The King, the House of Commons and the nation expected an immediate declaration of war. It did not happen. On the next day in the House of Commons there was a virtual all-party mutiny over the government's inaction and widespread fears of 'another Munich'.

Hardinge subsequently wrote, on 13 November 1940, his account of the events of 2 September, based on his notes of the time:

I was dining that night with Walter Monckton and happened to meet some Members of Parliament, including Major Nathan and one or two of the government whips. Having heard from them of the deplorable incidents in the House as a result of the Prime Minister's statement, I went to No. 10 immediately after dinner. There I found Simon and Anderson, who had been sent as a deputation from almost the entire Cabinet, assembled in the former's room at the House, to ascertain how it was that the Prime Minister's statement had been at complete variance with what had been agreed at the afternoon Cabinet meeting. They were told what had happened, but they made it quite clear that the Cabinet could not accept this indefinite postponement of the ultimatum, and in fact if it was adhered to the government were bound to be beaten in the House of Commons. A plan was therefore drawn up for submission to the whole Cabinet, which was hastily summoned at 11.30 p.m. I came back to Buckingham Palace to report to the King, after which I returned to No. 10. I waited until the end of the Cabinet and learned that agreement had been reached on a plan for Henderson to be instructed to see Ribbentrop at 9 a.m. the next morning, Sunday, September 3rd, and to say that if no assurance (which had been asked for on September 1st) for the withdrawal of German troops from Poland and Danzig had been received by 11 a.m. we should consider ourselves at war with Germany. I went back and reported this to the King at Buckingham Palace after midnight.[1]

Britain went to war with Germany the following morning.

Chamberlain's new government brought Churchill back to the Admiralty and Eden into the Dominions' Office, but the latter not in the War Cabinet. No offer was made to the Labour and Liberal leaders. This was not the National Government that the King had wanted: his relations with Chamberlain remained as before. Those with Churchill and Eden began with reservations on both sides. 'I find he [Eden] does not give me confidence,' the King wrote in his diary on 11 September, and, on 9 October, 'Winston is difficult to talk to but in time I shall get the right technique I hope.'

The King had started to keep a daily diary at the beginning of September – 'groaningly', as the Queen later remarked – and continued with it until January 1947. In the first entry he wrote:

[1] RA Hardinge Papers.

At the outbreak of war at midnight of Aug 4th–5th 1914, I was a midshipman, keeping the middle watch on the bridge of H.M.S. *Collingwood* somewhere in the North Sea. I was 18 years of age.

In the Grand Fleet everyone was pleased that it had come at last. We had been trained in the belief that War between Germany & this country had to come one day, & when it did come we thought we were prepared for it. We were not prepared for what we found a modern war really was, & those of us who had been through the Great War never wanted another.

Today we are at War again, & I am no longer a midshipman in the Royal Navy . . .

That evening he broadcast to the nation and Empire, rightly described by Wheeler-Bennett as 'a declaration of simple faith in simple beliefs', and all the more effective for that.

The outbreak of war immediately created a constitutional dilemma in South Africa comparable to that which had faced Byng in Canada in 1926. The governments of Australia and New Zealand had declared war on Germany straight away, without reference to their parliaments. In Canada, Mackenzie King did put the issue to the Canadian parliament, which on 9 September passed the motion to declare war without a vote.

But the South African Cabinet was deeply divided, the Prime Minister James Hertzog strongly favouring neutrality and his deputy Jan Smuts advocating intervention. Smuts had a seven-to-five majority in the Cabinet, but Hertzog, believing he could have a majority in parliament, took the issue to the House of Assembly on 4 September. After a two-day debate of great heat and passion, fifty-seven Members voted for Hertzog's motion of neutrality and eighty for Smuts' amendment for a declaration of war against Germany, with the proviso that South African forces should not serve outside Africa.

Hertzog did not resign, but asked the Governor-General, Sir Patrick Duncan, for a dissolution of parliament. Duncan was the King's representative, occupying the same constitutional position in South Africa as the King in Britain. Although George V had urged Baldwin not to dissolve in 1923, no modern British monarch had actually refused a Prime Minister's request for a dissolution, and the unhappy Byng precedent, and its consequences, had made a deep impression upon Stamfordham and then Hardinge.

But Duncan was exceptionally well-experienced in South African affairs, having first served as Viscount Milner's Private Secretary and having held senior ministerial offices under both Smuts and Hertzog before being appointed Governor-General in 1937.

He refused Hertzog's request, on the grounds that the Prime Minister was in a minority in his own Cabinet and in the House of Assembly, and that Smuts was confident that he could form a government that would have the support of the House and Senate – as he quickly proved he could. The new government declared war on Germany on 6 September.

Duncan's bold actions caused considerable nervousness in London. The King's representative had in effect compelled one Prime Minister to resign, after his advice had been rejected, and appointed another. It was now virtually axiomatic among the King's advisers that the days for such actions by a British monarch had long gone, and there was real concern that Duncan might have put not only his personal position in jeopardy but the reputation and authority of the King himself. But there was also the realisation that the circumstances were so exceptional, and the prospect of a bitterly divisive General Election so alarming, that Duncan had acted as a politician rather than as a constitutionalist.

But the precedent was a worrying one; when it was followed – although the circumstances were different – by Governor-General Sir John Kerr in Australia in 1975, these apprehensions were confirmed. The feeling in South Africa that Duncan had acted as a patriotic Briton rather than an impartial South African was intense, and in January 1940 Hertzog joined with the Nationalist Party in an attempt to pass a motion calling for the end of the war, which was defeated by only twelve votes in the House, although considerably more easily in the Senate.

The result was that many South Africans remained opposed to their country's involvement in the war, and hostile to Britain – as British servicemen were to discover. The bitter folk memories of the Boer War remained too fresh and too vivid.

Poland was swiftly and brutally defeated by the German invaders from the west and the Russians from the east. But, with the exception of the war at sea, which began immediately with the torpedoing of the passenger ship *Athenia* by a U-boat that had disobeyed official German policy, the Western Front was quiescent, and the anticipated air attacks on London and other British cities did not materialise.

The outbreak of war transformed the King's life, and was to dominate it totally for six years. Rather to his relief the royal peacetime rituals were abandoned and most of his staff were called up for military service, but he was initially unsure of his role.

He recorded on 9 September:

I paid a visit to the Central War Room to hear of the latest news on all fronts. Not much to report. The US Ambassador Mr Kennedy came to tea. He looked & was worried over the international situation. He was very busy over the victims who were killed in the *Athenia* when she was sunk by the German U-boat last Monday.

He looked at the war very much from the financial & material viewpoint. He wondered why we did not let Hitler have SE Europe, as it was no good to us from a monetary standpoint. He did not seem to realise that this country was a part of Europe, that it was essential for us to act as policemen, & to uphold the rights of small nations & that the Balkan countries had a national spirit. However, I wrote him a letter pointing out these things & he answered it very friendly-like. I was surprised as I had never seen him rattled before.

This was not the first indication the King had had of Kennedy's defeatism and total incomprehension of what the war was about, which infuriated and exasperated him. He knew that Kennedy had been a fervent supporter of Chamberlain and appeasement and American non-involvement in a European war, but he had expected that the American ambassador might have some understanding of the new situation and be sympathetic to the Allied cause. The revelation that he had neither caused an explosion.

Although the King could, and often did, express himself strongly – even violently – in person, he was cautious about doing so on paper, either in his diaries or in letters. But the original letter he wrote to Kennedy after this meeting – described later by Lascelles as 'a stinker' – was shown to Chamberlain and Churchill, who advised a milder rebuke; even so, the softened-down version was exceptionally sharp.[2] The original, unfortunately, does not seem to have survived. The Foreign Office jibe that 'I always thought my daffodils were yellow until I met Joe Kennedy' was described by Halifax as 'unkind but deserved'.

Before this meeting the King and Queen had accepted an invitation from Lady Astor for a farewell lunch at Cliveden for Mrs Kennedy and her children, who were returning to the United States. The Astors, of course, had no knowledge of the King's views on Kennedy, and were puzzled that while he conversed happily with Lady Astor's daughter-in-law he virtually ignored the Kennedys, who had been deliberately placed at the end of the table, well away from the King. It was some time before the younger Astors discovered the reason for the King's coldness towards the American.

Although the King did not know this at the time, Churchill's evaluation of Kennedy had been exactly the same, and he had begun his famous direct correspondence with Roosevelt, a course also followed by the King.

The problem of the Duke of Windsor, another doubtful ally, had also to be addressed.

The Duke had been as enthusiastic as the King had been relieved over Munich; unlike his younger brother he had continued to regard war with Germany as inconceivable, and still considered the Soviet Union to be the real enemy. He firmly believed that the war could have been avoided, without explaining how, and lost few opportunities of pointing out that Britain was fighting the wrong enemy.

On the outbreak of war the King ordered a plane to fly to the South of France to collect the Windsors and bring them back to Britain. They declined, but then accepted the offer of a destroyer to pick them up at Cherbourg.

The problem of his brother's role – especially with his known political views – greatly troubled the King. On 14 September there was a meeting which the King later described as 'very unbrotherly', and recorded in his diary that day:

[2] *The Lyttelton–Hart-Davis Letters*, Vol. 6 (Hart-Davis to Lyttelton, 31 March 1962, describing a lunch with the Lascelles at which Clementine Churchill was present).

I saw David on our return [from Port of London]. I had not seen him since he left England on Dec 11th in 1936. We talked for about an hour. There were no recriminations on either side. I told him I was glad the business matter was amicably settled, & he agreed. I found him the same as I had always known him. He looked very well & had lost the deep lines under his eyes. He was very glad to be back in England, he told me he had already seen Winston Churchill this morning. I expected that he had, as he was very confident about himself & as to what he was going to do now that he was home. He seemed to be thinking only of himself & had quite forgotten what he had done to his country in 1936.

He was ready to take up the military appointment I had offered him with the rank of a Major-General, although he did not want to have to hand back his baton as a Field Marshal for good. He asked me now that he had returned, would I not give him back his Regiments as Col-in-Chief & re-appoint him as Colonel Welsh Guards. I told him that I doubted whether this was possible just now, as it was too early yet to form an opinion . . . He did not ask about his mother or any female member of the family. He wanted to know what Harry & George were doing. He was anxious to stay here about a month before going back to France & I told him that that would be difficult. After he left me I wrote to the PM the gist of my conversation as he was going to see him tomorrow.

On the following day, the 15th, he wrote:

Mama came to lunch. She was very interested in what I told her about David, but had no intention of seeing him if she could avoid it. I was able to reassure her on this point.

I saw the PM this morning. He thanked me for putting him wise as to the line of argument to go on. He told me he had definitely put him off going to Wales as to the matter of his & her reception there but had suggested that he might be attached to one of the Home Commands for the moment. I told the PM I did not like the idea at all, & that the sooner he went to France the better for all concerned. He is not wanted here . . .

The Duke went to France, where he created more difficulties by visiting troops, taking salutes, and giving the impression that he was still King with Field Marshal rank. When these activities were limited on orders from London he reacted violently, and demanded a meeting at which he could accuse his brother to his face of 'duplicity, cowardice, and even personal hatred'.[3] But the King insisted that General Edmund Ironside be present, so the meeting did not take place, which was perhaps just as well. Beaverbrook urged him to return to Britain to 'stump the country' to champion a peace offer to Germany; when Monckton pointed out that this could be construed as treasonable the idea lapsed, but the Duke's palpable pessimism about the war made him as exhilarating company as Ambassador Kennedy.

Since his accession, the King had obstinately refused to follow his father's precedent of a Christmas Day broadcast, partly because he could not envisage any comparable quality or effect, and partly because he loathed broadcasting. This had been a mistake, because the King's annual broadcast had become an institution at the end of the reign of George V, and the refusal to continue this novel tradition had not only been a disappointment but had revived the rumours about the King's health and capacities. But he was eventually persuaded that the first Christmas of the war made it essential that he should resume his father's tradition. He hated the idea, argued against it vehemently, but eventually agreed.

This was to be the first of many ordeals for himself, his family and advisers. The process of preparing a text for him was in itself something of a nightmare, and with so many hands and minds involved, and so many drafts prepared, it was a wonder that the final versions were so good.

This was largely due to Lascelles, who had a most remarkable capacity for recognising what was, and what was not, in the character of the speaker. He, Logue and the Queen could see at once difficult words and phrases and false notes in the drafts from ministers and other advisers. He hated the lengthy and tortuous process as much as the King did, but considered it so important that he devoted himself to producing a text with which the King was reasonably happy. This was not easy. The business put the King into a bad temper, and he was seldom satisfied until the end of it. Even then, he dreaded the actual delivery.

[3] Ziegler, op. cit., p. 412.

The 'Dual Monarchy':
Prince Albert and Queen Victoria.

William Ewart Gladstone.

Benjamin Disraeli.

Robert, 3rd Marquess of Salisbury.

The return to royal magnificence: King Edward VII and Queen Alexandra, February 1910.

The Duke of York, the future King George V, lights a cigarette.

The troublemakers: H. H. Asquith (left) and Andrew Bonar Law.

George V at work in June 1918, with Stamfordham in attendance.

David Lloyd George and George V at Moy Hall, Inverness, summer 1921,
separated by their host, the Mackintosh of Mackintosh.

The Queen, Princess Royal, the King and Ramsay MacDonald
at Kempton Park Races, 1934.

Stanley Baldwin.

Prince Albert, naval officer, 1917.

The Duke of York's engagement to
Lady Elizabeth Bowes-Lyon, January 1923.

David *G.R.I.* *Bertie*

July 6ᵗʰ 1935.

The three Kings: the Prince of Wales, King George V and the Duke of York
after the RAF Review, July 1935.

Alexander Hardinge (left) and Alan ('Tommy') Lascelles.

A mistake. The King and Queen with Mr and Mrs Neville Chamberlain
on the Buckingham Palace balcony after Munich, 30 September 1938.

En route to Canada and the United States, May 1939.

With the Roosevelts at Hyde Park, New York state, June 1939.
From left to right: Eleanor Roosevelt, the King, Mrs James D. Roosevelt (the President's mother), the Queen and the President.

A trust abused: the King and Chamberlain
in Downing Street, 1 September 1939.

'Bobbety' (Lord) Cranborne: fiery
anti-Chamberlainite and friend of the King.

Sumner Welles (left), President Roosevelt's envoy, with Lord Halifax, March 1940.

A very near miss at Buckingham Palace, 13 September 1940.
Inspecting the damage with Churchill.

'The partnership': the King and Churchill in their prime.

Entering Valletta Harbour, Malta, June 1943.

he King with members of the War Cabinet, 1944. From left to right: Lord Woolton, Sir John Anderson, Clement Attlee, the King, Winston Churchill, Anthony Eden and Ernest Bevin.

'A friend of Americans': the King in France,
summer 1944, with US Generals Bradley (left)
and Eisenhower (right).

Victory in Europe, 8 May 1945. The King, Queen, Churchill and Princesses Elizabeth
and Margaret on the precarious balcony of the windowless Buckingham Palace.

The King and Clement Attlee, 15 August 1945.

The fatal tour: the Queen, a strained King and the Princesses in South Africa, 1947.

The last photograph. The King, with the Queen and
Princess Margaret, waves goodbye to Princess Elizabeth and
the Duke of Edinburgh at London Airport on 31 January 1952.

In private there were few signs of his stammer, but the tension of a public occasion revived it. As the broadcast would be live, the King had to be carefully rehearsed. The result was not always satisfactory, and steps were subsequently taken to amend the recorded versions transmitted for world listeners.

His first Christmas broadcast was peculiarly difficult as, apart from the war at sea, which, with the exception of the destruction of the pocket battleship *Graf Spee*, had not gone well (despite Churchill's grandiose claims to the contrary), little seemed to have happened. The dreaded air-raids had not yet occurred; all was indeed quiet on the Western Front; and many of the children evacuated into the countryside from the great cities, especially from London, were drifting home again. Apart from the black-out, Christmas 1939 had an unreal, semi-peacetime atmosphere. An American journalist called it 'the phoney war', and so it seemed.

But there came inspiration in the form of a then-unknown poem written by Minnie Louise Haskins which had been privately published in 1908. It was the King's idea to incorporate it at the end of his broadcast, to immense effect:

A new year is at hand. We cannot tell what it will bring. If it brings peace, how thankful we shall all be. If it brings continued struggle we shall remain undaunted.

In the meantime, I feel that we may all find a message of encouragement in the lines which, in my closing words, I would like to say to you.

'I said to the man who stood at the Gate of the Year, "Give me a light that I may tread safely into the unknown." And he replied, "Go out into the darkness, and put your hand into the hand of God. That shall be to you better than light, and safer than a known way."'

May that Almighty hand guide and uphold us all.

As George V, Baldwin, Franklin Roosevelt, and, unhappily, Goebbels, had demonstrated, radio was the most potent method of mass communication ever invented, but relatively few people in public life appreciated that it required techniques quite different from public speaking. Neither Churchill, Lloyd George, MacDonald, Hitler, Goering nor Mussolini grasped the simple point, that it is an intensely personal and conversational medium. Roosevelt's mastery of the 'fireside chat' was the example that attracted the King – and quite rightly. There was also something palpably endearing about the pauses and occasional hesitations which so worried the King and his advisers. The nervousness of the speaker communicated itself to the listener, but not to his disadvantage.

The King never got over his dislike of broadcasting, and never overcame what Wheeler-Bennett has rightly called 'his deep-seated repugnance' to the microphone. The composition of his broadcasts was invariably a hateful experience for everyone involved, and deeply shadowed Christmas Day for the King and his family. But the impact of those broadcasts was extraordinary, and, in the context of the war, even greater than that of his father. The words were the result of many people's efforts, but the final version was very much the King's, and the voice was clearly that of a good and decent man in a world that seemed to have gone mad and evil. And, as Lascelles once noted, the King was probably the only person who did not realise how effective a broadcaster he was.

But none, not even the little masterpiece hurriedly prepared for him in August 1945, equalled the impact of that first broadcast in the first Christmas of the war. The lines of the unknown Minnie Louise Haskins, a lecturer at the London School of Economics, became instantly famous and were reproduced on cards and widely published.

The war at sea, and the King's special interest in the navy, transformed his relations with Churchill. Things did not always go well at the beginning, the King recording in his diary on 9 October that 'I saw Winston Churchill later to tell him of my visit to the fleet. He seemed very sleepy, stifling yawns or trying to, or perhaps it was boredom!' It has often been claimed that the King and Queen were hostile towards him because of his role in the abdication crisis and his denunciations of Munich. In fact the King rather admired him for standing up for his brother, his moment of euphoria over Munich had been very short-lived, and he had been very grateful for Churchill's helpful support on the issue of the Duchess of Windsor's title in 1937.

It is true that they had not known each other very well, but this changed after the outbreak of war, and Churchill wrote in his own hand to the King in February 1940 that 'the knowledge wh. we all have at the Admiralty that Your Majesty watches every step we take with a keen & experienced eye is a stimulus in the heavy & anxious work we have in hand. By none is Your Majesty's compliment more treasured than by the vy. old servant of Your Royal House and of your Father & yr. Grandfather who now subscribes himself Your Majesty's faithful & devoted subject, Winston S. Churchill.'[4]

Churchill's flowery style, both in conversation and on paper, amused the King, but his congratulations upon Churchill's broadcasts and speeches were sincere. Also, while he felt cut off from other ministers, and not kept properly informed, Churchill was an exception. 'I hope Your Majesty will command me whenever there is a lull or indeed at any time, for it is always a gt. pleasure to come to tell Your Majesty about naval affairs and the service which you know so well,' he wrote on 15 April 1940.[5]

Although his relations with Churchill were improving, the war did not prevent the King becoming involved in other political tussles. The first such ministerial battle concerned the Secretary of State for War, Leslie Hore-Belisha. As the King has been accused of personal involvement in Hore-Belisha's resignation in January 1940, and even that he 'actively conspired to bring down the War Secretary',[6] his true role should be related. As always with Chamberlain, it was in fact minimal.

Hore-Belisha was a Liberal National, and a flamboyant self-publicist, now only remembered, if at all, as the Minister of Transport who introduced pedestrian crossings marked by orange lights, dubbed 'Belisha Beacons' by a newspaper, to Hore-Belisha's delight. At the time, however, he was considered a rising and important political personality of considerable potential. The fact that he was Jewish made him a somewhat unlikely member of an overwhelmingly Conservative government, but his abilities and energies were considerable. When he became Secretary of State for War in 1937 he set out to transform the conditions of service of soldiers and the army's organisation. In doing so he made many enemies in the higher echelons of the army, less so for his reforms than for his style and methods. Also, his much trumpeted 'democratisation' of the army – by appointing as a matter of policy more officers from the ranks – did not in fact produce better officers.

[4] RA PS GVI C 069/02.
[5] RA PS GVI C 069/05.
[6] Roberts, op. cit., p. 27.

The King had personal experience of Hore-Belisha's style.

On 4 May 1939 Hore-Belisha had written to Hardinge putting forward certain military appointments for the approval of the King, and re-instituting the posts of Inspectors-General of the Home and Overseas Forces. The King, about to sail for Canada, had given his approval, but then Hore-Belisha had told Hardinge he was having second thoughts. It then transpired that Hore-Belisha had not obtained Treasury, Prime Ministerial or War Office approval for the new appointments. Indeed, Lord Gort, the Chief of the Imperial General Staff, was strongly opposed to them. To make matters worse, Hore-Belisha had told General Ironside that he was to become the Inspector-General of Overseas Forces. Hardinge reported to the King after discussions in Downing Street and at the War Office that 'I gathered from Gort that Ironside is distrusted and unpopular among senior officers in the army. Gort is, as a matter of fact, very upset, and feels that Hore-Belisha wants to get rid of him. I am afraid H-B is an impossible person to work with or for.'[7]

The King officially professed himself 'much disturbed', and made it very plain that he did not expect to be placed in such a position again in the future.[8] The reality was that he was enraged by Hore-Belisha's arrogance, but had to accept Chamberlain's assurance that there would be no repetition.

On 11 October Hore-Belisha had then made a gratuitous statement in the Commons about the number of British troops and equipment being sent to France. 'This was rather stupid & quite unnecessary,' the King wrote in his diary. 'No one knew he was going to say it. H-B must always steal a march on his expert advisers if he can. He likes the limelight & personal kudos.' On the next day the King saw Ironside, who 'did not like H-B's statement in the H. of C. yesterday'. 'I told the PM that I was surprised at Hore-Belisha's statement. So was he, & he went on to say that H-B was having a bad time, as he had got up against John Simon & Burgin about army supplies. The 2 latter like himself are Liberals. I rather gathered he was not very popular anywhere.'[9]

Although the King was well aware of the bad relations between certain senior Generals – especially Ironside and Gort – and Hore-Belisha, he did

[7] RA PS GVI C 103/06.
[8] RA PS GVI C 103/08.
[9] Diary, 12 October 1939.

not 'intrigue' against the Secretary of State for War as has been claimed. If he did not care for him much, he was not alone in this.

But Hore-Belisha was undeniably a zealous and colourful minister who attracted favourable publicity and was also a leader of the Liberal Nationals, which gave him a considerable influence in the government. His Conservative colleagues disliked and distrusted him, but the fact was that he had shone out of the greyness of the pre-war Chamberlain government, although he was now seriously challenged by Churchill for public attention. Modesty was not part of his personality. He had been Secretary of State for two years, and although he had indeed been an energetic and reforming minister, the fact was that the British Army in 1939 was by far the weakest of the three services. This was not of course wholly his fault, but he had been the responsible minister, and the contrast between his posturing and the reality was evident to the soldiers.

In retrospect, Hore-Belisha's loudly expressed concerns about pill-boxes and the large gap between the western end of the Maginot Line and the North Sea coast seem fully justified, but the French were adamant that the Ardennes were impassable to large armies. And it would have taken considerably more and better pill-boxes to have withstood the German onslaught in May 1940, which came from a totally different direction (through the 'impassable' Ardennes) than the British and French had expected. But the problem was less one of strategies than personalities.

On 3 December the King recorded that 'I saw Ironside in the evening who told me that Gort and his Generals were furious at H-B's remarks which were not true and most unfair on the BEF [British Expeditionary Force]. He showed me the map of our front line & the place is covered with pill-boxes.' On 4 December Chamberlain reported to the King that 'I saw the CIGS [Chief of the Imperial General Staff] today, he gave me a very reassuring account of the line which he believes to be impregnable, but he says the ground is in a terrible condition, he never saw it so bad in the last war.'[10]

On the following day the King, with the Duke of Gloucester, Hardinge and Legh, crossed the Channel to Boulogne in HMS *Codrington*. 'During the two-hour drive to Arras Gort told me all about H-B's visit to him and how angry Gort was that he had made those untrue remarks to the War

[10] RA PS GVI C 047/27.

Cabinet. He resented them as H-B had seen troops and had not troubled to see the defences. H-B's remark that [General Maurice] Gamelin had told him that the French built pill-boxes in three days when Gamelin had said three weeks was the last straw. It appears that my visit is a timely one.'

The day after his return to London the King saw Chamberlain. He wrote in his diary:

> I saw the Prime Minister in the evening. He was interested in what I had to tell him of my visit to the BEF in France. I mentioned that Gort, his Staff & the Generals were upset by H-B's remarks, which they knew to be most unfair. I said Heads of Depts did not usually run down their own Dept. The PM told me he hoped to go to France himself next Friday & that he would have a talk to Gort on this matter, and also that he would go to Paris and hold a meeting of the Supreme War Council on Monday 18th Dec . . .
>
> I told Chamberlain that more skilled labour was needed in the BEF to cope with the building of pill-boxes & concrete defences, and the making of concrete runways on aerodromes. The number given me was 44,000 men needed. The shortage of billets was apparent to me, as the French have evacuated the civil population from further east into our area. The army are not very keen to have them as they are not soldiers & have no discipline & there is no room for them. The alternative is French labour, which means Poles & Czechs. But we have over one million unemployed over here. The PM told me he would mention it in France. We discussed the general situation.

On Wednesday 20 December the King wrote: '. . . I saw the Prime Minister after tea. He was pleased with his visit to France & all he had seen with the BEF. He had had good talks with Gort but he is not thinking of removing Hore-Belisha from the WO. He confessed & regretted the lack of young men to take on jobs in the Govt., which is due to their having been killed in the last war . . .'[11]

---

[11] Among those available for office, but not in the government, included Cranborne, Duff Cooper, Harold Macmillan, Swinton and Leo Amery. Cooper and Macmillan had had distinguished military records in the Great War, as did the Labour leader, Clement Attlee.

In a letter to his brother Gloucester on 3 January 1940, the King repeated that Hore-Belisha would stay, not knowing, nor having been told by the Prime Minister, that by the end of December Chamberlain had realised that a situation in which the leading army commanders actively detested their Secretary of State was intolerable, although he did not want to lose an energetic and able minister with such a prominent public profile.

On 4 January, the King being at Sandringham – the last time for many years – Hardinge was summoned to Downing Street to be told that there were to be some Cabinet changes that the Prime Minister wanted to recommend to the King. 'I had written them out and sent them off in their box,' Hardinge minuted the King, 'when I got a message to say that they had had to be altered, and I just managed to get the box stopped at the station.'[12]

Hardinge had been told that Oliver Stanley was to replace Hore-Belisha, and that the latter would be offered either the post of Minister of Information or the Presidency of the Board of Trade. Although neither Hardinge nor the King knew this, Halifax had pointed out the alleged difficulties of having a prominent Jew as Minister of Information; it would certainly not have seemed a disqualification to the King. But Hore-Belisha, Hardinge reported to the King, 'is v. upset about it. He has asked if he can postpone his answer until tomorrow morning. Oliver is at this moment being offered the War Office and will no doubt accept.'[13]

Chamberlain's attempts to keep Hore-Belisha in the Cabinet failed. He wrote to the King on 8 January to describe his meetings with Hore-Belisha and the latter's reaction to being told the reasons for his removal from the War Office. Hore-Belisha was particularly exercised by Chamberlain's mention of there being 'prejudice' against him, and wanted to know exactly what the Prime Minister meant. On being told there were those, 'not confined to the military side', who had taken offence at his 'brusque and inconsiderate manner', Hore-Belisha pointed out that such allegations could equally be levelled at him in another job, and that there was therefore no point in him accepting Chamberlain's offer of a move to a different department.

[12] RA Hardinge Papers.
[13] Ibid.

Chamberlain concluded: 'It may be that Your Majesty may see fit in any conversation you may have with him to give him some advice in this sense, as well as indicating your regret at the events which have made the change necessary and your hope that his absence from office will be no more than temporary . . .'[14]

But the King had little chance to build bridges with the ex-minister – Hore-Belisha was already claiming that he had been a victim of a royal conspiracy. Hardinge, also writing to the King on the 8th, noted that 'the PM wants Your Majesty to know that H-B is saying your attitude towards him had changed and that you were anxious for his removal. That is only what one would expect of him.'[15] And thus a legend, false but often perpetuated, was born. Far from showing the King's antipathy to Hore-Belisha, the episode merely demonstrated how little Chamberlain took the King into his confidence and how badly he kept him informed.

The spring of 1940 was a period of intense frustration for the King. Having written to Roosevelt about Anglo-American co-operation, he then recorded in his diary that 'Sumner Welles was shown a copy of my letter to President Roosevelt [presumably by Kennedy] & his comment was that he could not take it as one passage mentioned the collaboration of the USA with us & this will be taken to mean that we are asking the USA to help us in the war. I am very angry about it. It shows that the US administration & the USA are going to do nothing until after the presidential election.'[16]

Four days later he was lamenting, with full justification, that 'I am very worried over the general situation, as anything we do or try to do appears to be wrong, & gets us nowhere'. A minor reshuffle of ministers at the beginning of April was a deep disappointment to him, as 'there is no new blood coming in'. He had written to Chamberlain on 25 March that:

With regard to personnel, I realise that the arrangements which you outlined to me were of a purely preliminary & tentative kind,

[14] RA PS GVI C 047/29.
[15] RA Hardinge Papers.
[16] Diary, 13 March 1940.

but I cannot help feeling a little apprehensive of the criticism which might arise if there was not a leavening of younger men in such a War Cabinet.

I expect you have probably thought of this aspect of the matter already, but I felt that it was worthwhile drawing your attention to it as it would be a pity if it were to have a damaging effect on the reconstituted government as a whole.

I can well understand what a disagreeable task it must be, making changes among colleagues, & I sympathise with you very much in having to do it . . .[17]

Chamberlain, as usual, took no notice. The King's appeal had as little effect on his Prime Minister as his often repeated desire for a National Government, the King noting in his diary for 2 April that Chamberlain had told him that 'Attlee would not join in & the PM could not countenance conditions from Attlee as to the number of Depts in the Govt. with seats in the War Cabinet for the Labour Party'.

The political reality that the King had to face was that Attlee and Chamberlain loathed each other. A notably half-hearted, and wholly insincere, approach by Chamberlain to Labour after the German invasion of Poland had been curtly rejected on Attlee's emphatic instructions from his sick-bed; Chamberlain referred to Attlee in his diary as 'a cowardly cur'. The King's well-meant and sincere attempts to encourage a coalition foundered on this mutual dislike. And the King's difficulties in understanding, and communicating with, Attlee were to prove enduring. In this dilemma he was not to be alone.

On the war front, the period of relative inactivity ended in April 1940 with the German invasion of neutral Norway.

The British, worried about the provision of iron ore from northern Norway to Germany and German naval activity in Norwegian waters, including the sinking of British and neutral shipping, had informed the Norwegian government on 6 January that 'it would be necessary for His Majesty's naval forces at times to enter and operate in these waters'. The Norwegian reply to this Churchillian threat took the form of a private letter from King Haakon to his nephew King George, asking him to use his influence with ministers to reconsider this decision. The

[17] RA PS GVI C 047/30.

King had discussed the matter with Chamberlain, who seemed very ready to abandon Churchill's belligerency. But Churchill himself took no notice.

In March came the decisive *Altmark* incident. The *Altmark* was the auxiliary ship of the *Graf Spee*, and had on board 299 British merchant seamen captured from vessels sunk by the pocket battleship. After lurking in the South Atlantic for two months she had sailed by the northward route towards Germany; on 14 February she was spotted in Norwegian territorial waters by a British observation aircraft, and two days later was intercepted by a British flotilla commanded by Captain Philip Vian. She took refuge in a narrow fjord near Stavanger. When two British destroyers entered the fjord on the 16th, they were met by Norwegian gunboats who informed the British that the *Altmark* was unarmed and had already been inspected. The destroyers accordingly withdrew, but then Churchill ordered Vian to deliver an ultimatum to the Norwegians, and in the event of non-compliance to 'board *Altmark*, liberate the prisoners, and take possession of the ship pending further instructions'.

After some fierce resistance, in which four Germans were killed and five wounded, the prisoners were freed and brought home, to jubilant newspaper headlines and triumphant newsreels. Churchill's reputation soared higher, and the King wrote to him personally to congratulate him and the navy on this fine feat of arms.

It was, however, the first act in a drama that soon resulted in a major military setback for the British, the German occupation of Norway and the downfall of Chamberlain. Ironically, the true inspirer of this débâcle was to be the principal beneficiary. But despite the King's mounting alarm at what was already a deteriorating military situation, an increasingly critical press, and with Hitler's contempt for neutral states clearly demonstrated, there was no premonition of disaster at the Palace.

What was more accurately anticipated was a possible change of government, the resignation of a Prime Minister and the King's choice of his successor. As this preceded the dramatic events of 7–10 May, the professionalism and foresight of Hardinge were all the more remarkable.

As early as 29 March Lascelles had consulted Sir Stephen Gaselee of the Foreign Office about the right of the King to summon a person to form an administration. Gaselee consulted Professor Ivor Jennings, Professor Charles Webster and Professor Harold Laski without stating the source of the enquiry.[18] Hardinge's conclusions from these soundings was that 'the King need not ask the advice of the outgoing Prime Minister as to his successor, nor should the latter give such advice unless it is asked for. "Sending for" anyone after the resignation of the Prime Minister does not necessarily mean that this individual is going to be entrusted with the formation of a government, though this interpretation is likely to be put on it when he is one of the obvious candidates.'

He went on: 'It is common for the King to send for an elder statesman to consult, as King George V did AJB after Bonar Law's resignation . . . The only person who could make the formal offer of the post of Prime Minister to any individual is the King himself.'[19]

Thus fortified, Hardinge and Lascelles awaited events.

On 2 May Hardinge reported to the King that Oliver Stanley and Hoare had expressed concern over Churchill's increased responsibilities, adding, 'I am told too that Winston's attitude over all of them is part of an intrigue for him to oust Mr Chamberlain — but I cannot find any signs of a serious movement of this kind, and I hardly think it would have any parliamentary support. Moreover, I do not believe it.'[20]

Churchill was certainly not involved in any intrigue on his behalf, but others were. The results were seen in the Commons on 7–8 May.

The disastrous failure of the Norway campaign had brought to a head the increasing impatience with the government generally and Chamberlain in particular. The Labour leaders would not consider joining a government headed by him, and Conservative mistrust of Churchill remained strong. Although Hardinge did not anticipate an immediate crisis he realised that it could not be long postponed, reporting to the King on 7 May, the first day of the crucial two-day debate in the Commons on the Norwegian campaign:

> There is little doubt that the Government will get through the debate on the Norwegian campaign without much trouble, but the danger, as I see it, is that when the next reverse takes place, as it undoubtedly will, the country may demand the removal of the Government lock, stock and barrel, with the possible exception of

[18] RA PS GVI C 132/03.
[19] RA PS GVI C 132/09.
[20] RA Hardinge Papers.

Winston Churchill. Or, less drastically, they may insist on Churchill becoming Prime Minister of a Coalition Government. Each of these two courses would, in my opinion, be very undesirable, and the way to avoid them would be for the present Prime Minister to reconstruct the Government with the inclusion of the Oppositions. Such inclusion is bound to come in time and it would be much better for it to come before any serious disaster has occurred, and while the present Prime Minister is still in Office – for there is little doubt that the combination of Mr Chamberlain, Winston Churchill and Lord Halifax is about the best that can be obtained for the successful prosecution of the war.

I understand that the Prime Minister is prepared at any moment to invite the leaders of the Oppositions into the Government, but that the great stumbling block is the refusal of the Labour Party to enter any Government of which Mr Chamberlain is the head . . .[21]

Hardinge's advice was to propose that the King send for Attlee 'to impress upon him the very serious situation in which the country now finds itself, and the importance of the Labour Party taking their share of the responsibility for bringing the country safely through'.

The sequel was also recorded by Hardinge:

The King spoke to the Prime Minister on the lines of the attached memorandum [quoted above]. The Prime Minister thought that, if the King was prepared to take such action vis-à-vis the Labour Party, it would be well worth trying it. He advised His Majesty however, that such intervention would be more likely to be effective after the Labour Party Conference than before, as there might be a chance of the Labour leaders of their own accord accepting the offer to join, which still remained open – whereas Mr Attlee would be unable to give any definite answer before the Conference.

I think that this is probably right, though the chance of their joining the Government without any pressure would seem to me very faint.[22]

[21] RA Hardinge Papers.
[22] Ibid.

The opening of the debate had not gone badly for the government, and when Chamberlain saw the King on the evening of the 7th he smilingly said that he had not come to offer his resignation. The King recorded in his diary that Chamberlain told him that he

had seen Attlee & Greenwood this morning and had asked them about their coming into the Govt. They had said nothing. Knowing this, I sounded the PM on the question as to whether I could not help. Attlee had dined here on Monday, & I had found him easier to talk to. I told Attlee that on my industrial tours I was so impressed with the national spirit of the workers & that I had met representatives of the Trades Unions in leaders & shop stewards. Leading on from this I said to the PM would it help him if I spoke to Attlee about the national standpoint of the Labour Party, & say that I hoped that they would realise that they must pull their weight & join the Natl. Govt. The TUC are holding their Annual Conference this coming weekend at Whitsuntide. The PM suggested that I should wait until the Conference was over, as Attlee at the moment was not sure of their feelings. He [Attlee] might suggest joining in a Govt. with a new Prime Minister, not himself. I said that I felt what I call the great triumvirate, the PM, Halifax & Winston, could not be bettered, & that it would do the leaders of the Labour Party good to have to run a Dept in wartime & to have an insight into its difficulties. The PM said that if after the Conference nothing transpired & there was no hint from Attlee to him, then I could talk to Attlee. I told the PM that I did not like the way in which, with all the worries & responsibilities he had to bear in the conduct of the war, he was always subject to a stab in the back from both the H. of C. and the press.

On 8 May the debate went very badly indeed for the government, whose majority slumped to eighty-one, and concluded in tumult. Hardinge, on 11 May, recorded events as seen from his vantage point:

In the early morning after the Vote of Confidence, namely Thursday May 9th, I communicated with David Margesson [Chief Whip] and heard from him that, in consequence of the turn the debate had taken, it was agreed that the Government would have to be reconstructed on a broader basis. He was to see the Prime Minister early and would keep in touch with me during the day. Having heard nothing further I went to No. 10 to see Rucker[23] at 4.30 p.m. He told me that the Prime Minister, Halifax, Churchill and Margesson were at the moment discussing what approach should be made to the Labour Party. The idea then was that in the event of the Labour Party refusing to serve under Mr Chamberlain, the latter would resign, and, on the King asking his advice, he would recommend Lord Halifax. Subsequently the three Government leaders met Mr Attlee and Mr Greenwood and asked them (a) if they would join a Government under Mr Chamberlain, and (b) if not, whether they would serve under anybody else. They said that they would have to go to Bournemouth, where their executive was preparing for the Party Conference the following week, and would telegraph their answer by the afternoon of the following day, May 10th.

During the afternoon it transpired that Lord Halifax was becoming more and more definitely opposed to accepting the position of Prime Minister, and also that the Labour Party felt less disposed to serve under him than had originally seemed to be the case. I saw Rucker at my house before dinner, when he told me that Winston was now coming to be the most favoured candidate. I said, speaking entirely for myself, that I thought the King might want to try, once Chamberlain had resigned, to persuade Halifax to reconsider his decision, and I suggested that Rucker should mention this to the Prime Minister. We also touched on the question of the leadership of the Conservative Party, which Rucker told me was to be retained by Mr Chamberlain in any case. I pointed out to him that this would be quite contrary to the agreement that I had had with Margesson some time ago, that the man whom the King chose as his Prime Minister ought always to be elected as the leader of his Party. However, this was not a matter to which, at the time of a national emergency, too much attention need be paid.

[23] Arthur Rucker, Chamberlain's Principal Private Secretary, and a staunch Chamberlain loyalist.

On the morning of May 10th news was received that the Germans had invaded Holland and Belgium. It was generally felt that the fact that the greatest battle in history had broken out, on which the future of civilisation depended, altered the situation materially, and that in such circumstances the right person to lead the country was undoubtedly Mr Churchill. During the period of waiting for the reply from Bournemouth this opinion hardened and by the afternoon the choice seemed clear. I had seen Lord Lloyd the previous day and Lord Salisbury twice that day. The latter, speaking for his faction which comprised almost all the Privy Councillors in the House of Lords, was evidently afraid that the opening of the battle might be used as an excuse for delaying the reconstruction. He was insistent that, on the contrary, the necessity for immediate action was all the greater.

At about 5 p.m. I went to No. 10 to see Rucker. The reply from Bournemouth had just arrived, and was what was expected – (a) – no, (b) – yes.

On receipt of this the Prime Minister decided to resign, and I was informed that in the event of the King asking his advice as to his successor, he would *without hesitation* recommend Mr Churchill.

I came back and reported to the King. Shortly afterwards His Majesty saw Mr Chamberlain, accepted his resignation and asked if he would recommend Mr Churchill as his successor. Mr Chamberlain answered in the affirmative. After further thought Mr Churchill was asked to come to the Palace, was offered the post of Prime Minister and accepted.

Owing to the unusual circumstance that the Prime Minister had not been defeated in the House of Commons and that he made the decision to resign immediately after receiving the reply from the Labour Party, I felt that it would not be at all proper for me to make any contact with the Labour leaders, and therefore did not do so.[24]

The King had found the situation frustrating and uncomfortable, describing 9 May in his diary as 'an unprofitable day'. Chamberlain

[24] RA PS GVI C 129/001. Author's italics.

had told him on 30 April, as he wrote in his diary, that 'Winston still seems to be causing a good deal of trouble . . . The PM is having another talk with W. tonight, laying down what he can & cannot do without the War Cabinet's sanction.' But now Churchill's star was in the ascendant.

While the politicians conferred throughout the 9th, the King's principal source of information was Hardinge, and he himself was entirely sympathetic to Chamberlain, writing that 'the Conservative rebels like Duff Cooper ought to be ashamed of themselves for deserting him [Chamberlain] at this moment'. But, significantly, he did not criticise Churchill.

An intriguing, and unanswered, question remains. Why did Chamberlain not advise the King to send for Halifax? Halifax had emphatically withdrawn himself from contention, but his argument that it was no longer possible for a Prime Minister to be in the Lords could have been easily resolved, thanks to the highly flexible unwritten British constitution and the powers of the Royal Prerogative. As all parties, with varying degrees of willingness, were prepared to serve under Halifax, the use of the latter would not have caused any serious difficulties. But Chamberlain did not recommend him.

Halifax did not consider himself equipped to be a wartime Prime Minister and shrank from the possibility. This was not the result of moral, physical or political cowardice, but a realism about himself that was both honourable and right.

Andrew Roberts states that Lord Birkenhead, preparing his biography of Halifax, was told by Lascelles that 'when Chamberlain fell, the King felt he ought to send for Halifax. Alec Hardinge knew that Winston was the man, but had a hard job selling him to the King and the Queen was very anti-Winston.' No source is given for this, and it does not ring true on several counts. It is the case that Lascelles was indeed 'very anti-Winston', but after their better knowledge of Churchill since September 1939 neither the King nor Chamberlain was. Indeed, as has been related, the King's relations with Churchill had been good since 1937, and excellent since the outbreak of war. Hardinge's political influence with the King was limited, and even if the Queen had indeed been 'very anti-Winston' – which she was not, knowing her husband's increasing admiration for Churchill, although Queen Mary certainly was – the King did not depend upon her for political advice.

It is also stated, on the evidence of Harold Nicolson's unpublished diary for 6 April 1955, that Wheeler-Bennett had told Nicolson that, 'according to his research, the King "was bitterly opposed to Winston succeeding Chamberlain",' adding that 'the adverb employed is instructive'. It is true that the King would have preferred Halifax, but he was not 'bitterly opposed' to Churchill.

Halifax had been through fierce fires in India, and then the Chamberlain appeasement period had scarred him. He notably lacked arrogance; he was prone to self-doubt; he had an engaging lack of confidence. He was a kind, if sometimes sharp, decent man who never over-rated himself. Also, unlike Churchill, he wondered whether the war was winnable. He viewed the situation without optimism. Perhaps he was right, but an honourable and noble realist was not required as the leader of Britain in May 1940. And Halifax, to his eternal credit, realised this.

Although the King was 'disappointed' by Halifax's refusal to serve, 'as I thought that H. was the obvious man',

> then I knew that there was only one person whom I could send for to form a Government and who had the confidence of the country & that was Winston. I asked Chamberlain for his advice, and he told me Winston was the man to send for . . . I sent for Winston and asked him to form a Government. This he accepted and told me he had not thought this was the reason for my having sent for him. He had thought it possible, of course, & gave me some of the names of people he would ask to join his Government. He was full of fire & determination to carry out the duties of Prime Minister.[25]

And the King obtained, at last, the National Government that he had long wanted.

[25] Diary, 10 May 1940.

193

8

A NATION ALONE

———— ◆ ————

'I cannot yet think of Winston as PM,' the King wrote in his diary on 11 May. 'I met Halifax in the [Buckingham Palace] garden and told him I was sorry not to have him as PM.'

This was not only kindness to a valued friend and adviser; there were many others who shared his feelings. If there was a Churchill legend in May 1940 it was that of an unstable, erratic, wholly unreliable, egotistical opportunist, an impulsive and dangerous risk-taker whose long record of disastrous errors of judgement bulked rather larger in his critics' eyes than his many achievements. He had few friends and admirers at Westminster or in Whitehall, where his elevation caused almost universal horror. In Downing Street John Colville, the Prime Minister's Assistant Private Secretary, wrote that 'everybody here is in despair at the prospect [of Churchill]', and R. A. Butler was describing him as 'the greatest adventurer of modern political history', while Halifax gloomily referred to the likes of Churchill, Bracken and Beaverbrook as 'gangsters'. Lascelles later commented that 'the sad truth is that Winston did not like gentlemen'.[1] This, also, had some truth. But Germany itself was ruled by gangsters of an infinitely more evil hue.

Although the King would have favoured Halifax, he had, as noted, developed warm feelings towards Churchill and had realised something

---

[1] Interview with Halifax's biographer, Lord Birkenhead, quoted in Roberts, *The Holy Fox*, p. 187.

that what would now be described as the Establishment had not, that the appointment was immensely popular outside London political and official circles and was very quickly to become even more so. But neither the King nor Churchill anticipated the friendship and mutual respect that was to develop into the closest personal relationship in modern British history between a monarch and his Prime Minister.

Certainly, it did not begin promisingly. Although Chamberlain had, politically, not treated the King very well, their personal relationship had been good, and, as the King wrote to Queen Mary, 'I was able to confide in him.' The problem had been that Chamberlain had not confided in him.

The King's initial difficulties with Churchill arose over appointments to the new government, especially the apparently astonishing one of Beaverbrook as Minister of Aircraft Production. The King was dismayed, and wrote in his own hand to his new Prime Minister, commenting on Beaverbrook's bad reputation in Canada and adding, 'I wonder if you would not reconsider your intention of selecting Lord Beaverbrook for this post. I am sending this round to you at once, as I fear this appointment might be misconstrued. I hope you will understand why I am doing this, as I want to be a help to you in the very important & onerous office which you have just accepted at my hands.'[2]

This was not, of course, a veto on the appointment but a strongly worded suggestion, which Churchill ignored. It was in fact a very dangerous appointment with considerable potential for disaster, and over which Beaverbrook himself had initial doubts. But it turned out to have been inspired, although controversies still rage about the real value of his contribution. The balance of the verdict is strongly in Beaverbrook's – and Churchill's – favour. But the King's apprehensions were fully merited at the time. He had not yet appreciated Churchill's enthusiasm for dynamic buccaneers like himself.

The episode could be interpreted as a trial of strength between the two men, but the King's reaction had been a very human one. Neither Beaverbrook's private nor his public life appealed at all to the King, either in England or in Canada, and his mischievous involvement in the abdication had not been forgotten. There was also the point that his newspapers had been ardent supporters of appeasement long after

[2] Gilbert, *Finest Hour*, p. 316.

the King had lost faith in it, and had decried the possibility of war virtually up to its outset. Even Beaverbrook's commitment to the war effort had been doubtful, as his suggestion to the Duke of Windsor to lead a 'Peace Now' movement only a few months earlier had demonstrated. Beaverbrook always aroused intense emotions. There were those who admired and even loved him; there were many who feared him; and there were others who found him repellent. The King emphatically belonged to the latter school. But Churchill prevailed. The King almost certainly did not know that Beaverbrook had become a close friend of Roosevelt's, a fact of considerable political importance.

There were then complaints about Churchill's unpunctuality at coming to meetings with the King, which irritated both sides. The King, quite reasonably, disliked hanging around waiting for the Prime Minister to turn up. Churchill, equally reasonably, considered that the King did not appreciate that there was a desperate war going on, which the Allies were rapidly losing, and that the normal peace-time punctilio and formal-audience routine was impossible. But he gave the impression of the same dismissive attitude to the monarch that the King's father had experienced with Lloyd George, which was a wholly unfair charge. Churchill, operating under intense pressure and anxiety, behaved so badly and inconsiderately to colleagues and officials that his conduct drew a memorable rebuke from his wife. It seemed at the beginning of his historic premiership that all the doubts about his character and judgement were entirely justified.

Churchill did become seriously exasperated when the King objected strongly to making Brendan Bracken a Privy Councillor. It was true that Bracken had not held office of any kind, and held none at the time, acting as an informal but potent Parliamentary Private Secretary to the Prime Minister, but, as Churchill pointed out in a notably sharp response to the King's protest, Bracken had been one of his closest supporters in his wilderness years. He then added, with conspicuous asperity, that 'I should have thought that in the terrible circumstances which press upon us, and the burden of disaster and responsibility which has been cast upon me after my warnings have been so long rejected, I might be helped as much as possible'.[3]

The King immediately responded by agreeing to the recommendation

[3] Gilbert, op. cit., pp. 453–4.

– and came to like and admire the ebullient and often irreverent Bracken, although he was never fully reconciled to Beaverbrook – realising that he had tried his over-pressed Prime Minister too far, especially at such a time. But the incident did not improve Churchill's early relations with his sovereign. The King, however, had twice made his point. 'It is clear that the King has a mind of his own,' Colville wrote in his diary. Churchill, although victorious on both appointments, had noted the same fact.

Events now rushed forward with a terrible momentum as the German juggernaut swept through Denmark, Holland and Belgium. There was little the King could do except follow the stream of disasters with mounting dismay. On 13 May 1940 he was woken at 5 a.m. to be told that Queen Wilhelmina of the Netherlands was on the telephone. The King found this difficult to believe, but it was indeed her, begging for British aircraft to come to her country's assistance. The King passed on this appeal at once, but later in the day the Queen was again on the telephone, this time calling from Harwich, where she had arrived on a British destroyer. She said she fully intended to return to those parts of her country where there was still resistance, but the King and others persuaded her that the situation had become impossible. He met her personally at Liverpool Street Station and brought her to Buckingham Palace with only the clothes she was wearing. From the Palace she delivered two defiant broadcasts to her people. On 15 May the Dutch Army surrendered, and the juggernaut thundered on.

Belgian resistance was the next to falter under the onslaught. In this case King Leopold was both monarch and Commander-in-Chief, and on 25 May he realised that the situation was hopeless. The King received a long and poignant handwritten letter from 'Le Commandant de L'Armée Belge, Grand Carpentier Générale, Saint-Année, Bruges' that began, 'Your Majesty, Belgium has held to her engagement she undertook in 1937 by maintaining her neutrality and by resisting with all the forces at her disposal the moment her independence was threatened. Her means of resisting are now nearing their end . . . In spite of all the advice I have received to the contrary, I feel that my duty impels me to share the fate of my army and to remain with my people; to act otherwise would amount to desertion . . .'[4]

[4] RA PS GVI C 166/10.

Hardinge and the Foreign Office immediately prepared for the King a detailed telegraphed appeal to Leopold to leave his country at once, and go to either Britain or France, but he replied to the King, 'My dear Bertie, I feel sure I am doing the right thing and in the best interest of my country.'[5]

It was perhaps excusable at the time for Churchill and the British propagandists and press to excoriate the Belgian surrender as an act of perfidy and betrayal by Leopold. Unhappily, scapegoats are often necessary in politics and war, and Leopold was a highly convenient one. It was much less justifiable to repeat this vilification later, when passions had cooled, and the facts had become clearer. In his war memoirs Churchill was to repeat his statement to the House of Commons on 4 June that 'suddenly, without prior consultation, and with the least possible notice, without the advice of his ministers and upon his own personal act, he [King Leopold] sent a plenipotentiary to the German command, surrendered his army, and exposed our whole flank and means of retreat'.

The King, who had known Leopold since 1919, would have no part in this character assassination, which was, and was to remain, a sore point between himself and Churchill. Churchill had sent Keyes as his liaison officer to Leopold, who wrote angrily to Hardinge on 5 June protesting that the blame lay with the British plans to counter-attack southwards, and that he had suffered 'the humiliation of listening to such a shamelessly unfair statement' in the House of Commons.[6] Keyes had seen the King on 29 May – the day after the Belgian surrender – to explain Leopold's predicament. The King also sought the opinion of Gort and General Sir John Dill, who were equally sympathetic to King Leopold. He came to the conclusion that Leopold had conducted himself well as commander-in-chief, but had rather muddled up his twin roles, and certainly should have escaped and established a Government in Exile in Britain. The King also refused absolutely to remove Leopold's name from the roll of the Knights of the Garter, or to have his banner in St George's Chapel taken down. His attitude then and later was in marked and civilised contrast to that of his ministers.

But the main thrust of the German attack came through the Ardennes,

[5] RA PS GVI C 166/11.
[6] RA PS GVI C 166/16.

ignoring the Maginot Line, crossing the Meuse and sweeping westwards in a devastating arc towards the Channel ports. With complete German control of the air, the British losing many brave pilots in their useless Fairey Battle bombers – no match whatsoever for the German Messerschmitts – and the French Army in disarray, the British faced the appalling prospect of the total loss of their army – and with it, the war.

Few realised this except a small number, including the King and Churchill. Whatever differences between them rapidly evaporated. They were drawn together by the magnitude of the disaster that had befallen the British and French armies, and on 23 May Churchill told the King that it might well be necessary to evacuate the remnants of the British Expeditionary Force, losing all their *matériel*, and with the prospect of 'immense' losses. In fact Gort, on his own initiative, and whose army might well have been destroyed had he followed Churchill's disastrous orders for a southward offensive, began the evacuation from Dunkirk on 26 May.

This catastrophic situation made a broadcast by the King on the 24th all the more significant. This, on the occasion of Empire Day, had been under preparation for several days, and the King was understandably agitated by the real possibility that the rapidly changing military position might necessitate last-minute alterations. As Logue had taken him through the original draft, on which he was now thoroughly rehearsed, this could have caused serious difficulties. In the event it was decided to deliver it as it stood. It was a strong, and clear, denunciation of the enemy and his voracious ambitions for 'the overthrow, complete and final, of this Empire and of everything for which it stands, and after that the conquest of the world'. In his own style it was almost Churchillian in its resolution, and few of his listeners knew as well as he did how parlous the position of the BEF had become.

The King and Churchill often differed over their respective estimation of individuals. The Churchill–De Gaulle relationship was tempestuous; that between the latter and Roosevelt was bad, and got progressively worse.

The King was, from De Gaulle's arrival in London at France's darkest hour in June 1940 to raise the banner of the Free French, an admirer and staunch friend of this imperious, prickly and obstinate man. The King, as

De Gaulle later wrote with gratitude, gave him 'esteem and sympathy'. Eden, also, often took De Gaulle's side at difficult moments, of which there were many. It helped, of course, that the King and Queen and Eden spoke excellent French, whereas Churchill's was idiosyncratic and Roosevelt's non-existent, but the real difference was that the former three understood De Gaulle's character much better, and treated him not as an arrogant nuisance but as a great and proud man shouldering immense psychological as well as other burdens after the humiliation of his country. De Gaulle's biographer has reflected his subject's gratitude and admiration for the King.

Wars are not won by speeches or broadcasts, but in that terrible, and yet in so many respects magnificent, summer and autumn of 1940 the national resolution of the British people was inspired by those of Churchill and the King, and by their example.

It was understandable that the King and Churchill initially eyed each other somewhat warily. The Queen's attitude towards Churchill was cool, as was Lascelles' and that of the military; if not hostile, it was unapproving, for very obvious reasons. It was to change totally, but not immediately.

Colville has written that Churchill's 'respect for the monarchy amounted almost to idolatry', and his wife told him that 'you are Monarchical No. 1' and described him as the last believer in the Divine Right of Kings. But in fact his relations with successive sovereigns had been notable for a lack of deference on his part and considerable indignation on theirs. Edward VII, incensed by Churchill's speeches and his advocacy of large cuts in military expenditure, growled that his initials, WC, were appropriate. Churchill's description of the Peers in 1909 as 'a miserable minority of titled persons' prompted a furious royal protest. But Edward VII had a residual affection for him that George V certainly did not. Although his relationship with the latter had improved in later years it could hardly be described as warm; indeed, although the constitutional courtesies were maintained, the fact was that the two men disliked each other and George V always distrusted Churchill, while grudgingly conceding his abilities and application.

It did not help Churchill's cause that Lascelles had always detested him. In his diary in 1907 Lascelles had noted: 'Also there, Jack Churchill, almost as repugnant as his brother Winston,' and when Churchill returned from the Western Front in 1916 to resume his political career Lascelles described him as 'The Arch-Mountebank [who] has shown himself a supreme cad in his methods many times before,' and that 'it is only the harlequin-politician who can lay aside the King's uniform the moment it becomes unpleasantly stiff with trench-mud'. To be fair to Lascelles, this indignation was widely shared in the army. Lascelles also disliked Churchill's friend and adviser Eddie Marsh, who revelled in gossip about other people's indiscretions: 'I now know why some people think it worthwhile hating him,' Lascelles wrote in his youthful diaries, and the prejudice remained.[7]

These emotions were returned. When they had to work together it was an uncomfortable relationship. For four years Churchill refused to address Lascelles by his Christian name; when he did, he called him 'Alan', and not by his more familiar name 'Tommy', although later his letters did begin 'My dear Tommy'. Churchill was virtually the only person in political, social and family circles who called him first 'Lascelles' and then 'Alan'. As Lascelles knew, it was quite deliberate.

The Queen's doubts about the new Prime Minister were also very understandable. Churchill's many qualities did not include tactfulness, especially towards women – he had been a strong opponent of their being given the vote. He was impatient, even offensive, to others, without realising it. He simply ignored them, which could, and did, cause deep offence. He handled the Queen courteously but tactlessly, as he was to do with her elder daughter before she became Queen, and this was neither overlooked nor forgotten.[8] When Churchill came to appreciate the Queen's qualities of courage and cheerfulness under stress his attitude changed, but the fact was that he was always more comfortable in masculine political company. In this early stage of their

---

[7] Hart-Davis, *End of an Era – Letters and Journals of Sir Alan Lascelles, 1887–1920*, pp. 26, 196, 101.

[8] As Violet Bonham-Carter, who knew Churchill so well, wrote, his 'circle of friends contained no women. They had their own place in his life. His approach to women was essentially romantic. He had a lively susceptibility to beauty, glamour, radiance, and those who possessed these qualities were not subjected to analysis. Their possession of all the cardinal virtues was assumed as a matter of course.' (*Winston Churchill as I Knew Him*, p. 148.) She might have added that those who did not possess these qualities did not interest him at all, and he abhorred women politicians. Mrs Roosevelt was to prove the classic combination, and it is unsurprising that she disliked him so much.

relationship he saw the King as his sovereign rather than a political figure.

It was not long before they discovered, rather to their mutual surprise, that they had much in common. For one thing, the King, for all his devotion to his wife and daughters, shared Churchill's pleasure in male company, and in uninhibited intelligent political conversation of the kind that he had had with Roosevelt. They had both served in combat. Neither was deficient in physical courage, nor in a sense of humour. For his part Churchill also developed a trust in the King's integrity and resolution. It took some time, however, for this relationship to be transformed from official courtesy and respect into real friendship.

The King also had to get to know his new ministers, particularly the Labour and Liberal ones.

Ernest Bevin, Minister of Labour, was to become a firm favourite with the King, although initially he considered that Bevin knew surprisingly little about industry. When Bevin was sworn in as a Privy Counsellor on 15 May, the King noted in his diary that 'he had always excused himself from coming to see me when I had met other Trades Union leaders. Now I shall be able to send for him. He looks a strong man & a leader.'

On 28 May they had a much longer meeting, as the King recorded in his diary:

He told me he had a tough job. He was glad that relations between employers and workers were so good, which made his work easier of ordering employers to send their skilled people to help others, & the Trade Unions telling their men they must obey orders. I hoped he would not be too drastic to start with, but with the situation as grave as it is, I was sure everybody would understand. He delved into the past, even to Ramsay MacDonald's Labour Govt. of 1929–31 and said that we had never done anything with or for Unemployment, I said a War invariably brings two opposing forces in the country together, & especially at a moment like this. And we have got to get together for the Nation's safety. He is a strong man, & a capable one . . .

Bevin's experience had its limitations, but his capacity to learn, like

his memory, was prodigious. Also, he certainly never suffered from
nervousness in the presence of royals, although he was robustly courteous. His disregard for his own health was the despair of his doctor,
Dr Alec McCall, who claimed not to have found a sound organ in his
patient's entire body, apart from his feet. Bevin smoked and drank far
too much, and was seriously overweight. Indeed, to read Dr McCall's
pitiless diagnosis the wonder is that he survived the war, let alone the
post-war pressures as Foreign Secretary. But Dr McCall did his best,
while lamenting his patient's 'unruly and undisciplined' lifestyle. Bevin
introduced him to the King with the statement 'This is Alec. 'E treats my
be'ind like a dartboard.' The King, who had his own views on doctors,
roared with laughter, and it became Bevin's standard introduction of
McCall, who bore it remarkably well.

Bevin's openness and frankness, common sense, strength of character
and somewhat earthy good humour appealed to the King enormously,
even before he came to appreciate Churchill's qualities. But Churchill's
attitude was rather more that of the robust courtier, Bevin's that of the
practical friend. As with Churchill, the King did not mind his drinking at
all, even when Bevin crushed one of his expensive brandy glasses in his
huge fist, merely remarking, 'I suppose you'd like some more brandy,'
and providing another glass.

Other relationships were not so easy, the King writing on 15 May,
'I was very depressed all day. I saw Attlee in the evening. He looked
very shrivelled, & small & very tired, & said very little. I saw Archie
Sinclair [Liberal leader and Secretary of State for Air] later, and we
had an interesting talk. I don't like his political outlook, but he is
attractive . . .'

Attlee was a special case, and the King often despaired about his taciturnity and monosyllabic responses, usually grunted in a voice through
his pipe so low that it was difficult to hear. His references to 'Clam'
Attlee were not in any sense dismissive but vividly descriptive. On
Herbert Morrison he wrote on 4 December at Windsor that 'we
talked on many topics in a very amicable way. He asked if he could
stay here, which shows that now he is in the Govt. he wants to get
[to] know us. I am very glad of this as before the war they were
loth even to come & see me for a talk. Now that we are all in
the same boat, party factions are put aside – but for how long?'
He could never really trust or like Beaverbrook. He detested Hugh

Dalton,[9] and his attempts to conceal the fact were not always successful. This antipathy was not only the result of his dislike of Canon Dalton, Hugh's father, nor of the son's Socialist politics, but the fact that Dalton was, as Halifax described him, 'a naturally offensive creature'. Dalton's qualities of spirit and political courage were too often concealed by a bombastic and arrogant exterior and a recklessness that was eventually to bring about his downfall. The King's hostility towards Dalton, in which he was not alone, was to have significant consequences.

But, above all, the King welcomed the fact that he had a National Coalition government rather than a party one, and was determined to do all in his power to make it united and successful.

Churchill did not conceal from the King the near-disastrous situation in France. Calais, after a desperate, but essential, British resistance, had fallen. The French were disintegrating militarily, politically and morally. The BEF was fighting a fierce rearguard retreat towards Dunkirk, but after a meeting with Eden on 29 May the King wrote that 'I sent Gort a message for his troops telling him how magnificently they were fighting, & had an answer. I am so dreadfully sorry for these men, as I do not see how any but a small percentage can get out.'

But as a result of 'Operation Dynamo' 335,000 British and French troops reached Britain from Dunkirk in the greatest and most important military evacuation in modern military history. But the British returned home without most of their weapons and equipment. As Churchill sombrely told the House of Commons, 'Wars are not won by evacuations.'

The catastrophes continued. Italy entered the war on Germany's side on 10 June. France sued for an armistice on 16 June. The King wrote of Churchill on the 18th that 'he looked tired & was depressed over France. But he was full of fight over this country.' So was the King.

Churchill later wrote grandly but wrongly that 'the supreme question of whether we should fight on alone never found a place on the War Cabinet agenda', whereas there were five very long meetings – one lasting four hours – on exactly that subject. Given the gravity of the

[9] Minister of Economic Warfare, 1940–42; President of the Board of Trade, 1942–45.

situation this was not surprising, and the arguments of Halifax and Chamberlain that all options should be seriously considered were eminently sensible. But the fierce romanticism and patriotism of Churchill, vehemently and eloquently expressed in private as well as in public, overwhelmed reason. And in this emotional response to looming disaster he had a staunch ally in the King. It was the turning-point of their relationship.

Churchill's greatest immediate concern after the French surrender was the French Navy, and he asked the King to make a personal telegraphed appeal to President Lebrun, which he did on 22 June, to prevent it falling 'into hostile hands'. It was symptomatic of the chaos of the time that it reached the French President days later, and too late for it to have any possible influence. On 3 July the Royal Navy opened fire on French warships at Oran, with devastating results – and also to Anglo-French relations. But the sheer ruthlessness of the British operation sent a very clear message, and one that the Americans particularly understood. The British were going to fight.

The fall of France utterly changed the war. The British were no longer the blockaders but the blockaded. The loss of ships in Norway and at Dunkirk, reducing the number of operational destroyers to sixty-eight, made the need for immediate replacements imperative. They could come only from the United States.

The saga of the 'destroyers for bases' deal has often been related; what has been underestimated was the King's role. Roosevelt had raised the possibility in his talks with the King at Hyde Park, and the King had passed on the thought to Chamberlain and Churchill. Roosevelt was keen on having the Caribbean bases; the British desperately needed the destroyers. Churchill made the appeal direct to the President in June, reinforced by a personal letter to Roosevelt from the King. Perhaps the most crucial influence was that of the British Ambassador, Lord Lothian, who was a close friend of Roosevelt's.

The matter was dealt with speedily (given the situation in Congress and with a presidential election looming, remarkably speedily), although the British, and especially Churchill, were dangerously, if understandably, impatient and critical of what delays there were. The agreement was signed on 2 September. The first eight of fifty destroyers were handed over to the Royal Navy four days later. The ships were old, they rolled and wallowed alarmingly, and were much hated by their crews, but they had a long range.

What Roosevelt could not do was implement his statement to the King at Hyde Park that 'if London was bombed the USA would come in'. The aerial battle of Britain, the essential preliminary to the German invasion, began in earnest on 13 August 1940; the bombing assault on London began on 7 September, and was to continue throughout the winter, and not only on London. American support for Britain steadily grew, but necessarily fell short of 'coming in'.

Throughout the desperately close-run thing of the Battle of Britain the King travelled to fighter stations, army units and the newly created Home Guard. After the bombing of London began he and the Queen regularly visited the ravaged areas. At the beginning of September, with invasion apparently imminent, and with the Battle of Britain raging overhead, the King suggested to Churchill that instead of their regular formal audiences, whose frequency had risen sharply,[10] they should lunch together each Tuesday. At the beginning – the first lunch was held on 10 September – there were particularly trusted servants to serve the food and drink, but after a while, as their relationship developed to the point that they were discussing deeply secret matters, the King suggested that they serve themselves from a sideboard, with no servants, however trusted, present, and this was the arrangement for the rest of Churchill's premiership. From time to time the Queen joined them, but usually the King and the Prime Minister were alone together, sometimes for a long time. This was, as Churchill described it, 'a very agreeable method of transacting state business'.

It was through these regular weekly lunches – at which there was no nonsense about any repetition of George V's reluctant pledge, and sometimes interrupted by air-raids, when the lunch and discussion would be continued in the totally inadequate Palace air-raid shelter – that the two men came to know each other well, to trust each other implicitly,

[10] After the outbreak of war it was at first decided to have the audiences at 5.30 on Tuesdays and Fridays, later changed – in January 1940 – to Tuesdays only. Previously they had been on average only once a month, although the number rose at times of crisis. Edward VIII had only nine audiences with Baldwin in 1936; the King had had eleven with Baldwin and Chamberlain in 1937, sixteen with Chamberlain in 1938, thirty-nine with him in 1936, and fifty-five with him and Churchill in 1940.

so that, as Churchill later testified, he gave the King the most secret information in the government's possession. He also always told the King more frankly than any of his ministers, let alone parliament or the press, the grim realities of the war situation.

Churchill was the first politician since Roosevelt to take the King seriously and to welcome his counsel. With Roosevelt there had been his characteristic flattery, but in Churchill's case there was a sense of shared danger and deep commitment to a cause that at times seemed to be floundering towards disaster. They certainly agreed about the crucial importance of the United States to Britain's survival, which Chamberlain had never understood. They also knew the importance of setting an example. To the historian's regret neither kept a detailed record of these discussions, although the King's diaries are often revealing, and both were highly reticent about discussing them with their immediate staffs; neither Hardinge nor Lascelles was taken fully into his confidence at that time. Churchill has recorded how much he valued the King's advice and comments, but it is possible only occasionally to judge how much of it was taken. The creation of the George Cross and Medal was the first result, as will be seen, but there were to be others. Churchill, with his memories of Marlborough, later wrote, 'I valued as a signal honour the gracious intimacy with which I, as First Minister, was treated, for which I suppose there has been no precedent since the days of Queen Anne and Marlborough during his years of power.'

The changed relationship between King and Prime Minister exposed a cardinal point in the development of the monarch's political role – namely, that it had come to depend deeply upon the attitude of the Prime Minister towards the monarch rather than the other way round.

Chamberlain may have been courteous, friendly and helpful towards the King in private, but, politically, he had ignored him as comprehensively as Lloyd George had George V. In doing so, Lloyd George had made a great mistake for which he paid with his career. But Churchill was a devout royalist, who, in spite of his sharp disagreements with Edward VII and George V, revered the institution of monarchy. When he came to know the King much better, and his devotion to the institution was fortified by a respect and admiration that developed into real friendship, the political influence of the King was transformed from being virtually non-existent to becoming a major element in government. As the Labour leaders – with the conspicuous exception of Dalton – shared Churchill's high appreciation of the King's judgement and shrewd common sense, this further augmented his position. They did not invariably share Churchill's veneration for monarchy, but they admired the man.

This was subsequently a little-appreciated factor in the remarkable harmony of the wartime coalition. Although the King fully understood the rules, and never attempted to act as an umpire, the fact that unlikely men such as Bevin and Morrison valued his opinion and often acted upon it was significant. Morrison, indeed, to general amusement, became almost fawning in his attitude. But that relationship also had practical results. One example may be given.

It was the duty of the Home Secretary to make recommendations to the King on capital sentences – whether he should or should not accept or reject a plea for commutation of death sentences. This grim duty, which had caused Churchill much anguish as Home Secretary, was not at all a formality so far as the King was concerned, particularly when a certain woman was sentenced to death for murder. Of her guilt there was no doubt, and Morrison's frank opinion was that she deserved to hang, but he shrank from the press, public and political uproar that would inevitably follow the execution of a woman, particularly in the Labour Party, which had even then a strong abolitionist element. There was also the question of the impact on international opinion and the cynical use of the hanging of a woman by Goebbels' formidable propaganda machine.

Lascelles' diaries and papers vividly describe the dilemma, which exercised the King greatly, as he, also, saw the political implications if he refused to exercise the Prerogative of Mercy. He was also personally and morally repelled by the prospect of authorising the execution of a woman, however guilty.

There was an eager search in the Home Office and in the King's immediate entourage for strong extenuating circumstances; unfortunately, few serious ones could be found. But the King's view – that the sentence should be commuted to imprisonment – prevailed, to Morrison's evident relief.

The King had not overruled his Home Secretary, nor had he refused his advice, which in fact was not formally tendered until they had discussed the matter often and at some length. That the formal advice from the Home Secretary was mutually agreed was the result of the good relationship between them. It was very much a political rather than a legal decision, and on those grounds unquestionably the right one – and on others, as well.

For his part, the King looked forward to the Tuesday lunch with Churchill as one of the high points of the week, which only the absence from London of either men interrupted for four and a half years. Churchill's idea of conversation, as has often been remarked, was a monologue, but, like most stories about him, this does not tell the whole truth. In fact, on form, he was a dazzling conversationalist and a fascinating companion. He also had the great capacity of listening when he was interested, and was respectful of the opinions and judgements of others. What particularly impressed him about the King was the latter's total application to his job in every respect, not least in his careful and thorough reading of all documents put before him. Also, as matters progressed, and the King and the Queen travelled throughout the country – far more than Churchill or his principal ministers could – they were in a better position than most to assess the public mood.

These lunches and long man-to-man discussions also removed from the King the feelings of helplessness and irrelevance that had so depressed him. Chamberlain had told him nothing much beyond what he could read in the newspapers or hear on the radio; now he had a Prime Minister who told him everything and showed him everything. And Churchill's personality, style and high sense of the dramatic, which privately often made the King and Queen laugh, were as endearing as his courage and resolution. Churchill listened to the King, and increasingly confided in him, including ministerial appointments and the handling of difficult individuals and situations. The closeness and intimacy of their relationship has had no precedent in the history of the modern British monarchy. Furthermore, Churchill was the only one of the King's four Prime Ministers whom he came to address invariably by his Christian name.

Because the King and Churchill saw each other so regularly, and communicated through their private secretaries and secure telephone calls, their private correspondence, as opposed to the stream of official papers, was rather spasmodic, but increasingly warm. Thus, the King wrote to Churchill on 29 October that 'I am so sorry that everything nowadays is so worrying for you; there is not a bright spot anywhere. But I am sure something bright will turn up one day.'[11]

And Churchill memorably wrote to the King on 5 January 1941 that

Yr Majesty's treatment of me has been intimate & generous to a degree that I had never deemed possible. Indeed Sir we have passed through days & weeks as trying and as momentous as any in the long history of the English Monarchy, & even now there stretches before us a long, forbidding road. I have greatly been cheered by our weekly luncheons in poor old bomb-battered Buckingham Palace, & to feel that in Yr Majesty and the Queen there flames the spirit that will never be daunted by peril, nor wearied by unrelenting toil. This war has drawn the Throne & the people more closely together than was ever before recorded, & Yr Majesties are more beloved by classes & conditions than any of all the princes of the past. I am indeed proud that it shd have fallen to my lot & duty to stand at Yr Majesty's side as First Minister in such a climax of the British story . . .[12]

But their first lunch, on 10 September, was very nearly the last. Early that morning a bomb that had hit Buckingham Palace exploded, and blew out many of the windows. Three days later the King wrote in his diary:

We went to London [from Windsor] & found an Air Raid in progress. The day was very cloudy & it was raining hard. We were both upstairs with Alec Hardinge talking in my little sitting room overlooking the quadrangle; (I cannot use my ordinary one owing to the broken windows). All of a sudden we heard an aircraft make a zooming noise above us, saw 2 bombs falling past the opposite side of the Palace, & then heard two resounding

[11] RA PS GVI C 069/06.
[12] RA PS GVI C 069/07.

crashes as the bombs fell in the quadrangle about 30 yards away. We looked at each other, & then we were out into the passage as fast as we could get there. The whole thing happened in a matter of seconds. We all wondered why we weren't dead. Two great craters had appeared in the courtyard. The one nearest the Palace had burst a fire hydrant & water was pouring through the broken windows into the passage. 6 bombs had been dropped. The aircraft was seen coming straight down the Mall below the clouds having dived through the clouds & had dropped 2 bombs in the forecourt, 2 in the quadrangle, 1 in the Chapel & the other in the garden. The Chapel is wrecked, & the bomb also wrecked the plumber's workshop below in which 4 men were working. 3 of them injured & the fourth shocked. Looking at the wreckage how they escaped death is a wonder to me. E & I went all round the basement talking to the servants who were all safe, & quite calm through it all. None of the windows on our side of the Palace were broken. We were told that the bomb in the forecourt was a delay action (D.A.) bomb so we gave orders for all the east windows to be opened in case it exploded, & we remained in our shelter & had lunch there. There is no doubt that it was a direct attack on Buckingham Palace. Luckily the Palace is very narrow, & the bombs fell in the open spaces. The Chapel sticks out into the garden. It was a ghastly experience, & I don't want it to be repeated. It certainly teaches one to 'take cover' on all future occasions, but one must be careful not to become 'dugout minded'.

The reality had been far more serious than this laconic account indicated. The bombs had fallen very close to the royal couple, and had it not been for the fact that the remaining windows were open they could easily have been seriously injured by shards of broken glass, if not killed.

Very few people, not even Churchill, realised what a close shave it had been. He found the King 'exhilarated by all this, and pleased that he should be sharing the dangers of his subjects in the capital'. In fact, as always happens, the exhilaration was followed by delayed shock, which worried him, but was very understandable.

The Queen famously said, 'I am glad we have been bombed. We can now look the East End in the face.'[13] This remark has been ascribed to her skill at public relations, as though it was a contrived and clever comment rather than the sincere statement of her emotions it really was. Although she was much better than her husband in concealing her feelings in public, especially boredom and annoyance, and was untroubled by minor mishaps which enraged him, insincerity was not one of her defects. It was her spirit that was so important to him, and which made her so popular. There was much need of it in 1940 and 1941. Nor was it the case that the bombing 'caused little relative damage to the Palace';[14] it was in fact very considerable, and this was not the first time, nor by any means the last, that the Palace came under air attack. All the windows were boarded up, and, if not totally uninhabitable, the building remained for the entire war a gloomy, dark, unheated mausoleum, much hated by those who had to work there, not excluding the King and Queen.

When it was proposed in May 1941 by the Foreign Office that the Greek and Yugoslav Royal Families should receive refuge in London the King strongly protested, instructing Hardinge to write to Cadogan on 28 May that 'in the event of the Kings of Greece and Yugoslavia finding their way to this country in the near future, the King feels that the Ministers concerned should know that His Majesty has no means of putting them up now that Buckingham Palace is virtually out of

---

[13] A good example of the denigration to which the Royal Family has been, and is still, subjected, may be found on page 176 of Penelope Mortimer's *Queen Mother*, when she states: 'On 15 September a German bomber flew straight down the Mall and dropped two bombs in the forecourt of Buckingham Palace, two in the quadrangle, one on the Chapel, and one, carelessly, in the garden. The King and Queen lunched in the air-raid shelter, which Elizabeth had furnished with gilt chairs, a regency settee, a large mahogany table and a supply of glossy magazines . . . It was shortly after this that the Queen made the famous and outrageous claim that she was glad the Palace had been bombed, claiming that "it makes me feel I can look the East End in the face". Huddled in their flimsy Andersons, crammed into Underground stations, searching for Mums and the kids through last night's rubble, the people of the East End were genuinely impressed.'

The raid was on 13 September, not the 15th. The King and Queen were not having lunch. They were not in the air-raid shelter either, luxurious or otherwise, as only a makeshift one existed at the Palace. And the full fury of the Blitz had not yet hit London.

[14] Roberts, op. cit., p. 50.

commission as a residence and Windsor Castle is full up . . .'[15] When Cadogan suggested that the two monarchs might be accommodated for just a few days, Hardinge replied, 'The fact is that owing to the number of people called up from the King's establishment, the facilities for entertaining crowned heads have almost ceased to exist . . . This is entirely the case as far as Buckingham Palace is concerned, but at Windsor Their Majesties say that they could put up King Peter and one gentleman as well as one or two servants.'[16]

Nor was their protection on the ground much better. The experiences of King Haakon and Queen Wilhelmina had demonstrated the eagerness of the Germans to capture the monarchs of the nations they had conquered; these had escaped, but there was the sad example of King Leopold – to become even more sad – to emphasise the consequences if they did not. The amateurishness of the British at this stage was then exemplified.

A specially chosen unit from the Brigade of Guards and Household Cavalry was entrusted with the safety of the King and Queen at the Palace, allegedly on instant alert, to be summoned by a special alarm. Sceptical, King Haakon suggested that these arrangements be tested. In Wheeler-Bennett's account:

> Obligingly King George pressed the alarm signal and, together with the Queen, they went into the garden to watch the result. There followed anti-climax; nothing happened at all. An anxious equerry, dispatched to make inquiries, returned with the report that the officer of the guard had been informed by the police sergeant on duty that no attack was impending 'as he had heard nothing of it'. Police co-operation having been obtained, a number of guardsmen entered the gardens at the double and, to the horror of King Haakon but the vast amusement of the King and Queen, proceeded to thrash the undergrowth in the manner of beaters at a shoot rather than of men engaged in the pursuit of a dangerous enemy. As a result of this incident precautions were revised and strengthened.[17]

[15] RA PS GVI C 140/39.
[16] RA PS GVI C 140/41.
[17] Wheeler-Bennett, op. cit., p. 464.

It was a year into the war before either Buckingham Palace or Windsor Castle had any anti-aircraft protection, and the Palace's only 'shelter' was a small basement room; it was not until 1941 that an adequate one was built for the King and Queen and the Palace officials and staff.

It has also been written that 'during the Blitz the King and Queen left London every evening to join the Princesses at Windsor Castle'.[18] This rather unpleasant implication of abandoning the capital to its fate while the King and Queen fled to safety is not justified by the facts. The Blitz was not solely a night-time affair, as the events of 9 and 13 September demonstrated. Buckingham Palace was indeed 'battered', in Churchill's phrase, and was to become progressively more so, but the King and Queen doggedly used it as their London base throughout the war, although constantly advised not to by ministers and security advisers. And Windsor was hardly a haven of peace and safety; during the war over three hundred bombs, countless incendiaries and flying bombs fell on Windsor Great Park, and not even the massive Castle itself was impervious to danger, and not always from the enemy.

One dark late autumn evening in 1940 the newly arrived anti-aircraft artillery unit in Windsor Great Park was warned that an enemy bomber was rapidly approaching the Castle. When it was seen the guns opened up, but the aircraft escaped. The chagrin of the gunners at their failure was soon followed by a telephone call from an enraged commander of a nearby RAF station, one of whose Hampden bomber air-crews had complained of being fired on from the ground while returning to base from a training mission. The officer concerned – David Crouch, a future Member of Parliament – was ordered to present himself before the King immediately. Fearing at the very least a stern reprimand, and possibly a court martial, he did so. To his surprise the King first told him that he had been quite right to follow his orders, and that it was not his fault that the bomber had been wrongly identified. Nonetheless, he added, aircraft recognition was vital, and he passed over to the officer his own collection of wooden models of the principal British and German aircraft, with the advice that he and his men should study them very earnestly.

Then, in the summer of 1941, on a practice firing, a shell exploded prematurely, showering the two young Princesses with metal fragments while they were doing their French lessons on the South Terrace with

[18] Roberts, op. cit., p. 43.

their tutor, Viscomtesse de Bellaigue. No one was hurt, but, again, the King firmly took the side of the anti-aircraft battery, saying that practice was essential, whatever the risks.

In both incidents the King remembered, only too clearly, the events of the previous September.

With invasion apparently imminent, preparations had to be made for the safety of the Royal Family, and especially the two young Princesses. It was decided that the King and Queen would go to Madresfield, in Worcestershire, and the Princesses would be taken to Liverpool and thence to Canada, to ensure the succession if the King was killed in the fighting after the invasion in which he was determined to be involved. The Princesses' emergency luggage was prepared and packed at Windsor. This was only prudent planning for the worst, but neither the King nor the Queen considered it a serious possibility.

There was in fact very little pattern to the lives of the King and Queen throughout the war. They were constantly reacting to events, travelled a great deal throughout the country, often on the spur of the moment when a city was badly bombed – as was their visit to Coventry in November 1940 – or to military establishments. But the King placed great importance on his weekly investitures at the Palace, and the fact that his flag flew defiantly above it.

Amid all these mounting anxieties the Windsors were behaving rather oddly.

The Duke had left the Military Mission in Paris – although not without authority, as thought for a time in London – to join the Duchess at Antibes. After the French collapse they were driven to Spain, and became the responsibility of the British Ambassador, now Samuel Hoare. They installed themselves in the Ritz Hotel in Madrid before, under strong urgings from Churchill, moving to Lisbon. In fact Churchill, with the King's full approval, ordered the Duke to fly home in 'immediate compliance with the wishes of the government'. Windsor telegraphed back that, in the King's account in his diary for 30 June, 'He could only return to this country if his status and financial position were first regulated. The PM & I told him to obey orders. He is going to be very difficult, I can see.'

While the Windsors were still in Madrid the Germans went to remarkable lengths to keep them in Europe, and, judging from many contemporary accounts and recently disclosed British government papers, their hopes that the former King and his wife might provide useful propaganda for an Anglo-German peace settlement (on German terms) were not all that far-fetched. Patience with them in London snapped.

It was Churchill's solution that the Duke should be sent to govern some reasonably remote and certainly unimportant colony; the Colonial Secretary, Lord Lloyd (Lascelles' brother-in-law) was dubious, but suggested the Bahamas. Churchill jumped at the idea, and although the King fully shared Lloyd's doubts he saw the merits of the proposal. Halifax gave his approval, commenting drily, 'I am sorry for the Bahamas.' Although Windsor, now in Lisbon, continued to make difficulties, he eventually accepted. The King's letter to him expressing his pleasure was sympathetic, and in the circumstances warm and friendly, but the note of relief was unmistakable.

Another way in which the war occupied the King was in the matter of medals and honours, a great interest of his which he had certainly inherited. Prince Albert had instituted and designed the Victoria Cross; Edward VII had contributed the Order of Merit, and George V the Military Cross. He had also ended the situation in which the VC ribbon differed between the services. He had wanted to go further in rationalising military decorations, but Lloyd George, fully aware of the jealousies and competition between the services on these matters, persuaded him not to.

In 1939, entirely on his own initiative, the King had set up the Committee on Honours, Decorations and Medals in Time of War. It discovered a thoroughly confused situation, particularly in the case of medals available for bravery by civilians, each industry having its own. Very sensibly it was decided to start again, and the first result was the King's Commendation for Brave Conduct, but as civilians came increasingly into the front line in the Battle of Britain and even more in the Blitz the King did not think this was good enough. He was also incensed by the bland Whitehall view that civilians were not fighting 'in the face of the enemy'.

The results were the George Cross – the civilian equivalent of the Victoria Cross – and the George Medal. They were not only the King's idea, he also designed them himself, and had no difficulty in persuading Churchill of the urgent need for such recognition. It was to prove an inspiration.

The King took military and civil awards very seriously, and conferred as many as possible personally; almost throughout the war there was an investiture every week at Buckingham Palace. When the New Zealand Captain Charles Upham was recommended for a bar to his VC the King personally summoned his commanding officer to justify this very exceptional recommendation. His explanation totally satisfied the King, and the award was made.

The King's attention to awards, and thoroughness of his examination of recommendations, was demonstrated on several occasions, but a notable one was the award of the DSO to Captain Baker Cresswell, RN.

Baker Cresswell was commanding the destroyer *Bulldog* escorting convoy OB318 on 9 May 1941 when they came under heavy U-boat attack. But U-110, commanded by Captain Lemp, the destroyer of the *Athenia*, was trapped by a depth-charge attack and was forced to surface and abandon ship. Baker Cresswell's first instinct was to sink the stricken boat, but then he remembered a lecture describing the great value in 1914 of retrieving the German naval ciphers from the cruiser *Magdeburg*.

He accordingly ordered all action to cease and launched a whaler to rescue the U-boat crew who, after being taken aboard *Bulldog*, were sent below. Lemp and another officer realised what the British intended to do and attempted to swim back to the U-boat, but were shot in the water. The whaler then returned to the boat and brought back a veritable treasure-trove of documents and, most important of all, the naval Enigma machine with its list of settings. From then until February 1942, when the Germans added extra rotors, high-grade German naval signals could be read rapidly at Bletchley Park; this was resumed in November 1942 when HMS *Petard* captured the new rotors from U-559 in the Mediterranean. Baker Cresswell had taken the submarine in tow, but it had to be abandoned in a storm. The Germans assumed that their boat had been sunk and its crew killed; they never realised throughout the war − and for many years later − that their elaborate code system had been fatally compromised. Even the official history of the war at sea, published in 1954, made no reference to it, although its author, Captain Stephen Roskill, was permitted subsequently to tell the story.

So strict was the security surrounding this coup that very few were permitted to know about it. Churchill told the King, who felt that a higher award should be made than the recommended DSO. But this might have made the Germans suspicious, and when Baker Cresswell was presented to the King for his decoration the latter took him aside to tell him that his achievement was one of the most outstanding in the sea war, and to explain to him personally why a higher award could not be made.

King George VI now had a role, as his father had had in the Great War, but it was a very different one.

George V, for all his anxieties and problems between 1914 and 1918, had never had to contemplate the possibility of total defeat and a German occupation of his country. This was what his son had to do, although he never believed either would actually happen, despite knowing much more about how potentially catastrophic the position was than his subjects. This was not accidental. The Germans were to be given the clear impression that Britain was an arsenal, with a huge undefeated army now reinforced by Canadian divisions, a victorious air force and a mighty navy. It was a confidence trick, one of the greatest in history, and the King willingly played his part in this massive deception.

And, in the Second World War, although there were often disagreements and heated arguments, there was none of the harsh in-fighting between the politicians and the military that there had been in the First. Party politics fell into complete abeyance after the formation of the coalition; except on certain occasions, Churchill's leadership was unquestioned and admired; the Labour and Liberal ministers and the majority of MPs were loyal supporters of the government. The King became the symbol of this surge of national unity and resolution.

The developing relationship of mutual trust and affection between the King and Churchill can be clearly seen in the King's diaries.

On 23 July he wrote, 'I saw the Prime Minister after tea. He said "the man has not come yet", meaning Hitler's invasion. He was pleased with the RAF exploits, & what he had seen of the army defences. Winston was not very talkative. Many of his important problems are difficult to extract from him.' But the lunches changed things. On 22 October the King wrote, 'He was in good form & told me many things both of a serious & of a frivolous nature . . . I am getting to know Winston better & he is telling me more of his ideas.' On 12 November, after another Tuesday lunch, the King wrote of Churchill that 'I got him to tell me of the many vicissitudes of his own political career . . . which was most interesting & entertaining.' They discussed Baldwin; Churchill was, 'in his own genial way', rather dismissive, but 'I differ with Winston as I see SB in a different light from a non-political point of view, tho' 1936 everyone agrees was right. Winston admits this now . . .'

Also, they could, and did, speak freely about the continuing problems of the Windsors, who, on arrival in the Bahamas in August, at once complained of the heat, the lamentable condition of Government House – which 'would take two months to put into a habitable condition' – and declared that they would prefer to go to the Duke's ranch in Alberta while these essential improvements were made. The King noted in his diary on 27 August on these protests that 'W's answer was that he should remain in the Bahamas & stick to his new job. I hoped W. would always deal with D. like this, & he said he would.'

On 5 November they discussed the Greek situation, but also Windsor. 'We discussed D.,' the King wrote. 'Winston told me that D.'s ideas & his pro-Nazi leanings would have been impossible during the crisis of the last three years. D. was certainly dictatorial & obstinate if he could not get his own way, & felt frustrated in many ways under Papa's regime.'

These problems continued. 'At last W. understands what harm he can do,' the King wrote in his diary on 25 March 1941, after Windsor had given some unhelpful interviews to American journalists and had sought permission to visit the United States. 'D. has no mind of his own, it is all centred on Mrs S., his wife,' the King wrote. Churchill's reiterated suggestions, entirely contrary to his advice in 1937, that the Duchess should receive the title of HRH infuriated Hardinge and Lascelles, and did not improve his relations with the Queen. On this, the King was adamant, and Churchill gradually accepted the situation.

Other relations were warming. 'I like him much better,' the King wrote of Eden on 11 February 1941, after one of their first long discussions since Eden had replaced Halifax as Foreign Secretary;[19] 'He has grown out of his "know all" attitude at the FO before in 1937.' He was to become a great admirer of Eden, although the Queen, with significant shrewdness, doubted Eden's strength of character. She

[19] Halifax had replaced Lothian as British Ambassador in Washington. He – and Lady Halifax – had gone reluctantly, but, after a difficult beginning, were highly successful.

recognised the genuine charm, courage, professionalism and intelligence of an outstandingly talented diplomat; she also saw the flaws.

The change was symbolised by the death of Neville Chamberlain from cancer early in November 1940. While he had remained in the government as Lord President of the Council the King had continued to see him as 'an adviser & friend', and, as mentioned, he and the Queen visited him shortly before his death. But by then the Blitz had replaced invasion as the dominant concern, although in North Africa and in the Balkans new perils had dawned.

9

DISASTER AND SURVIVAL

T he Bagehot definition of the rights of a British constitutional monarch – to be consulted, to encourage and to warn – was now given an importance under circumstances unimaginable when Bagehot had written it and Stamfordham had later virtually sanctified it. George VI did not only have the duty of encouraging his ministers but the entire nation, as well as the Empire and possible allies – especially the United States – abroad. He also had to warn of the hazards, disappointments and losses of life that war would necessarily bring, and advise ministers about the possible consequences of their policies.

But his role had become considerably more substantial than this. Churchill gave him more information, and confided in him more greatly than any of his predecessors. He was made privy to all the great secrets of the war, and was accordingly far better informed than most members of the War Cabinet. He was thus given the ability to know. Knowledge does not necessarily bring with it power, but it does bring considerable influence, and King George VI between September 1940 and July 1945 was the most influential and significant British monarch of the century. That of Edward VII and George V had been considerable, and under-estimated. But neither had had the access to the quality and volume of information that George VI received, and certainly had not enjoyed the close personal relationship with their Prime Ministers that he had for five years.

There were many who had privately doubted whether the King had the capacity to fulfil these roles, although his successes in North America and his famous 1939 Christmas Day broadcast had diminished these doubts. The bombing of Buckingham Palace and the defiance shown by the King and Queen had changed many perceptions of them. Their constant visits to bombed cities, and their evident shock and distress at the casualties and damage, and unfeigned admiration for the spirit of the people transformed their position from remote respect to real popularity.

The crisis seemed to transform the King and Queen, as Harold Nicolson noted on 10 July after a private lunch with them at the house of Mrs Arthur James. 'I told the Queen today,' he wrote to his wife, 'that I got home-sick, and she said, "But that is right. That is personal patriotism. That is what keeps us going. I should die if I had to leave." She also told me that she is being instructed every morning how to fire a revolver. I expressed surprise. "Yes," she said, "I shall not go down like the others." I cannot tell you how superb she was. I anticipated her charm. What astonished me is how the King has changed. He is now like his brother. He was so gay and she was so calm. They did me all the good in the world.'[1]

But it was a hard slog – and was to become much harder, longer and fearsome than few had anticipated after the heady summer and autumn of 1940. For over two more years the King had to endure with his subjects a seemingly endless list of military disasters. In retrospect, the war proceeded through distinct phases to inevitable final triumph. At the time, however, it looked utterly different. If there was a strong belief in ultimate victory, there were to be many occasions when it seemed an article of faith rather than of reality. Between the summer of 1940 and the end of 1942 the British were fighting for survival. There were occasional successes, swiftly followed by severe reverses. The intervention in Greece ended in calamity; Crete fell; Malta was held, but at heavy cost in ships, aircraft and men. Rommel and the Afrika Korps nearly reached Cairo. The vital lifeline to North America was very nearly broken. Although the bombing offensive against Germany eventually developed into an awesome bombardment, the costs were substantial, and the results often seemed disproportionate to the losses of men and aircraft.

Although after Hitler attacked the Soviet Union in June 1941 the

[1] Nicolson, *Diaries & Letters 1939–45*, p. 100.

menace of the invasion of Britain definitely passed, the Soviet forces came perilously close to total defeat, and the U-boats nearly won the war against Britain on their own. Until the end of 1942 the advantage in the Balkans and the Middle East increasingly lay with the Germans, and the Mediterranean was an area in which the Royal Navy struggled grimly, and with heavy losses, to maintain its authority. Even after the United States entered the war in December 1941 following the Japanese attack on Pearl Harbor, this longed-for event was followed by a succession of military catastrophes for the British and American forces – the loss of Malaya, the abject and humiliating surrender of Singapore, the decimation of the British Far East fleet, the over-running of Burma by the Japanese, and their presence on the frontiers of India, itself in internecine turmoil.

The bad news was unremitting; the good only occasional. Thus when Churchill came for the Tuesday lunch at the Palace on 3 November 1942 he astounded the King and Queen by declaring, 'Sire, I bring you victory.' 'We thought he had gone mad,' the Queen later remarked. 'We had not heard that word since the war began.' Churchill was bringing the news of El Alamein. 'A victory at last,' the King noted on 4 November. 'How good it is for the nerves.'

They had, however, been forewarned that great events were at last on the way, as on 23 October they had hosted a dinner party at Buckingham Palace for Mrs Roosevelt, attended by the Churchills, Smuts and his son, Elliott Roosevelt, Winant, the American Ambassador, and the Mountbattens. After dinner they saw the new Noël Coward film *In Which We Serve*, based heavily on Mountbatten's own experiences. Churchill was acutely nervous, and kept asking for information from Downing Street. He eventually left to telephone to seek information about El Alamein, and returned singing 'Roll Out The Barrel' with gusto 'but with little evidence of musical talent', in the account of one present, who added, 'I wondered what their Victorian predecessors would have thought had they heard Dizzy or Mr G[ladstone] singing "knocked 'em in the Old Kent Road" in similar circumstances.'

But, before this, there had been no respite from tales of failure, however heroic.

As one hammer-blow succeeded another it was natural that even Churchill occasionally became depressed and angrily frustrated at the apparently unending misfortunes, defeats and humiliations that befell the British – and then the Allied – forces, and on several occasions at their Tuesday lunches it was the King who tried to cheer him up. But Churchill being 'down' seldom lasted long, and the King often marvelled at his extraordinary resilience.

In September 1941 the King openly demonstrated his total confidence in, and friendship for, his Prime Minister by appointing him Lord Warden of the Cinque Ports, with the privilege of residing at Walmer Castle at Deal, on the Kentish channel coast and therefore highly vulnerable. Churchill was delighted by the appointment – 'an extraordinary compliment far beyond my desserts to be included in that long line of Prime Ministers and eminent men who have across the centuries filled that office' – but was advised that it should not be announced that he would reside there until the end of the war: 'This seems most necessary as otherwise its proximity to the enemy's aircraft and indeed artillery might create a need for heavy structural repairs before very long.'[2]

Churchill's worst time was in 1942, before El Alamein, when, after the fall of Singapore in February and repeated failures in North Africa, criticism of his leadership became increasingly strong in the press and parliament. The King noted in his diary after the Tuesday lunch on 17 February that Churchill 'was very angry over all this, and compares it to hunting the tiger with angry wasps around him'. The King was so concerned that he asked Hardinge and Lascelles to test opinion, making it clear that his Prime Minister had his total backing and support.

Hardinge reported that the consensus was that although Churchill's leadership was unquestioned, he was doing too much, and that the strain was becoming obvious. Also, it was understandable that repeated defeats were undermining public confidence in the conduct of the war. He suggested that a government reconstruction was desirable, with which the King entirely agreed.

Some changes were made, and on 25 February Churchill sought, and received, a vote of confidence from the House of Commons. As the King shrewdly commented in his diary for 19 February, 'The H. of C. want Winston to lead them but they don't like the way he treats them. He likes getting his own way with no interference from

[2] RA PS GVI C 069/09.

anybody, and nobody will stand for that kind of treatment in this country.'

On 24 February Bracken told Hardinge that 'it was in large measure due to what the King said to the PM on Tuesday 17th that he made his drastic reconstruction of the government. He hoped therefore that HM could see his way to impress on the PM today that he now had the whole country behind him and that he *must* take more time off and leave more to Eden, Cripps, and Oliver Lyttelton. I reported all this to the King.'[3]

Eden also turned to the King, who agreed that Churchill needed 'some Super Chief of Staff'. But when he raised the matter at the Tuesday lunch 'the suggestion was *not* received with enthusiasm', as the King told Hardinge.

The relationship had its difficult moments, as when in November 1941 Edmund Ironside was appointed Field Marshal and raised to the Peerage without the King's prior knowledge or approval; indeed, he strongly opposed both appointments, but as they had been announced he had to acquiesce – but not without some cross exchanges between the Palace and Downing Street.

But when Keyes – not before time – was removed from his post as Commander of Combined Operations in October 1941, he was so incensed that he insisted on an interview with the King. This was granted, but, as Hardinge reported to Churchill on 10 October, 'As you may imagine, the person concerned had a good deal to say, but the King thinks that it probably did him good to blow off steam, and, of course, he got no change out of His Majesty.'[4]

On 5 May 1942, at the Tuesday lunch after the King's weekly investiture, they discussed the continuing problem of the Duke of Windsor, who was bored by the Bahamas and wanted to leave. 'Where can he go to & what job can he do?' the King wrote. 'He cannot come here anyhow, W. & I are certain of this, the Dominions don't want him, there is nothing he can do in America, & he wants a temperate climate to live in. W. suggests southern Rhodesia, which is vacant. But would they like it, & Smuts would have to be asked as well. It is a very difficult problem.'[5] A week

---

[3] RA Hardinge Papers.
[4] Ibid.
[5] Diary, 5 May 1942.

later Churchill vaguely suggested 'a mission to S. America'. Nothing came of these ideas. The Duke was ordered to stay in the Bahamas.

On 19 May they turned from this constant nuisance to the gravity of the war situation. 'Nothing is going right for us,' Churchill said. 'W. was not listening to what I had to say,' the King complained. Churchill proposed to replace Halifax with Beaverbrook as Ambassador in Washington and to send Sir John Anderson as Viceroy of India. The King did not think much of these ruminations, but, as he wrote, 'I found it was no use arguing with him in the state he was in.' Halifax stayed in Washington; as will be seen, Anderson did not go to India. But, as the King noted, his Prime Minister 'was in very bad form'.

Then Churchill enthusiastically agreed that the King should take the salute on 14 June in London for the American National Flag Day parade. The King was furious at being 'let in for this stupid parade', especially as Churchill had decided to absent himself. Again, there were sharp communications between the Palace and Downing Street. The lunches were not always agreeable occasions, but they did not lack frankness.

But by this time, events had moved on. Preoccupied as he was in 1941 by the precarious Russian military situation and the continued heavy shipping losses in the Atlantic, Churchill had given little attention to Japan. The King recorded in his diary after the Tuesday lunch on 29 July 1941 that Churchill 'does not think Japan will go to war with us or USA. Our combined freezing of assets & breaking commercial treaties have come as a shock to Japan.' On 17 August he wrote that Churchill had 'told Menzies[6] not to worry about Japan. FDR is sending a strong note to Japan & we shall back him up.' On 19 August, 'W. told me the Atlantic was much better, he thought that Japan would remain quiet,' and, after a discussion on 12 September with Halifax at Balmoral, 'He told me the American attitude towards Japan being a firm one, the Japanese will probably climb down. Winston is of the same opinion . . .' Churchill's comparison between the Italians and the Japanese – 'the Wops of Asia' – was instructive, but the situation was becoming so tense that he had dispatched the battleship *Prince of Wales* and the battle-cruiser *Repulse* to Singapore. They should have been accompanied by an aircraft-carrier, but it had been badly damaged and was being repaired in an American

[6] Robert Menzies, Australian Prime Minister.

dockyard. The British, Indian and Australian forces at Singapore were strongly reinforced, making it, on paper, a formidable armed fortress, while the arrival of a new battleship and escort seemed to strengthen greatly the already impressive Royal Navy presence in the area.

Roosevelt, however, was more troubled, writing to the King on 15 October that 'I am a bit worried over the Japanese situation at this moment. The Emperor is for peace, I think, but the Jingoes are trying to force his hand.' The King wrote in his diary on the 17th: 'The Japanese Govt. has resigned. Konoye has been replaced by Gen. Tojo. This may mean that Japan will enter the war,' and, on 27 October, 'It looks like war.' The King's apprehensions were more perceptive than others'. There was no premonition of impending disaster in either Washington or London.

It was from the radio at Windsor that the King learned, on 7 December, of the devastating Japanese air attack on the American naval base of Pearl Harbor in Honolulu. Worse was to follow, with Japanese attacks on Hong Kong and landings in Malaya. Britain and the United States declared war on Japan, and Hitler declared war on the United States. The conflict was now truly a world one.

On 9 December, at their regular Tuesday lunch, Churchill 'gave me the latest news from America which was dreadful. In Pearl Harbor three US battleships were sunk & three seriously damaged. There are now only two effective US ships in the Pacific, which means that USA has already lost command of the sea in the Pacific . . .'

On the next day the King was in South Wales with the Queen, visiting industrial centres, when Lascelles was called to the telephone to be told that both the *Prince of Wales* and *Repulse* had been sunk by Japanese air attack. The King was deeply shocked and upset, but determined that his programme should continue, and he gave no public sign of his distress at what he described in a letter to Churchill that evening as 'a national disaster'. He went on: 'I thought I was getting immune to hearing bad news, but this has affected me deeply, as I am sure it has you.'

Churchill's robust declaration that he had not become the King's First Minister of the Crown to preside over the liquidation of the British Empire at this stage looked distinctly hollow. Almost everywhere, the Empire was on the retreat. To face these mounting misfortunes with determination that they could and would be reversed was an immense test of national character, and it was one to which the British people responded.

Churchill, not an immodest man nor much afflicted by humility, always averred that it was the spirit, valour and optimism of the British people and their Commonwealth allies that were his inspiration. He marvelled at their fortitude, patience and ingenuity. He was often impatient at military commanders who lacked his aggressive spirit; he was too often over-impressed by those whose ambitions were unmatched by ability or resources; he had to make unpleasant compromises; he made mistakes. He ended the military careers of many, including Wavell and Auchinleck, to the enduring resentment of their friends, fellow officers and admirers; he seriously overrated Orde Wingate and Mountbatten, but they had the dash and eagerness he was seeking, and certainly found in Montgomery; he tried Brooke and Cunningham, and many others, sorely, but he provided the goad that was essential when boldness held the greater opportunities and cautious lethargy spelled potential disaster. Explaining to the King the removal of a certain General in North Africa, he succinctly described him as 'a very small agreeable man of no personality & very little experience'. It was, as it happened, a perfect description. Churchill's assessments of men were variable, but there were many occasions when they proved to be totally right. And in his resolute ardour to win he had a united people behind him.

The King *was* a modest man. He did not have a fraction of Churchill's power or authority. He had a tiny personal staff, infinitely smaller than that of a government minister. His London headquarters was a virtually uninhabited shell. He wrote his own letters and diaries; he made, and received, his own telephone calls. He, the Queen, and his small staff organised their travel arrangements. He read the newspapers without the benefit of a press office or cuttings service. He listened carefully to the BBC radio news broadcasts. Given deep secrets by Churchill, especially regarding the Ultra decrypts from Bletchley Park and the progress of the atomic bomb researches, he kept them. He operated essentially privately, even secretively. He was wary of confiding in anyone apart from Churchill and the Queen – and, later, Lascelles.

The burden of paperwork was in itself exhausting, but the King's demands to be kept informed were responded to by Churchill's orders. He was a modest drinker of alcohol, unlike several of his ministers, but a heavy smoker of cigarettes. His moods varied greatly, but his nerve never faltered. He once remarked to Lascelles – as he did to others – that 'I know we are going to win, but God knows how.'

He immersed himself totally in the war effort, while often pondering on the post-war problems, which had initiated the processes that led to the Beveridge Report in 1942. He was constantly restless and troubled, often by apparent trivialities. Swift to furious anger, he could be, equally suddenly, calm and amusing.

The Queen often conducted her own forays and travels, returning with important insights into morale and problems. She once went to an RAF weather station during the planning for a bombing raid. The meteorological expert concluded his exposition by announcing that the night was clear and cloudless. The Queen, looking out of the window, politely pointed out that it was pouring with rain and virtually impossible to see anything. Her frequent visits to bombed cities, towns and hospitals brought back not only stories of tragedy and courage but rich humour.

No one could claim, least of all the King, that he was an inspiring orator, or even that he had an inspiring presence. His subjects, meeting him for the first time – as so many tens of thousands were to do – were usually startled by how relatively small in stature and apparently diffident he was (the Queen, of course, being even smaller, although certainly not diffident). He could also be exceptionally tense on some occasions but surprisingly relaxed on others. Not even those closest to him could anticipate his moods, and there was one occasion in 1943 when his private secretaries confidentially consulted Lord Dawson of Penn about the King's 'Nashvilles'. Dawson, who did not examine the King, commented disconcertingly on the prevalence of epilepsy in the family history, but this was certainly not the opinion of the King's favourite homeopathic doctor, John Weir, nor, indeed, of Hardinge or Lascelles.

The simple fact was that the King was highly strung, and quite small things could send him into a brief paroxysm of rage. But, like Eden, who had a very similar temperament, he was remarkably calm at moments of real crisis. Lascelles, greatly daring but sure of his ground, once told him to his face that he reminded him of King Lear. Although the King's education had been limited, he understood the comparison, and his anger vanished into laughter.

What shone out of him, and was so clearly evident, were his decency, sincerity and determination. Those closest to him were devoted to him, protected him, and often worried about him. What they did notice was that the fact that he now had a real and important role had transformed him. He was not simply a ceremonial monarch, but an active participant in a desperate war.

His growing exasperation with Hardinge lay in the fact that he wanted to be active and innovative, while Hardinge was excessively cautious, and, in the King's opinion, negative. Churchill – and Lascelles – were of a more adventurous and understanding disposition.

What few recognised at the time, and which in retrospect is so evident, was that Hardinge's nerve and health had been severely and permanently affected by the abdication crisis. His subsequent reclusiveness and impatient solitariness, which so exasperated those who had to work with him, demonstrated that he had never fully recovered from the trauma of what he perceived as his failure as King Edward's Private Secretary – although few others blamed him.

What Churchill and Lascelles recognised was that the King had always had the rare quality of imagination. The Duke of York's camps had been one example of this; the eager acceptance of Roosevelt's invitation to Hyde Park and the establishment of the George Cross and Medal had been others. It was, for example, the King's idea to confer an immediate Victoria Cross posthumously upon Captain Fogarty of the converted merchant crusier *Jervis Bay*, which had saved thirty-three out of thirty-eight ships in his convoy by taking on, suicidally, the pocket battleship *Admiral Scheer* and the cruiser *Hipper*.

Indeed, the Tuesday morning Buckingham Palace investitures became as sacred to the King as his ensuing lunch with the Prime Minister. The former also required considerable preparation, as the King insisted on knowing about the achievements of the individuals he was personally honouring. All this took a great deal of time, which the King never begrudged. In 1945 he calculated that since the outbreak of war he had personally bestowed over 44,000 medals and decorations.

He and the Queen had gone immediately to Coventry when it was heavily bombed on the night of 13 November 1940, and thereafter as soon as possible to Southampton, Birmingham and Bristol – the precursor of many unplanned and hurried visits to badly damaged cities. During the war they travelled over 50,000 miles in the United Kingdom alone.

He and the Queen genuinely liked Americans, and admired their zest – Ambassador Kennedy, always predicting a British collapse, being a notable exception. When Roosevelt sent Harry Hopkins to Britain in January 1941, 'to see whether British morale was really as bad as Kennedy pretended', not only Churchill but the King and Queen soon put him right.

As the King and Churchill both knew, Hopkins' visit was crucial, not least because one of Kennedy's canards was that Churchill was anti-American and disliked Roosevelt personally. It was also vital to dispel the ambassador's portrait of a country and people being battered into despair and defeat.

Churchill applied all his charm and eloquence upon the distinguished guest, entertained him royally at Chequers, Downing Street and Ditchley, and took him to the heavily bombed Portsmouth and Southampton as well as London, and the as yet un-bombed Glasgow. Hopkins was amazed by Churchill's immense popularity wherever they went, the scale of the bomb damage, and the spirit of the people. He had been an admirer of the King and Queen since their 'astounding' 1939 visit and the Queen's kindness to his daughter, and his visit to Buckingham Palace was another great success.

The King particularly stressed to Hopkins the need for Churchill and Roosevelt to meet, as long telegrams were no substitute for personal discussion. There had already been some serious misunderstandings and resultant impatience and irritation in London and Washington that needed to be prevented in future, and it was important that the President and Prime Minister got to know each other. Churchill was equally keen, not least to dispel the Kennedy myths of his anti-Americanism and dislike of the President, repeatedly emphasising his American mother. What Churchill did not realise was that the President had taken a great dislike to him as a result of their unfortunate meeting in 1919, of which Churchill had no recollection.[7]

Hopkins' reports on his long British visit glowed with enthusiasm

[7] Roosevelt had been Assistant Secretary of the Navy; Churchill was Secretary of State for War. Roosevelt considered that Churchill had condescended to him and been offensively patronising – as he probably had. When Churchill was in New York in 1929 he asked to see the newly elected Governor; the Governor, Franklin D. Roosevelt, refused to see him.

for the British leadership, people and armed forces. He stressed the need for the two leaders to meet, and the processes whereby they did were begun.

Of course, the King's role had been of less importance than that of Churchill and his ministers – Hopkins was particularly impressed that the Cabinet and government contained so many Labour and Liberal ministers – but that he had met the King and Queen in Washington and had got on well with them greatly helped. Thus, the King again acted as a personal link with the American government.

The King later developed as good a relationship with the rising American star General Dwight Eisenhower as he had with the Roosevelts and Hopkins. Kennedy's successor, John Winant, was more difficult, although a vast improvement, having in June 1940 reported from London counteracting Kennedy's defeatist reports to Washington. But Winant and his wife were disconcertingly taciturn and shy, almost as difficult to converse with as Attlee – and, later, Wavell.

The King himself was more careless of his personal safety and comfort than those responsible for his security. When he and the Queen travelled by the Royal Train it was shunted in tunnels or in deep embankments for the night; as Lascelles once pointed out tartly, East Anglia was particularly ill-equipped with these protections. The King shared with Churchill great, and almost reckless, physical courage, taking the view that as millions of his subjects were exposed to many dangers he could not be exempt.

He was determined that, as far as possible, peacetime traditions should be preserved, although, mercifully, without the 'high-hat' ceremonies that he so detested. There could be no Court life, which was a relief, but the formalities were maintained and firmly recorded in the *Court Circular* and *London Gazette*. Meetings with Privy Councillors, ambassadors and dignitaries were duly reported. All important appointments, promotions and resignations were submitted to the King for his approval – not always easily given unless his prior agreement had been received. Churchill increasingly took him into his confidence about senior ministerial appointments.

After the Buckingham Palace shelter had been built in 1941 he and the Queen resumed their pre-war habit of small private dinner parties at the shattered and uncomfortable Palace. On 27 November he recorded in his diary that 'we spent the night at BP, the first since Sept 1940. We felt we had to break the idea that we could not stay there for reasons of security.' When Eleanor Roosevelt stayed at the Palace in October 1942 she was appalled by the conditions. She did not realise until later that she had been given the best bedroom available. The windows were boarded up, there was no heating, lighting was restricted to one bulb for each room, hot bathwater was limited to a few inches, and Lascelles later described to Michael Adeane the miseries of returning to the Palace after dinner 'to find that great, dark, draughty house uninhabited except for a few housemaids & footmen'. But the King and Queen stolidly and resolutely kept this gloomy, echoing and eerie monstrosity going.

It has been claimed that the Royal Family, while giving the appearance of sharing the nation's shortages, received special treatment, particularly in clothes coupons.[8] As so often, the truth was more prosaic.

When clothes rationing was introduced in 1941 the Queen asked the Keeper of the Privy Purse, Sir Ulick Alexander, to write to the President of the Board of Trade (Oliver Lyttelton) to ask if a supplement might be possible. 'Her Majesty and all other members of the Royal Family are naturally most anxious to abide by the clothes allowance regulations,' Alexander wrote on 25 June. 'At the same time I feel sure you can well appreciate that if they have to carry out many official functions, this necessarily leads to the purchase of more clothes than the regulation number of coupons would provide. I wonder if you would think this over and decide the best way to deal with this question. It will always be necessary for members of the Royal Family to hand over coupons for any clothes they may buy, as otherwise the firms they purchase them from will be unable to replenish their stocks.'[9] Lyttelton considered this request very reasonable. Alexander would be issued with 1,500 coupons for the year August 1941–August 1942 for

---

[8] See Ina Zweiniger-Bargeilowska, *History Today*, December 1993; Roberts, in *Eminent Churchillians* (p. 44), states, 'Far from sharing precisely the same position as the rest of the nation, it has recently emerged that the Queen and other members of her family each received on average over twenty times the number of clothing coupons above their normal ration.' This statement is the result of a simple error; he has extrapolated from the article that *each* member of the Royal Family received the number of extra coupons allocated for *all* of them and the ladies-in-waiting.

[9] RA PP (Treas.) GVI.

supplying to the royal ladies; 'The Queen has commanded me when doing so to emphasise the necessity that they should be used as sparingly as possible,' Alexander wrote to Lyttelton's successor, Sir Andrew Duncan, on 3 July.

They were indeed. Of the 1,500 coupons issued for the royal ladies for the year, only 1,092 were used. Of these, the Queen received 200, Queen Mary 250, the Duchess of Kent and the Duchess of Gloucester 250 each, and the Princess Royal 100. Additional coupons (1,248) were supplied for servants. The King in the year July 1942 to July 1943 asked for only 30 additional coupons, to enable him to buy new shirts.

It should be added that Alexander was indeed 'sparing' in his allocation to the royal ladies; when clothes rationing was ended in 1949 he had over 600 unused coupons. These facts do not confirm Dr Zweiniger-Bargeilowska's claim that this 'belies the image of the Royal Family's strict adherence to the fair shares policy'. Indeed, they flatly contradict it.

One later historian, commenting on the Queen's celebrated remark about 'looking the East End in the face' added somewhat waspishly, 'The East End, however, was not able to retreat to Windsor at the weekend to catch up on sleep, or to spend recuperative holidays in Norfolk and Scotland. Nor was the East End able to supplement its diet with pheasants and venison shot on the royal estates.'[10]

The reasons for using Windsor have already been described. Sandringham was closed in 1940 for the whole of the war, and, as the King's and Lascelles' diaries emphasise, the 'recuperative holidays' were few and were never uninterrupted. In August 1941 the King, Queen and the Princesses went to Balmoral for the first time for two years; in August and September 1942 they went there for longer[11] but their stay was ruined for them initially by terrible weather and then, on 25 August, by the death of the Duke of Kent when his aircraft, flying to Iceland, crashed in Scotland, killing everyone on board. It was a loss that affected the King deeply. Kent had caused his family many anxieties, but he had matured admirably after his marriage and his service in the RAF had been rightly praised, for which the King was grateful.

[10] Pimlott, op. cit., p. 63.
[11] In August 1943 the Royal Family stayed at Balmoral for five weeks, by far the longest break the King had throughout the war.

The aftermath to the Duke's death aroused considerable political controversy.

The King and the Queen, as Duke and Duchess of York, had attended the wedding of Prince Paul of Yugoslavia in Belgrade in October 1923, at which the Duke had been the Prince's best man. The bride, Princess Olga of Greece, was the eldest sister of Princess Marina, later Duchess of Kent.

Prince Paul had little interest in politics, but the assassination of his cousin King Alexander in Marseille in October 1934 compelled him to become Regent until his son Peter took the throne. It was a task for which he was quite unsuited even in quiet times, and the Balkans in 1940 and 1941 were notably unquiet.

In July 1940 the King, at Churchill's request, had tried to stiffen Paul's resolution against Nazi intimidation, but the German occupation of Romania and the Italian attack on Greece had deepened not only his personal depression at the course of the war but greatly increased the pressures on him for his country to join the Axis. King George tried to counter this with a long personal letter giving a positive account of the progress of the war, trying to encourage him, and praising him for his 'skill and patience'. But he could offer nothing in the way of practical military assistance.

By February 1941 the Regent's position had become desperate.

Hitler demanded passage through Yugoslavia for German forces coming to the assistance of the battered Italian army. On 1 March Bulgaria joined the Axis, and on the 4th Prince Paul gave Hitler an assurance that Yugoslavia would do the same. Churchill delivered a stern warning to the Yugoslav government, and the King, rejecting a Foreign Office draft, wrote another personal letter to Prince Paul urging him to stand firm, ending, 'We count on you.'[12]

There was no possibility of this. On 25 March Yugoslavia signed the Axis Pact in Vienna. The news was greeted with disbelief and then intense anger. A military coup ended the Regency and pronounced the accession of King Peter; it also abrogated the adherence to the Axis. On 6 April the Germans and the Bulgarians attacked. On the 17th the Yugoslav army surrendered.

For this disaster Prince Paul was cast in the same role as King Leopold

[12] Wheeler-Bennett, op. cit., p. 497.

had been. Churchill derided him as 'Prince Palsy', and blamed him personally for leading his country into 'shameful tutelage'. Even the King, who appreciated Paul's hideous dilemma more sympathetically, wrote, 'Poor Paul, he has a lot to answer for I am afraid for the present position of the Balkans.'[13]

Prince Paul and his family went into exile, first in Cairo and then under house arrest in Kenya, generally reviled until Neil Balfour was to restore the former Regent's reputation in 1980, his own memoirs having not achieved this.

The King decided that the grieving Duchess of Kent and her young children needed solace, and it was his decision that Princess Olga should be flown to Britain from Kenya to be with her sister. This compassionate action was strongly and widely condemned, not least in the House of Commons, where an unpleasant Conservative MP, Captain Alec Cunningham-Reid, not only denounced Prince Paul as a dangerous traitor but his dominating wife, also. Churchill publicly defended the decision, without revealing that it had been the King's and not his, but without much conviction.

The King was then concerned about the finances of the Kents. On this he received little sympathy and support, even among his private secretaries. The Duke had inherited a million pounds from his father, and his extravagances had been notorious. In these circumstances, and in the context of the times, the King's suggestion for a special Civil List income for the widow and her children was coolly received.

This might explain why the King was reluctant to receive special messages of condolence from both Houses of Parliament. He had returned to Balmoral after the funeral and a special private visit to the site of the fatal crash. He did not see why his first break since 1939 should be further disrupted by this unnecessary and unwelcome reminder of his family tragedy. Thus, the distinguished two-man deputation[14] had to find their way, escorted by an embarrassed Lascelles, to a shooting lodge in which the King was about to have lunch, to deliver their messages. The King sat down in the heather, took the documents and signed his replies.

[13] Diary, 24 September 1941.
[14] The Lord Chamberlain, Lord Clarendon, and the Vice-Chamberlain of the Household, Boulton.

As Lascelles and others realised, this apparent gracelessness and ill-temper, so untypical of him, indicated his tiredness and the strain of recent events. The bleak response to his invitation to Princess Olga and his attempts to help the Kents had not made his mood any lighter. The rather puzzled emissaries were provided with lunch at the lodge and driven back to the station for the long return journey to London.

As has been related, the King's original poor opinion of Eden had been completely changed by his performance as War Minister and then Foreign Secretary. Eden had been enormously popular since his star had risen dramatically in the early 1930s and then because of his resignation in February 1938. He still had his critics and detractors – principally in the Conservative Party – but had definitely emerged as a major national and international figure, his prestige almost on a par with Churchill's. The changed relationship was manifested in the King's diaries. Thus, on 30 April 1942 he recorded: 'Anthony Eden came to dinner. We discussed everything. He is very good at telling me things & I feel I can ask him about people frankly.'

A minister whom the King did not get to know well during the war was Sir Stafford Cripps, partly because he was abroad for a significant part of it, first as Ambassador in Moscow in 1940–42, and then on the sadly unproductive Mission to India in 1942. What the King saw of him he liked and respected, but it was not until he succeeded the disgraced Dalton as Chancellor of the Exchequer in 1947 that he came to know him well, and Cripps, the one-time left-wing firebrand, was able to render a notable service to the monarchy.

Churchill, meanwhile, was active as never before. It was before his journey to see Roosevelt off Newfoundland that Attlee had expressed his concern about the possibility of the Prime Minister's ship being sunk, to which Churchill had cheerily responded, 'I fear there will be no such luck.' But the same thought had occurred to the King, as Churchill became more and more enthusiastic about foreign travel and summit conferences. Aircraft were only too often shot down or crashed, warships were regularly sunk, and although Churchill's health seemed robust, his age, lifestyle and intense activity caused some concern, and with justification.

The King was not the only person worried about Churchill's health. He was now well past his mid-sixties and his medical record, including a near-fatal road accident in New York in December 1931, had its worrying aspects, including pneumonia and other respiratory problems. It was this concern that prompted a Cabinet request in 1941, strongly endorsed by the King, that he should have a personal physician; the choice fell upon Sir Charles Wilson, who became Lord Moran shortly afterwards.

While staying at the White House in late December 1941 Churchill had what might have been a minor heart attack while opening a heavy window. It was almost certainly not a cardiac arrest, but it was a warning sign nevertheless. In February 1943 he had mild pneumonia, but in mid-December, in Tunis, he had a much more serious attack, dealt with by the new drug M & B and over three weeks of rest. A milder pneumonia afflicted him on his return from conferences in Italy late in August 1944. Again, the magical M & B and his own resilience came to the rescue.

Given the severe strains of war and the burdens he carried, Churchill's wartime health record was remarkably good; much younger men collapsed under lesser responsibilities. Roosevelt's decline and relatively early death were certainly accelerated by the war. But Churchill was more careful of his health than was usually realised, and it was not until 1949 that he suffered the first of a series of strokes that were ultimately to end his life.

But the King and the War Cabinet were right to be worried about him. He had his critics in the Conservative Party and in parliament, and in some sections of the press, but no other British war leader of his stature and reputation seemed conceivable.

In retrospect it would have been as well if the King had been equally solicitous about his own health, but his confidence in his homeopathic doctor John Weir was total, and he seemed to be physically well, although sometimes looking frail. And his own energy matched that of his Prime Minister.

It was at a Tuesday lunch early in June 1942 that the King raised with Churchill the matter of his successor in the event of the latter's death. They agreed that Eden was the obvious choice, and Churchill would have left it at that, but the King insisted that Churchill write him a letter formally recommending Eden, and contributed to its drafting. In his war memoirs Churchill originally claimed that it was his own initiative, but the King firmly reminded him of whose idea it had been.

It was when Churchill and Eden began to travel together that a new possibility occurred to the King. What if both were killed; for whom should he send? There was no obvious Conservative minister of comparable stature. Attlee had by then the unusual title of Deputy Prime Minister, but he was the leader of a minority party in the Commons, and still, after several years as leader of the Labour Party, remained a somewhat obscure public figure, less well-known than Bevin, Morrison or Cripps. Also, for all his qualities of common sense and quiet diligence, he hardly resembled a great war leader.

To the King's considerable surprise, Churchill recommended the Chancellor of the Exchequer, Sir John Anderson, an Independent MP, already considered and rejected as a candidate for the Viceroyalty of India, as someone who could maintain 'the present harmonious coalition whose services will, the Prime Minister is sure, never be forgotten by Your Majesty or by the people, having regard to the extraordinary perils through which we have safely passed'.[15]

This recommendation was quite astonishing, particularly as Churchill seriously envisaged Anderson eventually becoming leader of the Conservative Party. But Churchill deemed Anderson 'well-qualified to sustain the existing all-party government'.

The King's papers and diaries are silent about his reactions to this advice, but Wheeler-Bennett's opinion that the King would have consulted the party leaders before making a choice seems eminently sensible and right, particularly given Lascelles' opinions of Anderson – and of Lady Anderson. Fortunately, the matter never arose.

British attitudes towards Russia have been extreme for over two centuries, ranging from barbarous tyrant to heroic allies. After 22 June 1941 the second view prevailed. In the opinion of many, including the King, this enthusiasm was carried rather too far. While he and Churchill recognised the importance of the Russian involvement in the war and in the Anglo-American war supplies through the grim and courageous Arctic convoys, they both had other memories and no illusions about the nature of the Soviet regime.

The Russian defence, and then assault, at Stalingrad produced some of the most savage battles of the entire war, and finally the German

[15] RA PS GVI C 069/55.

capitulation on 1 February 1943. The state of British feeling towards the Russians was manifested in large public meetings to commemorate Red Army Day on 21 February and to celebrate the great victory.

The suggestion was made to the King – by whom, it is not quite clear, but conveyed to him by Churchill – that the valour and terrible sacrifices of the people of Stalingrad should be recognised. Difficulties then arose over what would be an appropriate tribute. The idea of awarding the George Cross to the city was immediately dismissed by the King, on the grounds that it must be strictly limited to his subjects. A special Military Cross was suggested, but this was turned down because it was inferior to the GC and might be considered an insult by the Russians. After considerable argument the Foreign Office suggested a Sword of Honour, which the King considered a 'quite excellent' idea, and which he announced in a special message to President Kalinin on Red Army Day.

The King took considerable interest in the draft designs, finally choosing that of the Slade Professor of Fine Art at Oxford, Professor Gleadowe. When it was brought to Buckingham Palace in September it was not one of his better days. After looking somewhat cursorily at the magnificent object, the only question he asked of the proud designer and craftsmen was its cost. The King had not intended to give offence, and his mind was on other things; also, he did not wholly share the pro-Soviet emotions of the time.

But the Sword made a triumphal procession through the country, attracting unexpectedly huge crowds, before the King entrusted it to Churchill to present it on his behalf to Stalin at the Tehran Conference in November. Churchill recorded in his war memoirs that 'when, after a few sentences of explanation, I handed the splendid weapon to Marshal Stalin, he raised it in a most impressive gesture to his lips and kissed the scabbard. He then passed it to Voroshilov who dropped it.' Other witnesses said that Stalin in fact half-drew the blade and kissed the blade just below the hilt. His short speech was inaudible, as was his interpreter; the British had to assume that Stalin was expressing his profound gratitude. Tehran was the high point of the Churchill–Roosevelt–Stalin relationship; thereafter the balance of military and political power, and Roosevelt's illusions about Stalin, were to make Churchill the weakest of the triumvirate.

★　　★　　★

The question of who should succeed Linlithgow as Viceroy of India had troubled the King and Churchill for some time. Now the matter had to be resolved.

The subject first arose towards the end of 1942, when Churchill discussed it with the King at their weekly lunch on 1 December. At that point the favoured candidates were the British Ambassador to Egypt, Sir Miles Lampson, and Cranborne, with Sinclair as a possibility. Cranborne refused it, and Churchill then realised that Samuel would succeed Sinclair as leader of the Liberal Party, a prospect that did not attract him. Although the King considered that 'Lampson will do it well' (Diary, 1 December), this suggestion faded, as Lampson's role in Egypt was deemed too important.

The King, Churchill and Amery discussed the problem again in April 1943. It was not an enviable position, given the political turbulence in India and the menacing Japanese threat, but a crucially important one. As so often happens, the detailed and long debates produced the wrong result, from which much unnecessary misery and bloodshed ensued.

The name of Anderson, a suitably Olympian and inscrutable choice, had arisen, but was then rejected – one factor, although no doubt a minor one, being the personality of his wife, Ava, who was not deemed of Vicereine standard by some advisers. But Churchill also felt that he was more valuable in Britain, his regard for this dour and unattractive Victorian remaining a mystery. The more favoured name was that of Wavell, Commander-in-Chief in India between July and December 1941 and since then Supreme Commander, South-West Pacific, who had the advantage of being on the spot and highly regarded by the military, if not by Churchill. The King found Wavell's long 'oyster-like' silences disconcerting.

Then Churchill produced a startling new proposal. After speaking to Lascelles Churchill informed the King that, on Amery's advice, 'his mind is turning very decidedly towards Mr Eden. An appointment of this character might be the sole chance of lifting the whole Indian problem out of its present disastrous rut.'

He went on to say how he had at first rejected this suggestion

because of the evident loss which Your Majesty's Government at home, and he personally as Prime Minister, would sustain by Mr Eden's departure. Mr Churchill was however surprised to find that

Mr Eden was not only willing to go if he were strongly pressed, but was powerfully attracted to the idea of rendering this great service to the British Empire. Mr Churchill feels that it would be a dismal conclusion to all the glories which this war may bring our country if India were finally separated from Your Majesty's Dominions, and all that great story came to an ignominious end. Such a melancholy episode would dim our fame in this age to future generations. He therefore feels we must if necessary face inconvenience at home in order to place our most capable men in the decisive stations. No one has the qualities and reputation of Mr Eden, and there is no one whose appointment would excite so much world-wide interest and goodwill or would have so good a chance to reverse the downward drift of events.[16]

Hardinge was appalled, minuting to the King that 'I am convinced that AE cannot be spared. He is the only person who talks to the PM as an equal and can argue with him without there being a "row"! Whom would the PM get hold of to confide in and to discuss matters with at all hours of the day and night?'[17] Perhaps to fortify his case, he raised the spectre of Beaverbrook being recommended, and again suggested Sinclair.

In fact, unknown to Hardinge and Lascelles, the King and Churchill had discussed the matter at their lunch the week before, and the King noted on Hardinge's minute, 'I agree that Anthony should not go now. The PM was emphatic about that a week ago, but did say that Anthony, with whom he had discussed the matter, was willing to go if wanted to. PM was surprised at this.'[18] The King saw Eden on 9 June, and asked him about his views. 'He is ready to go if he must but he fears B[eaverbroo]k may return to the War Cabinet if there is a vacancy there. W. is now thinking of Wavell as Viceroy, & Auchinleck as C-in-C, & Oliver Leese as fighting general in Burma. These are the latest developments.'[19] The King did not dismiss the idea of Eden as

---

[16] RA PS GVI C 069/30, also Lascelles' almost identical memorandum to the King of 24 April (RA PS GVI C 200/03).
[17] RA PS GVI C 069/31.
[18] RA PS GVI C 069/32.
[19] Diary, 9 June 1943.

Viceroy, and was contemplating what appropriate titles Eden should receive that would not finish his political career.

Thus, the King's reactions to the proposal were unenthusiastic rather than hostile, although his doubts were made very plain, and he pointed out that Linlithgow had several months of his term of office left and there was no immediate urgency. Churchill wrote to him on 30 April that 'he does not remember ever to have had a more difficult question of this character to solve'.[20]

But even before the King's letter Eden had had second thoughts, as had Churchill. The King also personally urged Eden to stay, and the matter seemed to have been settled when Churchill made the suggestion in June that Eden should become Viceroy but remain in the government. 'He is thinking of Eden with a three-year term of office & frequent visits home,' the King noted with consternation in his diary. 'I asked him how he [Eden] could be in two places at once, as being Viceroy is a whole-time job.' Churchill thereupon dropped the idea, and Wavell was appointed on 19 June.

Wavell certainly did not share Churchill's romantic imperial opinions about India; he did not consider it possible, or even desirable, that British policy should be to retain control over India against the wishes of a large number of its people. At the very outset of his Viceroyalty he proposed to release the Hindu Congress leaders Gandhi and Nehru from prison as a conciliatory gesture; this was bold enough, but Wavell then wanted to appoint them as members of his Executive Council.

This provoked one of the King's more vehement 'Nashvilles', describing Wavell's proposals as 'suicidal'. Churchill, although he entirely agreed with the King over this suggestion, was politically more realistic, warning the King at a Tuesday lunch in July 1942 that it was almost the universal view in parliament that Indian independence after the war was inevitable. The King was astounded, and did not agree, saying, 'India has got to be governed, & this will have to be our policy.' More than ever he regretted that he had never visited India, and his attempts to do so were resisted by Churchill.

It was not the case that the King had vetoed Eden's appointment. Indeed, initially he had taken it very seriously, as had Churchill. It was unfortunate that their understandable desire to keep Eden at the Foreign

[20] RA PS GVI C 069/34.

Office, and knowing that he was Churchill's accepted successor in the event of Churchill's death, prevented what could have been an inspired appointment.

Wavell's was not. What was required in India was a sensitive politician and experienced diplomat, rather than a brave and fine soldier whose qualities did not include the ability to communicate. Excellent on paper, in conversation Wavell's shyness could be misconstrued as grim taciturnity and even limited intelligence. In the swirling tactics and mutual hostilities of Indian politics, confronted with men of the qualities of Gandhi, Nehru and the Muslim League leader Jinnah, he was lost and hopelessly out-manouevred. Harold Macmillan was right when he described Wavell as Viceroy as 'charming, sincere, cultivated – but no politician, and hopelessly bemused'.

Eden would surely have handled these complex, slippery, highly intelligent, superficially charming and inordinately vain men with more guile and success than Wavell could have possibly done. They might have met their match in Viceroy Eden, whose later warm and close friendship with Nehru was to be very different from Mountbatten's.

But the episode demonstated how totally the King's attitude towards Eden had changed. The man who 'could only read from his brief', who had, as the King thought, patronised him when he had acceded to the throne and who had irritated him as Foreign Secretary in 1937 by what the King resented as 'his know-all manner', had become in his eyes indispensable.

And thus, from very understandable motives, a great opportunity was lost.

The overwhelming Anglo-American victories in North Africa gave the King the opportunity of raising with Churchill in the Tuesday lunch on 23 March 1943 the possibility of him visiting the British, Dominion and American troops in Tunisia and possibly also Malta. Churchill was positive about North Africa, although hesitant on Malta, and so was the War Cabinet when the King dined with them in 10 Downing Street on 31 March. The plans were prepared for him to fly on 11 June in the York aircraft that had been specially converted for Churchill's use. He was to travel incognito as 'General Lyon'.

The King's excitement at his first trip abroad since December 1939 was tempered by his dislike of flying – a curious feature in a qualified pilot – and last-minute doubts about whether he ought to leave the country at all. There was also of course the possibility of his death, which he addressed by settling his personal affairs with his solicitor and appointing five Counsellors of State, to include the Queen.

He took with him Hardinge and Legh; Grigg and Sinclair travelled on another aircraft. The refuelling stop was due to be Gibraltar, but it was enveloped in fog and the pilot had to find a North African alternative. This he successfully did, awaking a startled station commander in the middle of the night, but the somewhat garbled messages reaching London caused the Queen considerable concern – 'of course I imagined every sort of horror', she wrote to Queen Mary, '& walked up & down my room staring at the telephone'[21] – before it was confirmed that the aircraft had been refuelled and had taken off again. It was an unpropitious beginning to what was eventually to be a very successful, if exhausting, visit.

In the King's absence Harold Macmillan discovered that few prior plans had been made for the King's programme, and none whatsoever for visiting the Americans, Hardinge taking the view that the King had come to see only his own troops. 'However,' Macmillan recorded in his diary, 'after a bit we persuaded them that they were wrong and that such an attitude would be an absolute disaster. Actually, General Lyon was merely tired and feverish. I do blame Alec, because he just doesn't seem to live in the modern world at all. He would have been out of date in the 1900s, and King Edward would have sacked him as outmoded then.'[22]

These, and other comments of Macmillan on Hardinge, were harsh and excessive, but the fact was that the eventual success of the visit owed very little to him. 'He is gradually waking up a bit,' Macmillan noted tartly, 'but he is a dreadful stick.'[23] It was Macmillan, supported by Legh, who had the inspired idea for a royal garden party for British and American officers and civilians, and, indeed, most of the arrangements had to be made almost on the spur of the moment, with Hardinge, characteristically, always raising difficulties and objections rather than proposing anything constructive.

There is no record as to whether there were any 'Nashvilles' between

---

[21] Wheeler-Bennett, op. cit., p. 568.
[22] Macmillan, *War Diaries*, pp. 120–1.
[23] Ibid, p. 122.

the King and Hardinge, but Legh was very much aware of the King's tension in private. What neither of them knew was that in London there was chaos, as Hardinge had taken the crucial official keys and had given Lascelles and Mieville no instructions during his absence about the Council of State and Wavell's appointment. For Lascelles this was the last straw.

But for the King the most important part of his North African tour was to visit Malta. He had been filled with admiration for its gallant defence against almost overwhelming odds by the garrison, the RAF pilots, and men of the Royal Navy and merchant marine who had suffered grievously in supplying it – and the heroic people of Malta. It was on his own initiative that he had awarded the island the George Cross in April 1942; when the Governor, General William Dobbie, collapsed under the intense strain the King personally invested him with high honours. His successor, Lord Gort, remained one of the King's favourites; when things looked desperate in July 1942 and surrender and evacuation seemed only too possible, the King had sent Gort a personal letter of support.

The King's confidence in Gort had proved fully justified. At considerable sacrifice, but at very heavy losses by the German and Italian air forces, Malta had not only held out but its defence had inflicted a major defeat on the German lines of communication. From near disaster a considerable victory had been achieved, and the King's eagerness to visit Malta to congratulate its defenders and citizens was deeply personal.

This journey, by sea, was hazardous. The Italian navy had not surrendered, its submarines were still active, and Malta was only sixty miles from enemy-held Sicily and its airfields, and within range of German aircraft on the Italian mainland. But the King was immensely anxious to try, and Admiral Cunningham did not consider the risks 'prohibitive'. On the night of 19 June the King was conveyed to Malta in the cruiser *Aurora*. It was a rough crossing, to add to the miseries of dysentery from which the King and his suite were suffering, but he was on the bridge when *Aurora* steamed into the Grand Harbour of Valletta at 8.15 on the morning of the 20th.

This was one of the most moving and important occasions of the war for the King. The garrison and people of Malta had been alerted to the King's arrival by loud-speaker vans at 5.30 a.m. When *Aurora* sailed into the Grand Harbour, with the King in white naval uniform saluting from the bridge on a glorious sunny morning, it was to a tumultuous and passionate welcome. The church bells pealed, the crowds were large and enthusiastic, the King personally presented Gort with his Field Marshal's baton, and did not mind at all that his uniform was made red by the scarlet geraniums – the only available flowers – thrown at him and into his car by the Maltese. The man so well-known, even notorious, for the perfection of uniforms and decorations only noted in his diary that the red posies were 'quite detrimental to my white uniform'. He had seldom looked more happy.

On his departure he said, 'I have been the happiest man in Malta today,' and wrote to his mother that 'the real gem of my tour was my visit to Malta'.

The King's concern for the island, its governors, garrisons and people, had been profound and totally genuine. His award of the George Cross had been one of his most imaginative gestures, and his enduring faith in Gort had been totally vindicated.

The King and his party returned to Northolt airport early in the morning of 25 June in Churchill's York. The King had lost a stone in weight, and was exhausted but exhilarated. He had been surprised by the enthusiasm of his reception by the British soldiers, and deeply moved by that in Malta. His diaries reflect his modest pleasure at the effect his unexpected appearances had made.

The crisis over his private office occurred after his return. Lascelles, finding it impossible to work with Hardinge, depressed by his lonely life in London, and trying to work in the draughty, bleak and virtually uninhabited Buckingham Palace, decided to resign after Hardinge had sent him a note so offensive that he felt he had no alternative.

Hardinge, clearly overwrought, exhausted and physically debilitated, told Lascelles that he, also, intended to resign. There was a fiery meeting between the two, when Lascelles suggested that they should consult Cranborne. At first Hardinge agreed, but then changed his mind, saying he wanted to consult his wife.

After doing so Hardinge sent the King a letter of resignation. The King wrote in his diary for 6 July that

it came as a great shock & a great surprise to me. Tommy Lascelles had had a long talk with him when he told Alec that he could no longer work with him. This was the outcome of AH's great secrecy over my N. Af. tour when he left no instructions to either Tommy or Eric M. over the Council of State or Wavell's appt as Viceroy. The latter question I dealt with myself with the PM & I had told E[ric] about it before I went away. I saw Tommy after dinner who explained the whole position to me & told me the cause of it. Both he & Eric had been kept so much in the dark by Alec as to what was going on & they had often complained that they had not enough work to do. Matters came to a head over this & Alec who has not been well for some long time & was utterly exhausted from the N. Af. tour, wrote me the letter from his house . . .

The King, to Hardinge's – and Lascelles' – astonishment, accepted Hardinge's resignation with alacrity. When Hardinge attempted to withdraw it and asked for sick leave for a few months, to which request Lascelles was sympathetic, the King was adamant. An awful correspondence then ensued, Hardinge justifying himself to an extent that clearly revealed he was gravely unstable. These painful letters merely confirmed the King's determination.

The King's record in his diary is that 'I replied accepting his [Hardinge's] resignation as I was not altogether happy with him & had always found him difficult to talk to & to discuss matters with. I knew & felt that he was doing me no good.'

This was not the response that Hardinge had expected. As the King wrote in his diary.

On Wednesday morning [7 July 1943] he asked me point blank if I really wanted him to resign. I told him I did, saying that I was very grateful for all he had done for me in the last seven years. It was difficult for me to have to do this but I know that I should not get the opportunity again. It came as a real shock to him I could see, & I am sure he expected me to say do go on three months' sick leave. After that I felt matters would be no better. I know I shall miss him in many ways, but I feel happier now it is over. Tommy Lascelles is going to succeed him.

As Lascelles' account also demonstrates, he was never part of any

'Hardinge must go' movement, and did not want the reversion for himself. Also, Hardinge was not dismissed, as has been alleged,[24] but did genuinely resign for reasons of health. The claim that the Queen was also responsible for Hardinge's downfall is correct only in that she was acutely aware, as were so many others, of the severe effects on her husband's nerves and temper from the complete incompatability between him and Hardinge. Her Private Secretary, Arthur Penn, wrote to Lascelles to express the fervent hope that the King 'under your more easy hand may develop a new, and very welcome, mellowness'.

The appointment of Lascelles as Private Secretary was not inevitable, but proved admirable. One problem was that he did not then get on particularly well with Churchill, and later noted in his retirement, as a footnote to his account of a particularly long and bibulous lunch at No. 10 on 19 July 1944, that 'Although W. is Joan's 1st cousin (once removed), we didn't actually get on Xtian name terms until about the end of 1944'. Lascelles would never forget Churchill's use of his Membership of Parliament to return from the Western Front to London in 1916, and they had never agreed – nor ever did – about Lascelles' former master, the Duke of Windsor. Lascelles wrote privately, many years later, that 'Winston's sentimental loyalty to the D. of W. was based on a tragic false premise – viz, that he really *knew* the D. of W. – wh. he never did.' Lascelles' admiration for Churchill as a war leader was very strong, but past disagreements and doubts were not fully assuaged.

This did not really matter, as the relationship between the King and Churchill and his ministers was now so close that there was no need for a conduit. But Lascelles' personal contacts in the official and political world were considerably better than Hardinge's, and far less formal. As events were to prove, he understood and appreciated Attlee rather better than the King or Churchill did.

He had been for some time the King's principal adviser on speeches and broadcasts, on which his skills were formidable, and much appreciated. He was not greatly awed by precedent or tradition, and his attitude to the role of the monarch in these extraordinary circumstances was a positive one.

It was in this that he was so refeshingly different from Hardinge. There were occasions when he resisted or questioned some of the

[24] Bradford, op. cit, p. 545.

King's ideas, and had no hesitation in saying so, but the latter welcomed his initiatives and imagination, and actively encouraged them. He totally lacked Hardinge's depressing negativity and formality. Although devoted to the King and Queen, he was never an obsequious courtier and never considered the monarchy as either a perfect or even a necessarily permanent institution.

Indeed, after his close relationship with Windsor, Lascelles regarded the Royal Family in personal rather than in institutional terms. To an extent that is underestimated, Edward VIII's failure, although Lascelles had anticipated it, had upset him for its human tragedy. He had written to his wife on 23 November 1936 that Edward VIII's abdication would be 'ultimately for the best – I'm inclined to think as the years went on the Hyde side would have predominated over the Jekyll – the pity of it all is heartrending . . . He will be the most tragic might-have-been in all history.'[25]

The King wrote in his own hand to Lascelles from Windsor Castle on 16 July, beginning 'My dear Tommy' to express his great pleasure at Lascelles' acceptance of his offer, his warm appreciation of the value of 'our countless talks' over the previous six and a half years, and to state his complete confidence in his new Private Secretary. He added that he wanted Lascelles to be sworn in to the Privy Council in his presence.

This was part of a remarkable correspondence and relationship, and one which was to develop further. There is nothing remotely comparable in the Hardinge Papers.

Churchill raised no objection to Lascelles' appointment, and their relations were to improve considerably. But one advantage, for the historian, and biographers of Churchill, was that Lascelles' new position brought him into much closer touch with the Prime Minister.

Now permitted into the real inner circle, Lascelles better understood the King's devotion to Churchill and the sheer enjoyment of his company at a time when there was not much else to enjoy. The war was far from won in July 1943.

After the initial contretemps over the appointment of Beaverbrook and the Privy Councillorship for Bracken in 1940, relations between the King and Churchill were so good that the latter, to a quite exceptional

[25] Lascelles Papers.

degree, consulted the King closely about ministerial appointments, and took his advice very seriously. Chamberlain had merely submitted his lists for the King's approval, which he took for granted, as had become the custom under Edward VII and George V; both had their views on individual politicians, but neither had been close enough to any of their Prime Ministers to have a decisive influence. George VI did.

An example of this occurred in September 1943, when the sudden death of the Chancellor of the Exchequer, Kingsley Wood, necessitated a government reshuffle. Wood was replaced by the ever-available and reliable John Anderson, but other changes were also necessary.

The King, with his immense admiration and affection for Cranborne, urged Churchill to make him Lord President of the Council. Lascelles, when the King told him of this, strongly represented to him that Cranborne would be wasted there and was ideal for Dominions Secretary. On reflection, the King agreed, and Lascelles was sent to Downing Street to find Churchill and Eden, each smoking large cigars, coping with the problem, Churchill considering the King's feelings about Cranborne as an order; Lascelles told him and Eden that the King had changed his mind, and wanted Cranborne to become Dominions Secretary. Eden entirely agreed, and Attlee became Lord President.

This was characteristic of the political interaction between the King and Churchill. The former's pressure on the Prime Minister to appoint Cranborne Lord President was entirely personal, as he would see more of him than as a senior minister not in the Cabinet. But Cranborne had been an excellent Secretary of State for the Colonies, and when Lascelles argued this point the King realised he was right. Meanwhile, Churchill had taken the King's views as in effect a command, and was trying to reorganise his government around this appointment when Lascelles arrived to tell him of the King's new opinion, which was decisive.

Although the King had no objection whatsoever to Attlee personally or politically, he would have been much happier with Cranborne, and it would, as it happened, have been a very good appointment. Although Cranborne often gave the impression of rigidity in moral and political issues, in private he was a man of immense charm, kindness and humour, and had already demonstrated a rare degree of political and personal courage. Even in later years, when he had moved somewhat alarmingly to the extreme right of the Conservative Party, the delight of his company, all the better for being quite unfeigned and entirely natural, gave much pleasure. His sense of duty, and deep religious convictions, were other bonds with the King and Queen.

Suddenly in late 1943 it seemed that after more than two years of nothing going right, the war situation was transformed. The North African war ended in Allied triumph. Sicily was captured, and the American and British armies landed in Italy. Mussolini was deposed in July, and on 3 September the Badoglio government agreed to unconditional surrender. The Italian navy sailed to Malta to surrender. The much-feared *Tirpitz* was severely damaged at its Norwegian anchorage by British midget submarines, and on 22 December the *Scharnhorst* was sunk at sea by the Royal Navy. The Battle of the Atlantic had been won. In the Far East, the surging Japanese advances had been decisively checked, and the British and Americans were preparing for the counter-attack.

But, as the King knew only too well, there was another side to this success. Both in Italy and on the Russian front the German resistance was fierce and was inflicting heavy casualties as they gradually retreated; the British and American bombing offensive on Germany remained costly, and Japan was a long way from being defeated. Although Churchill told the King that Germany might well be beaten before the end of 1944, he was doubtful whether Japan would be before 1946.

Also, with his vivid memories of Gallipoli and the Western Front, Churchill was unenthusiastic about the proposed Allied landings on the western European coast. But the massive build-up of American and Canadian armies and *matériel* in Britain, skilfully concealed, proceeded, as did the invasion plans.

Churchill was not alone in his doubts about the decision at the Casablanca Conference in January 1943 to invade western Europe, codenamed 'Overlord'. Smuts was a particularly strong critic of what was essentially an American plan, and which was already weakening the Allied advance in Italy, where the Germans now had a significant numerical superiority on the ground. He was also deeply suspicious of Russian ambitions in the Balkans. On 13 October, in London for a meeting of Commonwealth Prime Ministers, Smuts had a long talk with the King in which he urged concentration upon the Mediterranean, greater force to end the Italian campaign, and the occupation of Greece and Yugoslavia.

In both the King and Churchill – especially the former – he had willing recipients of his apprehensions. Churchill was due to continue his meetings with Stalin and Roosevelt at Cairo and Tehran, and the King invited him to dine with him and Smuts at the Palace on the 14th, following a long letter to the Prime Minister setting out his agreement with Smuts.

At this dinner Churchill emphasised that matters had gone too far for a change of strategy, and was optimistic about Overlord's chances of success. The King and Smuts had to accept his judgement, and Churchill assured them that the Chiefs of Staff, who had seen the King's letter, 'agree that Italy has got to be secured at all costs, before Overlord'.[26] With this, the King had to be content, but the sheer scale of the operation alarmed him when Montgomery and Admiral Sir Bertram Ramsay, the Allied naval Commander-in-Chief, briefed him. 'The more one goes into it, the more alarming it becomes in its vastness,' he noted after a briefing by Ramsay on 3 February 1944. But the die was cast. Although the King still favoured Smuts' Balkan strategy, and fully shared his scepticism about the Russians' intentions, he resolved to do eveything he could to assist in the success of Overlord.

The King's Christmas broadcast in 1943 reflected this cautious mood. 'As we were not downcast by defeat, we are not unduly exalted by victory. While we have bright visions of the future we have no easy dreams of the days that lie close at hand. We know that much hard working and hard fighting, and perhaps harder working and harder fighting than ever before, are necessary for victory.'

He then embarked upon the most formidable tour of Allied forces in Britain since the summer of 1940, and welcomed General Eisenhower – the newly appointed Supreme Commander of the Allied Expeditionary Force – at Buckingham Palace. The King had, of course, met Eisenhower several times before, and the new Supreme Commander had invited him to his headquarters. The King still considered that good Anglo-American relations were crucial, and was fully aware of the tensions between the senior commanders, not least those between Eisenhower and Montgomery.

Although the King liked flamboyant personalities he tended to be sceptical about their egotistical eccentricities, even Churchill's. He was

[26] Diary, 26 October 1943.

never convinced by Mountbatten's self-portrait of a genius of his time, and was seriously irritated by his constant promotion of the virtues of his nephew Prince Philip of Greece. He liked the dashing young naval officer, and invited him to Balmoral on leave, but Mountbatten's pushiness annoyed him, seeing only too clearly what his cousin's motives and ambitions were.

His admiration for Montgomery was also tempered by the General's inordinate self-esteem. When Alan Brooke remarked to him that he thought that Montgomery was after his job as CIGS, the King retorted, 'I thought he was after mine!'

It was Montgomery who produced the astonishing proposal that there should be a special service for the blessing of the men who would be taking part in Overlord at St Paul's Cathedral on 12 May, the anniversary of the Coronation, with the Coronation regalia displayed prominently. The King was disgusted by the idea, and it was witheringly dealt with by Lascelles, who produced from his capacious memory the words of the Younger Pitt in 1782: 'This is neither a fit time nor a proper subject for the exhibition of a gaudy fancy or the wanton blandishments of theatrical enchantment.' And that was that.

The King visited the fleet at Scapa on 10–13 May, and was particularly impressed by the Fleet Air Arm landings on the carrier *Victorious*, before returning to the extraordinary D-Day conference at St Paul's School in London on 15 May; Montgomery had been at school there, and had made it the headquarters of his 21st Army Group.

Churchill, Eisenhower, Montgomery and all the Allied commanders had rightly imposed intense security procedures. But for this meeting engraved invitations had been sent out as though for a formal peacetime dinner, to the King, Churchill, the War Cabinet, Smuts, the British Chiefs of Staff, and senior British and American officers – indeed any-one of military or political moment in the country. The conference was held in an ordinary classroom, and Lascelles spotted a message on the notice-board inviting sons of clergyman who were candidates for scholarships to apply to the High Master. He was not the only one who pondered on the consequences if a German bomb fell upon this eminent gathering.

The King and Churchill were accorded armchairs; the rest sat on the school benches. In deference to the King, Churchill and Eisenhower, Montgomery had waived his usual iron rule against smoking. Eisenhower made a short opening, then handed over the stage to Montgomery, whose bravura performance was followed by good presentations by Ramsay and Leigh-Mallory, and a notably poor one by the American air force commander, Spaatz, who had caused Eisenhower considerable difficulties and obstructions.

Then, to general surprise, the King walked to the platform and delivered a short speech,[27] without notes, and of which there is no record. There is, however, a version of it in his papers, although it is not clear whether these were provisional drafts or a later record. In his diary the King recorded that he had made a 'short impromptu speech' in which 'I stressed the fact that this was a "combined operation" of the forces of two nations, working together in friendly rivalry though in perfect harmony. No two nations (USA & Br. Emp) had ever worked so closely before.'[28]

On 30 May, at their weekly lunch, the King asked Churchill his plans for D-Day – the launching of Overlord. Churchill replied that he would be on one of the bombarding warships. 'I was not surprised,' the King wrote in his diary, '& when I suggested that I should go as well (the idea has been in my mind for some time) he reacted well & he & I are going to talk it over with Ramsay on Thursday. It is a big decision to take on one's own responsibility. W. cannot say no if he goes himself, & I don't want to have to tell him he cannot. So? I told E[lizabeth] about the idea & she was wonderful as always & encouraged me to do it.'

Normally Lascelles was equally supportive of the King's initiatives, but this proposal seemed to him to be insane. His approach on this occasion was indirect and subtle. Would the King advise Princess Elizabeth on the choice of the next Prime Minister if he and Churchill were killed in action? And how could the captain of the warship take a full part in the operation, which necessarily would involve danger, if he had the King and the Prime Minister on board?

[27] Stephen Ambrose, in *Eisenhower the Soldier*, p. 300, incorrectly states that the King spoke immediately after Montgomery. The King's notes are in RA PS GVI PS 09105, and are quoted in Wheeler-Bennett, op. cit., p. 600. These contain no reference to Anglo-American 'friendly rivalry', which has such an authentic touch that I have preferred the King's own version, especially as all accounts agree that he spoke fluently and without notes.

[28] Diary, 15 May 1944.

Both questions made the King think again. They agreed to sleep on it, and the following morning Lascelles told the King that neither he nor Churchill should expose themselves to this unnecessary and perilous act of bravado, and that he should write to Churchill to tell him so. By this point the King had come to the same conclusion, and wrote to the Prime Minister to dissuade him from his proposed adventure. The King added that he did not expect a reply, as they would both be seeing Ramsay on the following day.

Fortunately, both the King and Lascelles kept detailed records of this meeting.

Ramsay, who knew little about the background, explained that if Churchill sailed in the cruiser *Belfast* he would certainly be exposed to considerable dangers; also, as the ship would be bombarding some way offshore it would be difficult, if not impossible, to see anything. Ramsay and Ismay were equally hostile to the idea, but had no idea that the King might also be a passenger. When this possibility was put to Ramsay he vehemently denounced it. Churchill then added that the Cabinet would have to approve the King's participation, and that he would not recommend it to do so. But he himself was still determined to go.

When Lascelles remarked that it would be difficult for the King to find a new Prime Minister in the middle of Overlord, Churchill breezily retorted, 'Oh, that's all arranged for.' Lascelles then observed that no minister could leave the country without the King's consent: Churchill responded that he would be on a British warship and therefore on British territory; Lascelles said that he would be well outside territorial waters. This point was also swept aside. The King bluntly deprecated his Prime Minister going on a 'joy ride'; Churchill said that he had been on far more hazardous journeys since 1940; the King said that these had been necessary, this one was not. But Churchill would not be budged. He also greatly annoyed the King and Lascelles by declaring that it would be a fine thing for the King to lead his troops into battle 'as in the old days', having just said that the Cabinet would on his advice veto the idea.

By this point the arguments were becoming somewhat heated, and the King returned to the Palace from the Downing Street annexe deeply unhappy about Churchill's 'seemingly selfish way of looking at the matter. He doesn't seem to care about the future, or how much depends on him.'[29] Ismay came to see the King at the Palace to add his annoyance with Churchill. The King and Lascelles then drove to Windsor, angry and depressed.

Lascelles was not at all over-burdened with beliefs in the Royal Prerogative and Protocol, but the Prime Minister had flatly refused his monarch's advice and request and had produced spurious arguments. The King was much more worried about how the ship's captain could cope adequately with his crucially important duties as the commander of the bombarding force with Churchill at his side. Although the King and Churchill had had their differences, in the main the latter had followed the King's advice, and, indeed, had often sought it. Now, he was openly defying it.

Early on the following morning Ismay telephoned Windsor to say that Churchill was beginning to waver and asked if the King could send him another message. The King did so at once:

My dear Winston,

I want to make one more appeal to you not to go to sea on D-Day. Please consider my own position. I am a younger man than you, I am a sailor, & as King I am the head of all three services. There is nothing I would like better than to go to sea but I have agreed to stop at home; is it fair that you should then do exactly what I should have liked to do myself? You said yesterday afternoon that it would be a fine thing for the King to lead his troops into battle, as in old days; if the King cannot do this, it does not seem to me to be right that his Prime Minister should take his place. Then there is your own position; you will see very little, you will run a considerable risk, you will be inaccessible at a critical time when vital decisions might have to be taken; and however unobtrusive you may be, your mere presence on board is bound to be a very heavy additional responsibility to the Admiral & Captain.

As I said in my previous letter, your being there would add immeasurably to my own anxieties, & your going without consulting your colleagues in the Cabinet would put them in a very difficult position which they would justifiably resent.

I ask you most earnestly to consider the whole question again

[29] Diary, 1 June 1944.

& not let your personal wishes, which I very well understand, lead you to depart from your own high standard of duty to the state.

Yours very sincerely,

George R.I.[30]

This remarkable letter, rather more a rebuke than an appeal, was rushed to Downing Street before Churchill left to catch his special train, taking him and his staff to Eisenhower's new headquarters near Portsmouth.

By eleven that night no reply had been received.

By this time the King was incensed by Churchill's behaviour. Letters and meetings had had no effect, and he told Lascelles by telephone – the King being at Windsor and Lascelles back at the Palace – that he proposed to set off by car at dawn to Portsmouth to ensure that Churchill did not embark on *Belfast*.

This extraordinary possibility of the King personally barring the Prime Minister from boarding one of His Majesty's warships, and which would have been one of the more amazing episodes in the history of the British monarchy, was prevented by a telephone call from Lascelles to the special train, when Churchill, very grudgingly, and rather ungraciously, at last agreed to defer to the King's wishes.

Churchill saw in this not only an attempt to curb his freedom of movement but also a constitutional issue. His cool relations with Lascelles had not helped his mood. His somewhat surly letter of acceptance verged upon the impertinent:

Sir,

I cannot really feel that the first paragraph of your letter takes sufficient account of the fact that there is absolutely no comparison in the British Constitution between a Sovereign & a subject.

If Your Majesty had gone, as you desired, on board one of your ships in this bombarding action, it would have required the Cabinet approval beforehand & I am very much inclined to think, as I told you, that the Cabinet would have advised most strongly against Your Majesty going.

On the other hand, as Prime Minister & Minister of Defence,

[30] Diary, 2 June 1944; Churchill Papers.

I ought to be allowed to go where I consider it necessary to the discharge of my duty, & I do not admit that the Cabinet have any right to put restrictions on my freedom of movement. I rely on my own judgement, invoked in many serious matters, as to what are the proper limits of risk which a person who discharges my duties is entitled to run.

I must most earnestly ask Your Majesty that no principle shall be laid down which inhibits my freedom of movement when I judge it necessary to acquaint myself with conditions in the various theatres of war.

Since Your Majesty does me the honour to be so much concerned about my personal safety on this occasion, I must defer to Your Majesty's wishes & indeed commands. It is a great comfort to me to know that they arise from Your Majesty's desire to continue me in your service. Though I regret that I cannot go, I am deeply grateful to Your Majesty for the motives which have guided Your Majesty in respect of

Your Majesty's humble & devoted Servant & Subject,
Winston S. Churchill[31]

The King had not seen the matter as a constitutional one, although Lascelles had. 'I asked him as a friend not to endanger his life & so put me & everybody else in a difficult position,' the King wrote in his diary on 3 June.

Churchill had behaved throughout this episode thoroughly badly, and without consideration for anyone else. Having been understandably sceptical and fearful about Overlord he had become convinced that it would be successful, and was eager to take some public credit for the Allied triumph. He considered the risks negligible, but was, as always, willing to confront them. No admirer of Churchill should ignore his lifelong interest in self-publicity and heroic gestures. They formed part of his endearing charm, but could be maddening. By the evening of 3 June he had succeeded in infuriating everyone, from the King downwards, but had achieved nothing. And thus he sulked, while the King, with so many other anxieties, sighed with relief.

[31] Quoted verbatim in the King's diary, 2 June 1944. See also Churchill Papers.

10

FROM CHURCHILL TO ATTLEE

———

Overlord was due to begin at dawn on 5 June 1944, but the
weather was so bad that Eisenhower, making one of the bravest
decisions in modern military history, postponed it for twenty-
four hours. When the King was told of this he could imagine only too
vividly the feelings of the thousands of men involved, all prepared for this
momentous assault, now stood down until the weather improved. But
on 6 June D-Day took place. The recapture of Europe had begun.

Few of the King's broadcasts took more time and thought, preparation
and amendment than the one he made that evening. The themes of
prayer, dedication and intercession were entirely the King's, with the
advice and help of Sydney Woods, the Bishop of Lichfield, and the
rehearsals, again involving Logue, were intense.

At this historic moment surely not one of us is too busy, too young
or too old to play a part in a nation-wide, a world-wide, vigil of
prayer as the great crusade sets forth. If from every place of worship,
from home and factory, from men and women of all ages and many
races and occupations, our intercessions rise, then, please God, both
now and in a future not remote the predictions of an ancient Psalm
may be fulfilled: 'The Lord will give strength unto this people. The
Lord will give this people the blessing of peace.'

The D-Day fortunes were mixed, and subsequent progress was slow in the face of fierce German resistance and the problems caused by the terrain. Montgomery had said that he would be in Falaise, beyond Caen, on the first day. It took the British and Canadians over a month to capture Caen, which was by then in ruins. The Americans had a near-disaster at Omaha Beach, although they and the British and Canadians were more successful elsewhere. But on 13 June matters were going satisfactorily enough for Churchill to give the King the Cabinet's approval for him to visit Normandy, which he did on the 16th.

After seeing, and being briefed by, Montgomery the King returned that evening by cruiser, noting in his diary that 'it was most encouraging to know that it was possible for me to land on the beaches only ten days after D-Day', but he returned to a much less encouraging situation.

The British government had taken information of new German secret weapons seriously, and with good cause. On 13 June what the public thought were crashing German bombers – a Luftwaffe response to the Normandy landings having been anticipated by Londoners – caused no casualties and only limited damage. But on the night of 15 June 244 V-1 pilotless bombers were launched against London, of which 73 reached their target.

After the screaming Stuka dive-bomber in France in 1940 the V-1 was the most demoralising of the German air assault weapons, far worse than the Blitz and the later V-2 rocket. You could hear their chug as they flew towards you; then there was a chilling silence; then the explosion. The British counter-measures were of limited effectiveness, and although the V-1s were inaccurate – a fact that, ironically, made them even more feared when they started to fall upon villages in Kent, Surrey and Sussex as well as London – they caused considerable damage and casualties, and were, above all, unnerving. To take one particularly tragic case, one fell near Chartwell, Churchill's Kent home, and killed twenty-two homeless children and five adults in a refuge built specially for them.

The King was again under direct fire. Two V-1s fell and exploded close to Buckingham Palace, one in the garden close to the main building and another on Constitution Hill, destroying seventy-five yards of the Palace wall, and another obliterated the Guards' Chapel on nearby Birdcage Walk on 10 June, killing 119 and injuring another 102, several of whom later died. The King, Queen and Lascelles lost several friends and acquaintances in this disaster. Churchill ordered the Commons to return to Church House, from the more vulnerable, and already shattered, Palace of Westminster. On 8 September the first V-2s hit Chiswick, and then Epping. Prudence required that the Buckingham Palace investitures had to be temporarily abandoned – although not those elsewhere – and the King's Tuesday lunches with Churchill took place in the Palace air-raid shelter.

But it seemed – although wrongly – by mid-July that the V-1 menace had been successfully resisted, if not totally defeated, and the King felt that he could visit his troops in Italy, who considered, with some justification, that all the attention was being given to the Normandy fighting.

This visit took place between 23 July and 5 August – the departure of the King's party from Northolt was delayed by a V-1 exploding close to the airfield while they were waiting to take off. The King's tour of the front and visits to units of all nationalities was as exhausting as that of North Africa, but far better planned by Alexander, one of the King's favourite Generals. In eleven days King George travelled eight thousand miles by air and some one thousand miles by road. On one celebrated occasion Alexander organised a lavish lunch that began with caviar; the BBC reported dutifully that it was the King's first experience of army rations.

After the eventual comprehensive German defeat in Normandy, Paris was liberated on 23 August and Brussels on 3 September. On 11 October the King visited the victorious Montgomery at Eindhoven. Churchill was not at all keen on this, and dictated a letter advising against it. He showed it to Lascelles – another indication of their better relations – who persuaded him to amend it to one of guarded approval. The King and Lascelles flew in the Dakota of Sir Arthur Harris; this was, rather surprisingly, Lascelles' first aeroplane flight, which he disliked as much as the King did. It seemed that the path to the German mainland was open.

The King now wanted to repeat the exercise by visiting his troops in Burma, where the tide of war had also turned. Mountbatten, now the Supreme Allied Commander in South-East Asia, was keen, but Churchill again was not. The King, he argued, would have to make some statement on India's future, and the government was not then in a position to do so. The King protested that he would only be visiting his servicemen, and had no intention of making any political or constitutional statements. The 14th Army under General William Slim felt even more neglected by press and public attention than did Alexander's men in Italy, and called themselves, with some bitterness, 'The Forgotten Army'. The King knew this, but although other ministers thought he should go, Churchill was obdurate. The best that the King could obtain was an assurance that the visit was only temporarily postponed.

The war in Europe seemed to be coming to its end. The King took the salute in Hyde Park of representative units of the Home Guard, now disbanded, on 3 December, and broadcast to them that evening.[1] On the 19th he spoke at a dinner for the Regional Commissioners and their deputies, to thank them for their wartime work. On both occasions he emphasised the socially unifying aspect of the war, and his hopes for its continuation in peacetime. He began to make plans for the gradual restoration of royal ceremonials, on a modest scale, and new military uniforms.

But the war was by no means over. Montgomery's apparent master-stroke in an airborne assault on Arnhem ended in a major reverse after bitter fighting. The weather deteriorated in one of the worst European winters in living memory. In December the Germans launched a massive assault through the 'impassable' Ardennes again, taking the Americans totally by surprise. The ferocious Battle of the Bulge eventually ended in a complete Anglo-American victory, but with very heavy casualties, particularly for the Americans. There was also the psychological shock of realising that the Wehrmacht was far from defeated. They might have been drawing on their final resources, but these were still formidable.

In November Churchill had again raised the matter of the Windsors, urging the King that the Royal Family should bury the hatchet and formally 'receive' the Duchess in London: he also proposed that the Duke of Windsor should become Governor of Madras.

The King turned to Lascelles, who consulted Anderson and Bridges.

---

[1] Princess Elizabeth was about to launch the latest battleship, HMS *Vanguard*. The King suggested that it should be called *Home Guard*, in recognition of its loyal and dedicated service to the nation. Cunningham reacted violently to the idea, asking caustically whether the next warship should be named *Bomber Command*. The King's suggestion was withdrawn in the face of Cunningham's outrage, Lascelles for once in opposition to the King's imaginative proposal.

The King's personal views on the Windsors – especially the Duchess – had not changed, neither had those of Queen Mary nor the Queen, and they were unanimous that if the Windsors were officially restored to full royal status it might imply that the abdication had been a mistake. And the King could not forgive the offensive jibes by his brother and his wife about the Queen and his mother.

But these were private family opinions. If the Prime Minister, with the authority of the Cabinet, was advising the King that it was in the interests of the monarchy and Empire that he and his family should receive the Windsors – which would certainly include giving the HRH title to the Duchess, on which Churchill remained irritatingly persistent, despite his 1937 advice – this was a different matter.

Lascelles separated the two issues, concentrating on the constitutional point. Anderson was totally hostile to the Madras 'solution'. He also confirmed Lascelles' informal soundings that on this issue Churchill would be in a minority of one in the Cabinet, and that the Commonwealth governments, which would have to be consulted, would never agree. This was also Bridges' emphatic opinion. The Queen and Queen Mary made it very plain that they were not prepared even to meet, let alone formally 'receive', the Duchess then or at any time, but if Churchill insisted on making it a state rather than a family matter the Cabinet should tender its collective advice. As Lascelles by then knew, the Cabinet would not be supportive of Churchill's sentimental attachment to the Windsors.

Churchill, having been told the Madras option was impossible, then proposed that Windsor be appointed Governor of Ceylon. This was equally unacceptable. To make matters even more difficult, the French Ambassador, Massigli, told Churchill that the Windsors would be unwelcome in France – which the King and Lascelles regarded with scepticism, rightly as it turned out.

What remains astounding is that someone of Churchill's superlative qualities, and his now intimate friendship with the King, could have been so insensitive as to raise this storm at this time and in such a manner. But everyone was very tired and had been under intense strain for too long. Lascelles bluntly told Churchill that his constant harping on this matter might have a serious effect on the King's health, and that there were infinitely more crucial concerns than the future status and employment of the Duke and Duchess of Windsor.

The matter was not put before the Cabinet. Thus, the constitutional aspect never arose, but the problem remained nevertheless. The Windsors, somewhat noisily and unpleasantly, faded away. Their 1940 indiscretions were dealt with. They repaid this assistance by publishing articles and memoirs and bruiting their political and personal opinions, which were notably unhelpful and conspicuously ridiculous. 'I suppose she needs the money,' the King commented gloomily on another of the Duchess's semi-fictional effusions. But he had far more important matters to deal with, as he entered the most unhappy period of his life.

The last winter of the war was in many respects the worst of all for the British. The weather was vile, all the bombed cities were battered and drab, and the people were exhausted. At Yalta, in February 1945, Stalin extracted substantial territorial concessions from a much-aged Roosevelt – bluntly described by Ismay to Lascelles as 'gaga' – which Churchill could not prevent, of which the most shocking to the King and to many others was the effective handing over of Poland to a Communist puppet regime. This seeming act of betrayal of the people for whom Britain had gone to war caused considerable anguish in parliament and the press, and threatened the hitherto almost solid unity of the government. Stalin then proceeded to tear up the Yalta commitment to free elections in the European nations occupied by the Allies, Romania being another victim. Greece was ravaged by civil war, which required an urgent visit by Churchill and Eden to Athens, to the King's considerable alarm. The risks were substantial, and the King faced the not unlikely prospect of losing both his Prime Minister and Foreign Secretary. It was valuable to Churchill that Attlee strongly supported him in a very emotional and unhappy debate on Yalta in the Commons on 1 March, although the strongest opposition came from the Conservatives.

Churchill was well aware of the deep emotions that Yalta had aroused, not least with the King, and tried to urge Roosevelt to put pressure on Stalin. He did not fully realise how feeble and ill the President was, nor that Hopkins' health was also rapidly failing. The King's distrust of Russia made him apprehensive of the post-war world, but at the time the dramatic progress of the Soviet forces upon Berlin increased the popularity in Britain of the Soviet Union's contribution to victory.

The King, also, had no knowledge of Roosevelt's condition, and indeed there were still plans for the President to visit Britain: the King's last letter to him was written on 12 March to express his great pleasure at the prospect. On 11 April, however, came the wholly unexpected news of Roosevelt's death. The King ordered a week's Court mourning and attended the memorial service in St Paul's. Churchill had wanted to fly to Washington for the funeral, but with the European war approaching its climax the King persuaded him to remain in London. Eden went instead, and was to report on the unknown new President Truman in highly favourable terms, as did Attlee.

On 11 April the King also had the last of his many War Cabinet dinners at 10 Downing Street, with Churchill, Eden, Attlee, Woolton, Bevin, Morrison and Anderson. Lascelles was also present. Although everyone was very tired – Bevin twice falling asleep at the table, snoring loudly – the dinner and drink went on until 1.45 a.m., with Churchill and Bevin, when the latter was awake, on particularly good terms despite recent electioneering exchanges of views.

This was the last real gathering of the men at the heart of what Churchill rightly called 'The Great Coalition'. They had all been in it throughout the grim years, and deserved a good dinner, embellished with real Russian caviar and vodka, and Churchill's favourite champagne, Pol Roger.

It was their final reunion.

The last serious Luftwaffe air raid on Britain had been on 3 March; a forlorn venture, it was easily beaten off and did little serious damage, but it was an unpleasant shock – so much so that most people did not really believe the sirens. The last V-2 fell in Kent, killing one person and injuring twenty-three, on 27 March, and the final V-1 on the 29th. Mussolini was captured and executed by Italian partisans on 28 April, Hitler committed suicide on the 30th, and on 2 May the German forces in Italy surrendered. On 4 May the remnants of the Berlin garrison surrendered to the Russians.

But still the war obstinately refused to end on time. The King returned to the Palace on 6 May, expecting the following day to be VE – Victory in Europe – day, with his speech recorded and filmed, only to be told that the formal announcement would not be until the day after. As the King noted, all the preparations had been made outside the Palace, with the floodlights in place, and the balcony checked to ensure that it was safe to stand on. It had not been used since the King, Queen and Neville Chamberlain had appeared on it in September 1938, but although the rest of the Palace was in poor shape, with all the shattered windows boarded over, the balcony had survived. The King mentioned the possibility, not wholly in jest, of the dramatic conclusion to the war and to his reign if it disintegrated under the weight of himself, the Queen and Churchill. It was carefully inspected and declared to be battered but sound. The next day, 7 May, passed in widespread frustration, ended by a violent thunderstorm that reminded many of the night of 2–3 September 1939.

On the great day Churchill came to lunch at the Palace before making the formal announcement on radio and then in the House of Commons. Large crowds gathered outside the Palace to cheer the King and Queen and the Princesses – their first appearance on the famous balcony. (In the evening the Princesses joined the crowds to enjoy the celebrations with a party of young officers: 'Poor darlings, they have never had any fun yet,' the King wrote in his diary.[2]) There were eight balcony appearances on VE Day and several more in the evenings of the following two; on the 9th and 10th the King and Queen drove through huge and excited crowds in the bomb-blasted East and South London in an open horse-drawn carriage.

These popular triumphs, which genuinely astonished and moved the King and Queen, were followed by Thanksgiving services in London and Edinburgh and their receipt of an Address by both Houses of Parliament in the Royal Gallery in the Palace of Westminster. This, of course, required another speech, of which his biographer wrote that it 'was adjudged by many present to surpass in dignity and eloquence anything which they had previously heard from him'. Harold Nicolson, in contrast, admired the content but found the King's stammer 'almost intolerably painful to listen to', and noted that he often placed the emphasis on the wrong word or syllable.

Lascelles, Wheeler-Bennett's source, and always a critic of the King's delivery, considered it 'a great triumph', although he pointed out that

[2] One of the then young officers recalls that one of his most vivid memories of the evening was a spartan but very cheerful supper of cold ham in the bleak, poorly lit, and icy cold Buckingham Palace with the King and Queen and the Princesses. Years later he reminded the Queen of it. She remembered it well. 'Oh yes,' she said, 'wasn't it fun?'

the King had difficulty over the word 'imperishable'; when he referred to the death of the Duke of Kent, his voice faltered, giving the speech 'a really dramatic and moving quality'. Churchill, in Nicolson's account, 'with his sense of occasion, rose at the end and waved his top hat aloft and called for three cheers. All our pent-up energies responded with three yells such as I should have thought impossible to emanate from so many elderly throats.'[3]

The King wrote in his diary that he and the Queen were 'overwhelmed by the kind things people have said over our part in the war. We have only tried to do our duty during these five and a half years,' and added that 'I have found it difficult to rejoice or relax as there is still so much hard work ahead to deal with'.[4] But Lascelles recorded that the demonstrations of enthusiasm and gratitude to the Royal Family had given the King fresh confidence and diminished his chronic sense of frustration. Nonetheless, the King's sober reactions to the jubilation at the defeat of Germany were very understandable; Japan had yet to be defeated, and, to the King's unhappiness, the wartime coalition was disintegrating and party politics had returned.

The end of the war with Germany brought political confusion at home. Churchill had anticipated the end of the coalition as early as October 1944, when the close of the war in Europe seemed imminent. In a discussion with Lascelles on 3 October he had said that in this eventuality the King would be free to ask him, as the leader of the largest party in the House of Commons, to form a new government, which he would do. But he would not ask for an immediate dissolution, recalling with distate the 'khaki' elections of 1900 and 1918 (in both of which he had, incidentally, been a notable beneficiary), but would request one after an interval of several months.

The end of the coalition in May 1945 was, accordingly, a surprise neither to the King nor to Churchill, although both regretted it. Churchill had told the Commons on 31 October 1944 that 'we must look to the termination of the war against Nazism as a pointer which will fix the date of the General Election . . . Indeed, I have myself a clear view that it would be wrong to continue this parliament beyond

[3] Nicolson, op. cit., pp. 462–3.
[4] Diary, 18–20 May 1945.

the period of the German war.' The Labour leaders had agreed, but when the moment arrived Churchill's 'clear view' had changed, and he urged that the coalition should continue until the defeat of Japan. Attlee would agree only to a postponement until October.

Knowledge of the atomic bomb researches and forthcoming first test was so strictly limited that although the King and Lascelles knew of them, Attlee did not. Why Churchill kept his Deputy Prime Minister in the dark about this crucial development has never been satisfactorily explained. Nonetheless, Attlee initially agreed with Churchill, as did Bevin and Dalton, but Morrison, more accurately understanding the mood of the Labour Party, carried the majority of the National Executive to decide to withdraw from the coalition. Churchill was incensed by what he considered Attlee's perfidy, although, as Attlee's biographer has pointed out, he had only agreed to *recommend* continuation.[5]

The parliament had lasted for nearly ten years without an election, and without contested by-elections between the main parties since September 1939. In March and April 1945, with the war in Europe entering its final stages, Churchill, Attlee and Bevin had made distinctly partisan speeches, and the momentum for an early election, especially but not exclusively in the Labour ranks, accelerated.

The war with Japan was generally assumed to be far from over, and most military analysts, unaware of the atomic bomb, expected it to continue for a year; some expected it to continue for eighteen months. Even the very few who knew of the bomb did not know whether it would actually work and, if it did, how cataclysmic a weapon it would be. To politicians eager to return to their peacetime habits, and with the Conservatives confident of the electoral impact of Churchill's towering prestige and Labour eager for battle, the prospect of another year or eighteen months of unharmonious coalition was unappealing.

Churchill kept the King closely informed about the changing situation. The King was keen that the coalition should continue, and had noted without pleasure the clear signs of the return of partisan politics, but accepted that the position was untenable. Churchill proposed to Lascelles on 22 May by telephone that he should formally resign on the following day at noon and then call on the King at four o'clock to be requested to form a new administration. Churchill proposed this to emphasise that

[5] Harris, op. cit., p. 251.

the King had been given a period of reflection. The King agreed, but in the event certain unnamed 'pundits' (not Lascelles) decided that an interregnum of even four hours was undesirable, and that Churchill should both resign and be invited to form a new government at the same audience on the 23rd. Churchill thus formed a Conservative 'caretaker' government until the General Election on 5 July, whose decision could not be known until 25 July to allow time for the services' postal votes to arrive.

Churchill, as he told the King at lunch on 20 June, was deeply worried about the latter. When Lascelles took soundings they varied from James Stuart's estimate of a Conservative majority of 50, *The Times'* private forecast of only 20, and the Duke of Devonshire anticipating a Conservative defeat on the scale of 1906. These very differing assessments were conveyed to the King. With the exception of the Duke's gloomy prognostications, they pointed to, at best, a very modest Conservative victory – which was what Attlee and Bevin also expected. If the King was surprised by the outcome, he was by no means alone. His own opinion was that no party would have a clear majority.

Churchill and Eden took Attlee with them when they flew to Potsdam on 15 July for what was to be the last, and most futile, of the 'Three Power' summits, with the triumphantly menacing Stalin and the new President Truman. Eden described Attlee as a 'subdued and terse figure'. Eden himself was a deeply unhappy man. He had been too ill to take part in the General Election campaign apart from one radio broadcast, and the death of his elder son, Simon, in Burma had been a shattering personal tragedy. His marriage, which had been in severe difficulties for several years, was ending. If by no means a broken man, he was an exhausted and dispirited one. And even the ever-resilient Churchill admitted to intense weariness.

His election tours had been outstandingly successful, with huge and enthusiastic crowds, but his broadcasts and sharp exchanges of letters with Attlee had been less impressive. But, although not as confident as other forecasters, he told the King on his return to London on 25 July that he expected a Conservative majority of between 30 and 80. The King, with the information he had gleaned, was more sceptical.

But the 1945 General Election was uniquely difficult to foresee. The services' vote was only one of many imponderables. Some urban constituencies that still returned Members of Parliament had been bombed into near-oblivion. The Register of Electors was both inaccurate and out of date. It was, democratically speaking, a shambles. This was reflected in the result. With just under 12 million votes Labour won 392 seats; the Conservatives, with nearly 10 million votes, 189, although their Commons strength was greater than this with the Liberal Nationals and Ulster Unionists; the Liberals, with 2.5 million votes, only returned 12 Members of Parliament. The total votes cast put Labour into a significant minority; the distribution of seats gave them a huge majority. Attlee was as astonished as anyone in politics.

Although the scale of the Labour victory greatly surprised the King, and he was personally distressed for Churchill, understanding his emotions at this shattering rejection, he was, as his personal staff noted, very calm on 26 July.

It was as well that he was.

There was then a remarkable, and hitherto incompletely recorded, drama.

Wheeler-Bennett states: 'At four o'clock the Prime Minister asked Sir Alan Lascelles to call upon him [Churchill] at the Storey's Gate Annexe. His first inclination had been to postpone his resignation until after a Cabinet meeting on Monday, 30 July, but he later changed his mind and decided to resign that same evening.'[6]

There was much more to it than that. Shocked by his defeat, and especially by the scale of it, Churchill first spoke of remaining in office until the new parliament assembled, and returning to Potsdam. Eden and Chief Whip David Margesson protested strongly; Churchill then spoke of resigning the following week. Eden, who had returned to London with Margesson, urged immediate resignation.

In fact, as Lascelles' detailed record – written later that evening – emphasises, the King, having been told of Churchill's intentions, had expressed his own concerns. Lascelles went to see Churchill with a personal handwritten letter from the King that greatly moved Churchill, and supported Eden's and Margesson's arguments. Lascelles later reported to the King that Churchill had asked him to go to Downing Street and that he 'said at once that he had changed his mind' and would resign that evening.[7] But another account written

6 Wheeler-Bennett, op. cit., p. 635.
7 RA PS GVI C 254/002. This was written on or after 30 July.

that day states that Churchill was still talking about not resigning until the following week when Lascelles arrived, to find Eden and Margesson still urging immediate resignation, to which Churchill eventually agreed. The answer to this apparent confusion is that there were two visits by Lascelles, one at the King's request to convey his personal letter, at which Churchill was still strongly inclined to delay, and a second one, at Churchill's request, to inform Lascelles that he had changed his mind.

Understandably, the King was alarmed and perplexed at the varying messages from Downing Street. The factor that weighed most heavily with the King was the Potsdam Conference, and this was the central point he instructed Lascelles to emphasise to Churchill.

Churchill's own account of this day in his war memoirs is grievously inaccurate:

> In ordinary circumstances I should have felt free to take a few days to wind up the affairs of the government in the usual manner. Constitutionally I could have awaited the meeting of parliament in a few days' time, and taken my dismissal from the House of Commons. This would have enabled me to present before my resignation the unconditional surrender of Japan to the nation. The need for Britain being immediately represented with proper authority at the [Potsdam] Conference, where all the great issues we had discussed were now to come to a head, made all delay contrary to the public interest. Moreover, the verdict of the electors had been so overwhelmingly expressed that I did not wish to remain even for an hour responsible for their affairs. At four o'clock therefore, having asked for an audience, I drove to the Palace, tendered my resignation to the King, and advised His Majesty to send for Mr Attlee.[8]

This version bristles with errors. Japan seemed some way from defeat on 26 July. The successful testing of the atomic bomb did not guarantee that it would work in action, and the scientists and senior military advisers to President Truman were unsure how much damage it would inflict even if it worked; in the event they had considerably underestimated

[8] See Churchill, *Triumph and Tragedy*.

it. Nor was there any certainty at all that the fanatical element in the Japanese regime would abandon its determination to defend the Japanese mainland with the same suicidal ferocity it had already demonstrated on Okinawa, and in the deadly kamikaze attacks on American and British warships and transports.

Also, the new parliament was due to meet on 1 August; the first atomic bomb was dropped on Hiroshima on 6 August, the second, on Nagasaki, on the 9th; Japan did not surrender until Emperor Hirohito's decisive intervention on the 14th, so there would have been no possibility of Churchill announcing the Japanese surrender as Prime Minister unless he had advised the King to postpone the meeting of the new parliament – which Lascelles believed he fully intended to do. Far from not wishing 'to remain even for an hour' longer in office, Churchill had intended to remain in it for at least a week and to return to Potsdam, still as Prime Minister.

It was the combination of the pressures put upon him by the King (through Lascelles), Eden and Margesson that made him change his mind. Churchill was driven to the Palace at seven o'clock, not at four.

His official biographer, although accurate about the timing of Churchill's resignation, wrongly states that 'Churchill's mind was made up. He would not seek, as he was constitutionally entitled to do, to remain Prime Minister until the recall of parliament a few days later [in fact, nearly a week], and after the crucial concluding sessions of the Potsdam Conference.'[9] Both Churchill and his biographer are correct on the constitutional position. There is no need for a defeated Prime Minister to resign immediately, and the modern practice of them hurriedly abandoning 10 Downing Street and hastening to the Palace to resign at once, the successor lurking nearby to move in, is very recent. Attlee, with his own long political memories, did not think there was anything odd or improper in Churchill's original determination to stay on.

The arguments of the King, Eden and Margesson were different. After such a comprehensive electoral defeat it would look bad if Churchill appeared to be clinging on to office. Also, what influence could he have at Potsdam if he was perceived, rightly, as a defeated Prime Minister with no democratic authority? It would not have troubled Stalin, but the Americans were another matter.

[9] Gilbert, *Never Despair*, p. 108.

It was on this point that the King felt particularly strongly. Britain should be represented at Potsdam by the democratically elected leader of the majority party. The phrase 'lame duck' had not then become common political coinage, but it would have described Churchill's position. 'Dead duck' would have been even more appropriate. They all knew that Churchill was exhausted as well, a fact commented on by Truman and others at Potsdam. The shock of his defeat was immense, and although he concealed it admirably during the 26th the sense of unfair rejection by the British people after a unique premiership was understandably very strong.

To his great credit, Churchill gradually appreciated that the King, Eden and Margesson were right, and that he should leave with dignity and in style, which he did. His statement to the British people, issued to the press and read out on the radio, was a masterpiece of generosity and gratitude to them for 'the unflinching, unswerving support which they have given me during my task, and for the many expressions of kindness which they have shown towards their servant'.

Churchill had eventually written to Attlee during the late afternoon to inform him that he was going to resign at seven o'clock on the evening of 26 July, thus giving him the briefest of notice that he was about to become Prime Minister. There were already fevered machinations among Attlee's colleagues, principally fomented by Morrison, to have a leadership election before the King summoned Attlee to form a government, and which could possibly have succeeded if Churchill had adhered to his original, and even his second, intentions, in which case Attlee might well have never become Prime Minister at all.

Lascelles' diary relates the further events from his perspective after he had returned from Downing Street to Buckingham Palace to brief the King on the new timetable. He had expected the King to be indignant about this chaotic situation, but he found him calm and reasonable. The King recorded in his diary that evening:

I saw Winston at 7 p.m. & it was a very sad meeting. I told him I thought the people were very ungrateful after the way they had been led in the war. He was very calm & said that with the majority the Socialists had got over the other parties (153) & with careful management they could remain in power for years. He would be Leader of the Opposition. I asked him if I should send for Mr

Attlee to form a government & he agreed. We said goodbye & I thanked him for all his help to me during the five War Years.

Thus ended what Peter Hennessy has rightly called 'one of the greatest PM–monarch partnerships in British history'. The use of the word 'partnership' is particularly felicitous.

The King's diary account also confirms Lascelles' impression of Attlee's complete bewilderment at the rapid turn of events:

I then saw Mr Attlee [at 7.30] & asked him to form a government. He accepted and became my new Prime Minister. I told him he would have to appoint a Foreign Secy. & take him to Berlin. I found he was very surprised his party had won & had had no time to meet or discuss with his colleagues any of the Offices of State. I asked him whom he would make Foreign Secy. & he suggested Dr Hugh Dalton. I disagreed with him & said that Foreign Affairs was the most important subject at the moment & hoped he would make Mr Bevin take it. He said he would but he could not return to Berlin till Saturday [28 July] at the earliest. I told him I could hold a Council on Saturday to swear in the new Secy. of State.

This account is totally confirmed by Lascelles' immediate record, which states that the King 'begged' Attlee not to appoint Dalton as Foreign Secretary. The King told Churchill that he had been 'astonished' by the proposal. The audience with Attlee, as with Churchill, was surprisingly short. Churchill arrived at 7 p.m. and left at 7.25; Attlee was ushered in at 7.30 and left at 7.50. Within fifty minutes the entire British political situation had been transformed. As Attlee characteristically observed, 'It had been quite an exciting day.'

The Dalton episode requires some elaboration.

The King had expressed no objection to Dalton holding high office in the new government, although he personally detested him – a judgement in which he was not alone – but which in his case included memories of Canon Dalton and the young Hugh in his extreme Socialist period. The King also knew about his father's views on Dalton, having told Canon Dalton never to bring 'your anarchist son' into his presence ever again. Dalton in his diaries refers to the King's 'coldness' towards him in their official relations, and even referred to him as an 'inanimate' monarch, epithets which demonstrate only too clearly that the King was, with some difficulty, maintaining the constitutional courtesies.

The King's alarm concerned Dalton being Foreign Secretary. He was very well-informed about the horror of the Foreign Office at the prospect and Eden's dismay at the possibility; indeed, Eden had made it plain that he favoured Bevin as his successor. And, as the King's diary makes clear, Attlee's suggestion of Dalton was only a tentative one. He had, after all, not expected to be appointed Prime Minister so soon, and had had little time either to consult many colleagues or to clarify his own thoughts after his unexpected victory and speedy summons to the Palace.

Attlee later denied that the King's influence had been crucial in his decision to switch Bevin and Dalton. 'I naturally took into account the King's view, which was very sound,' he wrote in 1959, 'but it was not a decisive factor in my arrival at my decision,' and this has been accepted by his biographer, Kenneth Harris. Attlee even told him that he could not recall the King's intervention, an amnesia almost certainly deliberately manufactured to protect the King's constitutional probity and reputation, and probably also to impart to his own actions on 26–27 July a decisiveness and confidence that were not apparent to others.

By this point the King's political antennae were very acute, and his sources of information formidable. His respect and affection for Bevin had increased steadily during the war, but the key element was that, with his intense interest in foreign affairs, he had got used to working closely with two Foreign Secretaries, Halifax and Eden, whom he liked, trusted and respected. The prospect of working with Dalton was deeply unappealing, and this was made very clear to Attlee. If the King's views were not 'decisive' – although they probably were – they were highly important. When he met Dalton, now Chancellor of the Exchequer, and Bevin, now Foreign Secretary, on 27 July he expressed himself very pleased with these appointments. He was more pleased with the latter than the former.

It has to be added that the King's opinion of Dalton remained unchanged, as Hugh Gaitskell discovered in May 1951, when, as Gaitskell recorded in his diary, the King told him that 'there is really only one of your people that I cannot abide' – which, of course, was Dalton, not Aneurin Bevan, as Gaitskell had at first assumed. In fact, the King liked and admired Bevan. The dislike of Dalton was deep and long-standing, and it was personal rather than political. 'The Chancellor of the Exchequer,' he remarked with some fervour after Dalton had described his forthcoming 1946 Budget to him, 'smells like the town drain.' And he was not referring to his physical cleanliness, or to the contents of the Budget.

The King had his strong personal likes and dislikes, but he had few political favourites or foes, and had as many friends and admirers in the Labour and Liberal parties as he had among the Conservatives – perhaps more. But when he formed a dislike of someone it was hard to dissuade him of it, and when Dalton fell sheer in November 1947 the King found it difficult to conceal his joy.

Dalton's biographer Ben Pimlott has expressed surprise that the King, the 'least political of British monarchs and seldom given to advising Prime Ministers on any matter, should have held such passionate views on this one', which is a serious underestimation of the King's political interests and the impact of his advice and influence. If he had attempted to veto Dalton's appointment to the Cabinet this would have been stretching matters rather too far for comfort; by urging Attlee to think again about the Foreign Secretaryship he was quite properly expressing an opinion that he was not only entirely entitled to have, but which was shared by many others. And it was, as Attlee conceded, 'very sound' advice. Indeed, given Dalton's temperament and booming impetuosity, it is difficult to envisage him lasting very long at the Foreign Office, with hostile officials and a King who struggled with much difficulty to remain civil with him. He did not last all that long at the Treasury, either.

It was also a good example of the King's personal judgements on men. He was not, of course, infallible, but his assessments tended to be remarkably shrewd. He had not got to know Attlee at all well during the war, and he found his monosyllabic responses disconcerting after the freedom of conversation he enjoyed with most of his other ministers; but he liked and respected him, although remaining puzzled, as were so many others, by that remarkable conservatism in his private life and attitudes which contrasted so sharply with his political views. The King probably did not realise the intense respect Attlee had for him, and which was to be the basis for perhaps the most surprisingly and unexpectedly successful relationship the King had with any of his Prime Ministers.

Significantly, Lascelles was an early convert to Attlee because he recognised that Attlee's acute self-consciousness about his lack of physical presence belied his mental qualities, which were formidable. So was his resolution. As Lascelles was the first to recognise, the King and Attlee were ideally suited to each other, although neither realised it. Both were shy, nervous and very private men. They were also both deeply conservative in most matters, although liberal – indeed radical – in public affairs. Attlee had developed a deep regard for the King's courage and integrity; the King was only beginning to understand Attlee. But the unique bonds of his personal friendship with Churchill were irreplaceable.

On 31 July the King wrote two handwritten letters to Churchill, the first saying that 'my heart was too full to say much at our last meeting', and that he was 'shocked at the result [of the election] & I thought it most ungrateful to you personally after all your hard work for the people', and telling him that he had been 'astonished' at Attlee's original proposal of Dalton for Foreign Secretary and how he had told Attlee 'to think again & put Bevin there. I would like you to know this fact from me.'[10]

He later wrote on 31 July at greater length:

My dear Winston,

I am writing to tell you how very sad I am that you are no longer my Prime Minister.

During the last 5 years of War we have met on dozens, I may say on hundreds of occasions,[11] when we have discussed the most vital questions concerning the security & welfare of this Country & the British Empire in their hours of trial. I shall always remember our talks with the greatest pleasure & I only wish they could have continued longer.

You often told me what you thought of people & matters of real interest which I could never have learnt from anyone else. Your breadth of vision & your grasp of the essential things were a great comfort to me in the darkest days of the War, & I like to think that we have never disagreed on any really important matter. For all these things I thank you most sincerely. I feel that your conduct

[10] Churchill Papers, 2/360.
[11] The number of their Tuesday lunches alone was over 200.

as Prime Minister & Minister of Defence has never been surpassed. You have had many difficulties to deal with, both as a politician & as a strategist of war, but you have always surmounted them with supreme courage.

Your relations with the Chiefs of Staff have always been most cordial, & they have served you with a real devotion. They I know will regret your leaving the helm at this moment.

For myself personally, I regret what has happened more than perhaps anyone else. I shall miss your counsel to me more than I can say. But please remember that as a friend I hope that we shall be able to meet at intervals.

Believe me,

I am,

Yours very sincerely & gratefully,

George R.I.[12]

Churchill replied, also in his own hand, on 3 August:

Sir,

I have read w. emotion the letter of farewell wh. Yr Majesty has so graciously sent me. I shall treasure it all my life.

The kindness & intimacy with which Yr Majesty has treated me during these ever-glorious years of danger & of victory, greatly lightened the burden I had to bear. It was always a relief to me to lay before my Sovereign all the dread secrets and perils wh. oppressed my mind, & the plans wh. I was forming, & to receive on crucial occasions so much encouragement. Yr Majesty's grasp of all matters of State & war was always based upon the most thorough & attentive study of the whole mass of current documents, and this enabled us to view & measure everything in due proportion.

It is with feelings of the warmest personal gratitude to you, Sir, & devotion to the Crown that I have relinquished my Office & my cares.

Yr Majesty has mentioned our friendship & this is indeed a vy strong sentiment with me, & an honour which I cherish.

With my humble duty,

---

[12] Churchill Papers, ibid.

I remain Sir,
Yr Majesty's faithful servant & subject,
Winston S. Churchill[13]

The Churchills spent what they all assumed to be their last weekend at Chequers. Before going to bed on the Sunday night they all signed the Visitors' Book. Churchill was the last to sign, and under his signature he wrote 'Finis'.

But it was not the end, although it seemed so to everyone at the time. Churchill was destined to become the King's Prime Minister again, but very briefly. Neither the King nor Churchill was in November 1951 the man he had been between May 1940 and July 1945. By then, Churchill, in his seventy-seventh year, had suffered the first of his major strokes, and the King, although only fifty-five, was grievously ill and looked much older than his years. Thus, the deep and unique wartime relationship between this monarch and this Prime Minister was never to be re-created.

We may leave it at its apogee, which was in truth also its culmination. It was, indeed, 'Finis'.

[13] RA PS GVI C 069/59.

11

PEACE DENIED

———➤ ◆ ————

The King had hoped to meet President Harry S. Truman in London on the latter's way to Potsdam, but realised that this could not only arouse Stalin's suspicions but embarrass the new President. He then proposed to visit his troops in the British zone in Berlin and give a dinner for Churchill, Truman and Stalin. The President had no objection, but Stalin's reaction was churlish and unfriendly, and Montgomery bluntly stated that in view of the chaotic and hostile atmosphere in Berlin he could not guarantee the King's safety.

The King then invited Truman to stay at Buckingham Palace on his return from Potsdam to the United States. The President warmly accepted in principle, but explained that 'conditions in the United States may require my immediate return when the Conference is over'. The 'conditions' concerned the crucial decisions, and their aftermath, on the dropping of the atomic bombs on Japan.

The meeting between the King and President took place in Plymouth Sound on 2 August. The King embarked on the battleship *Renown*, where he gave lunch for Truman, Secretary of State Byrnes, and Admiral Leahy after a half-hour private meeting with the President. Each was impressed by the other, not least because both were in positions that neither had expected to hold.

Lunch was rather less successful, as Byrnes spoke openly about the atomic bomb, about which Leahy was sceptical, in the presence of the waiters, to the King's horror. He swiftly stopped discussion on what was the most secret subject in the war.

The King then boarded the USS *Augusta* to return the President's visit and to bid him farewell on his return to the United States. Four days later the first atomic bomb was dropped on Hiroshima. After this and the second attack, and despite fanatical opposition by the Japanese war party, the Emperor recognised the reality. Japan accepted unconditional surrender. The Second World War was abruptly and sensationally over.

This took the Palace, indeed everyone, by surprise. The end of the war in Europe had been long anticipated, and the King's VE Day speech had gone through the usual wearying rounds of numerous drafts and changes before the King was satisfied.

Now, on the eve of VJ Day, no speech had been prepared, even in draft form. Edward Bridges and Lascelles hurriedly conferred, and Bridges rapidly produced a draft. Lascelles, who confessed to having 'a jaded brain' and no ideas of his own, contacted Churchill at Chartwell, who responded by telephone with suggestions that Lascelles and Bridges considered tired, disappointing and uninspiring. Lascelles put all the drafts together and typed out his own version, which was essentially Bridges', and put it before the King. To his amazement the King professed himself delighted with it, and made only a few alterations. On the evening of 13 August the King's speech was relayed by loudspeakers to the crowd that had gathered outside the Palace, as well as on radio. Lascelles listened to it in the forecourt with the Halifaxes, in what Churchill described as 'a pin-drop silence'. Afterwards the King and Queen and the Princesses came on to the balcony for a deafening reception.

Lascelles had always argued that the best speeches were composed in a tearing hurry by as few people as possible, and now he was totally vindicated.

The euphoria of victory was short-lived, however.

The exultant Labour Party presented a formidable programme of nationalisation along with the repeal of the Trade Disputes Act and the Trade Union Act, with the promise of more to come. Aneurin Bevan was to create a National Health Service. The financial controls introduced during the war would be maintained. The stunned Conservatives at first could only grumble, but then began what was to be one of the most spectacular come-backs in British political history. Yet this seemed far away in the gloom of the winter of 1945–46.

The exultation died almost at once. American reactions to Churchill's dismissal by the electorate had been of astonishment and apprehension. Truman, having dealt with Attlee and Bevin at Potsdam, although he deemed them lesser men than Churchill and Eden, did not share the general American hostility to the new Prime Minister and government, but on 21 August he signed the document placed before him that ended Lend-Lease immediately. The British were aghast; the Russians considered they had been betrayed. By this blunder Truman unleashed a sense of burning resentment against the United States by its principal wartime allies and undid much of the goodwill and mutual trust that had built up since 1941. Truman came to deeply regret his thoughtless action, and was to redeem himself, but the immediate effects on the British economy were devastating, and revived the latent anti-Americanism in Britain, especially in the Labour Party.

Suddenly, there was no money for the great Socialist Revolution. This was a major part of the problem when the government appealed to the Americans for a loan, Congress expressing reluctance to lending money for such a cause. As a result, the terms seemed harsh, and although they later proved to be quite reasonable – and the key need was for immediate finance, which was met – they did not seem so in the context of the time. The Americans were widely and loudly denounced for their arrogance, ignorance and ingratitude. The unilateral ending of the exchange of information on atomic research by the Americans was an additional wound, and formed a vital part of the process whereby Attlee took the momentous decision – and a secret confined to very few – that Britain should develop her own atomic weapon.

Attlee handled the American hostility to Socialist Britain with considerable skill in a speech to the Congress on 13 November, but the damage had been done. The series of economic miseries that were to demoralise and eventually to destroy the post-war Labour government had begun.

The King strongly sympathised with Attlee, and was appalled by the Americans' actions. Like Attlee and Churchill, he had formed a high opinion of Truman, so that his casual signing of a document that he later admitted he had not even read seemed out of character.

What concerned the King now was that a virtually bankrupt country, still rationed, still suffering from severe shortages, still bomb-shattered, should be embarking upon an ideological crusade when what was needed was a practical approach to an exhausted people. He rightly emphasised the desperate housing situation – destined to be the greatest of the failures of the Labour government – and which he considered should have greater priority than abolishing legal restraints on trade unions (which the government quickly came to regret) and massive nationalisation.

Perhaps he was right, but he kept his opinions strictly private. Although Attlee invariably treated him courteously, and took careful note of the King's views, the latter's political influence, which had been so strong, was, perhaps inevitably, much diminished. He won some minor victories – Attlee agreeing that he should personally appoint Knights of the Garter, the Thistle and St Patrick, and that the Brigade of Guards should be retained at its pre-war strength, for example – and his advice was sought and usually taken by ministers, but his objections to domestic legislation were in effect ignored. His old sense of frustration was, accordingly, resurrected.

There was even some trouble over the royal servants, some of whom considered that their pay had not risen adequately during the war and wanted to join a trade union. Their claims had perhaps not been sensitively handled, and when the King learned of the dispute it was quickly resolved. He had always been the most considerate of employers and had not realised how inadequately his greatly diminished wartime staff had fared. He had had, after all, other preoccupations. But Dalton was proving unsympathetic over the Civil List, from which the royal staff was paid. With much goodwill on both sides, however, the King was able to resolve this potentially embarrassing dispute.

As the King surveyed the new situation, he asked himself the question, what was his role to be? The ceremonial one could only be gradually, and very cautiously, restored – like Buckingham Palace itself. The first formal dinner – in honour of the gallant Queen Wilhelmina – was not held until 30 July 1946, the King noting in his diary that 'we wore evening clothes & decorations for the first time since 1939' and that there were only forty people present. After the dramas of the war and his intimate involvement with his ministers, his life and position seemed suddenly to be empty, even irrelevant.

At first the King did not contemplate the new Labour government with much apprehension. He had come to know its leading members during the war, and, with the conspicuous exception of Dalton, had got on well with them, although Attlee's taciturnity had been a problem.

It was to remain one. On 24 August he gloomily wrote in his diary that 'Attlee still seems to be in a maze'. The contrast with Churchill's loquacity and ebullience was so marked that the King began to despair of getting on real terms with Attlee. Fortunately Bridges, Norman Brook and Lascelles had no such difficulties, and acted as useful mediums until Attlee and the King came to know and appreciate each other better.

The King's bafflement about Attlee was fully shared by Churchill, and for very much the same reasons. As Moran has written:

> Clem Attlee puzzles him. He cannot make him out, no one in his experience of politics has been quite like him. For one thing he cannot follow the working of Attlee's mind, any more than he can understand what is in the heads of those for whom Attlee speaks. Winston's temperament and upbringing make it difficult for him at any time to share the hopes and fears of the middle class. To make confusion more confounded, here, apparently, is a typical specimen of that section of the community which holds the most advanced, and in Winston's eyes, even subversive views about society and the Empire.[1]

Both the King and Churchill liked Attlee personally and admired many of his qualities, including his military record in the First World War and his imperturbable loyalty to the government in the Second. But, try as he could – and did – for some time the King found Attlee's silences and monosyllabic responses bewildering and frustrating.

The King was remarkably apolitical in the partisan sense, and the ending of the coalition and the return to full-blooded party warfare had saddened him, as has been noted. What disconcerted him was the realisation that this Labour government, unlike the first two, was genuinely Socialist, and prepared to embark upon a programme of massive nationalisation; there was also too much talk of the class war by Labour MPs, and even some ministers, for his comfort.

It has been claimed of the King that 'in private, he was unapologetically right-wing (his wife even more so), and was often moved to explosions of anger at the latest Socialist outrage, especially if he felt that he had

---

[1] Moran, *Winston Churchill*, p. 312.

not been consulted'.[2] This accusation is not accurate. The King was not 'right-wing' politically, either unapologetically or otherwise. If it were possible to give him a political label it would have been that of a progressive liberal, but his essential political attitudes were pragmatic and personal.

There was no danger of the King becoming partisan; what concerned him, and not only him, was that the new government's headlong dash into unprepared radical policies at a time of deepening economic stringency and international tension was both unwise and divisive. Emmanuel Shinwell, charged with the nationalisation of the coal-mining industry, which had long been a Labour Party commitment, found that no preparatory work had been done at all for this major undertaking. As he later wrote:

> I immediately took up the task of preparing the legislation for nationalisation of the mines. The miners expected it almost at a wave of a ministerial wand. The owners were hardly less anxious to get out of the pits – on terms. For the whole of my political life I had listened to the Party speakers advocating state ownership and control of the coal mines, and I had myself spoken of it as a primary task once the Labour Party was in power. I had believed, as other members had, that in the Party archives a blue-print was ready. Now, as Minister of Fuel and Power, I found that nothing practical and tangible existed. There were some pamphlets, some memoranda produced for private circulation, and nothing else.[3]

The essential difficulty that increasingly troubled the King was that he took his duty to encourage his ministers seriously, and found that there were aspects of the new government's policies that he did not agree with. In these circumstances, it was difficult for him to encourage them, or even warn them, 'as they are pledged to do it'. It was one of the great personal triumphs of his reign that few of his ministers realised his true feelings, which were strictly limited to a very small circle. Lascelles' reticence and exemplary relations with Labour ministers were,

[2] Pimlott, op. cit., p. 81.
[3] Shinwell, *Conflict Without Malice*, pp. 172–3.

if anything, even more remarkable. The Attlee problem, as Lascelles had foreseen it would, gradually improved, although as late as June 1951 the King was lamenting the difficulty of getting information from his Prime Minister. But if Attlee was reserved in conversation, he was very articulate on paper, and their relationship developed into warm mutual regard and genuine friendship; it was hard work on the King's side, but worth it; yet it is doubtful whether he realised the immense affection and regard Attlee developed for him.

The King, like his father, assessed politicians as individuals; like him, he preferred coalitions, and had found the wartime one the most congenial of his reign. Unlike Queen Victoria he did not maintain any political links with the Opposition; their relations were either personal or official. The personal ones remained strong, however. When the Churchills came for private dinner parties at the Palace they did so as friends, not as the Leader of the Opposition and his wife. Churchill was equally scrupulous. There was no possibility of the King becoming embroiled in the party fight, which he detested in any case.

His relations with Bevin were particularly good. Bevin's cynical, and indeed hostile, attitude towards the Soviet Union was quickly justified. The Cold War had in fact begun before Churchill's famous 'Iron Curtain' speech in March 1946 at Fulton, Missouri, which the King privately applauded – 'the whole world has been waiting for a statesmanlike statement'[4] – as did Attlee and Bevin, although in public, the government, wary of its left wing, was more critical. The Americans had gone home; the British had demobilised; the Russians had done neither. Furthermore, there was a noisy and not unsubstantial number of Labour MPs who constantly praised and defended the Soviet actions and denounced their own Foreign Secretary. But Bevin had the full support of his Prime Minister, the Conservative Opposition, and the King. He needed it.

The matter of honours for wartime services caused some difficulties.

The King had made clear his wish to confer the Knighthood of the Garter on Churchill in December 1944, but the latter had written to him on 19 December: 'I was touched and honoured by Your Majesty's kindness in wishing to confer the Garter on me at some future date. I

---

[4] Diary, 12 March 1946.

feel however that it would be much better that this high honour should not come to me while I am your First Minister, but, if ever, only on my retirement, when perhaps Your Majesty's gracious inclination would remain unchanged and my successors [as Prime Minister] would be willing to make the Submission.'[5]

The King had replied, in his own hand, on 24 December that he fully understood

your aversion to accepting any Honour while you are my Prime Minister & Head of my Government. As this is the case, I will wait a while, but I feel that The Country will expect me to give you a high Honour which they will acclaim as a fitting tribute for all your arduous work in this war, & which will still enable you to remain in the H. of C. Anthony Eden is your Chief Lieutenant as Foreign Sec. & I feel he should be offered it later when the tangles in Foreign Affairs have been cleared.[6]

The King had tried again when Churchill had formally resigned as Prime Minister in May 1945 when the coalition ended, and again when he resigned on 26 July, but without success. There was a note of good-humoured exasperation in his reports to Lascelles of Churchill's obstinate refusal to accept the highest honour that the King could bestow on a subject.

Eden had also declined, on the very understandable grounds that if his former leader would not accept then he could not possibly do so. At that time the Garter was not in the King's gift, but the Order of Merit was, and Attlee, when consulted, as a matter of courtesy, 'cordially approved' this recognition of Churchill's outstanding literary achievements. This honour Churchill did accept.

Both the King and Attlee took the matter of honours seriously, and this was a subject on which the Prime Minister carefully consulted the monarch. But he was not prepared to accept the King's recommendations without challenge. The King proposed an earldom for Cunningham and viscountcies for the other two Chiefs of Staff. Attlee deprecated this

[5] RA PS GVI C 069/53.
[6] RA PS GVI C 069/54.

division, and Lascelles agreed. So did the King when the point was made to him.

The King approved the revised list, which included the promotion of the head of Bomber Command, Sir Arthur Harris, to Marshal of the Royal Air Force. But, unlike the other senior commanders, he did not receive a peerage. Thus, the January 1946 Victory Honours List contained an impressive list of peerages for the senior service commanders, with the exception of Harris. He was, it is true, promoted to Marshal, thus giving him a good income for life, but the palpable snub to him and to Bomber Command by the new government aroused the wrath even of the pro-Labour *Daily Mirror*. Churchill protested strongly to Attlee, and asked that 'the omission may be repaired' before Harris left the country to live in South Africa, but Attlee categorically, and rather coldly, refused to consider it.[7]

The British have seldom demonstrated their perversity more clearly. The ever-increasing intensity of the Allied bombing offensive against Germany had been immensely popular, but when the war ended and the scale of the devastation was revealed, and especially what was regarded as the unnecessary destruction of Dresden, there was an extraordinary wave of self-reproach and even guilt, which was greatly increased by the strong participation of British scientists and technicians in the atomic bomb development. Harris was the scapegoat for this new revulsion.

But Churchill did not forget Harris, and when he became Prime Minister again he asked Bracken to contact Harris to tell him that a peerage was his for the asking, but Harris requested, and received, a baronetcy. The King did not live to see Harris' rehabilitation, but when, very belatedly, a statue of him was placed in London in 1992 Queen Elizabeth willingly agreed to unveil it. Even then, there were protests.

The King had ended the war physically and emotionally exhausted. He and the Queen had invested all their energies into a single purpose, and the strain upon the King had been manifest and constant. A real holiday had been impossible since December 1936, and now he was dealing with a new government in a rapidly deteriorating national and international situation that tried his nerves yet further. When Churchill took a long and much needed holiday in Italy after the 1945 election he

[7] Gilbert, *Never Despair*, p. 178.

returned rejuvenated, but after he had paid a courtesy call on the King the latter was furious, comparing the ability of politicians to take long sunlit holidays with his own situation.

This outburst to Lascelles confirmed Lascelles' opinion of his wisdom in persuading Smuts to invite the Royal Family to visit South Africa early in 1947. He had envisaged it as a relaxation, with some official functions. Unhappily, Smuts, approaching an election, and remembering the political impact of the royal visits to Canada and the United States in 1939, had different plans.

The King's health had caused few concerns at this stage, although, ominously, there had been leg problems with his sciatic nerve. He was under fifty when the war ended, and looked much younger. His family and those closest to him were used to his outbursts of temper and heavy smoking of cigarettes; but they had also seen him relaxing happily among those he loved and trusted. Although he had lived on his nerves for six years, so had many others.

But his ordeal had been much longer, and had begun in December 1936. He had dedicated himself to his unwelcome job with relentless devotion and determination. He had hoped that peace would allow him to step off the treadmill, but, if anything, it became worse. Britain was plunged into a post-war austerity and depression far less endurable than in war. Internecine political strife had broken out with a special venom, as though the wartime unity had never happened. Suddenly, everything seemed to be going wrong.

The King was not a Conservative, in the sense of favouring that party; indeed, as has been demonstrated, he was highly critical of the indifference of many Conservatives to the condition of the people, and his only serious disagreements with Churchill had been on these issues. He also had the unique advantage for a modern monarch in having known, and worked with, most of his new senior Labour ministers. Lascelles, somewhat to his surprise, found that he actually got on better with them than their Conservative predecessors, with the notable exception of Dalton. The King thoroughly approved of Bevin, and Eden's determination to maintain as far as possible a bipartisan foreign policy had the King's strong support.

One difficulty was personal. Although the King knew most of the senior members of the government, his attempts to get to know the others were, initially, less successful, and he set out his concerns to

Lascelles in a long and revealing correspondence from Sandringham over the Christmas of 1945, adding, 'I am not downhearted or pessimistic as to the future.'[8]

What was essential was that not only the King but his household should maintain strict political impartiality at all times and assist ministers to the best of their abilities. Lascelles, recalling Knollys' partiality, was particularly insistent on this among his immediate staff, knowing that any unguarded comment by any of them critical of the government, even in private company, could be construed as representing the opinions of the King himself. Lascelles was also more aware than the King was of what he called 'Buckingham Palace Paralysis', when nervous, and often awestruck, ministers and visitors became incoherent at the prospect of a meeting with the King. Lascelles could see this as they waited in his room; the King was astonished, as none of his wartime ministers and service chiefs had appeared to be overawed by meeting him, until Lascelles cited the case of Wavell. This particular problem, once identified, was speedily resolved.

The winter of 1946–47 had opened relatively mildly. Shinwell had informed the Cabinet, quite wrongly, that coal stocks were good. They might have been adequate for a normal British winter, but this one was certainly not. The Christmas and New Year periods were bleak and cold, but, compared to what followed, relatively benign. And then on 23 January the snow began, the temperature plummeted, and Britain was gripped by the most bitterly cold weather in modern records, and, thankfully, never equalled ever since, even in 1962–63. No one who lived through that winter will ever forget it.

Roads and railways, industries and schools were paralysed and closed. Large areas of the country were totally cut off. The electricity failed, the power-lines collapsed under the weight of ice and snow, as did the telephone lines. Those who had electricity were forbidden to cook between nine and twelve in the morning and between two and four in the afternoon. The River Thames froze solid, as did most other rivers, and the lakes. Agriculture was devastated, and the losses of sheep and cattle were terrible. But the human cost was even more grim. There are no reliable statistics of the numbers of premature deaths from the cold, but the mortality rate soared, especially among the elderly. The

[8] Lascelles Papers.

motor industry virtually closed down. Over two million people became unemployed. The RAF had to drop supplies to areas where food shortages had become critical. There was, in most of the country, simply no heat for housing, offices or schools, in an age when coal was the staple fuel for power generation and domestic use. Those who had gas-fired appliances fared marginally better than those who relied on electricity, most power stations having no coal.

By a supreme irony, the nationalisation of the mines had been much trumpeted on 1 January. Deaf to many warnings from his ministerial colleagues and civil servants, Shinwell had dismissed the possibility of coal shortages during the winter, believing that the mere fact of nationalisation would galvanise the miners into a huge increase in production. It did not. The reality was that the stocks were too low. When this became known a storm of vituperation fell upon the government in general and Shinwell in particular. The newspapers could print only four pages, and could not be distributed far, anyway, but they carried the same brutal message. The Conservatives seized upon the phrase 'Starve with Strachey [the Food Minister] and Shiver with Shinwell'. For once, such political invective had some justification.

The seemingly endless blizzards, accompanied with savage frosts and Arctic winds, marched on inexorably until the middle of March, when the snow melted and the floods began, their havoc exceeding even that of the snow and ice. And then it snowed again in April and even on 1 May. Even if the coal stocks had been as good as Shinwell had recklessly claimed, it would have been impossible to have moved them. Where there *were* coal stocks, the victorious wartime citizens and returned soldiers of Britain had to hack the frozen lumps from piles and convey them home in prams, buckets and wheelbarrows. The army, the RAF and rescue services had to work prodigiously from January until May just to maintain life.

These disasters, and the anger that the performance of the government aroused, had real and enduring political effects. Dalton was not the only minister who dated the collapse of confidence in the government from the winter crisis.

But it did not only affect the Labour government. When the Royal Family sailed for South Africa from Portsmouth on 1 February, on HMS *Vanguard*, which had escaped the unfortunate name that the King had suggested, the full scale of the catastrophe had not been appreciated. It was not only the snow and ice of that awful winter that was so demoralising, but its duration. By 1 February things were not good, but no one could have foreseen that this was only the beginning of the misfortunes. The north-east wind was to howl for a month.

Thus, as *Vanguard* steamed into sunshine and warmth, Britain was plunged into icy misery. The King had taken both Lascelles and Adeane with him, leaving the relatively inexperienced new Assistant Private Secretary Edward Ford at Buckingham Palace. But Attlee was in direct communication with the King, and the increasingly bad news from home cast a pall over the King's enjoyment of the voyage. He telegraphed statements of his sympathy and concern, but also received information that his absence from Britain was being openly criticised.

The King was severely disconcerted and depressed by this, and as the weather improved as *Vanguard* steamed south his unhappiness increased. He began to wish that he had never agreed to embark on the tour, especially when he saw the programme that Smuts had prepared for him. He spoke of cutting it down drastically and flying home, but Attlee realised at once that this would only make matters worse, as it would 'magnify unduly the extent of the difficulties we are facing and surmounting at home, especially in the eyes of foreign observers'. As the Queen pointed out, very sensibly, the King's hurried return would make people think that the situation was getting worse, and that, in any event, there would be nothing he could do about it. But the King chafed irritably.

As Kenneth Harris has rightly written: 'In the early days at sea the weather was rough, and the King, though previously regarded as a good sailor [which he certainly was not] spent most of his time in his cabin. When he emerged he was edgy, and sometimes ill-tempered. He found fault with day-to-day arrangements. When he left the ship to begin the tour, instead of being rested and relaxed, he was tense.'[9]

There were other problems. Wheeler-Bennett states that the royal party consisted of only eleven people. In fact there were thirty-four – as the group photograph demonstrates – and this in itself caused some difficulties in accommodation. Also, most of the crew were 'hostilities only' men, longing for demobilisation, and Rear-Admiral William

---

[9] Harris, *The Queen*, p. 79.

Agnew, who commanded *Vanguard*, was not a popular officer despite his distinguished war record. Indeed, when he took *Vanguard* to sea for gunnery practice after arrival at Cape Town there was a near-mutiny.

Vanguard, in short, was not a very happy ship. If the Queen and the Princesses enjoyed the voyage, the King did not. The combination of his unhappiness at being abroad at all while Britain was suffering so badly, and the prospect of what lay before him, made him tense and gloomy. In such a mood he was not easy company.

Smuts' programme was blatantly political, and was already arousing strong controversy in South Africa. Indeed, this aspect made a deep and enduring impression upon Princess Elizabeth, who realised that there was no such thing as a non-political Royal Tour. The Princess had told her parents of her love for Prince Philip and their wish to marry. The King's initial reservations about him – principally the result of Mountbatten's incessant and unwelcome eagerness – had gone, but he worried about how young his elder daughter was and hated the prospect of losing her. He and the Queen had urged a period of reflection, and almost the only aspect of the tour that had appealed to him was that they would be together as a family for two months. But neither he nor the Queen had any doubts that the young couple would change their minds, and this, to the King, with his devotion to his daughters, gave an additional poignancy to the tour.

Wheeler-Bennett described Dermot Morrah's *The Royal Family in Africa*, lavishly illustrated and published with remarkable speed immediately after the tour, as 'brilliant'. To a later reader its brilliance lay primarily in Morrah's near-genius with superlatives. The King, Queen and Princesses charmed everyone. Every occasion, formal or informal, was a triumph. The organisation was faultless. Everyone enjoyed themselves. Smuts wrote in his Foreword that 'their journey through the Union was to be more of a sustained triumphal progress than the sort of visit we had originally planned'.

There is no mention of the hostility of the Nationalist Party, which stubbornly boycotted events, or of the contemptuous indifference of the Nationalist press. The heat and fatigue were passed over, as were the King's justifiable annoyance at his South African bodyguards, whom he described – rather more accurately than he probably realised – as 'the Gestapo', and his manifest exhaustion on occasion. Morrah was an excellent scholar, but on this occasion he saw it as his brief to write about 'a sustained triumphal progress' rather than a two-month ordeal that had mixed receptions, which was the truth. The young journalist James Cameron, who also followed and covered the tour, was more realistic; as it ground on inexorably he became increasingly sorry for the King, and commented upon his loneliness and melancholy.

It would be wrong to go too far in the opposite direction to Morrah. There were good moments and some crowds were genuinely enthusiastic. The Royal Family put on a superb performance under increasingly difficult conditions. But the effort required taxed the King's patience and health severely. He lost an alarming amount of weight, and although apartheid had not yet been sanctified he saw enough to trouble him profoundly.

One instance which left a deep impression was the instruction that on giving medals to black South African servicemen he should not speak to them or shake their hands. The rule did not apply to white South African servicemen. The King objected strongly, but was advised that he must accept the instruction of the South African government. When he got on to British colonial soil, with great relief, the investitures of black servicemen and dignitaries were accompanied with personal chats and warm handshakes. It was noticeable that he was far happier and more relaxed outside South Africa, where the dictates of white supremacy reigned and where the presence of 'non-Europeans' was actively discouraged. In Swaziland the royal party was entertained by 15,000 tribal warriors, without a policeman in sight, whereas in Natal the Zulu warriors had been forbidden to carry spears and white policemen were present in force.

None of this was lost upon the King and Queen, and greatly increased the former's unhappiness. Cameron wrote of him that 'never was a man so jumpy'. He considered that his black subjects were just as important – and usually more welcoming – as his white ones, who were often hostile and morose. When in 1948 the Nationalists won the election, deposed Smuts and entered into the long nightmare of apartheid, the King and Queen were not surprised, and nor were their daughters. When the King agreed to visit South Africa again in 1952, for a genuinely convalescent visit, the grim process had only just begun in earnest. Princess Elizabeth would not visit the country until apartheid had been abolished and she herself was Queen; her mother never went there again. Sometimes considered, quite inaccurately, as rather reactionary and conservative, she abhorred racial discrimination as much as her husband. She was to remain eloquent – in private – on the subject of 'that dreadful apartheid'.

The long-term consequences of the Royal Tour were very different from those Smuts had intended. Of particular significance was the impact of the experience upon Princess Elizabeth.

The Princess had her twenty-first birthday on 21 April, and the occasion was made a public one, taking the salute at a march-past of the Cape Garrison, in the presence of Smuts, the Cabinet, and the entire Diplomatic Corps; she was then the guest at a rally of youth organisations, and in the evening, in Government House, she broadcast to the Empire.

This was not her first broadcast, but it was certainly the most important to date. In it she made her famous dedication to 'our great imperial Commonwealth to which we all belong'. This was a very significant phrase. Although the Empire was still very large it was obvious that India and Burma would soon become independent, and Ceylon – rather unwillingly, as it happened – would not be far behind. But, although the Empire was fading away, the dream of its replacement by a benevolent and harmonious Commonwealth of Nations which would treat non-white nations on the same basis as white ones had captured the King's imagination – as it had Attlee's.

The King and the Princess had taken great trouble over the text, and, as usual, Lascelles had been involved, but it had a very strong personal element, and its patent sincerity was moving; it also had a strong political content.

There were many in Britain – especially Churchill – who did not accept the ending of Empire, and especially the Far Eastern one after the sacrifices of the ultimately victorious war against Japan. If Churchill's fierce accusations of the government pursuing a policy of 'scuttle' embarrassed many of his colleagues, they received solid support elsewhere. The task was to reconcile the British to their imperial losses by the vision of the New Commonwealth. It was to be achieved, and Princess Elizabeth, as Queen, was to be one of its most ardent and effective practitioners and leaders. Indeed, she can be said to have saved it almost single-handedly. That task effectively began in South Africa in 1947.

The problem of the naturalisation of Prince Philip had proved remarkably difficult. His father, Prince Andrew, had been the youngest brother of King Constantine, who had been forced to abdicate in 1922 after the devastating Greek defeat in Turkey. The Revolutionary Committee summarily executed three former Prime Ministers, two former ministers, and the Commander-in-Chief of the army. As Prince Andrew had commanded one of the defeated Army Corps, he was destined for the same fate until the intervention of King George V saved him. He was stripped of his title and banished for life, and he and his family retreated to Paris. His marriage eventually foundered.

Prince Philip, however, was sent to England at the age of eight, to be brought up by Lord Milford Haven, the elder brother of Mountbatten. When Milford Haven died at the age of forty-six in 1938, Mountbatten took over the guardianship. Prince Philip was educated at Gordonstoun, in Morayshire, and entered Dartmouth in 1939, where he first met Princess Elizabeth. He had had a fine record in the navy in the war, but could not receive a permanent commission until he obtained British nationality.

The political and military turmoil in Greece complicated matters greatly. As often happens, the civil war was in many respects even worse than the war itself had been, and in Britain there were Labour MPs and newspapers that were sympathetic to the Communists and hostile to the return of the monarchy. The plebiscite of March 1946 restored the Greek monarchy, but this also caused delays. There was also the problem of Prince Philip's family's strong German connections, which came under hostile press and public attention when the rumours of his possible engagement began to circulate.

The ministers whom the King consulted, particularly the Home Secretary, James Chuter Ede, as well as Attlee, were helpful and sympathetic and had agreed to his naturalisation in principle by the end of 1946, but there was then much discussion about Prince Philip's new surname. Given the economic and other crises then plaguing the government, the amount of time devoted to this matter was somewhat surprising, but it was Ede who suggested he should take his mother's name of Mountbatten. Attlee warmly approved, although the King was initially doubtful, and the Prince even more so. As he later observed, 'I wasn't madly in favour . . . But in the end I was persuaded, and anyway I couldn't think of a better alternative.'

He insisted, however, that he should not be titled 'His Royal Highness', but merely Lieutenant Philip Mountbatten, RN. The King was impressed, and the naturalisation was confirmed in March 1947.

The announcement of the engagement was made on 10 July, and the wedding would be held on 20 November in Westminster Abbey.

One of many examples that Attlee was far more articulate on paper than he was in conversation was his charming letter of congratulation to the King, written on 10 July:

Sir,

My colleagues and I beg to present to Your Majesty and to Her Majesty the Queen our humble congratulations on the announcement of the betrothal of Her Highness, the Princess Elizabeth, and Lieutenant Philip Mountbatten, and to assure Your Majesties that they share the sentiments of pride and affection with which the announcement is welcomed.

Your Majesties have afforded to all your people a constant and graceful example of the felicity of a happy marriage and Mr Attlee trusts that, under God's guidance, the Princess and her Consort may also receive all such blessings and enjoy a long and happy life together in peace.

Mr Attlee, with his humble duty, begs to remain Your Majesties' humble and obedient servant.

C. R. Attlee[10]

There was a misunderstanding, then and later given an importance out of all proportion, relating to supplementary clothing coupons for the Princess's wedding dress and those of her bridesmaids.

When Ulick Alexander was asked for an estimate of those needed for what was, after all, a state rather than a private occasion, without taking serious advice he suggested 800. This turned out to be a grotesque over-estimate, and the figure was at once amended to 100 when the King and Queen learned about it. In view of probable newspaper and other criticisms of even this figure, no allowance was claimed, or made, for the Princess's trousseau. So far as clothing coupons were concerned, the Princess's wedding was somewhat frugal, as it was in other respects. But the magical, and mythical, figure of 800 extra coupons tends to be repeated.

The Labour government – with the exception of Dalton – was very

[10] RA PS GVI C 350/02.

understanding of, and sympathetic to, any royal requests, and raised no difficulties whatsoever over expenditure or coupons for a family that was resuming, in a strictly limited way, official state functions and duties. The King, for his part, made only the minimum requests for exceptional treatment. Attlee and Cripps knew this, appreciated it, and responded accordingly. Their discussions on these matters with Alexander and Lascelles were amicable and sensible. But politics, and personalities, nevertheless soured the relatively short period between the engagement and the wedding.

The problem was Dalton. Nineteen forty-six had been a year of success and achievement for him, in the face of grievous problems. Nineteen forty-seven had already been disastrous, and was to become even worse. Morrison had been so ill in the spring with thrombosis that he could well have died, and his recovery was slow. There was considerable concern over Bevin's health. Dalton himself was also unwell and was dispirited by consistently hostile press and Opposition criticism. He was outspokenly critical in semi-private about his Cabinet colleagues, including Attlee, and was nervous about the rapidly growing reputation and ambitions of Stafford Cripps. He still had his eyes covetously upon the Foreign Office.

These were not propitious circumstances under which to discuss the Civil List additions for the provision of Princess Elizabeth and her future husband. Nor was Lascelles, given his opinion of Dalton, which fully reflected that of his master, the ideal negotiator.

The discussions were unfriendly.[11] Dalton bore his grudges against the Royal Family keenly, and gave Lascelles the clear impression that he positively enjoyed causing difficulties and being obstructive. Lascelles sought a total of £50,000 a year for the couple from the Civil List. Dalton considered this not only excessive but that it could be substantially met from the King's savings on the Civil List during the war. The argument that the King's frugality should be used against him particularly enraged Lascelles. Fifty thousand pounds was indeed a very large sum, but most of it was necessary for the staff and expenses for the Heir to the Throne; the allocation for her husband was modest. Dalton's only contribution to the Cabinet meeting on 13 November was to present the then compromise for agreement, which was given.

---

[11] These are described in Pimlott, op. cit., pp. 128–31.

On the previous afternoon Dalton had presented an emergency Budget to the House of Commons. Just before he entered the chamber – still that of the House of Lords while the destroyed Commons chamber was being rebuilt – he gave the Lobby Correspondent of *The Star*, John Carvel, the essential points of his tax proposals. Carvel telephoned them to his newspaper. They appeared in the edition printed at 3.40 p.m., barely twenty minutes before Dalton announced them to the Commons.

It was unquestionably a serious blunder, but when Dalton made a full apology to the Commons on the following day more criticism was directed towards Carvel by Churchill and other Conservatives than against the Chancellor. But then the mood changed. Dalton had become almost a hate-figure to the Conservatives and much of the press, and the calls for his resignation rose. Dalton had few friends in the senior echelons of the Cabinet, and certainly Bevin and Morrison could not be numbered among them. Neither had Attlee forgotten Dalton's role in the attempt to remove him only two months earlier. He accordingly accepted Dalton's resignation and appointed Cripps as Chancellor.[12]

Lascelles was overjoyed at Dalton's humiliation and departure, and, apart from the personal aspect, Cripps was immensely more sympathetic to the problems of the royal incomes and expenditure: the Civil List problems that Dalton had created were swiftly resolved on the terms that Lascelles had proposed.

There was no direct involvement by the Palace in this episode, but Attlee had full knowledge of the King's opinion of Dalton, which he

[12] This extraordinary episode has been meticulously related in considerable detail in Ben Pimlott's biography of Dalton. A personal footnote can be added.

Carvel's son, Robert, was present at the conversation between his father and Dalton. John Carvel's reputation as a trusted Lobby Correspondent, however unfairly, never recovered, although Dalton had not said that their discussion was off the record. The general view was that it obviously was, and that Carvel had betrayed his source. In those far-off days this was considered unforgivable.

Bob Carvel became a greatly esteemed Lobby Correspondent himself, but never quite shook off the memories of his father's decision, which, however justified for a journalist gratuitously handed a major scoop, made him a figure of obloquy at Westminster. Bob was accordingly a model of discretion and deeply cautious. He was one of the last of the old-fashioned Lobby Correspondents, profoundly respected and trusted by colleagues and politicians. He once told me that he had spent his working life in the Commons getting over the resentment felt by politicians of all parties for his father's role in Dalton's downfall.

had come to share. As Pimlott has written, 'the simplest answer is the best one. The Prime Minister accepted Dalton's resignation because he wanted to be rid of him.'[13]

And Cripps was not the austere ascetic he has so often been depicted. He shared with the King an appreciation of good wine, and, like him, was a heavy smoker. Having been a turbulent *enfant terrible* of the Labour Party, now that he had reached his position of eminence his hitherto inadequately appreciated qualities of application, wit, intelligence and realistic common sense made him a royal, as well as a national, favourite. 'Austerity' was hardly a populist philosophy, but acceptable from someone who was almost miraculously transformed from high-minded controversial ideologue to thoughtful and eloquent realist. But the transformation had occurred some time before Cripps went to the Treasury.

It can be said with absolute certainty that anyone who succeeded Dalton would have been well regarded at the Palace, but Cripps was an outstanding success with the King personally, to the latter's genuine surprise, as until early 1947 he had regarded Cripps, whom he had not got to know at all well, somewhat bleakly. He now found that Cripps was someone he could talk to freely, frankly and informally, and with a response, like Bevin. His previous strong reservations about Cripps were totally removed. In this respect, at least, 1947 ended on a better note than it had begun, but there had been other political events in that turbulent year that had caused the King unhappiness and even grief.

[13] Pimlott, *Hugh Dalton*, p. 540.

12

THE END OF EMPIRE

———◆———

The sheer pace and scale of the Labour government's national-isation programme had worried the King as much as its content. In the parliamentary session of 1945–46 seventy-three Bills were introduced and passed – 'and they are not all minnows', Attlee proudly declared; 'some are very big fish'. They were indeed.

In that initial frenzy the Bank of England, civil aviation, the coal-mining industry, cable and wireless communications, road and rail transport, electricity and gas were all nationalised. The stunned Conservatives initially offered little resistance to this legislative avalanche, but then became more critical. The King protested about the former to Morrison in November 1945 and on the latter directly to Attlee. 'I told Attlee,' he wrote in his diary for 20 November, 'that he must give the people here some confidence that the government was not going to stifle all private enterprise. Everyone wanted to help in rehabilitating the country but they were not allowed to.' The King also raised other domestic topics, including the slow house-building programme, the shortage of clothing – 'I said we must all have new clothes, & my family are down to the lowest ebb' – and unofficial strikes in the gas industry in the winter of 1945–46, which the King described to Attlee as threats to 'the liberty of the subject'. As Attlee later wrote: 'Our policy was not a reformed capitalism, but progress toward a democratic socialism.' This was not an objective that attracted the King, but his personal relations with Attlee continued to improve, and on international affairs there were no disagreements.

At the beginning of 1947, the King stopped keeping his daily diary. The last entries reveal his mounting unhappiness and concerns; for example he noted on 28 January: 'I have asked Mr Attlee three times now if he is not worried over the domestic situation in this country. But he won't tell me he is when I feel he is. I know I am worried.'

The King had returned to Britain from South Africa to find his government and Prime Minister coping with the aftermath of the winter and floods, worsening relations with the Russians, and illness among Cabinet ministers. There was also discord, and increasing criticism of Attlee by his colleagues for his alleged indecision and unimpressive leadership. These difficulties were considerably mitigated by a glorious summer and a crucial turning-point in American strategy towards Europe. Truman, who had thoughtlessly caused such havoc by the casual ending of Lend-Lease in August 1945, now promulgated the 'Truman Doctrine' to save Greece and then inspired the Marshall Plan, which was to be the economic salvation of Western Europe, and seized upon at once by Bevin as 'a lifeline to a drowning man', as indeed it was. But when Molotov left Paris and the Marshall Plan discussions on 2 July this marked the real beginning of the Cold War; as Bevin reported to the Cabinet, 'the gloves are off, and we know where we stand with them'. The King thoroughly approved of the government's foreign policy and was greatly relieved by the dramatic change in American attitudes, but his domestic concerns remained.

Faced with mounting difficulties and a hostile press, the government introduced the Supplies and Services Bill, which gave it unprecedented powers in peacetime, denounced vehemently by the Opposition parties as taking totalitarian powers without recourse to parliament. The King had been led to believe that the Bill was not only necessary but was not a major piece of legislation. At Balmoral in August he read the parliamentary reports and the newspapers with mounting alarm, and wrote to Attlee for an explanation, offering to return to London 'if you think that my presence in London during the critical weeks ahead of us would be of assistance to you and to the country generally'.[1]

In an exceptionally long reply on 28 August Attlee justified the Bill, admitting that he had been taken aback by the ferocity of the attacks upon it by Churchill, which had claimed that it conferred dictatorial

[1] RA PS GVI C 350/04.

powers upon ministers. This Attlee strongly denied, and saw no reason for the King to interrupt his holiday. As Attlee explained, the Opposition leaders had been consulted before the introduction of the Bill: 'We had reason to believe that any grave apprehensions that they had held had been removed, and I was afterwards both surprised and sorry to see that the Leader of the Opposition should choose to take the opportunity to attack the government fiercely on the grounds that the Bill was designed for ends very different from those we had in mind . . .'[2]

Although this storm passed, the King's depression remained.

Attlee was not only under heavy pressure from Churchill and the Opposition but from within his own ranks. The causes were manifold. Bread rationing, the chaos of the awful winter crisis, the reintroduction of military National Service – bitterly opposed by the Labour left and the Liberals, and, under pressure, reduced from eighteen months to twelve – and the menacing situation in Europe eroded confidence in Attlee personally. Morrison, now recovered, began to intrigue again, together with Dalton, as did Cripps, who at least had the courage, on 9 September, to tell Attlee to his face that he should make way for Bevin.

Although accounts of this meeting vary, one version is that Attlee telephoned Bevin to say, 'Ernie, Stafford's here. He says you want my job.' Bevin replied that he did not. 'Thought not,' said Attlee, replaced the telephone, and offered Cripps the job of the government's economic overlord. Cripps accepted at once. What is certainly true is that Cripps emerged from the meeting in a greatly more powerful position than he had entered it, to the astonished mortification of Morrison and Dalton.

But so serious did the threat to Attlee seem that Edward Bridges and Norman Brook decided that the constitutional aspects of a change of Prime Minister should be put before Lascelles – and, through him, to the King. It should be remembered that the only occasion when a Labour Prime Minister had offered to resign had been in the extraordinary circumstances of 1931, when George V had refused to accept MacDonald's request. When he had resigned in 1935 he could hardly be described as a Labour Prime Minister. The question was whether the unique nature of the Labour Party would limit the King's choice of successor, and thereby reduce the Royal Prerogative.

[2] RA PS GVI C 350/05.

Bridges and Brook were so well-informed about the crisis that it is possible that Attlee had confided in them. More probable is that their exceptional knowledge of Whitehall politics had alerted them to the seriousness of the threat to Attlee.

On 9 September, the day of Cripps' crucial meeting with the Prime Minister, Bridges wrote to Lascelles:

> The case is a hypothetical one. Suppose that, the Labour Party being in Office, the Prime Minister decides that he wishes to resign and that some other member of his party should take his place. What is the procedure which should be adopted to bring about this change?
>
> I am told that it is the view of the Labour Party that they should in all circumstances choose their own leader. And in circumstances such as I envisage they would want to have a party meeting to choose a new leader who would then become the new Prime Minister.
>
> The point which has occurred to us is whether this procedure involves any unwarranted change in the part played by the Sovereign in the choice of the new Prime Minister . . .
>
> If, in the circumstances which I have envisaged, a Prime Minister who wanted to resign his Office were first to resign the leadership of the party and a new party leader were to be elected who would so to speak automatically take over the premiership from him, this would, I think, be a new precedent. Moreover, it would be a precedent which would put some restriction on the part which it is now open to the Sovereign to play in these matters. Hence my anxiety to put the point to you and to give you time to reflect on it . . .[3]

Lascelles did not reflect long, replying on the 11th that

> a prudent Sovereign should always, in these days, ensure that the man whom he is going to ask to be his Prime Minister has the full support of his own party and is not likely to come back to him (the Sovereign) and say that he cannot form a Government.

[3] RA PS GVI C 131/79.

In old days, the Sovereign appears to have relied largely upon private soundings, and to have been occasionally badly misled . . .

In that sense, therefore, a clear advance indication by the members of the party in power as to the man they want to be their leader is, it seems to me, a help to wise ruling by the Sovereign rather than a derogation of the Sovereign's power. It has been obvious for many years that it is no use the Sovereign sending for somebody who cannot command parliamentary support; therefore it is better that the Sovereign should have clear proof of who can command it; and the fact that, in nine cases out of ten, the Sovereign acts accordingly does not deny him the right to act differently in the tenth case should he think fit.

In fact, I should say that the definite and public adoption by the party concerned of a new leader is a more satisfactory, and more dignified way of doing business than all the secret and often inconclusive conclaves in Mayfair libraries which characterised such a Ministerial crisis as that of 1855. (Incidentally, wasn't the deposition of Lloyd George and the elevation of Bonar Law entirely the fruit of a 'caucus' meeting in the Carlton Club, which left the Sovereign practically no option in the matter?[4])

But in this problem, as in so many political problems, I think the right choice of words might be very important. While I am all in favour of a party meeting electing Mr X to succeed Mr Y as the party's future leader, I should deplore that meeting putting on record that it had nominated Mr X as the next head of HM government; that does seem to me an infringement of the Sovereign's prerogative – and a gratuitous one, for surely it can be taken for granted by any responsible party, commanding a parliamentary majority, that no Sovereign, save in very exception circumstances, would ignore their choice of their leader in making his own choice of his new Prime Minister?[5]

This sensible opinion rather begged the question of what course the King could take if Attlee made an emphatic recommendation for his

[4] This refers to the break-up of the Lloyd George coalition in October 1922: see pp. 72–3.
[5] RA PS GVI C 131/80.

successor while remaining party leader, citing the precedent of May 1940. And what would have been the situation if Attlee died without leaving any indications of his preferred successor, either to the King or to the party?

These imponderables remained hypothetical. That particular crisis passed, and Attlee's leadership was never effectively challenged again. But Bridges and Brook had been right to alert the King and Lascelles to the problem, and Lascelles' preference for parties to have fully accepted leaders rather than 'secret and often inconclusive conclaves in Mayfair libraries' was, ironically enough, prophetic in the cases of resigning *Conservative* Prime Ministers in 1957 and 1963. But then, political history is replete with ironies.

Churchill's attitudes towards India in the 1930s have been justly criticised, but he had, as has been related, accepted the inevitability of Indian and even – with great personal pain, given his father's role in the annexation of Upper Burma – Burmese independence in due course.

Whether the results would have been significantly different had he remained Prime Minister, or had his views prevailed, is highly controversial; they might possibly have been even worse than they were. But to describe the hurried British abandonment of India, its partition, and the subsequent appalling bloodshed, as a great achievement may be questioned. It was the lot of King George VI, and not Churchill, to 'preside over the liquidation of the British Empire'.

In reality he did not even preside. He was an unhappy, unwilling, eventually resigned but impotent onlooker, and in the crucial months between January and May 1947 he was on his South African tour. But no one, certainly not Attlee, had expected the incredible speed of events.

Attlee had more recent personal knowledge of India than Churchill, having been a member of the Simon Commission in the late 1920s. This experience had not convinced him that India was ready for self-government, as he told the King, but he had now come to the conclusion that it was inevitable. The problem was when, and under what conditions. The gulf between the leaders of the Hindu Congress Party and the Muslim League proved unbridgeable. On Wavell's initiative the government invited to London Jinnah and Liaquat Ali Khan, representing the Muslim League, and Nehru and Sardar Baldau Singh for

Congress. Nehru at first refused to come to London, but was persuaded to by a personal cable from Attlee. They arrived on 3 December 1946.

This gave the King hope that something might be achieved, having inherited his father's belief that sensible men working together could achieve sensible results. But although he had studied the reports of Linlithgow and Wavell, and had discussed the issues with Cripps before and after his abortive mission, the impossibility of compromise was brought home to him vividly when he gave a lunch for the four Indian leaders at Buckingham Palace on 5 December. He sat between Nehru and Jinnah. Nehru hardly said anything in response to the King's attempts at conversation, while Jinnah 'told me a great deal'. The conference broke up on the 8th without anything having been achieved.

Jinnah's obstinacy in insisting upon partition and the creation of Pakistan persuaded the British that this was the only possible solution. This was not an immediate, but a gradual, realisation that the government's favoured solution – an independent, Congress-dominated, unified India – was a political impossibility.

There was another factor which began to weigh heavily in London, especially with Churchill. In September 1939 Linlithgow had declared India at war with Germany without consulting Indian leaders. Congress had refused to support the war; the Muslim League and Sikh leaders had. Congress had then launched the 1942 'Quit India' campaign with the Japanese on the Indian borders, and rejoiced in British humiliations. They had seriously misjudged Indian opinion, especially in the Indian armed services, whose loyalty to the British was as total as their hatred of the Japanese. The Indian Army had a particular loathing and contempt for the pro-Japanese Indian National Army.

All the units in the Indian services, Hindu and Muslim, had fought valiantly together in the war, but the unhelpful role of Congress had not been forgotten. Jinnah may have been, as Attlee described him, 'a twister', but the credentials of the Muslim League were stronger than those of the Congress leaders. The sanctification of Gandhi had not yet begun.

The King, Attlee and Wavell were haunted by the prospect of an appalling civil war and the total collapse of British authority. The Muslim League's Direct Action Day on 16 August had led to the Calcutta massacre of thousands of Hindus and counter-killings of

Muslims, a ghastly foretaste of what was likely to happen on an even greater scale.

The failure of the London conference and the King's personal experience of the recalcitrance of the two sides had convinced him that there was no alternative solution, and that the days of the Indian Empire were numbered. Once he had come to that conclusion he accepted it. As it affected his position as King-Emperor he could have caused difficulties, but he went out of his way not to, which further increased Attlee's regard for him.

His discussions with Wavell had not gone well. Indeed, the Viceroy's taciturnity had been remarkable even by his standards, and made the King angry. On his return to India Wavell had urged a definite programme and a firm date for British withdrawal. He submitted a detailed plan for this, which finished his term of office. The King's reactions were the same as Attlee's. The King recorded in his diary for 17 December 1946 that 'Attlee told me that Ld Wavell's plan for our leaving India savours too much of a military retreat & does not realise it is a political problem & not a military one. Wavell has done very good work up to now but Attlee doubts whether he has the finesse to negotiate the next steps when we must keep the two Indian parties friendly to us all the time.' Attlee's real complaint was that Wavell had become 'defeatist', and his plan a 'policy of scuttle unworthy of a great power'. Attlee had also decided upon Wavell's successor – Mountbatten.

The Prime Minister had been greatly impressed by the fact that Mountbatten's assessment of the difficult Burma situation had proved right; it was also unquestionable that Mountbatten was a political animal who had acquired considerable prominence – and some notoriety – in India as Supreme Allied Commander. This had been one of Churchill's most controversial appointments, and one which he subsequently regretted bitterly. Mountbatten had established a huge headquarters in Kandy, in Ceylon, two thousand miles away from the theatre of action. Brilliant at self-publicity and handling the press, he was less impressive as a Commander-in-Chief. Alan Brooke was perhaps unduly hard when he wrote that 'seldom has a Supreme Commander been more deficient of the main attributes of a Supreme Commander than Dickie Mountbatten', but he was far from alone in this assessment.

The fact that he was the King's cousin could be seen as an additional asset, not least with the Indian princes, but could cause embarrassment if things went terribly wrong. At their meeting on 17 December 1946 Attlee put forward the idea rather tentatively to the King.

The King was taken aback. It was not the case, as Wheeler-Bennett has claimed, that Mountbatten was 'probably his closest personal friend';[6] it was at the time when Mountbatten was irritating him with his campaign on behalf of Prince Philip of Greece, and although the King admired his cousin's style and dash and undeniable achievements he distrusted his judgement and often over-bearing self-esteem. The King thought that there was something comical about Mountbatten's vanity, and his rapid enthusiasm for the new Labour government had not gone unnoticed in the Palace.

But the King at once saw the positive aspects of Attlee's proposal. It was going too far for his official biographer to state that he 'very warmly approved his choice'. He knew Mountbatten too well to do that. He did not oppose it, but, knowing his man, he emphasised to Attlee that Mountbatten 'must have concrete orders as to what he is to do'. This was wise advice. In the event, while the King was abroad on his South African visit, Mountbatten wrote his own orders – and then dramatically changed them.

There was also the snag that Mountbatten was genuinely reluctant to accept the post. He had, with some difficulty, persuaded the navy to allow him to continue his career, which had seemed an odd ambition for a former Supreme Commander and Service Peer. He was thus in a strong position to dictate his own terms, the most crucial of which was the establishment of a firm date for the transfer of power. Both Attlee and Wavell were extremely doubtful about the wisdom of this, but Mountbatten was emphatic, and his instructions stated that 'the date for the transfer of power is a flexible one to within one month; but you should aim at 1 June 1948 as the effective date'.

The announcement was made on 20 February 1947, Mountbatten having formally accepted on the 11th. Wavell had been given no hint while in London that his dismissal was imminent and his successor being discussed, and did not know until 13 February. But he had effectively signed his resignation on 17 January when he had rejected the government's suggestion that he should return to London for consultations.

[6] Wheeler-Bennett, op. cit., p. 710.

Attlee clearly signalled his intentions when he informed Wavell on 31 January 'that you may agree that the time has come to make a change in the Viceroyalty'. He accepted the decision with dignity, and Mountbatten, embarrassed by this treatment of a fine man, urged Attlee that his services should receive high recognition.[7] They did: Wavell was created an Earl.

Mountbatten's appointment had one unexpected sequel. Churchill hated what he called 'Operation Scuttle' and denounced this 'melancholy and disastrous transaction'. He was never to forgive Mountbatten for accepting the post and becoming a leading player in the rapid acceleration of the end of the Raj. Thus, when, on Mountbatten's strong recommendation, June 1948 became August 1947, Churchill's fury was augmented. Mountbatten's choice of the night of 14–15 August for Independence was simply because it was the second anniversary of the Japanese surrender. It was a catastrophic error, but Mountbatten had always been in a hurry, and the Labour government was equally keen to get the whole thing over with as soon as possible, at whatever cost. That cost in lives was claimed by Mountbatten to be 'only' 100,000, later revised to 200,000. The reality, as Ismay and others knew, was well over one million. Beaverbrook's persistent vendetta against Mountbatten now received a powerful ally. This prejudice stemmed from Mountbatten's disastrous Dieppe raid of August 1942, when of 4,963 men of the Canadian Second Division involved, 3,369 had been killed, wounded or taken prisoner. Mountbatten's part in his self-glorification in the superb Noël Coward film *In Which We Serve*, with its memorable opening shot of a copy of the *Daily Express* with the banner headline 'THERE WILL BE NO WAR' floating in an oily gutter, had not improved Beaverbrook's opinion of him.

By the time the King returned to Britain from South Africa at the beginning of May partition had become a reality. It was announced on 3 June; 15 August would be the date for the end of British rule in India. The speed of it all was breathtaking, and Mountbatten's role has been the subject of strong, and sometimes bitter, controversy ever since. The King asked for, and received, the last of the Union Jacks that had flown over the shattered Residency at Lucknow since the siege of 1857; he was also successful on a more important point – that the new India and

---

[7] Ziegler, *Mountbatten*, p. 358.

Pakistan should become members of the Commonwealth. On this he placed great importance, and Attlee entirely agreed.

Queen Mary, with her vivid memories of the 1911 Coronation Durbar, was almost inconsolable, although the King and Attlee ensured that the Crown of India, specially designed and made for King George V for that occasion, was retained for the Crown Jewels.

Mountbatten's pro-Congress and anti-Muslim bias, largely based on his friendship with Nehru, was then manifested when he became Governor-General of India, which confirmed the hostility of the leaders of the new Pakistan to him and increased their suspicions of his alleged impartiality over the border disputes – quite rightly, as later revelations disclosed. There was also a proposal by Churchill in 1949, which Attlee and the King took seriously, that the King should become President of India. This proposal did not proceed very far. Attlee wrote to the King on 13 February 1949 that 'it is unfortunate that Mr Eden should be away, as Mr Churchill's emotions on India tend to prevent him giving calm consideration to the larger problem of the future of the Commonwealth when the future of India is in question'.[8]

Nineteen forty-seven also saw Ceylon's independence as a self-governing dominion within the Commonwealth – with effect from February 1948 – and Burma's status as an independent republic outside the Commonwealth. There had been no significant Sinhalese independence movement on the scale of those in India and Burma; it was symptomatic of the government's determination to liquidate most of its Eastern Empire, leaving Malaya, Singapore and Hong Kong. The logic of this is somewhat difficult to fathom.

The King publicly accepted these astonishing developments. Within a matter of months, while he had been abroad on a tour that he had increasingly resented, decisions of enormous magnitude had been taken by his ministers – and his cousin – on which he had been barely consulted. If hundreds of millions of his subjects had been granted independence, they, and especially the most defenceless, had then been left to their own fate, which in too many cases meant violent death, and for others brutally enforced displacement and penury. It was difficult indeed to take pride in this abrogation of what Queen Victoria and Prince Albert, and his father and mother, had regarded, as he did, as a sacred trust to the

[8] RA PS GVI C 340/07.

protection of his Indian subjects, of whom the vast majority had been so loyal throughout the war.

These strong and very understandable feelings had to be, and were, publicly well-concealed. He retained a sense of resentment that Churchill had not permitted him to visit India, and Churchill's vehement strictures on the Indian 'scuttle' and Mountbatten's role were equally unhelpful to him, as the King could not be seen to be even faintly involved in a bitter dispute between his Prime Minister and the Leader of the Opposition, and one which now included his cousin.

Only very occasionally did the public mask of constitutional acquiescence to these miseries slip. When the King bestowed the Companion of Honour on Vita Sackville-West – the eminent author, poet, magical gardener and wife of Harold Nicolson – on 12 February 1948, he asked her about her childhood home, Knole. As Nicolson recorded: 'She said that it had gone to the National Trust. He raised his hands in despair: "Everything is going nowadays. Before long, I shall have to go."'

Yet another departure occurred a year later, when Eire declared itself a Republic and announced its decision to leave the Commonwealth. Despite the King's entreaties to 'stay in the family', he was unsuccessful, and the Conference of Commonwealth Prime Ministers went ahead in April 1949 without Irish participation. India, though, thanks to improved relations with Nehru and the agreement that allegiance to the Crown would cease to be a requirement of membership to the Commonwealth, stayed in – a considerable personal achievement by Attlee, Nehru, Mountbatten and the King.

Nineteen forty-eight opened busily. The House of Lords, with its large Conservative majority, had not emulated the Balfourian tactics of 1906–10, but a crisis arose over the proposed nationalisation of the steel and iron industries. Under the so-called 'Salisbury Rules', devised by the Conservative leader in the Lords, Lord Salisbury (as Cranborne had become), the Lords would not reject legislation contained in the 1945 Labour manifesto; iron and steel were considered to be outside the rules. Attempts at a negotiated compromise in February and March 1948, following the introduction of a Parliament Bill in November 1947 that curtailed the Lords' two-year delay powers to one, were unsuccessful.

The King, alarmed by the possibility of a repetition of the crisis that had caused his father and grandfather such prolonged anguish, let it be known that it was his wish that the Parliament Bill should not be contested. The result was an unembittered formality. The Lords rejected it both in September 1948 and in November 1949; under the 1911 Parliament Act it received the Royal Assent on 16 December 1949. It was agreed that the Steel Act would not be put into effect until 1 January 1951.

The fact that what could have been a harsh dispute was resolved relatively amicably was largely the result of the King's personal intervention. The government had made its point; so had the Lords. Churchill, who accepted the situation, pledged that a future Conservative government would repeal the iron and steel nationalisation, which it duly did.

In March 1948 it was announced that the King and Queen and Princess Margaret would be visiting Australia and New Zealand in the following year. This had been the King's ambition before the war, and it was one Royal Tour to which he looked forward eagerly, with his happy memories of 1927, which he considered had been one of the crucial turning-points in his life. On 26 April he and the Queen celebrated their Silver Wedding, driving to St Paul's in an open landau and in the afternoon being driven slowly in an open car through large, cheering crowds, and then repeatedly being called to the balcony of the Palace. The King professed that they had both been 'dumbfounded over our reception' and by the volume of letters and messages. An additional joy was that Princess Elizabeth, who had married on 20 November 1947, was now pregnant, her baby expected in November.

Thus, all seemed well. The atmosphere of desperate crisis at home and abroad that had dominated 1946 and 1947 seemed to have lifted. But all was not well with the King.

In January he noticed that he was suffering cramp in both legs, but did nothing about it except occasionally complain. By August he was experiencing considerable discomfort, and by October his left foot was numb all day and the pain made sleeping difficult. The problem then spread to the right foot, and, at long last, on 20 October, he summoned his Manipulative Surgeon Sir Morton Smart, who at once realised the condition was far more serious than cramp and called in the King's general medical adviser Sir Maurice Cassidy.

Sarah Bradford has, understandably, expressed some surprise that matters then proceeded so slowly, and has commented upon the ages of the

King's principal medical advisers. Smart was seventy, Cassidy sixty-eight, and Sir Thomas Dunhill, the King's oddly titled Serjeant-Surgeon, was seventy-two. Weir, on whose homeopathic wisdom the King had placed such faith, was in his seventieth year. Smart had been, according to the King's official biographer, 'gravely alarmed' on 20 October, but it was not until 30 October that the King was examined by Cassidy, Smart and Dunhill.

In that period there had been a State Visit by the King and Queen of Denmark, and the King had undertaken the first fully-fledged State Opening of Parliament since before the war. All this required a considerable amount of walking and standing, discomfort and pain. When his doctors examined him on 30 October 'all were agreed on the King's serious condition'[9] and decided to seek the opinion of Professor James Learmonth, Regius Professor of Clinical Surgery at the University of Edinburgh, and considered one of the foremost authorities on vascular problems.

But Learmonth did not see the King until 12 November, by which time the King, rejecting the advice of his doctors, had insisted on attending a Territorial Army review in Hyde Park and the annual Remembrance Day service at the Cenotaph, both of which, again, required long periods of standing.

The doctors were already sufficiently alarmed to strongly advise Lascelles that the Australia and New Zealand tour should be at least postponed, if not actually cancelled. It had reached such a stage in preparation that this was a very serious matter, and Lascelles knew how vehemently the King would react to it. Eventually a decision was postponed until Learmonth's examination. It was now over three weeks since Smart had been 'gravely alarmed'.

Learmonth was infinitely more concerned when he eventually examined the King. He diagnosed arteriosclerosis of such seriousness that gangrene might well set in and it might be necessary to amputate the King's right leg.

There was now no question of the Australasian tour taking place. The King at first fought this advice with all the tenacity and anger that Lascelles had anticipated. But because at that point his doctors considered amputation virtually unavoidable to save his life, and with the agreement

[9] Wheeler-Bennett, op. cit., p. 763.

and strong support of the Queen, the doctors won. The announcement was made on 23 November.

The medical bulletin was guarded, referring to 'an obstruction to the circulation through the arteries of the legs, which has only recently become acute; the defective blood supply to the right foot causes anxiety. Complete rest has been advised and treatment to improve the circulation in the legs has been initiated and must be maintained for an immediate and prolonged period. Though His Majesty's general health, including the condition of his heart, gives no reason for concern, there is no doubt that the strain of the last twelve years has appreciably affected his resistance to physical fatigue.'

He was in fact totally exhausted, and took to his bed without much resistance, greatly delighted by the birth of his grandson on 14 November.[10] Also, Learmonth's treatment seemed to work so well that the threat of amputation disappeared, and he was able to attend the christening of Prince Charles in Buckingham Palace on 15 December and to deliver his Christmas broadcast, expressing his warm gratitude and that of the Queen to the 'expressions of love and loyalty from our people', including those from Australia and New Zealand.

The Royal Family went to Sandringham for the New Year, where the King was allowed to go on short walks and, on 18 January 1949, to shoot in the morning provided that he spent the afternoon in bed. His morale rose rapidly, and he began to interest himself actively in political matters again. On his return to London he had meetings with ministers as well as his regular ones with Attlee and held an investiture. Rested, and greatly relieved that his illness had not been nearly as grave as it had seemed, he was cheerful and vigorous. But it was to prove a false dawn.

When his doctors, now swelled to six, and including Weir, consulted

---

[10] It had become a hallowed tradition that the Home Secretary should be present – not literally, but in the same building – for all royal births, and this had happened in the cases of the births of Princess Elizabeth at 17 Bruton Street in April 1926 and of Princess Margaret at Glamis Castle in August 1930. Both the King and the Home Secretary, Chuter Ede, wondered whether this procedure could not be dispensed with, and research revealed no justification for it. Thus, Prince Charles's birth did not have the official imprimatur of the Home Secretary, although the official announcement that Princess Elizabeth 'had been safely delivered of a Prince' sounded distinctly medieval.

together on 3 March after further assessment of their patient's progress, they concluded that his improvement could be maintained only if he lived the life of an invalid; they knew full well that he would never accept that. They accordingly recommended what in technical terms was 'a right lumbar sympathectomy operation'.

The King was furious. He had assumed that his treatment was working well and that the problem had been resolved; now he was faced with an operation which, although not serious in itself, was a massive inconvenience. But it was, as he reflected, infinitely better than an amputation. It was performed in Buckingham Palace by Learmonth in a specially established operating theatre on 12 March.[11]

Although the operation was considered a success, Learmonth's prognosis was not encouraging. The King would not have to live the life of an invalid, but there would have to be drastic changes in his lifestyle, both psychological and physical, if a second, and almost certainly fatal, thrombosis was to be averted. His smoking must be drastically curtailed, he must have more rest, and his official programmes kept to a reasonable minimum. As the Queen and his immediate private staff knew, nothing could prevent him worrying about political affairs at home and abroad, but his ceremonial and official duties could be restricted and conducted sensibly. By November his doctors agreed that he could undertake his coveted tour of Australia and New Zealand, with a greatly reduced programme, in 1952.

If 1948 and 1949 had been unhappy years for the King they had been politically difficult and dangerous for the Labour government. The withdrawals from India and Palestine – the State of Israel having been proclaimed in May 1948, almost immediately followed by a concerted Arab attempt to destroy it at birth – had been far from glorious, and considered by many to have been shameful and unnecessarily bloody.

[11] It had originally been intended that the operation should be performed in a hospital, and the Royal Masonic, very appropriately, was suggested. The King had no objection, although he remarked that he had never heard of a King going into hospital. When, in 1953, Eden, by then Foreign Secretary again, had to go into hospital for what was thought to be a relatively minor operation, but which was badly and almost fatally botched, Churchill expressed surprise, remarking that 'the King had been operated on on the kitchen table at Buckingham Palace'. It was in fact a fully equipped operating theatre.

The Russian blockade of Berlin had been eventually defeated by the Anglo-American airlift, but at times war had seemed very close. The return of the Americans to Europe, militarily as well as economically, marked the turn of the post-war tide, but although this is now obvious in hindsight it did not seem so at the time.

The economic situation got worse. The high hopes of 1948 had proved a chimera. In September 1949 Cripps and Bevin returned from Washington and Ottawa with good terms, but the pressures were such that Cripps had to announce the devaluation of the pound from the rate of $4.03 to $2.80 on 18 September. The meat and sugar rations were cut further, to predictable outrage. By the end of August the King was wondering whether there would be an imminent General Election before the end of the year and was apprehensive of 'another 1931 crisis'.

Attlee shared the King's opinion, although the latter's advice played no part in his decision to have a General Election early in 1950. The King's illnesses and slow recuperation had further diminished his political influence, although Attlee consulted him regularly and took his opinions seriously. But Attlee himself was exhausted and unwell; Bevin was not in good health at all; and, although it was not then realised, Cripps was a dying man.[12] They were all paying the physical price of ten years of unrelenting pressure, long hours, and disappointment. The adrenalin of war had long since dried up; the grim post-war grind was dispiriting for everyone involved.

The decisive voice was that of Cripps, who refused to consider another Budget until after the election – a characteristically principled action not followed by most of his successors at the Treasury. This effectively meant a February election, only Morrison dissenting, on the grounds that bad weather would affect the Labour vote more than the Conservative; in the event, the turnout of 84 per cent broke the previous record of 74 per cent in 1945.

Attlee wrote to the King, who as usual was at Sandringham for the Christmas and New Year break, on 5 January 1950, requesting

[12] Cripps resigned in October 1950, and died in 1951. Attlee removed Bevin from the Foreign Office in March 1951; he became Lord Privy Seal, but died within five weeks. He was succeeded at the Foreign Office by Morrison – 'Worst appointment I ever made,' Attlee later told his biographer, Kenneth Harris, an opinion endorsed then and later.

the dissolution of parliament on 3 February for an election on the 23rd.

To do this by letter was unusual, although not entirely unprecedented, and Attlee was invited to Sandringham on the 7th so that he could receive the King's assent personally. It was slightly surprising that Attlee, of all men – himself a stickler for formalities – had forgotten them on this occasion. The official announcement appeared on 10 January.

That election result, like that of 1945, took everyone by surprise. This time, Labour was confident of victory, although obviously not on the 1945 scale. For all its difficulties, the Labour government had also had its achievements, the greatest of all having been the creation of the National Health Service. Also, it had achieved the remarkable feat of having never lost a single by-election, a unique record that, very understandably, seemed to point to another Labour victory. This was also the opinion of the King and Lascelles.

But the Conservatives had rebuilt and revived themselves to a remarkable extent, and also went into the contest with enthusiasm and confidence. Their judgement was that the stampede to national-isation had been carried too far and too quickly, and had lost its popular appeal – an opinion strongly, but secretly, held by the King himself.

No one alive at the time is likely to forget the amazing night of 23 February and the interminable following day as the results were broadcast. At one point the Conservatives and Liberals were level with Labour; on four occasions the Labour lead vanished, only to creep forward again. It was not until the last result was declared after six o'clock in the evening of the 24th that it became clear that Labour had, just, been re-elected. Labour, with 46.1 per cent of the votes cast, had 315 seats; the Conservatives and National Liberals, with 43.5 per cent, had 298, 2 being returned unopposed; the Liberals 9 and the Irish Nationalists 2. The overall Labour majority in the Commons was only 5.

Although this narrow result did not in itself create a constitutional crisis, it certainly caused some potentially complex constitutional issues that could have involved the King.

The fluctuating fortunes of 23 and 24 February may have excited the nation, especially political commentators and journalists, but had been a nightmare for the King, noting that, 'Yesterday was one of the worst days of my life wondering what was going to happen.'[13]

The situation was now one of great uncertainty, and the King and his advisers urgently considered the possibilities. The first was that Attlee might ask for another dissolution. It would have been the King's decision whether to grant it, or to refuse and seek an alternative Prime Minister, as Attlee would certainly have resigned. The 1926 precedent, when the Governor-General of Canada, Lord Byng, had refused a dissolution to Mackenzie King and then had granted one to the Conservative leader, Arthur Meighen, at once came to Lascelles' mind. There was also the 1939 South African precedent to consider, when the Governor-General, Sir Patrick Duncan, had refused Prime Minister Hertzog's request.

Hardinge and Lascelles had studied the Byng precedent, on which Stamfordham had taken a keen interest, and Lascelles had detailed information on it. The conclusion was that although Byng had been technically and constitutionally within his rights to refuse the Mackenzie King request, he was wrong to then accept Meighen's. Lascelles' emphatic advice was that although he strongly defended the King's right to refuse a request for a dissolution, the uproar in Canada over Byng's actions – of which he had keen personal memories – and the subsequent overwhelming Liberal victory pointed to the political perils of such an action.

Hardinge had also prepared memoranda on the Duncan precedent, which was justifed by the facts that Smuts could, and did, acquire a parliamentary majority, and the exigencies of wartime made an election a highly unwelcome additional complication. It was the Byng precedent that most worried Lascelles.

Lascelles' papers also contained a long, and now very important, report on Churchill's views on Byng's actions, contained in a memorandum by Lord Bessborough of a discussion with Churchill in Ottawa in March 1932, and Churchill's discussions with Mackenzie King and Meighen. Churchill's view was that Byng had initially acted correctly, but then should not have granted Meighen his request.

As Lascelles quickly discovered, Churchill had not changed his mind, and told him that the 'new House of Commons has a right to live if it can, and should not be destroyed until some fresh issue or situation has

[13] Lascelles Papers.

arisen to place before the electors'.[14] The idea was floated by academic constitutionalists, who were in full cry in the press and on radio, that the impasse could only be resolved by an all-party conference, and the role of George V in 1931 was recalled – although seldom accurately.

Lascelles' strong personal political contacts and friendships now again paid significant dividends. Sent out by the King on a discreet journey of discovery, he returned with the hard information that Attlee was determined to meet the new House of Commons and would not ask for another dissolution unless defeated, that neither he nor Churchill wanted an all-party conference, and that the Conservative leaders were not at all anxious for another immediate General Election. He therefore concluded that the so-called grave constitutional crisis was largely artificial, and that the King would not be called upon to make major decisions, at least not for the time being.

On 27 February Attlee had an audience with the King and confirmed what he had told Lascelles – that he would continue as Prime Minister unless and until his government was unable to carry its essential business through the House of Commons. But, as Lascelles realised only too well, this was not an academic matter at all. Also, as he frankly told the King, his assessment might well be wrong. The Conservative leadership might not want another immediate General Election, but their exultant followers, so close to power, might well do so. Attlee would resign after a Commons defeat, and might even – although this was highly improbable – advise the King to send for Churchill. If the King had declined Attlee's request for a dissolution, and then gave one to Churchill, the Byng precedent would become only too relevant.

Alternatively, Attlee might not resign and simply ask for a dissolution. Although, Lascelles argued, the King would be technically justified in refusing, given the parliamentary realities, Lascelles wrote that 'there does not seem to be sufficient reason here for the sovereign to break the precedent followed by his predecessors for more than a century by refusing his Prime Minister a dissolution'. Again, the Byng precedent 'undoubtedly left in certain quarters in Canada a considerable legacy of bitterness against the Crown'.

Lascelles also advised the King that if he did grant Attlee a dissolution it must be on the condition that it could only be after the passage of a

Minimal Finance Act to make provision for the national finances until a new government was formed. But Lascelles' conclusion was: 'To sum up, then: it does not seem probable that the government will be faced with resignation during the next few weeks, but even if this should happen the only difficult problem which the King might be called upon to solve is the decision to grant or to withold a dissolution; in present circumstances the arguments in favour of granting it seem to outweigh those against it.'[15]

Not content with this private advice, which the King entirely accepted, Lascelles took it upon himself to write a letter for publication in *The Times* under a pseudonym, only telling the King that he was the author after it had been published on 2 May 1950.

The King was amused and grateful rather than irritated, although it could have been interpreted as carrying self-confidence rather too far, particularly as the Editor knew who the author was. But in those days such confidences were kept. The *Times* letter ran:

Sir,
    It is surely indisputable (and common sense) that a Prime Minister may ask – not demand – that his Sovereign will grant him a dissolution of Parliament; and that his Sovereign, if he so chooses, may refuse to grant this request. The problem of such a choice is entirely personal to the Sovereign, although he is, of course, free to seek informal advice from anybody whom he thinks fit to consult.

    Insofar as this matter can be publicly discussed, it can be properly assumed that no wise Sovereign – that is, one who has at heart the true interests of the country, the constitution, and the Monarchy – would deny a dissolution to his Prime Minister unless he were satisfied that: (1) the existing Parliament was still vital, viable, and capable of doing its job; (2) a General Election would be detrimental to the national economy; (3) he could rely on finding another Prime Minister who could carry on his Government, for a reasonable period, with a working majority in the House of Commons. When Sir Patrick Duncan refused a dissolution to his Prime Minister in South Africa in 1939, all these conditions were satisfied: when Lord

[15] RA PS GVI C 320/021.

Byng did the same in Canada in 1926, they appeared to be, but in the event the third proved illusory.

I am, &c.,

SENEX

This letter has been so often commented upon as demonstrating Lascelles' wisdom and unparalleled experience that the oddity of one of his qualifications for refusing a dissolution, that a General Election 'would be detrimental to the national economy', has tended to be overlooked. He was harking back to the 1931 crisis, but was making a claim for the royal powers that involved a personal judgement by the monarch on the state of the economy, and, in that case, a personal political judgement that had gone beyond the economy. It was certainly a bold claim, and it was strange that it went unchallenged.

13

THE LAST PHASE

———— ▸ ————

C ommunist North Korea, armed, encouraged and assisted by the
Soviet Union, invaded the South on 25 June 1950. The Soviet
Union had absented itself from the UN Security Council in
protest at the exclusion of Communist China, which enabled the rapid
passage of a resolution calling for its members to ensure the withdrawal
of the North Korean forces and to assist in this. Attlee responded strongly
to what he called 'this naked aggression'. British forces were committed
to what was to develop into an especially vicious war, and one which
the North Koreans nearly won in the first weeks.

Although the Conservative Opposition supported the government's
action and its increased defence expenditure, the situation in Korea was
so perilous and the domestic political situation in Britain so tense that
serious differences soon became evident.

Attlee reported to the King on 18 August in a handwritten letter:

Sir,
Mr Churchill, Mr Eden and Mr Clement Davies came to see
me yesterday to ask that Parliament should be recalled next week.
Mr Bevin was with me.

I explained that we had decided on the date of September 12th
in order that we might put to the House our full proposals and
indicate the reasons which weighed with us in our not suggesting
an earlier date.

Mr Churchill talked at considerable length on the dangers of the present situation mostly on the lines of his last speech in the Defence debate in the House.

I was unable to find any substantive reason for an earlier recall as it did not seem to me that another debate without definite action to be taken by the House would be useful.

Mr Churchill showed considerable annoyance and suggested that in not accepting this date the Government was acting dictatorially. I was unable to accept this view as it would seem that Mr Churchill's demand might be considered as an attempt to dictate to the Government.

Mr Clement Davies has issued a statement in which he sets out his reasons and I wondered if Mr Churchill proposes to broadcast . . .[1]

Mr Churchill certainly did, and at the end of August there was an acrimonious exchange of radio broadcasts in which Churchill denounced Attlee's refusal to recall parliament immediately, for sending too little military assistance to the Americans and South Korea, and too tardily, and for having sold military equipment to the Soviet Union. Attlee responded with cold asperity, remarking on Churchill's poor attendance at the House of Commons, and describing him as 'a prima donna full of querulous complaint against the people of this country for not having continued him in power'. The King was not alone in deploring these rancid exchanges at a time of major international crisis. The debate on 12–14 September was not much better. The government announced a further increase in the defence budget and the extension of National Service. The Conservatives said again that it was all too little and too late.

But within days the situation seemed to be dramatically transformed when the American United Nations Commander, General MacArthur, achieved one of the most astounding coups in modern military history, a brilliantly conceived and highly hazardous American amphibious landing behind the enemy lines on the west coast of Korea at Inchon. The hitherto hard-pressed American, South Korean and Allied forces in the south now advanced rapidly and the North Koreans were routed, driven back across their border, suffering heavy casualties. It seemed

[1] RA PS GVI C 350/11.

that the Korean War, already exceptional in its brutality and loss of life, was over.

But the government's domestic problems continued, in an atmosphere of ill-temper and recrimination, particularly over steel nationalisation. And then Cripps, grievously ill, tendered his resignation as Chancellor of the Exchequer.

This was a heavy blow to the government, and it was a notable tribute to his stewardship that Britain was able to dispense with Marshall Aid in December 1950, before any of the other recipients, and two years ahead of the target date.

Attlee wrote to the King on 17 October, again in his own hand, that 'the departure of the Chancellor is a serious loss to the government and it is not easy to fill his place'. He went on:

> It is, I think, generally desirable that the Exchequer should be in the charge of a senior Minister of long experience, but in these days it is, I think, important that the Chancellor should be well versed in all the technicalities of finance, especially as he has very often to deal with experts from foreign countries.
>
> With the exception of the Foreign Secretary, who could not, I think, be spared from his present post, I do not think that any of my senior colleagues have the necessary qualifications, as I do not think it would be desirable to bring back Dr Dalton.
>
> The President of the Board of Trade [Harold Wilson] is a possible choice, but he is very young & I should prefer to leave him where he is.
>
> I am, therefore, inclined to suggest Mr Gaitskell and the Chancellor of the Exchequer agrees with this view. He is very experienced in financial matters and has done well in the House of Commons. He made a very good impression on the Commonwealth Ministers at the recent conference and also in his talks in Paris.
>
> It will not, I think, be possible to preserve secrecy for long as to the Chancellor's position. I shall wish, therefore, to make the change this week.[2]

Gaitskell was the preferred choice of both Cripps and Dalton, but it

[2] RA PS GVI C 350/14.

was to prove a disastrous error. Gaitskell had several qualifications for this remarkable promotion only five years since his election to parliament, but he had not yet established himself in the Labour Party, and was considered to be significantly right of centre. He had been an able deputy to Cripps, and knew the Treasury, but in a party perhaps over-impressed by seniority and experience it was considered an astounding preferment.

After Attlee himself, Cripps and Bevin, Aneurin Bevan had been one of the great successes of the government, although his sometimes vitriolic assaults on the Conservatives, especially one in which he described them as 'lower than vermin', had been highly counter-productive and had offended Attlee. But he was in every respect a far more substantial political figure than Gaitskell. He was in his prime, a politician of the first rank and experience, with the towering achievement of the National Health Service to his undying credit. He expected, and deserved, promotion. As Attlee knew, he also loathed Gaitskell.

Bevan wrote to Attlee to express his 'consternation and astonishment'; in private, as Douglas Jay, the Financial Secretary at the Treasury, has recorded vividly, he was incensed and 'began to pour forth with uncontrolled passion a torrent of vitriolic abuse on the head of Attlee for daring to make such an appointment'.[3] Morrison, who had supported it, lived to deeply regret it. So did Attlee, although it is unreasonable to criticise him for not anticipating the full extent of the personal and political repercussions that were to tear the Labour Party apart. Gaitskell had many qualities, but, far from being 'the desiccated calculating machine' of Bevan's imagination, was a highly emotional man of uneven judgement and temperament. The King was not the only person who found him difficult to understand, although he tried. As Gaitskell's diaries later revealed, there was a failure of comprehension on both sides.

The war in Korea then went appallingly wrong. MacArthur's triumphant advance into North Korea collapsed when the Chinese army intervened in massive strength. His forces hurled back, and suffering grievous casualties, MacArthur's arrogance deteriorated into near-panic. Three days after the launch of his lauded final offensive to end the war he confronted what he called the 'complete destruction' of his army. He called for reinforcements of 'the greatest magnitude', a naval blockade of

[3] Jay, *Change and Fortune*, p. 202.

China, and a bombing offensive against Chinese territory. Truman and his advisers had no intention of widening the war, but on 30 November 1950 the President held one of the most disastrously sensational Press Conferences in presidential history.

Truman publicly stifled the doubts about MacArthur's judgement that were surfacing in many minds, and defended him. But, when asked whether the phrase 'we will take whatever steps are necessary to meet the military situation' included the use of atomic bombs, Truman replied, 'That includes every weapon we have . . . It [the atomic bomb] is one of our weapons.'

The White House Press Corps, which held the President in high regard, unlike some other journalists and their proprietors, was stunned. They did not misrepresent Truman in their reports. As his latest biographer has written, 'Truman's answers had been devastatingly foolish.'[4]

Although the British and Commonwealth – Canada, Australia and New Zealand – military commitment to the United Nations forces in Korea was nowhere near as considerable as that of the Americans, it was considerable enough for concern, 1,263 being killed and 4,817 wounded, but the real worry was that the war would escalate out of control. This alarm was not confined to the Labour Party. On 30 November Attlee told the Cabinet that as Bevin was too ill to travel to Washington he would go himself to see Truman, leaving on the evening of 3 December.

The King wrote to him in his own hand on the 2nd:

My dear PM,

I am writing on the eve of your departure for America for your talks with President Truman, to wish you all success.

I know that you have contemplated this visit for some time & I feel that this is the right moment when, as Head of my Government in the UK, you can explain to the President the true picture as we see it of the present world situation.

I wish I could have told you this personally, but events nowadays happen so quickly. I have been very worried lately about affairs in general, so I am very glad that you will be able to put our case fairly & squarely before the President . . .

I am quite confident that you will be able to deal with all the

---

[4] McCollough, *Truman*, p. 822.

important outstanding problems & I trust that your visit will not
be too exacting.

I shall look forward to our next meeting in London with much
anticipation.

I am Yrs v. sincerely,

GR[5]

Attlee replied, also in his own hand, that 'Your Majesty's gracious letter
gave me much encouragement to deal with the tasks before me'.[6]

Attlee's meetings with Truman have been described and analysed in
some detail by his biographer and the admiring but suspicious Secretary
of State, Dean Acheson. The Labour mythology that Attlee talked
Truman out of using atomic weapons and thereby saved the world
belonged to electoral campaigning hyperbole. What he did achieve was
a firm commitment that the conflict would be confined to Korea. He
certainly tried to get an assurance from Truman that the United States
would not use atomic weapons without consulting its allies, and at one
point did so until Acheson intervened. His proposal that the British and
American forces should be evacuated was not accepted either, but he did
commit Britain to a greatly enlarged defence programme, the burden
of which was to provoke Bevan's resignation (along with Wilson and
John Freeman) over Gaitskell's Budget proposals to introduce further
NHS charges. Thus, Attlee's achievements in Washington, which were
considerable, came to be shadowed by the crisis that effectively ended
his government and condemned the Labour Party to thirteen years in
the political wilderness.

Throughout the spring and summer of 1951 the King tried to follow
Learmonth's advice and regime, but it was a time of much worry for
him. The Korean War had expanded into one of great savagery, and
on 11 April Truman took the sensational step of dismissing General
MacArthur. There was crisis in Persia, with the nationalisation of the
Anglo-Iranian Oil Company. At home, the government's precarious
Commons majority was under daily threat.

The King fulfilled the minimum public functions permitted to him

[5] RA PS GVI C 350/15.
[6] RA PS GVI C 350/16.

by Learmonth – now Sir James, personally knighted by the King in his bedroom in his dressing-gown and slippers, remarking as he produced his concealed sword that 'you used a knife on me, now I'm going to use one on you' – including opening the Festival of Britain, Morrison's pet project, on 3 May. But on that occasion, on the steps of St Paul's, and at a special service in Westminster Abbey on 24 May for the Knights of the Bath, he looked dreadful. When, on that evening, he went to bed with influenza his doctors took their opportunity of giving him a full examination.

Their initial diagnosis, they told the King, was pneumonitis in the left lung, to be treated with penicillin and prolonged rest. He convalesced first at The Royal Lodge, and then at Sandringham and Balmoral in August. But the August weather in Scotland was cold and wet, and he complained of a chill and sore throat. After his doctors examined him on 1 September they persuaded him to return briefly to London for further examination and X-rays.

Sir Horace Evans had become the King's physician in 1949, at the age of forty-six. X-rays the King had had in May revealed a shadow on the lung that had worried him more than he had disclosed to his patient. He had hoped that it was indeed pneumonitis, and would be cleared up by penicillin, but was suspicious. He now consulted Clement Price Thomas, a specialist on malignant diseases of the chest. After the X-rays on 8 September they decided that a bronchoscopy to remove tissue from the lung for examination was necessary. This was undertaken in Buckingham Palace on 15 September. Evans' fears proved justified: the growth was malignant.

The only possible course then was the removal of the left lung. No mention was made to the King or in the public bulletins of cancer.

Learmonth's principal apprehension for his patient was thrombosis. He believed that it was probable that the cancer was limited to the left lung, and that the operation – performed by Price Thomas on 23 September 1951 – would be entirely successful. He was proved right on both counts. The King did not die of lung cancer, as has been often alleged, but of his old enemy, the blood-clot that had so nearly killed him in 1948–49.

It does not seem that Attlee had any premonitions of disaster, but it was characteristic of his regard for the King that the forthcoming visit to Ceylon, Australia and New Zealand – postponed from 1949 – was a major factor in his decision to have the General Election before the King left.

There were, of course, other reasons. The Labour government, with its tiny Commons majority, had been further damaged by the resignations of Bevan, Wilson and Freeman and the parliamentary situation was becoming almost intolerable as the Conservatives ruthlessly used every device to keep the Commons business going as long as possible, with all-night sittings becoming almost the norm. Attlee himself was exhausted after more than ten years in high office, and as early as 27 May had written to Morrison telling him that he proposed to hold the election in October. He felt strongly that to delay it would be unfair to the King, and against the national interest.

This decision was Attlee's, and among his senior colleagues only Morrison demurred. Whether the King knew of this is very unlikely, as on 24 June he noted that he had told Attlee that he hoped he would ask for a new mandate before he went to Australia and New Zealand, as he could not leave the country with such an unstable situation in the Commons; Attlee told him that he would ask the King for a dissolution in the autumn, but did not give a date.[7]

Were it not for Attlee's May letter to Morrison and the subsequent consultations with his colleagues, this note might give the wrong impression that the King was trying to accelerate the General Election to accommodate his travel plans. Neither he nor Attlee at that point realised how ill he was; both considered the visit important, and recognised that the absence of the King at a time of political turmoil at home was an impossibility.

The King then heard nothing on the matter from his Prime Minister for over two months. Attlee, who had been on holiday in Norway, broke his mysterious – and, indeed, inexplicable – silence on this vital subject on 6 September in response to an anxious letter from the King, when he wrote:

I have been giving much anxious thought to the question of a General Election. Among the factors to which I have given particular attention was the need for avoiding any political crises while Your Majesty was out of the country.

[7] RA PS GVI C 350/18.

I have come to the conclusion that the right course would be to have a dissolution of Parliament in the first week of October. A later date would, I think, be undesirable as November is seldom a good month [for elections] from the point of view of the weather.

I should, therefore, like to make a submission to Your Majesty in about a fortnight's time for the prorogation and dissolution of Parliament in the first week in October.[8]

In this process the King's health had not been a factor. Indeed, when he was told that he must have an operation, he told Lascelles to write to Attlee to record the fact that on 1 September 'he had no conception that his physical condition might make it necessary for him to abandon this tour; indeed, he still believes today, on the eve of his serious operation, that he will be able to carry out his tour more or less as planned'.

It is very probable that this letter, to be put 'on record in our secret archives here . . . So that there is no misinterpretation of recent events by historians in the future,' was Lascelles' idea.[9] He knew how serious the King's condition was, but also knew his determination. It was not a dishonest letter, because it faithfully reflected the King's optimism, but historians are rightly wary of letters written for the record, and this is no exception.

Polling day was on 25 October 1951, just over a month after the King's operation. There was a very real possibility that neither Labour nor the Conservatives would have a majority, and Lascelles consulted Anderson and Salisbury on what the King's course might be. Anderson suggested that if Labour was returned with a bare majority the King should suggest to Attlee that he should try to form a National Government – the 1931 scenario that the King so dreaded – and that if he declined, as he almost certainly would, also remembering 1931, and decided to face the Commons he should do so. Anderson also considered that Churchill, in the same position, would take the same course. But Anderson considered that the Conservatives 'would come back with a 30/40 majority', Lascelles reported to the King, '& that seems to be the most general opinion'.[10]

In the event the Conservatives and their allies won 321 seats, Labour

[8] RA PS GVI C 350/23.
[9] RA PS GVI C 340/016.
[10] RA PS GVI C 340/040.

295, the Liberals 6, and others 3. Much has been made of the fact that the total Labour vote (13,948,605) was greater than that of the Conservatives and allies (13,717,538), but this does not take account of the facts that, for the last time in British General Elections, several Conservative-held seats were uncontested, and that in some others no Conservative candidate opposed Liberal ones, and Conservative voters were advised to vote Liberal. Tactical voting is not as recent an innovation as has often been suggested.[11]

Certainly Attlee did not cavil at the result, and went to the Palace at 5 p.m. on the 26th to resign. The King had developed a strong affection and respect for him, and expressed his gratitude and admiration, which he demonstrated by conferring upon the retiring Prime Minister the Order of Merit.

At 5.45 Churchill arrived, to become Prime Minister again. Sadly, there is no extant record of what must have been for both men a moving occasion. The King no longer kept a diary, and Churchill never did. Churchill, through Moran's sources and knowledge and from a letter Lascelles had written him, knew that the King had been operated on for lung cancer. The King himself did not: the word was not mentioned to him.

But Churchill quickly discovered, as he had before, that the King was not disposed to accept his recommendations lightly. He baulked at Eden being designated 'Deputy Prime Minister', although both Attlee and Morrison had been so titled. This had nothing to do with his opinion of Eden; it was the principle that concerned him. The King was anxious not to let this unofficial designation become established, and thereby limit his freedom of choice of Churchill's successor. Churchill withdrew the recommendation.

The King was too weak to be able to discuss Churchill's appointments with him, or to take leave of the outgoing ministers individually, although each received a personal letter of thanks for their services. When the new parliament met on 6 November the King's Speech was read for him by the new Lord Chancellor, Lord Simonds.

---

[11] The February 1974 General Election was a more serious test of the British electoral system, when the Conservatives had a small majority of the national vote over Labour − over 200,000 − but four fewer seats in the Commons. In that election all seats were contested.

*   *   *

The King had no premonitions of an early death. Nor did his doctors. When Churchill later movingly declared that 'during these last months the King walked with death, as if death were a companion, an acquaintance, whom he recognised and did not fear', this was not, strictly speaking, true, although it could be fairly ascribed to his previous experiences. He had been delighted by the success of a visit to Canada and the United States of Princess Elizabeth and the Duke of Edinburgh, marked by his appointment of them both to the Privy Council. His doctors were pleased by his recovery. On 31 December Churchill sailed for the United States. He had wanted to fly to Washington, but Moran thought this unwise at his age, and asked Lascelles for the King's support, which the King willingly gave him. Rather to his surprise, Churchill accepted it. This was destined to be their last meeting and exchange.

For the first time the King's Christmas Day broadcast was pre-recorded in sections, the whole operation taking over two somewhat exhausting hours. Apart from a slight hoarseness, few noticed anything different from his 1950 one, which had been notably confident. He had wanted to do it again live, but was persuaded that this was not practicable until he was fully recovered.

Christmas 1951 at Sandringham was very happy. The family, now expanded by the birth of Princess Anne, rejoiced in the King's recovery, and he began shooting again. He wrote personal letters to Truman and Eisenhower. He, the Queen and the Princesses and the Duke of Edinburgh went to a performance of *South Pacific* at Drury Lane. Plans were well advanced for a convalescent trip to South Africa in March; on 29 January his doctors pronounced themselves 'very well satisfied' with his condition. Having seen his elder daughter and her husband off at London Airport on 31 January – the Princess and Duke were to conduct the long-delayed Australasian tour on his behalf – he and the Queen returned to Sandringham on 1 February 1952.

If he had looked ghastly at the airport in the photographs, the reality had been much less alarming. He was described as 'jaunty', enjoying champagne. He was on excellent form at Sandringham, shooting conspicuously well. February 5th was a particularly good day, followed by a good dinner, and an early night at 10.30.

At 7.30 the following morning his valet, bringing in his tea, found him dead. Lascelles telephoned Edward Ford with the coded phrase they had agreed, 'Hyde Park Corner last night', instructing him to inform Churchill and Queen Mary. Churchill was 'shattered' by the news; Colville, returned to his service, found him stunned, with tears in his eyes. The task of telling Queen Mary fell to Colville's mother, one of her ladies-in-waiting, before Ford went in.

The shock of the King's unexpected death was immense, and evoked perhaps Churchill's finest and most deeply felt broadcast tribute. In it he revealed, for the first time, the narrowness of the escape of the King and Queen from serious injury in the bombing of Buckingham Palace in September 1940. In his tribute in the Commons on 11 February, Churchill described the King's demeanour in the dark days of 1940, and how he had 'lived through every minute of this struggle with a heart that never quavered and a spirit undaunted'. Attlee's tribute, in his very different style, was equally moving, and in some respects even more touching coming from such an outwardly unemotional man now so deeply and visibly moved by the King's death. A deep silence seemed to fall, and almost wordless queues of mourners braved the intense February cold to file past the catafalque in Westminster Hall and to line the streets of London and Windsor for the funeral procession. The grief was widespread and sincere. De Gaulle, for the time being a private French citizen, out of office, and, it seemed, permanently so, attended to honour the man who had shown him such kindness and understanding in France's most desperate and humiliating hour. The card attached to the Cabinet's wreath, in Churchill's writing, stated simply, 'For Valour', the inscription on the Victoria Cross.

These tributes emphasised that the mourning was for a man, not the passing of the senior member of an institution. The United States House of Representatives was not a likely candidate for honouring the institution of the British monarchy, but it carried unanimously a resolution of sympathy and adjourned in respect.

Princess Elizabeth, now the Queen, was in Kenya with her husband on their way to Australia when she received the news. She and the Prince flew home at once, to be met at London Airport by a sombre phalanx of elderly men, headed by Churchill and Attlee.

Her accession to the Throne was as unexpected, and infinitely more tragic, than that of her father's. And he had been forty, she was twenty-five. The story of how she assumed her duties and responsibilities and put her own personality upon the monarchy will be for future historians to recount.

The small 'Royal Family' was uniquely close. It was a devoted, and usually light-hearted, quartet, and the loss of its adored leading member was, for a time, almost insupportable and unendurable. It is not given to many to inspire such love. Queen Mary never recovered from the loss of her second son, and her long life ended on 24 March 1953. There had been no reconciliation with the Duke of Windsor. He had not appeared overly grief-stricken at the funeral of his brother, and wrote some harsh things to the Duchess about his mother, but Philip Ziegler has, quite fairly, balanced these cruel denunciations with other evidence that the Duke was genuinely distressed by the loss of the first woman he had loved. She had made it plain that nothing was to interrupt the Coronation of Queen Elizabeth II, which took place in June.

This occasioned the new Queen's splendid rejection of the unanimous advice of the Cabinet, the Archbishop of Canterbury and the Duke of Norfolk, who, as the Earl Marshal, was responsible for the organisation of state occasions. The advice was that the ceremony in Westminster Abbey should not be televised. The Queen – and the Duke of Edinburgh – insisted that it should, with the exception of that part in which she took communion. Churchill was considerably taken aback by this emphatic rejection of ministerial advice, but accepted the Queen's wishes, taking the sensible line that, 'After all, it was the Queen who was to be crowned and not the Cabinet. She alone must decide.' The Cabinet formally withdrew its recommendation. 'Thus it was,' Jock Colville recorded with amused admiration, 'that the new 26-year-old sovereign personally routed the Earl Marshal, the Archbishop of Canterbury, Sir Winston Churchill and the Cabinet, all of whom submitted to her decision with astonishment, but with a good grace.'

The royal couple were less successful in their desire to stay in Clarence House and to use Buckingham Palace as an office and place of official entertainment and ceremonies. The Palace had been substantially repaired after its wartime damage, but retained its old daunting character. But on this matter Churchill was adamant: the Palace was the official London residence of the sovereign and had been so since the accession of Queen Victoria, and had been the symbol of indomitable British resistance and resolution during the war. This was all very well, but Churchill's fond memories were as a visitor, not as a resident. But the symbolic aspect was important, as the Queen agreed. Windsor Castle, however, retained its dominant place in her heart.

Assessments of the monarchs since George IV have been of considerable quality, and generally favourable and sympathetic. The officially approved biographers have been shrewdly chosen, and, although not given totally a free hand, censorship has been rare,[12] and access to the Royal Archives has been generously given.

This new openness and preservation of the royal papers has been in marked and welcome contrast to the appalling incendiarism of the diaries and journals of Prince Albert and Queen Victoria and the papers of Edward VII and Queen Alexandra. These perceptions of monarchs and their spouses as people rather than distant representatives of an institution has certainly reduced what Lascelles praised as the 'mystique' of royalty, but in an age of media intrusion and manipulation that would have happened in any case.

Emphasis has been placed in this narrative upon the individual characters of monarchs and their political attitudes and interests, and their relationships with politicians. The most actively political were Queen Victoria and Prince Albert, who both strayed dangerously into partisanship. King Edward VII – and Edward VIII, when Prince of Wales – perhaps travelled abroad too much, and King George V too little, but in his case, given the problems he confronted, there was much to be said for being at home and available, and concentrating on domestic rather than international issues. His attitude was very similar to that of Attlee, who in his retirement expressed puzzlement why Prime Ministers travelled

---

[12] Elizabeth Longford was asked not to publish Queen Victoria's account of her wedding night; Harold Nicolson was asked to delete unkind references to the Kaiser; I was asked not to reveal the salary of the tutor to the Prince of Wales, the future Edward VII, in my biography of Prince Albert. None of us had any difficulty with these requests. The claims by A. N. Wilson in *The Decline and Fall of the House of Windsor* of deliberate manipulation of the record are not substantiated by those given access to the archives. The critical frankness of the biographies of Edward VII and Edward VIII by Philip Magnus and Philip Ziegler, and of Queen Victoria by Elizabeth Longford and Cecil Woodham-Smith, defy this allegation, as do the biographies of George V by John Gore and Harold Nicolson. That by Kenneth Rose was not officially blessed, but was certainly approved of, as was Sarah Bradford's sensitive biography of George VI.

abroad so much to meet foreign potentates, remarking that, 'In my day, they came to see me.' This was certainly true of George V.

Although his second son rather shared his insularity, being perfectly happy with living in his own country, and certainly not an enthusiastic traveller to foreign parts, his visits to Australia and New Zealand in 1927, to East Africa in 1924–25 – 'quite an ordinary private visit' – and to Canada and the United States in 1939 demonstrated an interest in imperial matters that his father had lacked, in the sense of actually going to places and meeting people. Apart from his Durbar visit to India, George V had loved his Empire from a distance. George VI wanted to know it at closer range. The Second World War of course precluded this, although it was only Churchill's obstinacy that prevented him visiting India. The South African tour of 1947 was a good idea that went sadly wrong, and was very badly timed, for reasons wholly out of the King's control. The much-desired return visit to Australia and New Zealand never happened.

Queen Victoria and Edward VII were devoted Francophiles; George V was not; nor was Edward VIII, who was more attracted to the United States and Germany, and who, although he lived for many years in France, like many British ex-patriates, never bothered to learn the language properly. George VI and Queen Elizabeth spoke excellent French, although their visits were only occasional. But their love of France, and dislike of Germany, had its political importance, especially in their positive and friendly attitude towards De Gaulle.

King George V's anti-American prejudices were certainly not inherited by his sons. In the case of the Prince of Wales and the Duke of Kent this might be considered unfortunate; in that of King George VI it was to be a major advantage. He enjoyed the company of Americans and was happy with them. The breezy informality and respectful good humour of American servicemen of all ranks – and the quality of their uniforms – impressed and amused him. It was a refreshing change from suffocating deference and tedious protocol.

This was the key to his relationship with Churchill. It was serious, and often grim, but although Churchill was a punctilious admirer of the institution of monarchy he was also a puckish one. He rated the monarchy very highly; but he also rated himself very highly. This could have caused resentment, as it had in the cases of Edward VII and George V, but did not with George VI.

Churchill, who cheerfully described himself to the King as 'conceited but not arrogant', would have been disconcerted had he known the amusement he gave to the Royal Family. They respected and admired him immensely, and regarded him as a true friend and a great man, but there were aspects to Churchill's personality and flamboyant style that they found irresistibly funny.

There was also the fact that Churchill was a superlative actor, striding the stage in whatever role he desired or created, and never happier than under the arc-lights of attention, whether greeted with applause or abuse. The attention, and the publicity, were what mattered. The King was very different in temperament, preferring the quieter life, but the Queen also enjoyed the stage, as did her younger daughter. They were naturals, and thus saw Churchill rather more clearly than most people did, and enjoyed him all the more for his innate theatricality and sense of drama.

The Royal Prerogative of choosing the Prime Minister was preserved until 1963. In January 1957, on Eden's resignation on the urgent advice of his doctors, the Queen consulted Churchill, and Salisbury and Lord Kilmuir took soundings of the Cabinet. The Conservative Whips also sought opinions of back-bench MPs. Eden gave no advice to the Queen on his successor, although his preference was for R. A. Butler, less as a result of any enthusiasm for him than his long-standing mistrust of Harold Macmillan, now augmented by the latter's performance during the Suez crisis. But if this had been inconsistent, it had been considerably more emphatic than Butler's, whose somewhat distant and aloof role had revived old memories – not least in Churchill's mind – about Munich.[13] The Cabinet soundings were overwhelmingly for Macmillan; so were those of the Parliamentary Party; Churchill's advice was the same.

Nonetheless, this was a controversial decision that exposed the Queen to some muted criticism. With all the wisdom of hindsight it would have been as well if the Conservative Party had been warned by the Queen's advisers that the monarch should never again be put in such a position when a Conservative Prime Minister resigned. The opportunity was not taken.

The dilemma that some had foreseen occurred in October 1963, after

[13] Butler had been Halifax's Under-Secretary at the Foreign Office, and was regarded as significantly more pro-appeasement than his master.

the sudden illness and resignation of Macmillan. On Macmillan's advice to the Queen, she invited the Foreign Secretary, the Earl of Home, to form a government. Controversies still swirl about the justification for this advice, and Home, like Bonar Law in October 1922, was doubtful whether he could do so. If Butler had refused to serve he might well have not been able to, but Butler agreed, to the dismay of his closest adherents, and Home became Prime Minister.

The Queen was assured that Macmillan's nominee, Lord Home, had the strong support of the Cabinet and most of the Parliamentary Party, a claim vehemently denied by, among others, Iain Macleod and Enoch Powell, who refused to serve in the Home government. Blame did not fall upon the Queen personally, but the furore resulted in the Conservative Party creating rules for the election of its leader by Members of Parliament. These were devised by a Conservative back-bench MP, Humphry Berkeley, and put into effect by Home; the first election under these rules was when Home resigned the party leadership in July 1965 – the Conservatives having narrowly lost the October 1964 General Election – and Edward Heath was elected.

It could be argued that this action further seriously reduced the monarch's political power of choice of Prime Minister. In reality, it confirmed what had become the practice, and finally removed the monarch from personal involvement in leadership crises. This should have been anticipated in 1957.

As has been related, it had been the growth of organised parties in the mid-nineteenth century that had completely changed the royal position. In a situation of political chaos the sovereign's choice of Prime Minister gave him or her a decisive voice. After the 1860s this was no longer the case, as Queen Victoria realised. Her detestation of Gladstone personally and his policies at home and abroad increased greatly after 1876, but she could not, and did not, deny him the premiership in 1880, 1886 or 1892.

Her choice of Rosebery as Gladstone's successor was certainly a personal one, but at the time it was popular, and not least in the Cabinet, wearied by the ponderous machinations and diatribes of Harcourt. And Rosebery was a major political figure with an immense following. The fact that his brief premiership was an almost total failure was not Queen Victoria's fault, although she certainly had not contributed to assisting his peace of mind or diminishing self-confidence.

There was also no demur when Balfour succeeded Salisbury and Asquith followed Campbell-Bannerman. George V had a more difficult choice in December 1916, but Law's disinclination to serve made Lloyd George's appointment natural and inevitable, although not, in the King's personal opinion, desirable.

Neither Edward VII nor George V got on well personally with their Prime Ministers – with the conspicuous exception of George V and Ramsay MacDonald – and George V's preference for his military friends in the First World War had its dangers, and certainly did not improve relations with Lloyd George, but his political antennae were often sharper than those of the politicians. His fears of revolution now seem exaggerated; but in the context of 1917–19, with monarchies and empires tumbling in Russia, Germany and Austria-Hungary, and under severe threat elsewhere in Europe, they were by no means misplaced. And he was, although steeped in the old ways, a natural conciliator and pacifier, which was no bad thing in the turbulent and unhappy 1920s.

His invitation to Law to form a government in October 1922 was considerably more controversial, as was that of Baldwin in 1923. Law's refusal until he was sure he could form a government and was formally elected Leader of the Party disconcerted the King, but it was the course followed by Home in October 1963; in both cases it made sound political sense.

The King's choice of Baldwin rather than Curzon was probably wrong in terms of experience and ability, but it demonstrated the King's political shrewdness. The 1922 General Election had returned the Conservatives, but demonstrated the growing power and popularity of the Labour Party, and the until-then unthinkable prospect of a Labour government. The inadequate and confused guidance the King received from Law and other Conservative politicians effectively left the choice to him, and he was convinced that it was politically impossible to have a Prime Minister in the Lords. The acute divisions in the Conservative Party meant that he had had perforce to turn to an inexperienced, although popular, senior Commons minister. The principle was right; the actual choice more dubious. But the more formidable alternatives were at the time, by their own decision, unavailable.

Perhaps George V's greatest political achievement was to welcome the first Labour government warmly and courteously, and to make real personal friendships with Ramsay MacDonald and Jimmy Thomas. That with the former had its consequences in the August 1931 crisis, when the King's role was a dominant and crucial one. His conduct then has often been considered a masterstroke; later judgements have been much more critical – but we now know what happened in the 1930s under the palsied leadership of MacDonald and Baldwin. The King's desire for national unity was certainly confirmed by the electorate in the 1931 General Election. The monarch's political position was in reality far stronger at the end of his reign than it had been for the first ten years of it, and reflected his character and sagacity. His great fear was that his eldest son would wreck everything.

We can now appreciate how fully justified this apprehension was. Edward VIII's defenders have blamed his parents, as he did, for his inadequate education and for their coldness towards him. The first charge has some justification, but they could not be held responsible for the deterioration of his character, which was as apparent to others as it was to them. Parental demonstrativeness towards their children was not a common feature of the Victorians, but it has not been unknown in previous or later generations. Queen Mary, it is true, remains an enigma, but she was a considerably more worldly and warm person than she is usually depicted. The prolonged illness, and eventual death, of her youngest son was a profound sadness to her. She treated the tragedy with outward and characteristic stoicism; but she never lost an opportunity of privately visiting his grave and praying beside it. She was not uncritical of her other sons, but loved them greatly and was proud of them until her eldest one, in her eyes, betrayed his family and his country. This she could never forgive, and it was an immense personal tragedy for her.

The events of 1936 were largely dictated by Edward VIII's all-devouring passion for Mrs Simpson, but the King's tangled private life was part of a much larger problem which had greatly troubled Hardinge, Lascelles, Legh and others of the King's immediate circle long before Mrs Simpson had made her appearance.

The more we know of the political views of Edward VIII confirms the opinion that in the context of the 1936–39 European situation his political role could well have been active, ill-informed and probably disastrous. He was, or perhaps became, a feeble person. There had been qualities of courage and character, but they had been tragically dissipated. And this degeneration had long preceded the arrival of Mrs

Simpson. His brief reign demonstrated not only his impetuosity and indolence but his dislike of taking advice that was uncongenial to him, especially from the Foreign Office.

He would certainly have supported Chamberlain's appeasement policies ardently and openly, as he surely would have demonstrated his intense hostility to the Soviet Union. All the evidence is that he would have been the most overtly political of modern British monarchs, offending not only the critics of appeasement but those elements in the Labour Party who, however foolishly and ignorantly, considered Russian Communism as only another version of British Socialism.

Churchill, his strong and ill-considered supporter in the crisis of November–December 1936, later recognised that Edward VIII's pro-German prejudices and acceptance of Nazi rule would have made his position well-nigh untenable if he had been on the throne in 1940. He might well have been the last British monarch.

It is conceivable that Edward VIII might have learned the constitutional and political limitations of his position and kept his real thoughts to himself, but no one who knew him well believed this. The threat to abdicate if he did not get his own way was a deliberate challenge to his elected ministers, and gave to the November 1936 crisis a crucial constitutional and political aspect that has often been underrated, and certainly was by Churchill at the time. It was the interview when the threat was made that so deeply shocked Baldwin, and precipitated the crisis. As Lascelles constantly reminded people, and emphasised in his diaries and unpublished portrait of the King, 'he thought he would get away with it'.

If he had, and the Cabinet – strongly supported by the Opposition party leaders – had not held firm to its conviction that in matters of such magnitude the sovereign must bow to the advice of his ministers, the consequences would have been interesting indeed. It is also somewhat difficult to imagine the Britain of the late 1930s rapturising over Queen Wallis. The Guardian Angel that hovers over Britain rendered a notable service in December 1936. The claims by his admirers that Edward VIII would have made a great King if he had been allowed to be do not stand up well to examination.

Sensible historians often marvel at the sheer element of luck, for good or ill, in human affairs. It was certainly fortunate for the British monarchy that the Duke of Clarence did not succeed to the Throne and that his younger brother did. Of the four sons of George V the best one succeeded: the mordant wit who advocated the raising of statues to Mrs Simpson in gratitude for her role in a national deliverance expressed a widespread opinion, fortified by subsequent knowledge.

It was also a strange combination of circumstances that brought together George VI, Roosevelt and Churchill in terrible and dangerous times. George VI wholly lacked his elder brother's self-assurance and confidence, and had shown little interest in politics, but he had no prejudices, and did not claim knowledge in matters of which he was ignorant. Honest modesty is not a disability; nor is straightfoward common sense. He made up for what deficiencies he had by sheer hard work, moral strength, and application. As has been described, the later charge against him that, by praising Chamberlain and presenting him to the exultant crowds on the balcony at Buckingham Palace on his return from Munich, he gave a royal endorsement to appeasement and thereby plunged the monarchy into political dispute and danger, is not sustainable. If he had made a mistake in the euphoria of the moment – in which he was not alone – he realised quicker than most that the perils had not miraculously disappeared.

The royal visits to Canada and the United States in 1939 and the friendship with the Roosevelts had real political importance, comparable to Edward VII's Paris triumph and George V's role in the 1921 Irish Treaty. These were to pay handsome dividends; it is difficult to put a price upon goodwill and personal friendship between Heads of State.

But the key relationship of the King's reign was with Churchill.

As it was Halifax who had played a considerable part in the King's abrupt change of attitude to Munich, it was not surprising that the King favoured him as Prime Minister in May 1940, as almost everyone did, before the full cataclysm of the looming disaster in France was apparent, even to Churchill.

This was not as grave a misjudgement as has been usually assumed. Halifax was a man of real quality, with moral and physical courage of a high order, and a devoted public servant of great integrity, intelligence and achievement. But he also possessed the exceptional political merit of self-realism. He knew in his bones that he was not the man for the hour. By removing himself from the contest that he could easily have won he rendered another great service – perhaps the greatest of all – to the state.

The King's political influence while Chamberlain was Prime Minister was virtually non-existent. Initially, so was it with Churchill. How that official relationship swiftly developed into close friendship, mutual respect and profound trust has been described. What needs to be emphasised again is how rare a phenomenon it was, the only comparisons being Queen Victoria's relationship with Melbourne, and, later, Disraeli; Prince Albert's with Robert Peel; and George V's with MacDonald.

And there were echoes of his father's friendship with, and admiration for, Jimmy Thomas, in George VI's relationship with the considerably more estimable Ernest Bevin, during and after the war. Although the King privately hated most of the domestic legislation of the 1945–51 Labour government, he strongly supported and encouraged its foreign policy and his Foreign Secretary. The fact that he made devoted monarchists out of Attlee and Morrison and an admirer in Aneurin Bevan reflected their admiration for him as a man.

Ben Pimlott has claimed that 'the acceptance of a cypher-monarchy, almost devoid of political independence, began in 1936'. These are rather strange conclusions. The monarchy had not had 'political independence', in the sense of being a politically independent force, for over a century before Edward VIII's abdication, and neither George VI nor his successor can be described as 'cypher-monarchs'. Nor is it fair for Pimlott to write of George VI that he 'was ideally suited to the task of doing very little, conscientiously'.[14] It was the fact that he did too much, and exhausted himself in the process, that shortened his life.

With the notable exception of Edward VII, no British monarch since George IV has much relished the panoply of monarchy. Queen Victoria actively and emphatically rejected it, to considerable criticism. George V and VI accepted it as part of the job, and undertook it dutifully, if unenthusiastically. Edward VIII hated it, and consequently did it badly.

It is often argued that as the ceremonial aspect of the British monarchy has increased immensely in the twentieth century, its real influence has diminished – a reflection of Britain's drastically changed position in the world from imperial power to European offshore island. What has really happened is that, with one exception, the occupants of the British

[14] Pimlott, op. cit., p. 40.

Throne since the accession of William IV have skilfully accommodated themselves to changing realities. There have been some dark moments. Mistakes have been made. There have been surges of criticism, reasonable or otherwise. Nonetheless, after centuries of turmoil and social and political revolution, the creation, and then the loss, of a vast Empire, two terrible and near-disastrous world wars, the grievous reduction of wealth and position, and their laborious re-creation, Britain and the British monarchy have survived.

And this great achievement was not accidental. Triumphs of character, national and personal, never are.

There was another tribute to George VI that especially moved his family.

On 1 July 1956 a memorial to the King on Garrowby Hill in Yorkshire was dedicated by the Archbishop of York. It is a figure of Christ on a cross twenty feet high, with a base bearing the inscription:

> TO THE GLORY OF GOD, AND IN MEMORY OF
> GEORGE,
> KING,
> SERVANT OF HIS PEOPLE
> 1895–1952

It was Edward Halifax's tribute to his friend and monarch, and the perfect epitaph not only to an individual, but to the tradition he had inherited. And he left, as the French Ambassador, Massigli, reported to his government, 'a throne more stable than England has known throughout almost her entire history'.

From monarch-as-despot to monarch-as-servant is no degradation of the role of the sovereign. Indeed, it can rightly be regarded as an advancement.

SELECT BIBLIOGRAPHY

——— ➤ ———

A s Vernon Bogdanor has commented in his Bibliography to *The Monarchy and the Constitution* (OUP, 1995), 'Of the vast mass of books on the monarchy, few have much to say on constitutional issues.' Frank Hardie's *The Political Influence of the British Monarchy, 1868–1952* (Batsford, 1970) was the sequel to his pioneering work on the political influence of Queen Victoria, but can hardly be described as definitive, or even very profound. Nonetheless, he merits high praise for having seen something that had eluded all others, and which considerably influenced me in my researches into Prince Albert's previously neglected political role, and on this work.

Queen Victoria has been the subject of numerous biographies, some of considerable quality, and especially those by Elizabeth Longford and Cecil Woodham-Smith, although Monica Charlot's *Victoria, The Young Queen* (Blackwell, 1991), her first volume, may well supersede them. The fact that none is wholly satisfying on the political side is more the result of the lamentable destruction of most of the Queen's journals and those of Prince Albert than to the inadequacies of the authors, although their interest in other aspects of the Queen's personality and reign obviously played some part. My biography of Prince Albert (Hamish Hamilton, 1983) also suffered from this incendiarism, as did Philip Magnus's excellent biography of Edward VII (John Murray, 1964).

George V was well served by John Gore and Harold Nicolson, but even better by Kenneth Rose (Weidenfeld & Nicolson, 1983).

Frances Donaldson's perceptive biography of Edward VIII (Weidenfeld & Nicolson, 1974) is rightly highly esteemed, as is Philip Ziegler's admirable and shrewdly objective official biography (Collins, 1990). As with his biography of Mountbatten (Collins, 1985), it is a memorable exercise in objectivity and self-restraint – one of those occasions when the biographer becomes increasingly disillusioned with his subject but very successfully maintains a judicial fairness.

Both the Duke and Duchess of Windsor wrote their accounts of their lives and adventures, and have been bravely supported by Michael Bloch. I can only say that the more I have discovered about this couple the more grateful I am for the events of November–December 1936.

It would not be right to say that Sir John Wheeler-Bennett became disillusioned with his subject in his official biography of George VI (Macmillan, 1958), but that he did not really understand him and that this was a duty conscientiously fulfilled rather than a pleasure. He also lacked Nicolson's marvellously languid and feline literary skills, and it was Rose's access to Nicolson's notes and material that gave his biography of George V its special qualities. Sarah Bradford's unauthorised biography of George VI (Weidenfeld & Nicolson, 1989) is very good on his early life and development, and, if it is less sure-footed on the reign itself, particularly on the political aspects, it certainly holds the field.

Political biographers have also tended to play down, or even to ignore entirely, the political role of the monarchy, notable exceptions being Robert Blake's biography of Andrew Bonar Law, *The Unknown Prime Minister* (Eyre & Spottiswoode, 1955) and David Marquand's biography of Ramsay MacDonald (Jonathan Cape, 1977). Gladstone's and Rosebery's difficulties with Queen Victoria have been well catalogued by Colin Matthew, Philip Magnus, Roy Jenkins, myself, and by Arthur Ponsonby in his biography of his father, *Henry Ponsonby: His Life from His Letters* (Macmillan, 1942). This highly informative book aroused disproportionate royal ire on its publication, particularly on the part of Queen Mary, and remains the only biography of a royal Private Secretary, although Helen Hardinge's *Loyal to Three Kings* (William Kimber, 1967) tactfully and loyally puts the case for her husband; Harold Macmillan in his *War Diaries* (Macmillan, 1984) gave a considerably harsher judgement – rather excessively so.

Both Baldwin and Neville Chamberlain have rather eluded their biographers, although David Dilks may remedy the latter deficiency.

Although the King's relationship with Churchill is referred to by Martin Gilbert in his monumental work, it is perhaps not given the importance that it merits. The King's private diaries are the only records of their Tuesday lunch discussions. Attlee's memoirs, *As It Happened* (Heinemann, 1954) are, characteristically, wholly uninformative, and Kenneth Harris's biography (Weidenfeld & Nicolson, 1982) is a valiant attempt to fathom the mystery; if it does not fully succeed, this is unsurprising.

Vernon Bogdanor's quiet and thoughtful work on the monarchy and the constitution has already been referred to, and is indispensable to an understanding of the modern monarchy. It is a subject that has attracted a substantial number of books, of very varying quality, and particularly some biographies of the Queen and Queen Elizabeth the Queen Mother. But even the better attempts – especially those of Elizabeth Longford, Kenneth Harris and Ben Pimlott – can be described as premature, while Sarah Bradford's did not live up to the high promise of her biography of George VI. Of many of the others the less said the better.

Andrew Roberts, the biographer of Lord Halifax, has given a surprisingly hostile, even contemptuous, portrait of George VI in his otherwise perceptive essays in *Eminent Churchillians* (Weidenfeld & Nicolson, 1994). Some of its more notable inaccuracies have already been referred to. Others, including John Charmley, have taken up his theme that the King and Queen were passionately pro-Appeasement and anti-Churchill, in defiance of much evidence to the contrary. The reaction to royal hagiography may be understandable, and fashionable in some quarters, but it can be carried too far, especially when it is unsupported by the facts. There are other examples, from far less serious sources, Penelope Mortimer's book on the Queen Mother being a prime instance.

This book is heavily dependent upon documents and information from several sources that I have been permitted to see and know, but from which I have not, for copyright and other reasons, been able to quote directly. This may dissatisfy purists, eager for source references, but it is not the first occasion on which I – and other historians and biographers – have accepted that access to confidential papers and information does not carry with it the right to publish them. The important fact is that the historian should be able to give an authentic account.

I can only add the sombre note that my researches have been such, and the material gathered so voluminous, that this work could easily have been much longer.

INDEX